Governing Risks in Modern Britain

Tom Crook • Mike Esbester
Editors

Governing Risks in Modern Britain

Danger, Safety and Accidents, c. 1800–2000

palgrave
macmillan

Editors
Tom Crook
Oxford Brookes University
Oxford, United Kingdom

Mike Esbester
University of Portsmouth
Portsmouth, United Kingdom

ISBN 978-1-137-46744-7 ISBN 978-1-137-46745-4 (eBook)
DOI 10.1057/978-1-137-46745-4

Library of Congress Control Number: 2016938643

Printed on acid-free paper

This Palgrave Macmillan imprint is published by Springer Nature
The registered company is Macmillan Publishers Ltd. London

Acknowledgments

This volume arises out of a conference held at Oxford Brookes University in 2013. The editors would like to thank all those who participated in the conference and to acknowledge the financial support of the following institutions: Oxford Brookes University; the University of Portsmouth and, in particular, the Centre for European and International Studies Research; the Wellcome Trust; and the Economic History Society of the UK. Mike would also like to thank his family, particularly his wife Nicki and daughter Rosie, for their support and patience in the latter stages of preparation. Finally, Mike and Paul Almond gratefully acknowledge the Institution of Occupational Safety and Health, which has funded the research project 'The Changing Legitimacy of Health and Safety, 1960–2015', from which their chapter is drawn. They also thank their research assistants, Carmen D'Cruz and Laura Mayne.

Contents

1 Risk and the History of Governing Modern Britain, c. 1800–2000 — 1
Tom Crook and Mike Esbester

Part I Early Risk Societies — 27

2 Risk, Prevention and Policing, c. 1750–1850 — 29
Francis Dodsworth

3 Rethinking the History of the Risk Society: Accident Reporting, the Social Order and the London Daily Press, 1800–30 — 55
Ryan Vieira

Part II Environmental Risks — 77

4 Artificial Britain: Risk, Systems and Synthetics Since 1800 — 79
Chris Otter

5 Danger in the Drains: Sewer Gas, Sewerage Systems and the Home, 1850–1900 — 105
Tom Crook

6 **Public Health and Public Safety: Disinfection, Carbolic and the Plurality of Risk, 1870–1914** 127
Rebecca Whyte

7 **Risk, Time and Everyday Environmentalism in Modern Britain** 149
Timothy Cooper

Part III Mobility and Leisure Risks 169

8 **Drunk Driving, Drink Driving: Britain, c. 1800–1920** 171
Bill Luckin

9 **Risk on the Roads: Police, Motor Traffic and the Management of Space, c. 1900–50** 195
Chris A. Williams

10 **'Maximum Supervision': Risk, Danger and Public Water in Post-War Britain** 221
Glen O'Hara

Part IV Occupational Risks 247

11 **Risk, Responsibility and Robens: The Transformation of the British System of Occupational Health and Safety Regulation, 1961–74** 249
Christopher Sirrs

12 **Il/Legitimate Risks? Occupational Health and Safety and the Public in Britain, c. 1960–2015** 277
Paul Almond and Mike Esbester

13 **Conclusion: Governing Risks in Britain and Beyond** 297
Arwen P. Mohun, Thomas Le Roux, Tom Crook, and Mike Esbester

Index 309

List of Figures

Fig. 5.1	'Water-closet with arrangements all faulty, compared with w.c. with the faults remedied.' Plate XVI in T. Pridgin Teale, *Dangers to Health: A Pictorial Guide to Domestic Sanitary Defects* (London, 1878). Published with the kind permission of the Bodleian Library, Oxford	120
Fig. 6.1	Total deaths due to carbolic (accidents and suicides), 1863–1914. Figures derived from the *Annual Reports of the Registrar-General of Births, Deaths and Marriages* for England and Wales	139
Fig. 6.2	Total suicides and accidental deaths due to carbolic, 1863–1914. Figures derived from the *Annual Reports of the Registrar-General of Births, Deaths and Marriages* for England and Wales	140
Fig. 10.1	RoSPA, *The Water Safety Book* (London, 1976), p. 4. Published with the kind permission of the Royal Society for the Prevention of Accidents	239
Fig. 10.2	RoSPA, *Be Water Wise* (n.d., 1980s), p. 2. Published with the kind permission of the Royal Society for the Prevention of Accidents	240
Fig. 11.1	The proportion of workers covered by principal health and safety laws in 1972 (millions of workers). Lord Robens, *Safety and Health at Work: Report of the Committee. 1970–2* (2 vols, London, 1972), I, p. 5	253
Fig. 11.2	The 1966 Aberfan disaster. *Welsh Office: A Selection of Technical Reports Submitted to the Aberfan Tribunal* (2 vols, London, 1969), I, p. 33. Published with the kind permission of the Bodleian Library, Oxford	264

Notes on Contributors

Paul Almond is Professor in the School of Law at the University of Reading, where he researches and teaches contemporary criminal law, criminology, and health and safety regulation. His book *Corporate Manslaughter and Regulatory Reform* was published in 2013 by Palgrave Macmillan and constitutes the first major contextual study of the Corporate Manslaughter and Corporate Homicide Act of 2007.

Timothy Cooper is Senior Lecturer in History at the University of Exeter. He completed his doctorate at the University of Cambridge and was Research Fellow at the Institute of Environmental History at the University of St Andrews. He works on historical political ecology and in particular the relations between everyday life and the environment. He has published on the social and environmental politics of waste, including in journals such as the *Social History of Medicine*, *Technology and Culture* and *Historical Research*, and is currently collaborating on an oral history project on the *Torrey Canyon* disaster.

Tom Crook is Lecturer in Modern British History at Oxford Brookes University. He has published a number of articles on modern British governance in journals such as *Social History*, *Urban History* and *Past & Present*, as well as a number of edited collections, including (with Glen O'Hara) *Statistics and the Public Sphere: Numbers and the People in Modern Britain, c. 1800–2000* (2011). He is currently completing a study of Victorian and Edwardian public health.

Francis Dodsworth is Senior Lecturer in Criminology at Kingston University, London. His research explores the history of crime and security in modern Britain, particularly crime prevention and self-defence. It engages with Michel Foucault's insights into the genealogy of discipline, security and liberal government, and the work of Norbert Elias on the civilizing process. He has published a number of articles in these areas, including in journals such as *Social History* and *Journal of Historical Sociology*. His most recent publication is an edited collection of sources on the emergence of the idea of policing in eighteenth-century England, which was published in 2014.

Mike Esbester is Senior Lecturer in History at the University of Portsmouth. His research has been funded by the Arts and Humanities Research Council and focuses on understandings of safety and accident prevention in late nineteenth- and twentieth-century Britain. He is currently writing a monograph on the safety of railway workers between 1871 and 1948. He is Co-Principal Investigator, with Paul Almond, on a major research project funded by the Institution of Occupational Safety and Health, looking at ideas of legitimacy surrounding health and safety in post-1960 Britain.

Thomas Le Roux works at the French National Centre for Scientific Research, where he leads a research programme on the history of industrial accidents and risks in modern France and England. His research focuses on environmental history and the history of industrial nuisances and risks in the eighteenth and nineteenth centuries, and he is especially interested in comparing France and England. His recent publications include *Le Laboratoire des pollutions industrielles: Paris, 1770–1830* (2011).

Bill Luckin is Research Professor in Urban History at the University of Bolton and an Associate at the Centre for the History of Science, Technology and Medicine at the University of Manchester. An urban, technological and environmental historian, he has published widely on a range of topics, many of them relating to London in the nineteenth and twentieth centuries. He is currently working on two projects: a history of drink driving and a co-edited volume on the urban-environmental history of the capital between 1800 and 2000. His most recent book is *Death and Survival in Urban Britain: Disease, Pollution and Environment, 1800–1950* (2015).

Arwen P. Mohun is Professor of History and Chair of the Department of History at the University of Delaware. She is known for her work on gender, technology and labour. Her major publications on these topics include *Steam Laundries: Gender, Work, and Technology in the United States and Great Britain, 1880–1940* (1999); and (co-edited with Nina Lerman and Ruth Oldenziel) *Gender and Technology: A Reader* (2003). Her most recent book is *Risk: Negotiating Safety in American Society* (2013), which explores the changing ways in which Americans have understood and managed everyday risks from the beginning of the eighteenth century to the present.

Glen O'Hara is Professor of Modern and Contemporary History at Oxford Brookes University. He is the author or editor of a series of books and articles on post-war Britain, including (with Helen Parr), *Harold Wilson and the Labour Governments of 1964–1970: The Modernisation of Britain?* (2006), and *Governing Post-War Britain: The Paradoxes of Progress, 1951–1973* (2012). He is currently working on a book entitled *The Politics of Water in Post-War Britain*, which will be published by Palgrave Macmillan in 2016.

Chris Otter is Associate Professor of History at Ohio State University. He is the author of *The Victorian Eye: A Political History of Light and Vision in Britain, 1800–1910* (2008) and is currently completing his second book, *The Vital State: Food Systems, Nutrition Transitions, and the Making of Industrial Britain*.

Christopher Sirrs is a PhD candidate at the Centre for History in Public Health, London School of Hygiene and Tropical Medicine. With a background in the history of medicine from University College London, his research concentrates on the historical development of the British system of occupational health and safety regulation between 1961 and 2001, including the origins and work of the Health and Safety Commission and the Health and Safety Executive. His research is supported by the Economic and Social Research Council.

Ryan Vieira has published articles on the historiography of accidents and the temporality of political culture in *History Compass*, *History and Theory* and the *Journal of Liberal History*. His book *Time and Politics: Parliament and the Culture of Modernity in Britain and the British World* (2015) studies the transnational history of procedural modernization in the British House of Commons and the parliaments of the settler colonies between 1811 and 1913.

Rebecca Whyte completed her doctorate at the University of Cambridge in 2012, which was entitled 'Changing Patterns of Disinfection in England and Wales, c. 1840–1914'. Her research examines the development of ideas, practices and problems in public health disinfection. She currently works for the Scottish government as a policy advisor.

Chris A. Williams is Senior Lecturer in History at the Open University. He has worked on various aspects of police history in Britain and the British Empire, and his publications include *Police Control Systems in Britain, 1775–1975: From Parish Constable to National Computer*, which was published in 2014. Among his broadcast work has been the role of academic consultant on the BBC's *Wartime Farm* and as the originator of the Radio 4 series *The Things We Forgot to Remember*.

CHAPTER 1

Risk and the History of Governing Modern Britain, c. 1800–2000

Tom Crook and Mike Esbester

This book is about the history of governing risks in modern Britain. To write such a history is itself a risky endeavour, given the variety of problems any such account might encompass. Back in 1998, the sociologist Anthony Giddens began a public lecture by asking: 'What do the following have in common? Mad cow disease; the troubles at Lloyd's Insurance; the Nick Leeson affair [and the collapse of Barings Bank]; genetically modified crops; global warming; the notion that red wine is good for you; anxieties about declining sperm counts.'[1] His answer was that they were all considered 'risks' and were steeped in conflicting accounts regarding their origins and consequences, causes and effects. All attested to the way in which risk permeates our lives, he went on. Risks might be financial and

[1] A. Giddens, 'Risk and Responsibility', *Modern Law Review* 62 (1999), p. 1.

T. Crook (✉)
Department of History, Philosophy and Religion, Oxford Brookes University, Tonge Building, Headington Campus, Gipsy Lane, Oxford OX3 0BP, UK

M. Esbester
School of Social, Historical and Literary Studies, University of Portsmouth, Milldam, Burnaby Road, Portsmouth PO1 3AS, UK

T. Crook, M. Esbester (eds), *Governing Risks in Modern Britain*,
DOI 10.1057/978-1-137-46745-4_1

technological as much as environmental and medical, and personal and local as much as national and global. In what he called the 'risk society', after his fellow sociologist, Ulrich Beck, there was no escaping uncertainty, no relief from stumbling, anxiously, into the future. And yet, it might be said, we hardly need an eminent sociologist to remind us of something we confront daily. Confirmation of the diversity of contemporary risks can be found in the pages of our newspapers, where we might read of those relating to an impending terrorist attack, another economic recession, burglary and physical assault, or the side-effects of a particular medicine. We read, too, of accidents involving cars, workplace machinery, leisure pursuits, and household gadgets and chemicals.

We begin by emphasizing this abundance of concerns—the multiplicity of problems that have been, or might be, characterized as 'risks'—simply to affirm at the outset that this volume does not pretend to exhaust its subject matter. Rather, the focus is on the regulation and representation of a particular set of risks, dangers and accidents that are of a physical and everyday sort. Simply put, it focuses on threats to the human body and, to a lesser extent, property, as these emerged in spaces such as homes, streets, workplaces and sites of recreation. The omissions are thus many. It does not attend, for instance, to the history of financial bubbles, crises and speculative risk taking, a facet of economic historiography that has enjoyed a renaissance in recent years.[2] Nor, again, does it concern the intensified risks and dangers that accompanied the eruption and execution of mass warfare—whether on the battlefield or, in the twentieth century, on the home front as well—and how this experience impacted on the development of the state and everyday life.[3] Nor, finally, does it present any detailed studies of practices of insurance, either of a commercial or a compulsory, state-sponsored sort.[4]

Yet, to speak of omissions is to assume that the historiography of governing risks has a determinate scope and shape, a settled sense of what

[2] See, for instance, J. Levy, *Freaks of Fortune: The Emerging World of Capitalism and Risk in America* (Cambridge, MA, 2012); N.H. Dimsdale and A. Hotson (eds), *British Financial Crises since 1825* (Oxford, 2014); and C. Bilginsoy, *A History of Financial Crises: Dreams and Follies of Expectations* (London, 2015).

[3] Recent accounts include D. Edgerton, *Warfare State: Britain, 1920–1970* (Cambridge, 2006); M. Harrison, *The Medical War: British Military Medicine in the First World War* (Oxford, 2010); and J. Bourke, *Wounding the World: How Military Violence and War-Play Invade Our Lives* (London, 2014).

[4] See footnotes 43–45 below.

it might or should encompass and what it might or should exclude—something which has yet to be established. In any case, even our focus on the field of regulating everyday risks and physical dangers is varied and complex enough to pursue the central aim of this volume: namely, to advance the work of rethinking how modern Britons have been governed since the turn of the nineteenth century. In so doing, this book helps to situate the present in some much-needed historical perspective, not least by exploring when, how and why regulating risks became such a central and obsessive dimension of governing. The ambitions of the book, however, are principally historiographical and the broad argument is twofold. The first aspect is that risks, dangers and accidents constitute a useful means for rethinking some of the dynamics and dilemmas of governing modern Britain, beyond recourse to a state that grows or diminishes, intervenes or neglects, or is more or less 'liberal'. The second aspect is that these dynamics and difficulties stem—to paraphrase Friedrich Engels' famous formulation—not only from the government of persons, but also from the *administration of things*: machines, technologies and infrastructures; consumer products and forms of property; natural and artificial substances; and the environment, man-made or natural and unspoiled.[5]

The remainder of this chapter offers three brief discussions. The first concerns the historiography that this volume at once builds on and seeks to refresh and take in new directions. The second concerns contemporary theorizations of risk. Although the argument of this volume is informed by recent historiographical developments, it is also inspired by innovations in adjacent disciplines, notably in the social sciences, where a substantive body of literature has emerged on the subject of risk (and not least the seminal work of Beck invoked by Giddens above). The third discussion is more historical and concerns some of our key terms—in particular, 'risk', 'danger' and 'accident'—and the shifting assumptions and material cultures that have accompanied their changing uses and salience. We then outline the chapters that follow and the structure of the volume as a whole.

[5] The phrase is taken from Engels' *Socialism: Utopian and Scientific*, first published in 1880 and translated into English in 1892. The passage is as follows: 'State interference in social relations becomes, in one domain after another, superfluous, and then dies out of itself; the government of persons is replaced by the administration of things, and by the conduct of processes of production.'

Histories of Welfare and Risk

In some respects, the history of governing everyday risks, dangers and accidents has already been dealt with by historians of modern Britain—and even, one might argue, in abundance. Labour historians, for instance, have long been interested in the advent of official state inspectorates for factories and mines during the early Victorian period and their variable success thereafter in enhancing the welfare of workers and preventing industrial accidents.[6] Key legal developments such as the Workmen's Compensation Act of 1897, which established routine procedures of financial redress for some of those injured at work, have also attracted attention.[7] More broadly still, since the 1950s, historians have been charting the development of the welfare state and the growth of collective responsibility for risks and dangers that are thought to lie beyond individual control, in particular, unemployment, sickness and accidental injuries—or what some historians now term the history of 'the social' and the 'socialization of risks'.[8] The institutional milestones are well known; foremost among them are the 1911 National Insurance Act and the founding of the National Health Service in 1948.

More might be said on this front. Clearly the history of governing physical and health-related risks in modern Britain is not virgin territory—far from it, and valuable work continues to appear in the vein of welfare historiography.[9] Equally, of course, everything depends on how questions

[6] Among other accounts, see P.W.J. Bartrip, 'British Government Inspection, 1832–75: Some Observations', *Historical Journal* 25 (1982), pp. 605–26; and Robert Gray, *The Factory Question and Industrial England, 1830–1860* (Cambridge, 1996).

[7] See especially P.W.J. Bartrip and S. Burman, *The Wounded Soldiers of Industry: Industrial Compensation Policy, 1833–1897* (Oxford, 1983); P.W.J. Bartrip, *Workmen's Compensation in Twentieth Century Britain: Law, History and Social Policy* (Aldershot, 1987); and R. Fitzgerald, *British Labour Management and Industrial Welfare, 1846–1939* (London, 1988).

[8] The literature on the history of the welfare state is enormous. See the bibliography in the most recent synthesis, D. Fraser, *The Evolution of the British Welfare State: A History of Social Policy since the Industrial Revolution*, 4th edn (Basingstoke, 2009). On the history of 'the social' see J. Vernon, *Hunger: A Modern History* (Cambridge, MA, 2007); and K. Brückweh, D. Schumann, R.F. Wetzell and B. Ziemann (eds), *Engineering Society: The Role of the Human and Social Sciences in Modern Societies, 1880–1980* (Basingstoke, 2012).

[9] This is especially true of occupational health: P. Weindling (ed.), *The Social History of Occupational Health* (London, 1985); P.W.J. Bartrip, *The Home Office and the Dangerous Trades: Regulating Occupational Disease in Victorian and Edwardian Britain* (Amsterdam, 2002); A. McIvor and R. Johnston, *Miners' Lung: A History of Dust Disease in British Coal Mining* (Aldershot, 2007); and C. Mills, *Regulating Health and Safety in the British Mining Industries, 1800–1914* (Farnham, 2010).

are formulated and posed, and how particular problems and points of reform are set within a broader interpretive framework. The history of the welfare state is a case in point. Since the demise of the so-called classic post-war welfare state during the 1980s, scholars have been busy revising and refreshing our sense of what happened and how. This has partly involved mobilizing new sources and recovering actors and activities hitherto overlooked, and there is much of this in what follows in this volume. But it has also involved matters of interpretation. For some time now, historians have been emphasizing the gradual and contested nature of state-formation in modern Britain and the absence of any 'modernizing' teleology or trajectory. From Edwin Chadwick in the nineteenth century to William Beveridge in the twentieth, the actions of key reformers have been shown to be more politicized and peculiar than was assumed by earlier accounts.[10] Likewise, the idea of a 'Victorian revolution in government', first advanced by Oliver MacDonagh in the 1950s, no longer serves as a key point of reference.[11]

In a similar spirit of puncturing 'heroic' narratives of necessary progress, historians have pointed to the 'mixed' nature of governing and the way that it mobilized an eclectic array of agents.[12] There was no linear assumption of power by experts and officials, whether employed or directed by a central state. Rather, there flourished—and persisted—complex networks of agency that also embraced local and voluntary actors, as well as those of a commercial and transnational sort. The 'I', too, has featured in recent accounts of power, to the extent that scholars have sought to recover the encouragement and co-option of the self-governing capacities of individuals. The growing use of the term 'governance' is one indication of this, where it refers to a diffuse field of agency that extended far beyond a state.[13]

[10] See especially C. Hamlin, *Public Health and Social Justice in the Age of Chadwick: Britain, 1800–1854* (Cambridge, 1998); and J. Harris, *William Beveridge: A Biography*, 2nd edn (Oxford, 1997).

[11] O. MacDonagh, 'The Nineteenth-Century Revolution in Government: A Reappraisal', *Historical Journal* 1 (1958), pp. 52–67. A useful overview of the historiography is P. Mandler, 'Introduction: State and Society in Victorian Britain', in P. Mandler (ed.), *Liberty and Authority in Victorian Britain* (Oxford, 2006), pp. 1–21.

[12] This is especially so in relation to the history of welfare and 'mixed economies' of provision. See A. Kidd, *State, Society and the Poor in Nineteenth-Century England* (Basingstoke, 1999); and M.A. Powell, *Understanding the Mixed Economy of Welfare* (Bristol, 2007).

[13] See, for instance, R.J. Morris and R.H. Trainor (eds), *Urban Governance: Britain and Beyond since 1750* (Aldershot, 2000); and L.M.E. Goodlad, *Victorian Literature and the Victorian State: Character and Governance in a Liberal Society* (Baltimore, MD, 2003).

The terms 'liberalism' (for the Victorian period especially), 'social democracy' (for the inter- and post-war periods) and even 'neoliberalism' (for the post-1970s) have also been redefined and put to new uses to uncover the political stakes of what we now call 'welfare reform' and 'health and safety'.[14] The new common sense is that governing modern Britain was an altogether more contested, confused and contingent enterprise than was previously thought: more messy, multi-faceted and multi-layered.

The chapters contained in this volume endorse and deepen the thrust of this revisionism. They do so in various ways, but none situate their particular subject matter in terms of the evolution of a welfare state, even if they concern matters of health, security and safety. They also affirm that governing has always been deeply problematic and, crucially, not just in terms of generating contest about the limits of the state and how 'big' or 'small' it should be. But whereas the categories of 'welfare' and 'the state' have come under sustained scrutiny in relation to their meaning and interpretive utility, this is not true of 'risks', 'dangers' and 'accidents'. Historical works that place these concerns centre stage are still relatively few.

A key intervention in this respect was Roger Cooter and Bill Luckin's collection, *Accidents in History*, published in 1997. As Cooter and Luckin argued in their introduction, though 'accidents can seem nearly as pervasive as the air we breathe … there is hardly a comparable subject in which historical investment has been so meagre'.[15] Accidents barely constituted a 'minority interest'. Only a handful of articles had sought to pose the problem of 'the accidental' in an historical and critical fashion, notably Karl Figlio's 'What is an Accident?', published in 1985.[16] Their point was not that accidents per se had been overlooked; rather, it was that accidents had been marginalized as significant sites of power and contested

[14] See, among other accounts, P. Joyce, *The Rule of Freedom: Liberalism and the Modern City* (London, 2003); S. Gunn and J. Vernon (eds), *The Peculiarities of Liberal Modernity in Imperial Britain* (Berkeley, CA, 2011); J. Callaghan and I. Favretto (eds), *Transitions in Social Democracy: Cultural and Ideological Problems of the Golden Age* (Manchester, 2006); J. Hinnfors, *Reinterpreting Social Democracy: A History of Stability in the British Labour Party and Swedish Social Democratic Party* (Manchester, 2006); D. Harvey, *A Brief History of Neoliberalism* (Oxford, 2007); and D. Stedman Jones, *Masters of the Universe: Hayek, Friedman, and the Birth of Neoliberal Politics* (Princeton, NJ, 2012).

[15] R. Cooter and B. Luckin, 'Accidents in History: An Introduction', in R. Cooter and B. Luckin (eds), *Accidents in History: Injuries, Fatalities and Social Relations* (Amsterdam, 1997), p. 1.

[16] K. Figlio, 'What is an Accident?', in Weindling (ed.), *The Social History of Occupational Health*, pp. 180–206.

meanings, and as deeply historical and social in themselves. 'The "accident"', they concluded, 'far from being "accidental" or wholly arbitrary in occurrence and meaning is, in fact, historically contingent, as well as germane to our understanding of some of the most fundamental features of social, political, cultural and material life.'[17]

What was only a 'minority interest' in the mid-1990s, however, is no longer so. Certainly the study of everyday risks, dangers and accidents has yet to emerge as a recognizable subfield of modern British studies in the way that the history of the welfare state once was, which is now served by multiple summative and general surveys. Indeed, in terms of genres of historiography, the work that has appeared is, to varying degrees, of a cultural, medical, urban, industrial, technological and environmental sort, and not all of it concerns Britain. Nonetheless, two complementary developments might be highlighted. On the one hand, new histories of 'the accident' have emerged, notably in relation to modern forms of transport, such as railways and automobiles, but extending to industrial machinery and even water networks and reservoirs.[18] As Ryan Vieira has recently suggested, surveying the literature on the subject, accidents are no longer seen as a 'motor of progress', as unfortunate teething problems that are eventually resolved on a predestined path towards greater safety and security. Instead, historians have sought to recover the assumptions—about society and human agency in particular—that structured the very idea and representation of 'accidents', as well as their problematic status as a *product* rather than a negation of 'progress' and the onset of growing levels of material and technological complexity.[19]

[17] Cooter and Luckin, 'Accidents in History', p. 12.

[18] See especially R. Harrington, 'Railway Safety and Railway Slaughter: Railway Accidents, Government and Public in Victorian Britain', *Journal of Victorian Culture* 8 (2003), pp. 187–207; B. Rieger, *Technology and the Culture of Modernity in Britain and Germany, 1890–1945* (Cambridge, 2005); M. Aldrich, *Death Rode the Rails: American Railroad Accidents and Safety, 1828–1965* (Baltimore, MD, 2006); J. Burnham, *Accident Prone: A History of Technology, Psychology and Misfits of the Machine Age* (Chicago, 2009); J. Moses, 'Contesting Risk: Specialist Knowledge and Workplace Accidents in Britain, Germany and Italy, 1870–1920', in Brückweh, Schumann, Wetzell and Ziemann (eds), *Engineering Society*, pp. 59–78; S. Ewen, 'Socio-technological Disasters and Engineering Expertise in Victorian Britain: The Holmfirth and Sheffield Floods of 1852 and 1864', *Journal of Historical Geography* 46 (2014), pp. 13–25; and M. Esbester and J. Wetmore (eds), '(Auto) Mobility, Accidents, and Danger', special issue of *Technology and Culture* 52 (2015).

[19] R.A. Vieira, 'The Epistemology and Politics of the Accidental: Connecting the Accident's Intellectual and Cultural Historiography', *History Compass* 11 (2013), pp. 227–34.

On the other hand, historical studies of the formation and regulation of risks and dangers—of which accidents represent an actualization, a shift from the potential or probable to the real—have also begun to emerge. This was already apparent in Cooter and Luckin's volume, which included chapters on 'hazards' and 'risk management', but it is a focus that has become much more pronounced and articulate since then. The most notable instance is Arwen Mohun's *Risk: Negotiating Safety in American Society*, published in 2013.[20] It is the first study of its kind to integrate a variety of practices around a single risk-based narrative of broad chronological sweep. Beginning with fire prevention in the eighteenth century, it moves through the regulation of industrial and railway accidents in the nineteenth, before exploring road safety and gun control in the twentieth. The guiding thread is that 'technological change did not, by itself, determine how Americans understood and managed risk. Instead, the physical characteristics and cultural meanings of specific kinds of man-made hazards intertwined in a process of "mutual shaping"'. As Mohun sees it, risks are a product of both. 'Taken separately', she writes, 'neither the characteristics of technology nor the ideas and actions of individuals and organizations can adequately explain what caused Americans to change how they negotiated risk. The full nature of the process becomes clear only by examining both technology and culture.'[21]

Mohun's analysis comes in the wake of similarly focused accounts, of varying interpretive dispositions, including of a literary sort. Elaine Freedgood's *Victorian Writing about Risk: Imagining a Safe England in a Dangerous World*, for instance, has detailed the way in which a variety of texts—from handbooks on hospital reform to travelogues of Alpine mountaineers—constructed risk as something that could be either banished entirely in England or experienced voluntarily in perilous worlds of adventure abroad.[22] Others, again, are of a medical and institutional sort. One notable instance is William G. Rothstein's *Public Health and the Risk Factor: A History of an Uneven Medical Revolution*, which has offered an account of changing ideas of etiological causation, and in particular how they converged on one of the biggest killers of the twentieth century,

[20] A.P. Mohun, *Risk: Negotiating Safety in American Society* (Baltimore, MA, 2013).

[21] *Ibid*., pp. 6–7.

[22] E. Freedgood, *Victorian Writing about Risk: Imagining a Safe England in a Dangerous World* (Cambridge, 2000). See also P. Fyfe, *By Accident or Design: Writing the Victorian Metropolis* (Oxford, 2015).

coronary heart disease.[23] More instances might be given. Evidently the history of risk has been—and still might be—approached in various ways. What recent accounts share, however, is the broad premise that risks and dangers should be understood as fully historical phenomena, shaped as much by evolving material infrastructures and social conditions as by evolving cultural norms, economic interests and forms of expertise. It is the same premise that has informed the recent historiography of accidents noted above.

Theories of Risk and the 'Risk Society'

The chapters contained in this volume also share this premise, even if they develop it in different ways. All, however, contribute to the development of what remains a fledgling field of the historiography of modern Britain, and it is here in particular where the book seeks to generate debate and new points of departure. But the broad conviction that risk should be foregrounded as an object of focused historical research is also inspired by the fact that for some time now, it has functioned as an object of sustained *theoretical* reflection, and especially in the social sciences, where it has given rise to an enormous and varied literature. As Jens O. Zinn sets out in the introduction to his collection of essays, *Social Theories of Risk and Uncertainty*, it is now possible to isolate no less than five strands of this literature, most of which have emerged since the 1980s. These include Ulrich Beck's risk society thesis; Foucauldian governmentality perspectives; systems theoretical approaches, as pioneered by Niklas Luhmann; and those of an anthropological kind, largely based on the work of Mary Douglas.[24] Overall, Zinn concludes, what is at stake here is not the proposition that perceptions of risks and accidents, and practices relating to their regulation, are at once real—that is, related to variables that are physical,

[23] W.G. Rothstein, *Public Health and the Risk Factor: A History of an Uneven Medical Revolution* (Rochester, NY, 2003). See also T.L. Alborn, *Regulated Lives: Life Insurance and British Society, 1840–1920* (Toronto, 2009); and V. Berridge, *Marketing Health: Smoking and the Discourse of Public Health in Britain, 1945–2000* (Oxford, 2007).

[24] J.O. Zinn, 'Introduction: The Contribution of Sociology to the Discourse on Risk and Uncertainty', in J.O. Zinn (ed.), *Social Theories of Risk and Uncertainty: An Introduction* (Oxford, 2008), pp. 15–16. The other strand is 'edgework' theory, which looks at voluntary risk taking. Further summative accounts include D. Lupton (ed.), *Risk and Sociocultural Theory: New Directions and Perspectives* (Cambridge, 1999); and P. O'Malley, *Risk, Uncertainty and Government* (London, 2004).

demographic, technological and environmental—*and* socially embedded in shifting power structures and norms of behaviour. Rather, the debate is about the precise nature of this 'co-production' and relative degrees of 'realism' and 'constructivism'.[25]

The authors assembled here much prefer the richness of the historical record to the kind of theoretical intricacies that distinguish this literature. Certainly the volume as a whole has no particular theoretical axe to grind, and with good reason. For one thing, much of this literature is of a contemporary focus, concerned with developments over the past 30 or 40 years. We live in many 'ages', of course—'age of the internet', 'age of globalization' and so on—but this literature is partly an interrogation of the present and what has been dubbed a new 'age of risk'.[26] Equally, beyond the broader conundrum that Zinn suggests is central, this literature pulls in markedly different analytical directions. Douglas, for instance, advances a resolutely cultural approach, which views scientific and popular knowledge of modern risks as but a variation on a longstanding anthropological problem: namely danger, and how to manage that which undermines social cohesion and shared understandings of what is taboo and threatening.[27] Conversely, for systems theorists such as Luhmann, risk relates not to particular dangers or anxieties, such as environmental pollution or industrial technologies; rather, our modern obsession with risk is a product of a generalized structure of decision-making that evolved with the decline of any 'exterior' points of reference, such as God or a Great Chain of Being, and a waning sense of divine agency and providence.[28] Instead, in a development that Luhmann suggests began during the nineteenth century, modern societies practise a risk-based culture of administration based on the assumption of contingent human agency, whereby the principal guide for future (contingent) decisions are the consequences of past (contingent) decisions. All 'subsystems' of modern society, whether political, economic,

[25] J.O. Zinn, 'A Comparison of Sociological Theorizing on Risk and Uncertainty', in Zinn (ed.), *Social Theories of Risk and Uncertainty*, pp. 168–209.

[26] See especially U. Beck, *Ecological Politics in an Age of Risk* (Cambridge, 1995); A. Petersen and D. Lupton, *The New Public Health: Health and Self in the Age of Risk* (London, 1996); and C. Coker, *War in an Age of Risk* (Cambridge, 2009).

[27] It is an approach that builds on her seminal *Purity and Danger* published in 1966. See especially M. Douglas and A.B. Wildavsky, *Risk and Culture: An Essay on the Selection of Technological and Environmental Dangers* (Berkeley, CA, 1982).

[28] Luhmann's major statement here is *Risk: A Sociological Theory*, trans. R. Barrett (Berlin, 1993).

legal or techno-scientific, are rooted in the actions of agents that have, in some form or other, calculated the risks of taking decisions.

Crucially, neither the work of Luhmann nor that of Douglas is especially, if at all, historical. Luhmann's account, as with his broader systems theorizing, is self-consciously abstract and based on the insights of information theory. Douglas' work is unapologetically anthropological, seeking in fact to blur the distinction between 'pre-modern' and 'modern' cultures of managing danger.[29] This is not true of all the literature, however. A more developed sensitivity to the historical record is especially evident in the governmentality strand, which has focused on how risk emerged as a key 'technology of government' in the realms of social welfare and the development of the modern state.[30] All of these accounts affirm the growing responsibility of the state for unfortunate human events, such as sickness, unemployment and crime. Yet they do so by focusing on the technical expertise and practices that underpin this process, which in fact have no *necessary* connection with a state, even if they might be—and were and continue to be—co-opted by the state.

In particular, these accounts suggest that risk is a product of new ways of reckoning with people in statistical terms, which reformulate accidental and harmful events such as theft, unemployment and sickness in a twofold fashion. First, statistical techniques enumerate these events as part of long-term sequences that afflict groups of people rather than individuals per se; second, they thereby transform actual, individual events into manifestations of collective, calculable probabilities. As François Ewald, the French historian of welfare, has detailed, insurance schemes, whether voluntary or compulsory, constitute one of the most notable instances of risk as a modern technology of government.[31] The key quality here is that risks are calculable, which means that they can also function as financial capital; or rather, as calibrated payments into necessarily collective schemes, thereby allowing security for the subscribers as well as individual compensatory payments when a virtual, collective risk becomes an actual event for a particular person. Other work in this vein, notably by

[29] See also, and respectively, N. Luhmann, *Social Systems*, trans. J. Bednarz (Stanford, CA, 1995); and M. Douglas, *Risk and Blame: Essays in Cultural Theory* (London, 1992).

[30] For a summary, see P. O'Malley, 'Governmentality and Risk', in Zinn (ed.), *Social Theories of Risk and Uncertainty*, pp. 52–75.

[31] See especially F. Ewald, 'Insurance and Risk', in G. Burchell, C. Gordon and P. Miller (eds), *The Foucault Effect: Studies in Governmentality* (Chicago, 1991), pp. 197–210; and F. Ewald, *L'État providence* (Paris, 1986).

Robert Castel, Nikolas Rose and Pat O'Malley, has looked at how actuarial formulations of risk emerged as a new means of rationalizing efforts to police crime during the latter stages of the twentieth century.[32] Crudely, so they suggest, practices have shifted from confining and treating subjects classified or convicted as 'dangerous' to pre-emptively targeting calculable 'risk' variables that either produce dangerous individuals or undermine their rehabilitation.

Of the above, Ewald's work on the birth of the French welfare state (*l'État providence*) is by far the richest in empirical terms, and it has formed a point of reference in a handful of works dealing with the history of insurance and workmen's compensation.[33] But if, for Ewald, the history of risk should be traced in terms of the development of specific rationalities of government over the nineteenth and twentieth centuries, he has not shied away from asserting the central role that risk plays in contemporary society. 'Risk', Ewald has written, 'presents itself as the modern approach to an event and the way in which, in our societies, we reflect upon issues that concern us. Risk is the single point upon which contemporary societies question themselves, analyse themselves, seek their values and, perhaps, recognize their limits.'[34] It is a position similar to that of Luhmann noted above: namely, that risk now forms the key point of reflection in all areas of administrative decision-making. It is the work of the German sociologist Ulrich Beck, however, that has done most to advance the thesis that managing risk is the defining feature of contemporary society. The prominence of his work stems from just this: the emphatic assertion that risk constitutes the singular thematic around which we might understand not only the administrative obsessions of our recent past and present, but also the social, political and environmental transformations that have taken place.

[32] R. Castel, 'From Dangerousness to Risk', in Burchell, Gordon and Miller (eds), *The Foucault Effect*, pp. 281–98; P. O'Malley, 'Risk, Power and Crime Prevention', *Economy and Society* 21 (1992), pp. 252–75; N. Rose, *Powers of Freedom: Reframing Political Thought* (Cambridge, 1999).

[33] P. Baldwin, *The Politics of Social Solidarity: Class Bases of the European Welfare State, 1875–1975* (Cambridge, 1990); G. Steinmetz, *Regulating the Social: The Welfare State and Local Politics in Imperial Germany* (Princeton, NJ, 1993); and G.W. Clark, *Betting on Lives: The Culture of Life Insurance in England, 1695–1775* (Manchester, 1999).

[34] F. Ewald, 'Risk in Contemporary Society', trans. J.-M. Dautrey and C.F. Stifler *Connecticut Insurance Law Journal* 6 (1999), p. 366.

First published in English in 1992, Beck's *Risk Society* has inspired voluminous commentary among sociologists and political scientists.[35] Quite whether Beck offers an accurate diagnosis of the present has been much debated, but for historians, the most striking aspect of his work is his delineation of the changes that have occurred *within* modernity, which he couches in terms of two distinct 'epochs'.[36] Briefly, Beck posits an initial 'industrial modernity', born in the nineteenth century, which replaced a pre-industrial world where accidents, dangers and natural catastrophes were viewed in fatalistic and providential terms. Industrial modernity, by contrast, though it produces novel risks and dangers—among others, environmental pollution, unemployment and technological injuries—nonetheless assumes that these can be rationalized and managed, whether through further technological advances or through the work of a welfare state. Furthermore, the key axis of struggle in industrial modernity is class and the social distribution of wealth.

The second phase, which began to develop following the Second World War, constitutes an intensification of the first, giving rise to a new and more radical modernity. Crucially, whereas dangers were previously 'residual', to the extent that they were considered amenable to government, they now become integral. In the risk society, Beck argues, 'progress' is inherently problematic and is 'reflexively' interrogated as such; that is, as the very cause and source of risks and dangers rather than as the means through which they might be resolved. Much as in the first phase of modernity, these dangers are recognized as man-made. Yet, such are the human-technological powers over nature, and such is the speed and density of global interconnections, that these risks assume an indeterminate form. Risks become difficult to confine to local and even national spaces (for example, the risk of radiation poisoning from nuclear accidents), science becomes increasingly unable to specify the effects of new technologies and substances over the long term (for example, genetically modified food), and politicians struggle to locate causes and culpable agents amid a global swirl of people, goods and information. Meanwhile, the class antagonisms of the industrial era are superseded by political struggles to define and eliminate dangers, which move to the centre of collective conflict.

[35] U. Beck, *Risk Society: Towards a New Modernity*, trans. M. Ritter (London, 1992).

[36] On the reception of Beck's theory, see M.P. Sørensen and A. Christiansen, *Ulrich Beck: An Introduction to the Theory of Second Modernity and the Risk Society* (London, 2013), Chapter 8.

This is only to sketch what has been and remains a vibrant field of theoretical reflection, but it is evidently the case that no single historiographical agenda emerges from the literature described above. It is much too abundant for this. What, then, does it offer historians and what might we take from it? The literature certainly offers what might be called some basic rules of thumb: for instance, that risks and accidents are social and political phenomena as much as physical and environmental; or, again, that their regulation is bound up with struggles to define what is legitimate and illegitimate, tolerable and intolerable, preventable or not—analytical insights that are already evident in the emergent historiography of risks and accidents outlined above. But it also represents an opportunity to contribute towards contemporary debates, inviting reflection on the novelty of the present and begging questions about when and how governing risks became a key feature of modern societies. This is surely much needed, for there is no sign that risk is diminishing as a topic of debate in the social sciences. Crucial here is the historical task of challenging more abstract and presented-centred approaches to risk by developing more patient, textured and precise studies of the past. Another is generating new and more empirically satisfying periodizations and patterns of development.

Historians in fact have already begun this work, challenging Beck's account in particular. The main line of argument is that there was no clean break between a 'first' and a 'second' modernity.[37] Already in the nineteenth century, 'progress' was considered as inherently, and not just incidentally, problematic. Even what today we would call 'climate change' was a source of anxiety. More broadly, attempts to regulate the risks and dangers generated by urbanization and industrialization were subject to the competing claims of experts and members of the public. Then, as now, the management of risks was a hugely confused and contingent process. The work of Beck forms a point of reference in some of the chapters that follow here and certainly the volume as a whole suggests that our present 'age of risk' is not as novel as some sociologists and political scientists have claimed.

[37] See especially S. Boudia and N. Jas, 'Risk and "Risk Society" in Historical Perspective', *History and Technology* 23 (2007), pp. 317–31; J.-B. Fressoz, 'Beck Back in the 19th Century: Towards a Genealogy of Risk Society', *History and Technology* 23 (2007), pp. 333–50; F. Locher and J.-B. Fressoz, 'Modernity's Frail Climate: A Climate History of Environmental Reflexivity', *Critical Inquiry* 38 (2012), pp. 579–98; T. Cooper and S. Bulmer, 'Refuse and the "Risk Society": The Political Ecology of Risk in Inter-war Britain', *Social History of Medicine* 26 (2013), pp. 246–66; and Mohun, *Risk*.

Most of all, the theoretical literature suggests that we can and should develop a more foundational sense of the importance of risk in the past and a more expansive sense of how it has been governed. Among other things, the literature is at once a symptom of and a reflection on the exhaustion of any grand narratives of progress and promises of greater human security and safety. Regardless of any particular theories or arguments, it thus encourages historians to look again at the past and to view the production of risks as part of what is evidently a longstanding and constitutive—as opposed to temporary and incidental—feature of modern societies, even if the production of these risks assumes different forms and intensities over time. Equally, this literature suggests that governing risks is something that extends far beyond a state or even experts. Although the state is not entirely absent, it is but one actor among many that struggles to define and regulate the multiple hazards generated by a technologized, industrialized society, including politicians, businesses, corporations, pressure groups and families. Furthermore, these accounts are populated by non-human as much as by human agents: that is, the often fraught—and sometimes devastating—relations of the latter with machines, technological infrastructures, artificial substances and the natural environment. To put it another way, this literature encourages an altogether diffuse and eclectic sense of what governing is, and where we might locate the production and regulation of risks.

'Risks', 'Dangers' and 'Accidents': Meanings and Context

This volume embraces this eclecticism, seeking new connections and shared dynamics between areas of regulation and objects of anxiety that have often been examined in isolation. The argument of the book is partly inscribed in the variety of problems that it brings together. These extend from designing gas-free domestic plumbing networks and regulating the sale of carbolic acid in the nineteenth century to policing motor traffic accidents and encouraging the safe enjoyment of open waters in the twentieth—evidently diverse endeavours, reacting to and seeking to shape the emergence of very different technologies and popular habits, and yet, equally, all concerned with the regulation of risk and the management of danger.

The chapters also share a common historical context and a common language of 'risks', 'dangers' and 'accidents'. It is a sign of the contemporary prominence of risk-based practices that scholars and safety practitioners have debated the precise meanings of these terms (and in some cases in quite rarefied ways).[38] Certainly, one distinction insisted upon today is between risk on the one hand, and danger or hazard on the other. As Britain's Health and Safety Executive points out, a danger or hazard is anything that may cause harm and injury, such as a corrosive chemical or an electricity socket, whereas risk refers to the likelihood or chance that someone will be harmed by a danger and how serious that might prove to be.[39] This was not a distinction insisted on in the past, even if it might be glimpsed in places. *Johnson's Dictionary*, published in 1755, for instance, defined risk as 'hazard; danger; chance of harm'. Danger meant 'risk; hazard; peril'.[40] Later dictionaries offered much the same definitions as Samuel Johnson's pioneering work and in most contexts the terms were deployed quite loosely, if not always incorrectly, together—much as they are today. 'No one voluntarily incurs injury; but risks, apparently small, frequently turn out to be serious hazards', urged one safety pamphlet published in 1914 by the Great Western Railway Company. 'Why take the risks?' it added. 'Always choose the "Safety" method of doing your work.'[41] The examples might be multiplied.

Indeed, loosely or otherwise, these terms were deployed with growing frequency. This partly reflected a transformation in the organizational complexity and technological density of British society. Four developments might be highlighted. One is pronounced demographic growth and urbanization. In 1801, 80 % of a population of 15 million resided in rural areas. A century later, 80 % of a population of 41 million lived in towns and cities—a percentage that is roughly the same today, albeit with a population of over 62 million. The remaining three developments are tightly interwoven. The first is industrialization and the emergence of heavy industries in the nineteenth century, such as shipbuilding and mining, followed by lighter forms in the twentieth, such as the manufacture of consumer electronics. The second is the advent of new technologies and forms of energy. From the 1830s, steam engines powered railway locomotives; internal combustion engines followed, propelling cars and aeroplanes. Natural gas was mobilized in order to light streets and to heat

[38] An excellent summary is B. Heyman, M. Shaw, A. Alaszewski and M. Titterton, *Risk, Safety and Clinical Practice: Health Care through the Lens of Risk* (Oxford, 2010), Chapter 1.

[39] www.hse.gov.uk/risk/controlling-risks.htm (date accessed 10 November 2015).

[40] S. Johnson, *A Dictionary of the English Language* (London, 1755), pp. 'Dan' and 'Ris'.

[41] The Great Western Railway Company, *The 'Safety' Movement* (London, 1914), pp. 4–5.

homes. Electricity was later mass produced, relying on power stations that burned coal and even, from the 1950s, harnessed the energy from nuclear reactions. The third development is the emergence of a wealth of new material resources. Iron, coal and cotton-based textiles remained important, but they were joined by substances whose production required much greater industrial might and scientific ingenuity, among them steel, aluminium, rubber, plastics and petroleum.

Of course, all of these developments were part of and helped to produce a society characterized by advancing prosperity, material comfort and higher living standards. Life expectancy increased markedly, as Britain underwent an epidemiological transition from infectious to chronic diseases during the early twentieth century.[42] Yet, besides the variable nature of this progress according to class and region, these same developments also produced a suite of new problems and novel dangers and risks. Prior to their decline, infectious diseases such as smallpox, diphtheria and scarlet fever were rendered more unruly and devastating by the speed and density with which people mixed and moved around. New technologies and work practices introduced new ways of dying. Train crashes and air disasters represent the most dramatic instances, but they formed only a fraction of the injurious and deadly possibilities that were now realized, not least a great seam of unspectacular, if no less deadly, 'industrial diseases', a term that became common in the Edwardian period. More might be said in this vein. The point is that a discourse of risk and danger was not a matter of cultural invention; it reflected a profound transformation in the physical fabric and material culture of British society.

To affirm this dimension, however, is not to occlude the importance of equally profound changes in ways of thinking about the world and practices of governing. Risk is a case in point. We might well be sceptical of claims made by the likes of Beck and Luhmann that risk is a defining feature of modern societies. Yet they find (perhaps unlikely) allies in historians of science and, in particular, historians of statistics and theories of probability. Work on this front is immense, and although much of it is concerned with methodological innovations in the social and natural sciences—and especially new ways of assessing causality—it has also argued that these innovations were part of broader cultural and administrative

[42] An excellent summary of this transition is S. Szreter and A. Hardy, 'Urban Fertility and Mortality Patterns', in M. Daunton (ed.), *The Cambridge Urban History of Britain: Volume III, 1840–1950* (Cambridge, 2000), pp. 629–72.

transformations; or, to quote one study of this sort, the advent of an 'empire of chance'.[43] Beyond laboratories and the computations of social scientists, the most signal manifestation of this was the insurance business. As Lorraine Daston and Robin Pearson have argued, the business took off in the seventeenth and eighteenth centuries, and at this point operated according to rudimentary, even intuitive, ideas of probability, which bore little relation to the use of numbers.[44] All this changed in the nineteenth century with the birth of 'actuarial science', which transformed risk into a matter of number crunching and statistical time series.[45] Here especially risk was understood as a matter of probability—of quantifiable degrees of chance—and it extended everywhere. As early as 1867, one handbook was able to detail the precise actuarial practices that surrounded shipping, fire, life and personal accident ('casualty') insurance, a field of application that would only expand thereafter.[46] As Ewald has noted: 'Today, it is hard to imagine all the things that insurers have managed to invent as classes of risk ... [and] always, it should be said, with profitable results.'[47]

Ultimately, so these accounts argue, the pervasiveness of actuarial risk and its seemingly endless applications is a reflection of a world divested of any sense of divine superintendence or providence, at least at the level of collective institutions (individual beliefs are another matter, of course). Instead, the assumption is that the world operates according to statistical laws, patterns and regularities, which themselves might be modified by acting on underlying conditions and causal factors. This latter aspect is crucial, for growing reference to risks and dangers also reflected the assumption that they might be assessed and managed, magnified or reduced, by the actions of humans. The very practice of insurance is an exercise in calculating and governing risk, and it was a practice that was eventually collectivized and socialized under the responsibility of the

[43] G. Gigerenzer et al., *The Empire of Chance: How Probability Changed Science and Everyday Life* (Cambridge, 1989). See also T.M. Porter, *The Rise of Statistical Thinking, 1830–1900* (Princeton, NJ, 1986); I. Hacking, *The Taming of Chance* (Cambridge, 1990); and P.L. Bernstein, *Against the Gods: The Remarkable Story of Risk* (New York, 1996).

[44] L. Daston, *Classical Probability in the Enlightenment* (Princeton, NJ, 1988), Chapter 3; R. Pearson, 'Moral Hazard and the Assessment of Insurance Risk in Eighteenth- and Early-Nineteenth-Century Britain', *Business History Review* 76 (2002), pp. 1–35.

[45] T.L. Alborn, 'A Calculating Profession: Victorian Actuaries among the Statisticians', in M. Power (ed.), *Accounting and Science: Natural Inquiry and Commercial Reason* (Cambridge, 1996), pp. 81–119.

[46] C. Walford, *The Insurance Guide and Hand Book* (London, 1867).

[47] Ewald, 'Insurance and Risk', p. 199.

state and an enormous bureaucracy: the National Insurance Act of 1911, for instance, also created a number and numbered card for each skilled worker. But the manifestations are of course multiple, extending indeed to all those reforming and regulatory initiatives historians have collected together under the broad rubric of 'welfare' and the 'welfare state'.

It would be pointless to summarize these here. They are well known and, as this volume contends, building on the historiography described in the first section, 'the state' was not the only agent involved in the government of risk. For our purposes, we might note three developments. The first is informational—namely, the mass of knowledge that emerged concerning risks, dangers and accidents. In 1837, for instance, the registration of death and cause of death was placed on a comprehensive footing with the establishment of the General Register Office, paving the way for the timetabled production of mortality reports according to annual and quarterly rhythms. Reporting dangers and accidents also became routine. The obligation to report accidents in factories was imposed in 1844 and applied to smaller workshops in 1878; in 1895, it became compulsory to report both fatal and non-fatal accidents at work. Similarly, the compulsory notification of infectious diseases began in a handful of towns in the mid-1870s, and by the mid-1890s was being practised throughout the country.[48] None of this informational intensity would diminish in the twentieth and twenty-first centuries. Recent developments include the refinement of the Reporting of Injuries, Diseases and Dangerous Occurrences Regulations (RIDDOR) in 2013, which require 'responsible persons' such as employers and teachers to report a range of cases, including accidents that lead to death or incapacitating injury; occupational diseases (e.g. carpal tunnel syndrome); incidents relating to carcinogens and mutagens; dangerous occurrences (e.g. fires); and gas leaks.[49]

The second development is the specialization and professionalization of safety as a field of concern. The factory, railway and mines inspectorates, established in 1833, 1840 and 1842, respectively, were home to the first

[48] P.W.J. Bartrip and P.T. Fenn, 'The Measurement of Safety: Factory Accident Statistics in Victorian and Edwardian Britain', *Historical Research* 63 (1990), pp. 58–72; G. Mooney 'Public Health versus Private Practice: The Contested Development of Compulsory Infectious Disease Notification in Late Nineteenth-Century Britain', *Bulletin of the History of Medicine* 73 (1999), pp. 238–67.

[49] Health and Safety Executive, *Reporting Accidents and Incidents at Work: A Brief Guide to the Reporting of Injuries, Diseases and Dangerous Occurrences Regulations 2013* (London, 2013).

officials specifically charged with protecting safety and we might trace a line here to perhaps the most significant institutional development of the twentieth century, the establishment of the Health and Safety Executive in 1974. Yet safety as a distinct practice and ideal was also developed by multiple actors beyond the state. Drawing on the early twentieth-century American 'Safety First' movement, for instance, the British railway industry introduced a 'Safety Movement' in 1913, which aimed to instruct workers in ways of avoiding accidents.[50] This educational approach spilled over into the mining and shipbuilding industries, which also made use of safety committees comprising representatives of workers and managers. Beyond the workplace, voluntary bodies began to promote safety in homes, schools, parks, streets, swimming pools and beaches—indeed, few sites escaped some kind of attention. Formed in 1916, the London 'Safety First' Council was followed in 1923 by the National 'Safety First' Association, which in 1941 became the Royal Society for the Prevention of Accidents (RoSPA). Meanwhile, growing numbers of 'safety engineers' and 'safety officers' were appointed, eventually leading to the establishment in 1945 of what would become the Institution of Occupational Safety and Health, which is still today the principal professional home for Britain's safety experts.

A third development is technical and concerns the scale of governing. Paradoxically perhaps, amid reference to an increasingly abstract and impersonal state, we find a descent into the specification and maintenance of myriad, maddening technical details, and especially those relating to complex machinery and technological systems. Victorian engineers obsessed, for instance, about the best way to combine safety and efficiency in the construction of domestic and industrial boilers. Flues, pipes, cylinders, feed pumps and safety valves: the design of each was debated and refined as engineers sought to secure boilers that were less likely to explode. Yet, even with sound design and construction, all could agree that maintenance was essential: in 1854, the Manchester Steam Users' Association was formed to promote regular practices of inspection and repair.[51] Once more, this only intensified during the twentieth century. Routine maintenance and risk assessment by safety engineers became

[50] M. Esbester, *The Birth of Modern Safety: Preventing Worker Accidents on Britain's Railways, 1871–1948* (Aldershot, forthcoming).

[51] P.W.J. Bartrip, 'The State and the Steam-Boiler in Nineteenth-Century Britain', *International Review of Social History* 25 (1980), pp. 77–105.

central to the functioning of the aeronautical, oil and nuclear industries, where the consequences of minor technical faults could be—and sometimes were—catastrophic. But it was manifest across the entire technological spectrum, extending to relatively modest forms of machinery. Annual 'MOT' tests for motor vehicles, for instance, were introduced in 1960. Initially the tests applied to vehicles that were over 10 years old and involved rudimentary checks of brakes, lights and steering columns. In 1967, the testable age was reduced to 3 years, something supplemented by a gradual expansion in the number of components subject to inspection, which now include tyre treads, wheel bearings, seat belts, indicators and brake lights.

Crucially, all of the above developments can be seen in the history of the term 'accident' and the status of 'the accidental'. Prior to the nineteenth century, the term 'accidental' referred to non-essential qualities of beings and things, a connotation evident in the meaning of 'accidents', which referred to events with no necessary or identifiable causation. They were, to quote *Johnson's Dictionary* once more, that 'which happens unforeseen ... [by] chance', and accordingly provoked a sense of fatalism and fate.[52] Their growing frequency, however, combined with their investigation, gradually led to accidents assuming a 'normalized' status, to quote Cooter and Luckin, whereby they were recognized as an unfortunate but recurrent facet of urban-industrial society.[53] In 1850, for instance, the tireless technological enthusiast Dionysius Lardner published his *Railway Economy*, a treatise that sought to provide a comprehensive guide to this emerging industry. Tellingly, it contained a chapter entitled 'Accidents on Railways', in which Lardner classified and enumerated the injuries and fatalities so far, distinguishing between those that were 'beyond the control' of passengers and railway employees, and those 'which might have been prevented'. Much else followed, including figures relating to the 'ratio of risk' on British and Belgian railway lines.[54]

Yet, as Lardner's text suggests, if accidents were increasingly regarded as recurrent and regular, even normal, they were not necessarily regarded as unavoidable or inevitable. Instead, fitfully, the fatalism of earlier centuries was displaced by the assumption that accidents were preventable.

[52] Johnson, *A Dictionary of the English Language*, p. 'Acc'.

[53] Cooter and Luckin, 'Accidents in History', p. 5.

[54] D. Lardner, *Railway Economy: A Treatise on the New Art of Transport, its Management, Prospects and Relations, Commercial, Financial and Social* (London, 1850), Chapter 14.

This was most obviously manifest in the emergence of safety as a diffuse field of voluntary and official endeavour. But it was also evident in legal enactments such as the Workmen's Compensation Acts of 1897 and 1906, which insisted on employer liability in the event of an accident—or, in other words, that employees had the right to enjoy a safe working environment and that if accidents occurred, it represented a failure on the part of employers, thereby rendering someone responsible.[55] Corporate manslaughter and homicide laws are but the most recent manifestation of this kind of legal rationalization of the accidental. Even so, as scholars have suggested, the modern reappraisal of the accident is a subtle and complex one.[56] On the one hand, we know that they will happen, just not to whom, when and where precisely. As statistics suggests, a more or less regular number of accidents happen every year. They are patterned and predictable, albeit at a *general* level (which is why they can seem quite random at the level of the individual). On the other hand, we seek to assert our control over accidents in particular places and moments, and assign responsibility for their prevention. Ultimately, what binds these two strands of governance together is the idea of risk—or, rather, and more actively, the idea that governing risks involves working vigilantly on habits, dispositions, propensities and probabilities.

Outline of Chapters

It should be stressed once more that this book does not seek to exhaust its subject matter. The chapters that follow, for instance, make only limited reference to actuarial techniques, legal innovations and methodological advances in statistics and public medicine—all of which, as the above sketch suggests, have a crucial bearing on the governance of risks, dangers and accidents of a physical and everyday sort. Even so, the world of popular habits, spaces and technologies makes for a rich historical field in itself, providing ample material for rethinking the nature of modern British society, moving beyond the state as the principal horizon of analysis and, most of all, probing when, how and why regulating risk became such a central and obsessive dimension of governing. Ultimately, it is hoped that the

[55] Useful discussions include Figlio, 'What is an Accident?' and Ewald, 'Insurance and Risk'.

[56] See especially R. Hamilton, *Accident: A Philosophical and Literary History* (Chicago, 2007).

volume will contribute to defining just this: namely, some of the critical coordinates of this emerging area of historiography and a better sense of the thematic concerns that might lend it coherence. We summarize these concerns in a co-authored conclusion (along with Arwen Mohun and Thomas Le Roux), before then outlining some of the key historical dynamics and tensions that might help to situate Britain in a comparative and connected international framework.

The preceding chapters are organized into four parts. We begin in Part I, entitled Early Risk Societies, with two chapters that directly address questions of genesis and periodization. Francis Dodsworth's chapter examines the origins of what contemporary analysts call 'risk-based policing'. But whereas sociologists and criminologists locate the emergence of this particular style of policing in the latter half of the twentieth century, Dodsworth boldly argues that it began in the mid- to late eighteenth century. It was at this point, he suggests, when a set of actuarial and informational practices combined to fashion a new kind of policing, one that was self-consciously risk-averse and 'preventive', and concerned with the threat posed by 'dangerous' sections of the urban population. Ryan Vieira then examines the press and the emergence of what he calls the 'single accident article' during the 1820s, something that would later become a crucial component of the cultural mechanisms developed to ease popular anxieties over the dangers of an increasingly technologized society. His point of departure is the work of Beck and the assumption that the cause of this might be sought in the hazards introduced by early industrialization. In fact, Vieira suggests, the explanation should be sought in social and cultural rather than technological and economic changes, and in particular the declining authority of the aristocracy.

The chapters by Dodsworth and Vieira suggest that historians can work productively both with and against ways of theorizing the 'risk society'—they suggest in fact that the benefits lie in doing both. They also challenge disciplines such as sociology to develop more sensitive appreciations of the past and more sophisticated genealogies of our present 'age of risk'. This challenge continues in the remaining three parts, which are grouped thematically in terms of particular arenas of governance and the location and generation of risks. The next part, Environmental Risks, opens with a chapter by Chris Otter. This chapter also contributes to debates on periodizing the risk society, ranging as it does across the first (c. 1750–1830) and second (c. 1880–1930) Industrial Revolutions. Otter's main concern, however, is with the nature and dynamics of modern risk environments rather than with the genesis of specific risk-based practices. In particular, he urges the importance of material transformations in terms of understanding the production of risks in modern Britain, arguing that the advent of complex technological systems and industrialized chemistry engendered more hazardous and unpredictable relations between humans and non-humans. Ultimately, the advent of an 'artificial Britain' made possible a radical transformation in human experiences of danger and pain, death and uncertainty. Like Vieira, Otter engages with the work of Beck, but here the critique is levelled at Beck's disregard of the local, and his neglect of the embodied and situated nature of technological and synthetic risks.

The next two chapters by Tom Crook and Rebecca Whyte examine developments within the field of Victorian and Edwardian public health. Crucially, both point to the dangers and risks produced by measures otherwise designed to manage them. As Crook details, although cesspools constituted a source of pollution and disease, the ambitious and complex water-borne sewerage systems that replaced cesspools generated a novel danger of their own: the presence of sewer gas in homes and streets. It was not, however, solely a sanitary danger; as Crook suggests, it also constituted a significant challenge to middle-class ideals of sensory civility and domestic privacy, which is one reason why sewer gas caused such public alarm. Whyte's chapter demonstrates that the use of chemical disinfection was similarly fraught and troublesome. On the one hand, as a matter of both municipal and domestic practice, chemical disinfectants emerged as a crucial means of managing the risks and dangers of infectious diseases. On the other hand, these new and more widely available substances were, by design, supposed to be deadly, thus generating the risk of poisoning and injury—risks that were realized in a spate of carbolic-related suicides during the 1890s. How to balance public safety and public health proved immensely difficult and controversial.

There is much in both chapters to support Otter's argument regarding the development of infrastructural and synthetic risks, and how this relates to the advent of a more complex material-technological environment. The chapters also consider the place of experts and officials in governing risk, a theme further and more pointedly developed in the next chapter by Timothy Cooper in the context of what he calls 'everyday environmentalism' in twentieth-century Britain. In particular, the chapter seeks to offer a new way of understanding the politics of risk in modern Britain. For Cooper, this politics is not only rooted in spatial considerations regarding the location of environmental hazards, but also concerns time and different kinds of temporal exposure, from confronting immediate and catastrophic disasters on the one hand to living with more modest, if permanent, hazards on the other. At root, struggles regarding the regulation of risk are struggles regarding the integrity and durability of everyday life—and these are struggles, Cooper argues, that cannot be understood without reference to the demands of capitalism.

The technologically complex and 'artificial' society explored in Part II was also a more mobile and leisured society; or, rather, a society where locomotive mobility and various leisure pursuits—including driving itself—combined to generate a novel set of risks that played out in streets and sites of recreation. This is the subject of Part III, entitled Mobility and Leisure Risks, which contains three studies. It opens with Bill Luckin's chapter on 'drunk-driving' and the often fraught interrelations of pedestrians, alcohol and an expanding number of horse-drawn vehicles. It explores an era when determining whether or not an errant driver was drunk was a haphazard, impressionistic and sometimes comic affair. At this point, there was no necessary equation between alcoholic impairment and criminal negligence. Yet, as Luckin argues, this was not necessarily out of place in an already 'pro-motorist' culture, where the rights of road users trumped those of pedestrians—and, indeed, it was a culture that would prove remarkably resilient amid the increasingly busy streets of Britain's towns and cities. Much like the chapters by Vieira and Crook, it encourages a socially embedded understanding of 'the accidental' and 'dangerous', and the abiding importance of class.

The next chapter by Chris A. Williams moves into the early twentieth century and concerns the advent of mass, motorized automobility. His focus is the growing role of the police in regulating motor traffic accidents, thus shedding further light on the place of experts and officials in governing risks. Rising numbers of fatalities and injuries on Britain's roads certainly prompted greater levels of police intervention, gradually eroding the more lenient and ad hoc culture of regulation described in Luckin's chapter. Yet, as Williams argues, although the police opted for power and responsibility over traffic, they sought to do so on their own terms, ultimately privileging spatial and engineering solutions. To put it another way, choices were made, in keeping with their professional interests and considerations of bureaucratic convenience and manpower resources. The risks that accompanied the onset of a more affluent and mobile society are further explored in the chapter by Glen O'Hara, which recovers the multiple anxieties and policy initiatives that attended swimming in and playing near open waters. The principal danger here was drowning and, as O'Hara argues, it is a danger that can only be properly understood in the context of rising standards of living and concerns about the 'correct' use of leisure time, especially among the young. It was also a danger that attracted the regulatory work of all manner of agents, among them charities, schools, local authorities and safety professionals, all of which sought to encourage more responsible parenting practices and safety-conscious children. Here, as elsewhere, governing risk involved reckoning with popular habits and targeting the self.

The final part concerns the workplace and is entitled Occupational Risks. As noted above, much has been written on the emergence of industrial risks in the nineteenth and early twentieth centuries, and the slow and contested gestation of an 'industrial welfare' regime. The two chapters in this part explore developments in post-war Britain and, in particular, the creation and work of Britain's Health and Safety Executive (HSE), still the nation's pre-eminent authority when it comes to governing risk in the workplace—and indeed much beyond. Christopher Sirrs' chapter presents a fresh reading of the genesis of the 1972 Robens Report, which outlined the regulatory philosophy of what would become the HSE two years later. It offered, he suggests, a vision of governance that was very much of its time, reflecting a movement of regulatory attention over the 1960s towards safety management by employers and workers themselves, and the need for health and safety to be accepted as an integral part of everyday industrial practice. Curiously, perhaps, the state, in the form of the HSE, was also to be a custodian of industrial 'self-regulation'. Building on Sirrs' chapter, the next chapter by Paul Almond and Mike Esbester explores how the governance of health and safety broadened still further, particularly from the mid-1980s, when it began to reach beyond employers and employees to embrace the public at large. This partly reflected the changing economic structure of the UK and the growing scope of health and safety regulation, but it was also embedded, they argue, in the rise of neoliberalism and a more aggressive anti-regulatory agenda. The tabloid refrain 'health and safety gone mad' has achieved considerable currency in recent years. This chapter details the complex reasons for such popular antipathy, and how the regulation of health and safety came to embrace a multiplicity of actors. It once more demonstrates the importance of governance as a central theme in understanding risk and the regulation of everyday dangers in modern Britain.

PART I

Early Risk Societies

CHAPTER 2

Risk, Prevention and Policing, c. 1750–1850

Francis Dodsworth

Until the 1970s, modern policing was generally understood to have emerged with the creation of London's Metropolitan Police in 1829 under the auspices of Sir Robert Peel. Such accounts relied on a Whiggish narrative of organizational progress, whereby customary practices were gradually replaced by those that were more rational and professional, and better suited to combatting the rising crime and social dislocation produced by urbanization during the late eighteenth and early nineteenth centuries. From the 1970s, this was challenged by a body of scholarship that portrayed the birth of modern policing as a response not to rising crime rates, but to the emergence of the working classes and associated fears of political revolt. From this perspective, the police were acting as agents of 'social control', suppressing political opposition and collective action, enforcing bourgeois moral values, and aiding the appropriation and monetization of communal resources in the service of capitalism.[1]

[1] For a guide to this literature, see C. Emsley, *The English Police: A Political and Social History* (London, 1996) and his 'Filling in, Adding up, Moving On: Criminal Justice History in Contemporary Britain', *Crime, History and Societies* 9 (2005), pp. 117–38.

F. Dodsworth
Faculty of Arts and Social Sciences, Kingston University, London,
Penrhyn Road Campus, Kingston upon Thames, Surrey KT1 2EE, UK

T. Crook, M. Esbester (eds), *Governing Risks in Modern Britain*,
DOI 10.1057/978-1-137-46745-4_2

Recent work has contested both of these interpretations by demonstrating that the development of modern policing took place over a much longer time-span than the late eighteenth and early nineteenth centuries, even if this period is still regarded as a key point of transition. In fact, organized, paid policing began to emerge in London in the late seventeenth century and developed in fits and starts over the next 100 or so years. Methods of discipline, principles of selection, the use of uniforms and patrols, and even the formation of a nascent detective force: all predated the founding of the Metropolitan Police.[2] These more pragmatic, empirical studies of policing development have certainly undermined the grand narratives of progress and class struggle that framed earlier histories, and yet, in so doing, they have also lost something of their narrative and interpretive ambition. In general, these accounts have relied on what John Styles has termed a 'problem-response' model of change, whereby developments in policing are linked, quite directly in some cases, to shifting patterns of crime, with little attempt to understand the links between the construction of crime as a 'social problem' and wider transformations in cultures of governing.[3]

This chapter moves back in the other direction, seeking to reconnect the very real anxieties contemporaries expressed about these changing patterns of crime with a wider transformation in governmental culture.[4] It is argued that although changing patterns of crime may have provided the impetus for developments in policing, they did not define or determine the ways in which this change took place. Indeed, the very idea that 'crime' was a problem that could be 'managed' was itself relatively novel and was part of an embryonic culture of risk management that emerged during the period 1750–1850. This culture was perhaps most evident in the fledgling insurance industry and the growth of a variety of mutual and

[2] J.M. Beattie, *Policing and Punishment in London, 1660–1750: Urban Crime and the Limits of Terror* (Oxford, 2001); J.M. Beattie, *The First English Detectives: The Bow Street Runners and the Policing of London, 1750–1840* (Oxford, 2012); A.T. Harris, *Policing the City: Crime and Legal Authority in London, 1740–1840* (Columbus, OH, 2004); E.A. Reynolds, *Before the Bobbies: The Night Watch and Police Reform in Metropolitan London* (Stanford, CA, 1998).

[3] J. Styles, 'The Emergence of the Police—Explaining Police Reform in Eighteenth- and Nineteenth-Century England', *British Journal of Criminology* 27 (1987), pp. 19–20. Beattie, *The First English Detectives* is particularly insistent on this.

[4] C. Gordon, 'Governmental Rationality: An Introduction', in G. Burchell, C. Gordon and P. Miller (eds), *The Foucault Effect: Studies in Governmentality* (Hemel Hempstead, 1991), pp. 1–51.

friendly associations, but it is also evident in the development of modern policing.[5] This chapter does not pretend to offer an exhaustive account of this process; rather, it sketches some of the key historical elements—some of the novel practices, forms of language and reforming aspirations—that constitute something like the genealogical roots of risk-based policing.

The aim is twofold. The first is to recover a neglected aspect of the birth of modern policing in Britain. Reading some revisionist accounts that portray police history as the history of social control, one might be forgiven for forgetting that a central dimension of police reform was an attempt to prevent and cope with victimization. Modern policing emerged at a time when there was no public prosecutor and when becoming a victim of crime could have severe financial as well as personal and physical consequences. Policing practices were developed in order to either prevent, or reduce the likelihood of, theft and loss of property, and as a means of spreading the costs of victimization. This is not to claim that all aspects of policing can be explained by this process: 'police' was a broad concept with many facets.[6] But we should not overlook the key concerns of contemporaries: namely, to protect themselves against the risk of robbery, burglary and the costs of pursuing justice. The second aim of the chapter is to contribute towards—and complicate—a largely sociological literature that places the birth of risk-oriented policing firmly in the late twentieth century. This chapter suggests that, in fact, risk management has in some senses been an aspect of modern policing from its inception. The roots of the 'risk society', then, lie much deeper than this literature assumes. The chapter therefore begins by engaging with these recent debates and the shifts towards risk-based police practices that are claimed to have taken place only recently, in the latter stages of the post-Second World War period.

[5] On the cultural history of insurance, see T. Alborn, *Regulated Lives: Life Insurance and British Society, 1800–1914* (Toronto, 2009); G. Clarke, *Betting on Lives: The Culture of Life Insurance in England, 1695–1775* (Manchester, 1999); N. Henry and C. Schmitt (eds), *Victorian Investments: New Perspectives on Finance and Culture* (Bloomington, IN, 2009); L. McFall and F. Dodsworth, 'Fabricating the Market: The Material Promotion of Life Assurance in the Long Nineteenth Century', *Journal of Historical Sociology* 22 (2009), pp. 30–54.

[6] F. Dodsworth, 'The Idea of Police in Eighteenth-Century England: Discipline, Reformation, Superintendence, c. 1780–1800', *Journal of the History of Ideas* 69 (2008), pp. 583–604; M. Neocleous, *The Fabrication of Social Order: A Critical Theory of Police Power* (London, 2000).

Policing the 'Risk Society'

In 1997, Richard Ericson and Kevin Haggerty published their groundbreaking work *Policing the Risk Society*, in which they argued that present-day policing was no longer about enforcing social order by controlling crime through the detection and punishment of individual offenders. Rather, it was now largely concerned with using techniques and technologies of surveillance to assess and manage risk, with the aim of providing security against threats.[7] They argued that the police have come to assume a central place in the wider government of risk in society and that day-to-day police work now operates according to the logic of risk, as evident in an array of 'rules, formats and technologies'.[8] Instead of focusing on the generation of information about specific criminals based on the personal connections of detectives or patrolling the streets in order to deter criminal acts, the role of the police has increasingly become one of risk assessment through technical-statistical procedures and the communication of this information to other agencies, among them health services, neighbourhood watch organizations and insurance companies. Policing is no longer concerned with the enforcement of order through the physical presence of 'Bobbies on the beat'; it now 'consists of the public police coordinating their activities with policing agents in all other institutions to provide a society-wide basis for risk-management (governance) and security (guarantees against loss)'.[9]

The kind of practices deemed crucial here include the use of crime statistics not to understand the background causes or motivations of crime, but to inform the identification of criminal risk factors and risk populations; the practice of 'actuarial justice' in which sentencing is dictated less by the severity of a (past) offence and more by the (future) risk of reoffending; the role of the insurance industry in encouraging property holders to fortify their houses, invest in security technologies and report incidents to the police; the primacy of 'networked' connections and information sharing between the police, members of the public, fire and rescue services, local authorities and the probation service (as in the Neighbourhood Watch schemes of the 1980s and more recently Community Safety Partnerships); and the growth of electronic forms of surveillance, which enable the

[7] R.V. Ericson and K.D. Haggerty, *Policing the Risk Society* (Oxford, 1997).
[8] *Ibid.*, p. 14.
[9] *Ibid.*, p. 3.

permanent monitoring of 'risk zones'—all developments that have been documented in the work of a number of other criminologists and sociologists, who also identify a decisive shift in policing during the last 30 years.[10]

In making this argument, Ericson and Haggerty attempt to synthesize two prominent theoretical frameworks for understanding modern government through risk: Ulrich Beck's 'risk society' thesis and work inspired by Michel Foucault, which is generally referred to as the 'governmentality' approach. As Chapter 1 of this volume has detailed, Beck suggests that a 'risk society' has displaced an earlier 'industrial modernity'. It inheres, Beck argues, not only in exposure to novel technological dangers and the threat of global catastrophe, but also concerns the anxious anticipation of these dangers, their calculation in advance and formulation in actuarial and probabilistic terms (as 'risks'), and the ongoing informational processing of risks and their 'reflexive' politicization as products of human endeavour and 'progress'. Foucauldian accounts also highlight the significance of government through risk in the contemporary world, but they posit a much longer genealogy, tracing these developments back to the nineteenth century, linking them to the widespread use of statistics and in particular actuarial techniques for the assessment of risk among populations.[11]

This domination of the governmental imagination by risk is argued to have had a direct impact on policing, displacing the 'crime-fighting' model of police work that characterized the early to mid-twentieth century, based on a reaction to events in the past and knowledge of known offenders. Instead, policing has become concerned with the future-oriented management of risk.[12] Contemporary policing is said to be concerned with managing statistically calculable harms through actuarial techniques, as

[10] Similar transformations are charted in D. Garland, *The Culture of Control: Crime and Social Order in Contemporary Society* (Oxford, 2001) and N. Rose, 'Government and Control', *British Journal of Criminology* 40 (2000), pp. 321–39.

[11] Classic Foucauldian studies are F. Ewald, 'Insurance and Risk' and R. Castel, 'From Dangerousness to Risk', in Burchell, Gordon and Miller (eds), *The Foucault Effect*, pp. 197–210, 281–98; P. O'Malley, 'Risk, Power and Crime Prevention', *Economy and Society* 21 (1992), pp. 252–75 and his 'Risk and Responsibility', in A. Barry, T. Osborne and N. Rose (eds), *Foucault and Political Reason: Liberalism, Neo-Liberalism and Rationalities of Government* (London, 1996), pp. 189–207.

[12] P. O'Malley and S. Hutchinson, 'Reinventing Prevention: Why Did "Crime Prevention" Develop so Late?', *British Journal of Criminology* 47 (2007), pp. 373–89. On modern policing as 'crime fighting', comparable to the concept of firefighting, see P. O'Malley, *Crime and Risk* (London, 2010), p. 38.

well as tactics of ongoing surveillance, pre-emption and anticipation. Risk, furthermore, is contrasted to 'uncertainty', which refers to futures that are infrequent or unique, and with 'dangerousness', which is concerned with the habits, personal qualities and criminal dispositions associated with known deviant subjects.[13] Individual moral reformation of the offender is no longer the goal of either policing or penal policy; rather, the aim is to manage and monitor a permanent stratum of criminal behaviours and malign possibilities that inhere in groups of people and patterns of activity. This approach to governing crime is defined by the sociologist Nikolas Rose as an 'actuarial regime' of 'control' in which there is no attempt to transform the soul of the offender; rather, the concern is simply to control their behaviour—their actual conduct rather than some inner moral quality. Offenders are treated not as individuals, but as an aggregate, with the focus on the risks and crime rates associated with particular groups, such as the urban poor.[14] As part of this same reconfiguration of the governance of crime, police officers have joined an array of other 'knowledge workers', among them social workers, health visitors, education welfare officers and probation officers, all of whom are concerned with assessing and managing the risk posed by the behaviour of those judged 'socially excluded'.

Clearly there have been significant transformations in the government of crime and the practice of policing in the recent past. As part of their daily praxis, police officers now routinely engage in practices dubbed 'risk management' and 'risk assessment': indeed, they monitor offenders variously classified as 'high', 'medium' or 'low risk'. Likewise, the technological revolution of the late twentieth century has enabled masses of data to be collected, stored, processed and shared through CCTV and IT systems. Nevertheless, in making these claims for a radical transformation in the nature of policing, scholars such as Rose, and Ericson and Haggerty are doing more than noting the technological transformation of police work; they are writing this transformation into a more general argument about a shift from (criminal) 'dangerousness' to (criminal) 'risk'.[15] The key point of reference here is Robert Castel's exploration of the transformation of mental health care in France and the USA, which turns upon a contrast

[13] P. O'Malley, *Risk, Uncertainty and Government* (London, 2004), pp. 5, 13–16.

[14] Rose, 'Government and Control'.

[15] Castel is a point of reference for a number of criminologists and sociologists writing on these subjects, but see especially Ericson and Haggerty, *Policing the Risk Society*, pp. 38, 40, 74 and 104–5; O'Malley and Hutchinson, 'Reinventing Prevention'; and Rose, 'Government and Control'.

between disciplining dangerous individuals, something that he argues characterized reformatory practices in the nineteenth and early twentieth centuries, and managing population-based risks, which he suggests began to emerge during the 1970s. Henceforth it was no longer a question of dealing with a danger embodied in a particular individual, but of identifying and managing a series of risk factors—such as social background, poverty, physical health, habits and environment—distributed across and common to groups of mentally ill patients. Indeed, for Castel, the subject as such, as a singular object of reformation and discipline, has been dissolved into a series of calculable, manageable elements of risk.[16]

However, if this is a good account of the transformation of the government of mental health and, indeed, of imprisonment and punishment, the attempt to argue for a transition to what Castel calls a 'post-disciplinary' order simply does not fit the history of policing so neatly.[17] Policing was never especially, if at all, concerned with disciplining or reforming individuals per se, and so it seems difficult to claim a shift comparable to that in the field of mental health or penal policy, where the management of dangerous individuals through face-to-face relationships and personalized intervention practices has been displaced by an assessment of population-based risk factors and their relative frequency. As Marxist criminologists and historians might remind us, from a very early period, the focus of modern policing was on the 'dangerous classes' and groups within larger populations deemed to be especially threatening.[18] A generalized, impersonal and increasingly class-based sense of criminal danger was central to the development of modern policing and formed a crucial part of a growing climate of anxiety that attended the onset of rapid urbanization in the eighteenth and early nineteenth centuries.[19] One element of the history of risk-based policing thus resides in the emergence of a class-based sense

[16] Castel, 'From Dangerousness to Risk'.

[17] *Ibid.*, p. 293.

[18] Recent work in this area includes D. Philips, 'Three "Moral Entrepreneurs" and the Creation of a "Criminal Class" in England, c. 1790s–1840s', *Crime, History & Societies* 7 (2003), pp. 1–24; A.L. Beier, 'Identity, Language and Resistance in the Making of the Victorian "Criminal Class": Mayhew's Convict Revisited', *Journal of British Studies* 54 (2005), pp. 499–515; and S. Jankiewicz, 'A Dangerous Class: The Street Sellers of Nineteenth-Century London', *Journal of Social History* 46 (2012), pp. 391–415.

[19] D. Lemmings, 'Introduction: Law and Order, Moral Panics and Early Modern England', in D. Lemmings and C. Walker (eds), *Moral Panics, the Media and the Law in Early Modern England* (Basingstoke, 2009), p. 2.

of danger and a 'social' concept of the criminal characteristics of larger populations.

We can trace the development of this concept back to the eighteenth century. As a number of historians have detailed, before the huge growth in newspaper publishing from the mid-1700s onwards, narratives about crime tended to take a particular 'authorized' and largely religious form. An exemplary instance is the 'last dying speech' literature, such as the accounts of the lives of condemned criminals compiled by the Ordinary of Newgate, the chaplain of Newgate Prison.[20] Texts of this sort offered an account of crime that emphasized the universality of sin and the certainty of Divine justice and providential judgment. They were also focused on the fortunes of particular individuals with the aim of providing a salutary warning about the ease with which a wrong turn in life could lead anyone into crime, no matter what their station.

However, as Malcolm Gaskill has suggested, providential arguments concerning crime went into decline during the early eighteenth century, when they were displaced by a greater emphasis on the action of human and environmental forces.[21] Other scholars have suggested that the emergence of a new genre of writing about crime, namely the newspaper article, called into question many aspects of these traditional accounts. The pattern of crime reporting in newspapers emphasized the perspective of the victim and, with a focus on unsolved and violent offences, undercut comfortable ideas of inevitable justice or any sense of agency for the victim, whose helplessness in the face of barbarity was often to the fore.[22] As David Lemmings puts it, this was not a 'universalist human story of providence and judgement; rather it [was] concerned with the particular threats that the anonymity of the modern city posed to the personal

[20] See L.B. Faller, *Turned to Account: The Forms and Functions of Criminal Biography in Late Seventeenth- and Early Eighteenth-Century England* (Cambridge, 1987); A. McKenzie, *Tyburn's Martyrs: Execution in England, 1675–1775* (London, 2007).

[21] M. Gaskill, 'The Displacement of Providence: Policing and Prosecution in Seventeenth- and Eighteenth-Century England', *Continuity and Change* 11 (1996), pp. 341–74. See also Clarke, *Betting on Lives*, p. 3, where a similar decline of faith in providence is noted regarding the insurance industry.

[22] P. King, 'Newspaper Reporting and Attitudes to Crime and Justice in Late Eighteenth and Early Nineteenth-Century London', *Continuity and Change* 22 (2007), pp. 73–112 and his 'Making Crime News: Newspapers, Violent Crime and the Reporting of Old Bailey Trials in the Late Eighteenth Century', *Crime, Histoire & Sociétés/Crime, History & Societies* 13 (2009), pp. 91–116; E. Snell, 'Discourses of Criminality in the Eighteenth-Century Press', *Continuity and Change* 22 (2007), pp. 13–47.

welfare and economic assets of the middle classes. It was a discourse of risk and social problems', which were thereby amplified in the public sphere.[23] One aspect of this was a shift from a concept of crime underpinned by the idea of sin and the fortunes of an individual sinner to one in which crime was learned through temptation, association and habituation in particular social environments. Furthermore, it was a concept associated disproportionately with certain social groups, particularly the urban poor, who were identified as the 'dangerous' source of criminality.[24] As early as the late eighteenth century, then, crime was being defined as a problem of populations as much as individuals. Accordingly, much effort was taken to engage with the contexts within which this 'dangerousness' developed.

This development is itself important in relation to a genealogy of risk. Central to Beck's 'risk society' thesis is the idea of 'reflexivity', whereby risk is conceptualized, to quote Anthony Giddens, as a 'consequence of modernity'—which is to say, that the conditions that generate both actual risks and the sense of threat and uncertainty that attend them are understood as a consequence of the social and technological changes associated with progress and modernization.[25] However, it is clear that a self-conscious awareness that processes of modernization generate their own problems is by no means unique to the late twentieth century, especially in the field of crime. Two of the earliest and most prominent writers on the idea of 'preventative police'—who were also among the first to develop a clear definition of crime as a 'social problem'—were Henry Fielding, the Bow Street Magistrate, and Patrick Colquhoun, one of the first stipendiary magistrates introduced by the 1792 Middlesex Justices Act. Both Fielding and Colquhoun identified the source of the crime waves they imagined were occurring around them in socio-historical developments, and in particular the advent of a 'commercial society', the 'love of luxury' and the rise of 'movable property'.[26] Commerce, commodification and urbanization were all identified not only as harbingers of a new world, but as forces that, by their very nature, gave rise to and encouraged criminality. This

[23] D. Lemmings, 'Conclusion: Moral Panics, Law and the Transformation of the Public Sphere in Early Modern England', in Lemmings and Walker (eds), *Moral Panics*, p. 255.

[24] F. Dodsworth, 'Habit, the Criminal Body and the Body Politic in England, 'c. 1700–1800', *Body and Society* 19 (2013), pp. 83–106.

[25] A. Giddens, *The Consequences of Modernity* (Cambridge, 1990).

[26] See F. Dodsworth, 'Police and the Prevention of Crime: Commerce, Temptation and the Corruption of the Body Politic, from Fielding to Colquhoun', *British Journal of Criminology* 47 (2007), pp. 439–54.

perspective continued to flourish in the nineteenth century, when anxieties about crime and the condition of the poor continued to be directly related to processes of modernization, specifically industrialization, urbanization and the loss of traditional patterns of life.[27] Indeed, this viewpoint was increasingly combined with attempts to quantify the dangerous classes in terms of their criminal habits and actions, and how these correlated with particular urban districts and streets, and variables such as age and levels of education, pauperism and employment.

Attempts to quantify the nature and extent of criminal 'dangerousness' draws us into another dimension of the debate around risk-based policing: its relation to statistics and mathematical aggregation. Proponents of the argument that risk-based policing only emerged in the late twentieth century are aware that even from the earliest times, policing was concerned with the social dynamics of crime, as well as crime prevention through deterrence, correction and forms of information-based surveillance.[28] Nonetheless, they still contend that contemporary policing is different because it is concerned with statistical aggregation and actuarial modes of thinking. It is argued that these aspects properly define risk as distinct from looser notions of 'dangerousness' and 'uncertainty'. Castel is again a key point of reference here in relation to the concern with aggregation. Unlike dangerousness, Castel argues, which is concerned with a generalized condition of uncertainty rooted in a particular subject, risk is concerned with 'factors, [with] statistical correlations of heterogeneous elements', in which there is no subject of intervention, only a calculus of probabilities concerning multiple behavioural traits.[29] The association of governing risk with the use of statistics, meanwhile, is particularly prominent in the influential work of another Foucauldian scholar, the French historian of welfare François Ewald. In particular, Ewald argues that the history of risk is inseparable from the history of insurance, which itself is an essentially statistical technology for rationalizing and collectivizing

[27] See, for example, C. Emsley, *Crime and Society in England, 1750–1900*, 2nd edn (London, 1996), pp. 56–120; and M.J. Wiener, *Reconstructing the Criminal: Culture, Law and Policy in Nineteenth-Century England* (Cambridge, 1990). See also the documents in P. Lawrence (ed.), *Policing the Poor: The Making of the Modern Police, 1780–1914, Volume 3* (London, 2014).

[28] O'Malley and Hutchinson, 'Reinventing Prevention', pp. 373–4. See also O'Malley, *Crime and Risk*, pp. 2–3.

[29] Castel, 'From Dangerousness to Risk', p. 288.

risk among groups of subscribers and the specification of contributory premiums.[30]

Historically, however, it is questionable whether this straightforward alignment between governing risk and the use of statistical evidence holds true, even in the apparently exemplary case of insurance. Geoffrey Clarke, for instance, has pointed out that insurance emerged in the late seventeenth century as a 'bold effort to extend human control over accident, ill fortune, and indeed over uncertainty itself'.[31] He notes that early insurance clubs were like friendly societies, with simple principles of redistribution and no collection of statistics or reference to probabilities, let alone sophisticated actuarial calculations.[32] In contrast to Ewald, Clarke argues that there is no reason to define 'true' insurance in statistical terms.[33] Even if the history of risk was essentially the history of insurance—and it is not clear that we should accept this assertion—it does not necessarily follow that the history of insurance is inseparable from the history of statistics.

Moreover, Pat O'Malley points out that, even in the present day, the boundaries between (calculable) risks and (unknowable) uncertainties are often indistinct and that crime prevention practices are based as much on common-sense understandings of uncertainty and possible danger as on specific calculations of risk. Indeed, he has offered an array of different conceptions and practices of the management of uncertainty, ranging from 'prudentialism'—or the setting aside of financial resources against the threat of future harm—to the use of professional judgment, ordinary foresight, suspicion and even 'rules of thumb'.[34] Given that the distinction between governing risk and governing uncertainty is unclear in the present day, it is surely unreasonable to expect the distinction to appear in the past, either in thought and conception or as an operational principle of policing practices.

To give this argument more concrete form, we might pay closer attention to the example used by O'Malley and Stephen Hutchinson, who draw a contrast between the history of fire prevention and the history of preventive policing. They identify a shift in fire prevention from an early concern with 'firefighting'—that is, a concern with containing and extinguishing

[30] Ewald, 'Insurance and Risk,' in Burchell, Gordon and Miller (eds), *The Foucault Effect*, pp. 197–210, particularly p. 207.

[31] Clarke, *Betting on Lives*, p. 1.

[32] *Ibid.*, p. 6.

[33] *Ibid.*, pp. 6–7.

[34] O'Malley, *Risk, Uncertainty and Government*, pp. 16, 21, 23.

fires and saving lives, modelled on a masculine protective role—to fire prevention. The latter, they suggest, emerged from about 1850 and was manifest in the installation of sprinkler systems and fire hydrants, and the regulation of dangerous technologies such as steam boilers. The formation of the British Fire Prevention Committee in 1897 drew together insurers, engineers, architects and surveyors into a structured network of governance.[35] Policing, by contrast, continued to operate in a 'crime-fighting' mode until the late twentieth century, at which point crime prevention became the dominant ethos, leading to the establishment of the organizational structure characterized by Crime and Disorder Reduction Partnerships (now Community Safety Partnerships) introduced in 1998.[36]

Certainly, throughout the late nineteenth and early twentieth centuries, the police viewed their activities in terms of masculine notions of protection, and detectives especially saw themselves as involved in crime fighting.[37] However, we might contend that in the same period many municipal firefighters saw their daily practice as firefighting, despite the preventive apparatus around them.[38] More importantly, what O'Malley and Hutchinson's account overlooks is the fact that crime fighting was only ever one relatively minor part of police work, primarily focused on the very small detective departments; most policing has always involved a much broader 'social' function. Furthermore, not only was the activity of the police concerned with more than fighting crime, but 'the' police were also far from being the only agents involved in 'policing' in the broad sense.[39] In fact, a large number of organizations—ranging from philanthropic,

[35] Malley and Hutchinson, 'Reinventing Prevention', pp. 376–80. It is notable that although inspection is noted in the 1870s, their references to actuarial practices cite only early twentieth-century sources (pp. 377–8).

[36] On the recent history of crime prevention, see A. Crawford, *Crime Prevention and Community Safety: Politics, Policies and Practices* (London, 1998); D. Gilling, *Crime Prevention: Theory, Policy and Practice* (London, 1997); G. Hughes, *Understanding Crime Prevention: Social Control, Risk and Late Modernity* (Buckingham, 1998).

[37] On police detection and masculine notions of protection, see F. Dodsworth, 'Men on a Mission: Masculinity, Violence and the Self-Presentation of Policemen in England, c. 1870–1914', in D.G. Barrie and S. Broomhall (eds), *A History of Police and Masculinities, 1700–2010* (Basingstoke, 2012), pp. 123–40.

[38] We might add that long before the late nineteenth century, fire prevention itself was a concern of municipal corporations and other agencies concerned with building regulations and design.

[39] On the broader 'social' work of the 'police', see Dodsworth, 'The Idea of Police'; and Neocleous, *The Fabrication of Social Order*.

temperance and housing reform associations to workhouses, orphanages and schools—were active in attempting to understand and ameliorate the conditions that produced the 'dangerous classes'. If we want to understand the prevention of crime, we need to explore all those issues around the policing of morals and poverty that were so characteristic of the reform programmes of these eras. We need to incorporate the activities of what might appear to be peripheral organizations, such as societies for the prevention of vice, or the Charity Organization Society (established in 1869), which have been subject to so much historical attention, but are ignored by criminological work on crime because they appear to be concerned with something else—and yet the reduction of crime was a central part of their concern.[40]

There is a history of preventive policing, then, that extends beyond 'the' police. Equally, even the history of policing organizations directly concerned with managing criminal activity is a history of the long-term development of practices of risk management, with the collation and circulation of information about criminals and crime at the heart of that process. As we shall now see, although it would be overstating the case to argue that we can identify a fully developed 'risk-based' model of policing before the late twentieth century, we can certainly trace its roots in organizational forms and practices that are, in the words of O'Malley once again, 'loosely risk-based': practices that demonstrate a concern for preventing rather than simply reacting to or 'fighting' crime, for patrolling and identifying dangerous populations, and for managing the risks of becoming a victim of crime.[41]

Entrepreneurial Organizations

What, then, of practices—of novel types of crime prevention and risk-based forms of organization? The mechanisms that were developed to assuage anxieties about the consequences of commerce and urbanization were closely connected to techniques of insurance devised to manage uncertainty in other contexts. In fact, developments in policing and

[40] The connections are clear in Lawrence (ed.), *Policing the Poor*, but see also A. Hunt, *Governing Morals: A Social History of Moral Regulation* (Cambridge, 2000); G. Stedman Jones, *Outcast London: A Study in the Relationship between Classes in Victorian Society* (Oxford, 1971).

[41] O'Malley, *Crime and Risk*, pp. 25–6.

insurance were contemporaneous, and the new policing institutions and forms of crime control were clearly established as systems for the communal dispersal of risk and, in particular, the risk of becoming a victim of crime and the costs of pursuing justice. They were the more socialized, communal administrative complement of the more social and reflexive understandings of crime noted above.

Before the introduction of permanent, paid systems of policing in England, the responsibility for reporting and prosecuting an offence lay with the victim. The victim would report the issue to a local peace officer, either a constable or a magistrate. The role of constable was not a salaried position, but a parochial office, filled by unpaid gentlemen, serving their parish, manor or town as part of their 'civic duty' for a year.[42] The role of magistrate, or justice of the peace, was likewise a position of social status, filled by unpaid, propertied gentlemen.[43] Prosecution was also the responsibility of the victim, and if there were legal proceedings, these would have to be paid for. It was common, particularly in London, in instances of theft or other serious criminal offences, for the victim to employ a private thief-taker to recover their property or apprehend the offender for them.[44] Similarly, a number of enterprising magistrates developed something of a trade in justice and managed to make a profit from what was often an onerous as much as an honourable office.[45] All of this only served to increase the potential costs for the victim.[46] Many of the early developments in policing were designed to make pursuit and prosecution cheaper and easier for victims. These included the offer of rewards, which enabled the development of entrepreneurial and semi-professional constables and

[42] F. Dodsworth, '"Civic" Police and the Condition of Liberty: The Rationality of Governance in Eighteenth-Century England', *Social History* 29 (2004), pp. 199–216 and his 'Masculinity as Governance: Police, Public Service and the Embodiment of Authority, c. 1700–1850', in M.L. McCormack (ed.), *Public Men: Masculinity and Politics in Modern Britain* (Basingstoke, 2007), pp. 33–53.

[43] N. Landau, *The Justices of the Peace, 1679–1760* (Berkeley, CA, 1984).

[44] See Beattie, *Policing and Punishment in London*, pp. 226–58; R. Paley, 'Thief-Takers in London in the Age of the McDaniel Gang', in D. Hay and F. Snyder (eds), *Policing and Prosecution in Britain, 1750–1850* (Oxford, 1989), pp. 301–40; T. Wales, 'Thief-Takers and their Clients', in P. Griffiths and M.S.R. Jenner (eds), *Londonopolis: Essays in the Cultural and Social History of Early Modern London* (Manchester, 2000), pp. 67–85.

[45] N. Landau, 'The Trading Justice's Trade', in N. Landau (ed.), *Law, Crime and English Society, 1660–1830* (Cambridge, 2002), pp. 46–70.

[46] D. Hay and F. Snyder, 'Using the Criminal Law 1750–1850: Policing, Private Prosecution and the State', in Hay and Snyder (eds), *Policing and Prosecution*, pp. 26–7.

thief-takers, as well as the development of an elaborate 'official' body of thief-takers in London, the Bow Street Runners, pioneered by Sir John Fielding between the 1750s and 1780s.[47] However, these costs escalated in the later eighteenth century owing to the increasing use of lawyers in the trial process, and it is surely no coincidence that this period coincided with the increasing adoption of novel methods for coping with the potential cost of crime.[48] The responses to this situation were various, but all of them constitute a dispersal of risk across the community.

Two of these might be highlighted. One option was for groups of residents to contribute from their own pockets to the cost of hiring the services of their usual parish watchmen beyond normal hours or seasons of service.[49] In the early eighteenth century, the constables of some Westminster parishes were collecting voluntary contributions to finance the nightly watch outside of their usual season (between the quarter days of Michaelmas (29 September) and Lady Day (25 March), the start of the new year). This practice was still continuing in London in the 1770s, when the constables of the parishes of St Giles in the Fields and St George, Bloomsbury, are recorded collecting voluntary contributions and a number of parishioners appear to have raised subscriptions to pay a different set of watchmen of their own choosing. Similar schemes to supplement protection included hiring other kinds of patrols that were not tied to the beat system. In 1749, during the mid-century crime wave, parishioners in Islington raised a subscription to hire soldiers alongside the watch.[50] Such schemes also existed outside London.[51] As late as the 1820s, the 106 watchmen of the Birmingham commission of police worked only 7 months of the year, but they were allowed to continue and collect pay on their rounds in the summer months at the discretion of the residents, something that was described as 'universally practised'.[52]

Of more significance in terms of the present chapter, however, is the formation of prosecution associations. Essentially, these were insurance

[47] See Beattie, *Policing and Punishment* and *The First English Detectives.*

[48] D. Philips, 'Good Men to Associate and Bad Men to Conspire: Associations for the Prosecution of Felons in England, 1760–1860', in Hay and Snyder (eds), *Policing and Prosecution*, p. 125.

[49] See Beattie, *Policing and Punishment*, pp. 169–225.

[50] P. Rawlings, *Policing: A Short History* (Cullompton, 2002), pp. 66, 68, 69, 71.

[51] *Ibid.*, pp. 74–5.

[52] Manchester Central Reference Library, Local Studies Unit, 'Reports of the Police Establishments in Various Towns' [1828–9], M9/30/9/1, p. 5.

schemes assembled by groups of individuals which enabled any member of the association who was a victim of crime to use the pooled resources to hire the mechanisms of restitution. These included covering the costs of the pursuit of offenders either by a constable or a third party, the costs of advertising the theft of particular goods in the press, and the costs of mounting a prosecution. Some associations could be more proactive and act to root out offenders, and some even paid their own bodies of watchmen.[53] All prosecution associations required annual subscriptions and offered rewards for the recovery of property and for the conviction of offenders for particular offences. For example, the Potton (Bedfordshire) association offered rewards of £5 5s for the conviction of burglars, 10s 6d for the conviction of turnip thieves and £1 1s for the conviction of window breakers.[54]

The prosecution association as a form dates back to the seventeenth century and took its place alongside a variety of mutual assurance associations and voluntary movements against vice and immorality, which also sought to unite communally to prosecute offenders.[55] This was contemporaneous with the widespread adoption of maritime, fire and life insurance (although interestingly burglary insurance failed to prosper as a field until the late nineteenth century).[56] Despite this long heritage, however, the prosecution association took off most notably in the period 1780–1850, during which time there were probably more than 1000 such organizations in operation across the country.[57] Peter King's analysis of Essex in the 1780s and 1790s suggests that the average association covered seven

[53] See P. King, 'Prosecution Associations and their Impact in Eighteenth-Century Essex', in Hay and Snyder (eds), *Policing and Prosecution*, pp. 171–210; A. Schubert, 'Private Initiative in Law Enforcement: Associations for the Prosecution of Felons, 1744–1856', in V. Bailey (ed.), *Policing and Prosecution in Nineteenth-Century Britain* (London, 1981), pp. 25–41.

[54] *Potton Association, for the Protection of Property, and Punishment of Offenders, within the Parish of* Potton, *and the adjacent Towns, Parishes, and Places, not exceeding the Distance of Six Miles from* Potton*: Instituted the 23rd Day of February, and by Adjournment to the 3d* [sic] *March, 1790.*

[55] Philips, 'Good Men to Associate and Bad Men to Conspire', p. 121. On moral reform, see Hunt, *Governing Morals*, pp. 28–76.

[56] On the history of burglary insurance, see H.A.L. Cockerell and E. Green, *The British Insurance Business, 1547–1970: An Introduction and Guide to Historical Records in the United Kingdom* (London, 1976), pp. 47–8, 55–6; E. Moss, 'Burglary Insurance and the Culture of Fear in Britain, *c.* 1889–1939', *Historical Journal* 54 (2011), pp. 1039–64.

[57] Philips, 'Good Men to Associate and Bad Men to Conspire', pp. 120–1.

or eight parishes and comprised about 27 members, numbering more than one in ten of the commercial, professional, gentry and farming households. The 1000 or so members of prosecution associations in east and central Essex were responsible for between 10 and 15 % of prosecutions.[58]

Historians have long referred to these organizations as forms of insurance and indeed contemporaries described themselves in similar terms.[59] The Stoke Ferry (Norfolk) association, for instance, 'unanimously agreed to sustain and bear in equal shares, the costs, charges and expences [sic] attending all and every prosecution', the association having been formed because 'many Felonies are committed by Persons who escape Punishment by Reason of the great Expences [sic] attending the Apprehension and Prosecuting them'.[60] The West Bromwich association constantly used the phrase 'mutually and reciprocally covenanting' as a description of its activities.[61] Thomas Dimsdale of the Barnet General Association drew a comparison between the urge to establish prosecution associations, often occasioned by the panic surrounding notorious crimes, and the establishment of fire insurance: 'It is like the fire-offices in London; a great fire in a neighbourhood increases the insurance all round.'[62]

Information, Prevention and Local Policing

The above might be characterized as entrepreneurial forms of organization against the growing risks of crime that attended modernization. They also contained a communal element, to the extent that they sought to socialize the costs of either preventing or prosecuting crime, something premised—as in nascent forms of insurance—on the assumption that all those who subscribed were equally at risk. Crucially, they were slowly complemented by analogous, if more formal and official, responses

[58] King, 'Prosecution Associations and their Impact in Eighteenth-Century Essex', pp. 188–90.

[59] The link between prosecution associations and insurance is made in Hay and Snyder, 'Using the Criminal Law, 1750–1850', pp. 26–7; and Philips, 'Good Men to Associate and Bad Men to Conspire', pp. 121, 125–6, 139.

[60] *Articles of the Association, for the Prosecution of Horse-Stealers and other Felons, within the Parishes of Stoke-Ferry, and Towns adjacent, in the County of Norfolk* (Lynn, 1808), pp. 3–4. The same argument is made in *Rules, Orders, and Regulations of Crowle Association for the Prosecution of Felons* (Howden, 1814), p. 3.

[61] *Copy of a Deed of Association for the Prosecution of Felons* (Birmingham, 1773).

[62] Quoted in Philips, 'Good Men to Associate and Bad Men to Conspire', p. 126.

from local and national levels of government. In the process, the organs of government were themselves transformed, so that local and national authorities were 'governmentalized' according to a similar, loosely risk-based rationality; that is, the state (in the form of Parliament at least) and local government were transformed into mechanisms for the government of populations by absorbing these administrative principles.[63]

One of the ways in which this process took effect was through petitions to Parliament for acts for the 'improvement' of the government of particular areas. In 1735 two wealthy parishes in Westminster worked together to secure an act of Parliament that enabled them to levy a compulsory watch rate. Over the next three quarters of a century, almost all other parishes in Westminster gradually followed this example, and in 1774 the Westminster Watch Act laid down basic standards for the number, pay and general duties of these watchmen.[64] The watchmen were supposed to patrol the streets at night, calling the hours, checking doors, windows and locks, looking out for 'suspicious characters', and generally concerning themselves with public order and morality, including the lure of prostitution.[65] As provincial towns developed, the process of petitioning for local 'Improvement Acts'—also known as 'Lighting and Watching' and 'Police' acts—was copied across the country, allowing for the establishment of what were often known as 'improvement' or 'police commissions'.[66] The jurisdiction of these bodies extended from individual parishes to whole boroughs or cities and, from the late eighteenth century, they became a popular means for active urban elites to energize the government of their town and improve its paving, lighting and watch systems, or what together was often understood as 'police', in the broad sense of the term then still

[63] On the 'governmentalization of the state', see M. Foucault, 'Governmentality', in Burchell, Gordon and Miller (eds), *The Foucault Effect*, pp. 87–104.

[64] For the transformation of the watch in the eighteenth century, see E.A. Reynolds, *Before the Bobbies: The Night Watch and Police Reform in Metropolitan London* (Stanford, CA, 1998).

[65] Beattie, *Policing and Punishment*; Reynolds, *Before the Bobbies*; and R. Paley, '"An Imperfect, Inadequate and Wretched System?" Policing London before Peel', *Criminal Justice History* 10 (1989), pp. 95–130.

[66] Manchester was one such commission that was termed a 'police commission'. For a study of this body, see F. Dodsworth, 'Mobility and Civility: Police and the Formation of the Modern City', in G. Bridge and S. Watson (eds), *The New Blackwell Companion to the City* (Oxford, 2011), pp. 235–44.

in use.[67] Between 1760 and 1799, no less than 400 commissions were established across Britain.[68]

Having been established by acts of Parliament, these bodies were permitted to charge rates on the local population, which in practice were often connected to the established levels of the poor rate. Such public systems of watching and policing, paid for from the local rates, obviously constitute a method of distributing the potential cost of crime to an individual over the whole (rateable) community, albeit one that was distinct from the voluntary prudentialism of prosecution associations. Although there was an element of choice in terms of a local community resolving to lobby for an act of Parliament, once that act was passed, the payment of rates was compulsory and participation in the system was not at the discretion of the individual. By spreading the cost of policing and good order generally through the rateable population, it constituted a more socialized form of risk reduction, one which also made free provision for the poor. It made for a significant and genuinely novel development: John Beattie, for instance, has identified the shift from rotational systems of civic enlistment to rate-paid policing and watching as the most fundamental change in the way in which such services were provided in the modern period.[69]

It is thus possible to point to a general and geographically diffuse reconfiguration of policing as a 'loosely risk-based'—and, indeed, loosely collective and preventive—enterprise. Nonetheless, London remained the focal area of administrative anxieties and reforming efforts, and although not all of these efforts came to fruition in the short or medium term, what was achieved, as well as the way in which reform was discussed, is significant in terms of the genealogy being advanced here. Of particular interest are the various schemes for the improved collection and dissemination of information in order to enhance the self-consciously 'preventive' capacities of policing. The pioneers are well known, namely the Fielding brothers, Henry and John, who during the 1750s established the Bow Street Magistrates' office as a kind of hub of crime prevention and justice. The Bow Street office not only functioned as a court room where Londoners

[67] The classic study of these organizations in England remains S. Webb and B. Webb, *A History of English Local Government, Volume 4: Special Bodies for Special Purposes* (London, 1922). For Scotland, see D. Barrie, *Police in the Age of Improvement: Police Development and the Civic Tradition in Scotland, 1775–1865* (Cullompton, 2008).

[68] D. Eastwood, *Government and Community in the English Provinces, 1700–1870* (Basingstoke, 1997), p. 66.

[69] Beattie, *Policing and Punishment*, p. 84.

could watch justice being dispensed. It also functioned as a bureau of information, which included a register of offenders and a record of all stolen goods, and was the operational home of the Bow Street Runners, London's first detective force. The Runners became famous for knowing the haunts and proclivities of the city's more prolific criminals, but they were only one component of a broader culture of prevention and detection that turned on the generation and sharing of information. John Fielding was in regular correspondence with magistrates all over London and the provinces, gathering and collating information on the latest crimes and criminals, and then distributing the latest digests. Indeed, in 1771, he established the journals the *Quarterly Pursuit* and the *Weekly or Extraordinary Pursuit* in order to publicize stolen goods, wanted criminals and the rewards available for their capture. These publications later became the *Hue and Cry* in the 1790s and then the *Police Gazette* from 1839—a title that is still published today.

The Gordon Riots of 1780 served to catalyse further reflection and reforming initiatives. For several days in June, a mob took control of the streets in what turned into a violent protest not only against Catholicism, but more widely against symbols of authority. A number of buildings associated with law and order were destroyed, notably Newgate Prison and Bow Street Magistrates' office. The riot was brought under control only after the imposition of military force and the killing of at least 200 people. The first substantive reforming effort that followed came in 1785, when the government submitted an unsuccessful bill for the improvement of the police of London and Westminster, which would have established a state-funded (via a parliamentary grant) police force for the whole of the metropolis. It foundered on the opposition of the City of London and concerns about the potential for the state to oppress the people.[70]

The introduction of the bill, however, prompted debate about the reform of policing, not least its better coordination and how to advance the work and aspirations of the Fielding brothers. Authors, for instance, promoted general systems of 'superintendence' and a 'chain of connection' between activities intended to manage, license and regulate the

[70] D. Philips, '"A New Engine of Power and Authority": The Institutionalization of Law-Enforcement in England, 1780–1830', in V.A.C. Gatrell, B. Lenman and G. Parker (eds), *Crime and the Law: The Social History of Crime in Western Europe since 1500* (London, 1980), pp. 155–89.

'variety of dangerous and suspicious trades' that threatened morality and gave rise to the temptation to commit crime.[71] One of the more ambitious visions of an administrative system was put forward by the mathematician George Barrett, who later came to fame as an actuary for the Hope Life Office insurance company, where he developed a series of tables relating to life expectancy that were used by Charles Babbage in his more famous work on the subject. In fact, Barrett's only published work was his intervention in the 1780s, in which his interest in questions of demography and mortality intersect with the practical government of populations through police. Barrett envisaged a national system for the collection and circulation of information about crime.[72] The central office was to be based in London and each local branch, or 'register office', would be composed of boards of commissioners, police officers, messengers, clerks and solicitors. Each office would help to generate, and be in receipt of, a national weekly circular of information relating to criminal activities, whilst local surveillance was to be exercised through the generation of certificates regarding the movement and residence of people. It was a scheme that aimed to promote 'good order', 'public welfare' and 'safety', and it proceeded in a particular fashion, he argued, 'not by the introduction and increase of penal laws, which are already too numerous, but by establishing salutary and adequate modes of prevention'.[73]

Ultimately the debates of the 1780s did not lead to the establishment of a new, general police system for London. They were not entirely without consequence, however: in 1792, the Middlesex Justices Act extended the principle of the Bow Street office pioneered by the Fieldings across the metropolis, creating seven Police Offices staffed by three salaried magistrates and six constables.[74] Further modest reforms followed. One of the new stipendiary magistrates introduced by the 1792 act, Patrick Colquhoun, conducted a prominent campaign for police reform and

[71] See Dodsworth, 'The Idea of Police'; and F. Dodsworth (ed.), *The 'Idea' of Policing: The Making of the Modern Police, Volume I* (London, 2014), which excerpts and introduces many of the contributions to these debates.

[72] G. Barrett, *An Essay Towards Establishing a System of Police, on Constitutional Principles* (London, 1786); R. Brown, 'Barrett, George (1752–1821)', *Oxford Dictionary of National Biography*, available at: www.oxforddnb.com.oxfordbrookes.idm.oclc.org/view/article/1523 (date accessed 11 November 2015). See also Dodsworth (ed.), *The 'Idea' of Policing*, pp. 149–58.

[73] Barrett, *An Essay*, pp. 60–1.

[74] See Beattie, *The First English Detectives*; and Reynolds, *Before the Bobbies*.

successfully established the Thames Police in 1800 on similar principles.[75] Wider attempts at police reform in London were, however, less successful: in 1799, a police bill was drafted but never introduced, and parliamentary select committees in 1812, 1816, 1818 and 1822 failed to prompt the change that reformers hoped for.

Nonetheless, the link between policing, crime prevention and the circulation of information remained an established point of reference. Indeed, this did not preclude visions of reform modelled along the lines of insurance companies. One example is the prominent barrister Henry Alworth Merewether writing in response to the 1816 select committee, where he described his plan for a new police in the following terms: 'it is almost a sufficient description of it to say, that the system which the writer proposes, is one of "*insurance against robbery*"'.[76] The scheme was in some respects similar to the prosecution associations discussed above and Merewether was at pains to stress the voluntary nature of subscription, although he recommended that whole parishes should subscribe to it using the money that they currently paid to watchmen. He explicitly defined the idea of a unified form of urban policing in terms of insurance:

> that the unity and simplicity of this plan should be preserved, which is esteemed essentially necessary, in order to secure to it promptitude of action and systematic arrangement of information, it is most strongly recommended that there should be one superintending *general office of insurance* incorporated by a gratuitous act of parliament.[77]

Merewether recommended that shares of £100 should be taken in this office, which would pay out bonuses in terms already established for fire insurance offices. Continuing the link between insurance against risk and the organization of information within London, he identified a key problem as a failure to circulate information between the watchmen and the police offices; the solution was to establish minor offices throughout the city, regulated according to the plan of the central 'insurance office' and intended to collect and communicate local information to the general office.[78] Indeed, the scheme was to stretch across the country, forming

[75] On Colquhoun, see especially Dodsworth, 'Police and the Prevention of Crime'.

[76] H.A. Merewether, *A New System of Police, with Reference to the Evidence Given to the Police Committee of the House of Commons* (London, 1816), p. 13, emphasis in original.

[77] *Ibid.*, pp. 13–15, 18–19, emphasis in original.

[78] *Ibid.*, pp. 9, 27.

something like a national prosecution association, with offices in every town or city communicating with the central office.[79] Like many of his contemporaries, Merewether was concerned not so much with regulating the conduct of individual criminals, but with monitoring a variety of sites and conditions that rendered crime more likely, among them poverty, the prevalence of receiving houses and 'low public houses', and the state of prisons.[80] His principal complaint was that 'the chief employment of the present police establishments is rather in the *detection* than the *prevention* of crime'.[81]

In 1829 the question of London's police was raised once again and this time the Metropolitan Police Act was passed with surprisingly little opposition. It created the institution still in existence today and equipped the Home Office with direct control over London's policing.[82] On the introduction of this 'new' police in 1829, the central concern with the circulation of information and the management and surveillance of crime-related dangers and risks remained. The circulation of information from police constables on the beat, through their sergeants, inspectors and superintendents, right up to the Commissioners of Police at Scotland Yard, was a crucial aspect of the policing of early Victorian London. The compilation of reports regarding any incidents encountered during the day provided Commissioners with a general picture of patterns of crime, something that was supplemented, following the establishment of a Detective Department in 1842, by the keeping of records on known criminals.[83]

Practices of this sort further intensified over the course of the nineteenth century. The passage of the Habitual Criminals Act in 1869 subjected those who were not sentenced to prison to 7 years of supervision by the police to ensure they had not returned to their criminal ways, while the Prevention of Crimes Act of 1871 enabled 'ticket of leave' men released from prison to be returned if their behaviour was suspect. This act also led to the creation of the Habitual Criminals Register, which recorded all convicted offenders and was housed at the Criminal Record Office,

[79] *Ibid.*, pp. 35–8.

[80] *Ibid.*, pp. 53–5.

[81] *Ibid.*, pp. 6–7, 57, emphasis in original.

[82] Uniquely in England and Wales, the Home Office directly controlled the Metropolitan Police until the creation of the Metropolitan Police Authority (2000) under the Greater London Assembly.

[83] F. Dodsworth, 'The Institution of Police in Britain, c. 1750–1856: A Study in Historical Governmentality' (PhD thesis, University of Manchester, 2002).

a repository that was ultimately augmented with fingerprint records and details of modus operandi.[84] Other examples include preventive activities in relation to 'moral' issues thought to be directly related to crime, such as prostitution and drunkenness. The police were central to the implementation of the notorious Contagious Diseases Acts of 1864, 1866 and 1869, which enabled the police to arrest known or suspected prostitutes in ports and garrison towns. Once arrested, they could be subjected to a forcible examination for venereal disease, which in turn could result in their detention in hospitals for months at a time.[85] Police officers were also involved in the administration of the Habitual Drunkards Act of 1879. The act entailed the circulation of information about known and regular drunkards encountered by the police and allowed for those drunks judged suitably 'habitual' to be committed to an asylum for extended treatment.[86] All were loosely risk-based practices, combining information management and surveillance by way of preventing the future occurrence of crime.

Conclusion

This chapter has sought to make an intervention in two bodies of literature, both of which make claims, either directly or indirectly, about the history of policing. The first of these is a large body of literature in criminology and sociology that draws on the 'risk society' thesis of Beck and Foucault's work on governmentality as a way of explaining recent transformations in policing. This literature mobilizes an historical narrative in which the 'traditional' approach to policing, based around the concept of 'crime fighting', has been displaced by a new focus on the prevention of crime and the management of risk. According to this account, traditional crime fighting is a mode of government focused on maintaining order through a physical presence on the streets coupled with individualized discipline following acts of transgression. The orientation here is firmly on the individual and towards the past. This has been replaced with a system of policing focused on surveillance and information gathering, with the aim of assessing and managing the risk of future acts of criminality

[84] S. Petrow, *Policing Morals: The Metropolitan Police and the Home Office, 1870–1914* (Oxford, 1994).

[85] See the classic study by J.R. Walkowitz, *Prostitution and Victorian Society: Women, Class and the State* (Cambridge, 1982). See also Petrow, *Policing Morals.*

[86] Petrow, *Policing Morals.*

through the use of statistics drawn from an analysis of populations, as opposed to individual offenders. Rather than disciplining individuals, the rationale is one of controlling potentially risky behaviour, with an orientation towards the future.

It is clear that the statistical, predictive and often computerized forms of surveillance and risk assessment that Castel terms 'systematic pre-detection' are indeed novel contributions to the government of contemporary society, and particularly the practice of policing.[87] However, this chapter has sought to suggest that although these technical innovations are important and in many ways transformative, it would be a mistake to see them as the point of creation of a culture of risk management and prevention per se. Crime prevention and risk management cannot be reduced to these particular techniques and technologies for their exercise: both have a much longer history, dating back to the eighteenth century.

In making this claim, the chapter makes a second intervention in recent debates on the history of modern policing, in particular those accounts which locate the development of paid, professional and organized police services in the series of crime panics that convulsed late eighteenth and early nineteenth-century England. The importance of these events is not denied. However, it is argued that the occurrence of these panics, and perhaps even real crime waves, in no way determined the response that police reformers devised. Rather, the particular form taken by policing organizations as they developed over the period between 1750 and 1850 was closely related to a wider culture of risk management, something that was most apparent in the growth of insurance as a field of governance. This culture of risk management was marked by declining faith in providential intervention in human affairs, growing awareness of insurance and the possibility of socializing costs and risks, and a reflexive understanding that processes of industrialization, urbanization and commodification had negative as well as positive social consequences, evident at the level not only of individuals, but also of populations. Clearly, then, long before computerized models of risk assessment, people were engaged in the future-oriented management of perceived threats emerging from populations undergoing radical change. Far from modern policing being displaced by a culture of risk management and crime prevention, we might argue that it was in fact a product of that culture in the first place.

[87] Castel, 'From Dangerousness to Risk', p. 288.

CHAPTER 3

Rethinking the History of the Risk Society: Accident Reporting, the Social Order and the London Daily Press, 1800–30

Ryan Vieira

Ulrich Beck's risk society thesis is among the most influential theoretical frameworks within the growing multi-disciplinary scholarship on risk. As Chapter 1 in this volume has suggested, the theory is premised on a particular historical narrative. In the period prior to the rise of industrial capitalism, Beck claims, the concept of risk was absent. Danger and accidents were local, non-politicized phenomena that were primarily understood in terms of providence or misfortune.[1] The onset of mass industrialization drastically transformed this situation by producing new hazards that were man-made. Danger became risk and a wide array of institutions and practices for managing and reducing risk emerged. In this 'first modernity',

[1] U. Beck, *Ecological Enlightenment: Essays on the Politics of the Risk Society* [trans. M. Ritter] (Atlantic Highlands, NJ, 1995), p. 20.

R. Vieira
McMaster Innovation Park, Suite 305, 175 Longwood Road South, Hamilton, ON, Canada

T. Crook, M. Esbester (eds), *Governing Risks in Modern Britain*,
DOI 10.1057/978-1-137-46745-4_3

risk was understood as 'residual'.[2] It was a limited quantity of danger, its effects were manageable through systems of insurance, and it was understood as something that could be continually reduced as techniques of accident prevention progressed. By the mid-twentieth century, however, this orientation to risk began to break down in the face of the global dangers of the 'atomic age'. Whereas the earlier risk regime reinforced a confidence in progress, the situation of late modernity was defined by a 'radical uncertainty' that led to a questioning of the basic premises of modern life.[3] The key question of social and political organization no longer centred on the 'wage conflict' or how the spoils of progress should be distributed, but rather on the 'ecological conflict' and who should bear the responsibility for the disasters arising out of modern technology.[4] According to Beck's theory, then, the prevalence of risk discourse in our contemporary culture and the tremendous significance of risk for the ways in which we organize society and politics are the products of an historical teleology driven primarily by technological change and consisting of three epochal transitions: roughly, pre-modern (prior to 1850), modern (1850–1950) and late modern (1950–present).[5]

While the risk society thesis has long been a subject of scholarly debate among social and political theorists, the historical narrative upon which it stands has recently attracted the attention of historians as well. Though this body of historical scholarship is still small, it typically centres on two general points. The first is that the historical development of risk and risk management is substantially less linear than is presumed in risk society theory. The concept of risk and practices of risk management long predate mass industrialization, and many of the ideas about risk that Beck associates exclusively with the late twentieth century can also be found in the nineteenth century—something also evident in this volume in

[2] U. Beck, 'The Reinvention of Politics: Toward a Theory of Reflexive Modernization', in U. Beck, A. Giddens and S. Lash (eds), *Reflexive Modernization: Politics, Tradition and Aesthetics in the Modern Social Order* (Stanford, CA, 1994), p. 5.

[3] U. Beck and J. Willms, *Conversations with Ulrich Beck*, trans. M. Pollak (Cambridge, 2004), p. 29.

[4] Beck, *Ecological Enlightenment*, pp. 4–5.

[5] A large section of Beck's risk society theory also hinges on a social process of individualization that is driven by economic change. I have omitted reference to this aspect of risk society because it is beyond the scope of the historical analysis provided in this chapter.

the chapters by Dodsworth, Crook and Whyte.[6] The second is that the regime of risk management that developed during first modernity had an important cultural component that Beck and other risk society theorists have neglected. Along with new institutions and practices for limiting accidents, new forms of narrating accidents emerged that circulated on a mass scale and worked to alleviate anxieties over modern danger.[7] By examining the conceptualization of risk and the operation of risk management strategies at particular historical epochs, historians have helped to produce a more complex narrative than the one Beck first postulated.

The purpose of the present chapter is to build on this nascent body of historiography through a different strategy. Rather than examining the history of risk and danger in the context of one of Beck's epochs, this study is located at a liminal point in that narrative, a moment of historical transition. Specifically, this chapter focuses on the 1820s, when a significant quantitative expansion of accident reporting occurred in the nationally circulated daily newspapers of London. At the same time, accident reporting moved away from grouping multiple accidents together under a single headline and began instead to present longer narrative accounts of individual disasters—or what is here termed the 'single accident article'. These shifts form part of the broader transformation associated with the transition to a peculiarly modern culture of danger and risk in Britain. The growth of accident reporting during this decade represented the beginning of a trend towards a mass public fascination with accidents, and the single accident article which emerged during these years would later become an important component of the cultural mechanisms developed to ease popular anxieties over the hazards of the industrialized world. Yet, as we shall see, the relationship between industrialization and the expansion of accident reporting in Britain was much more contingent, and the

[6] A.P. Mohun, *Risk: Negotiating Safety in American Society* (Baltimore, MA, 2013); J.-B. Fressoz, 'Beck Back in the 19th Century: Towards a Genealogy of Risk Society', *History and Technology* 23 (2007), pp. 333–50.

[7] E. Freedgood, *Victorian Writing about Risk: Imagining a Safe England in a Dangerous World* (Cambridge, 2000); M. Sanders, 'Manufacturing Accident: Industrialism and the Worker's Body in Early Victorian Fiction', *Victorian Literature and Culture* 28 (2000), pp. 313–29; J. Bronstein, *Caught in the Machinery: Workplace Accidents and Injured Workers in Nineteenth-Century Britain* (Stanford, CA, 2008), Chapter 3; B. Rieger, *Technology and the Culture of Modernity in Britain and Germany, 1890–1945* (Cambridge, 2005); P. Sinnema, 'Representing the Railway: Train Accidents and Trauma in the Illustrated London News', *Victorian Periodicals Review* 31 (1998), pp. 142–68.

boundaries between modern and pre-modern cultures of danger more fluid, than Beck's risk society theory presumes.

This chapter argues that it was not the technological hazards of industrialization that drove the transformation of accident reporting, but rather the pressures that industrial modernity placed on the ways in which Britons imagined the structure of their society. In particular, it was the perceived emergence of a new 'middle class' and the simultaneous cultural erosion of the aristocracy's social authority that was the principal factor behind this transformation. As the cultural imagining of British society became more contested, discursive spaces where alternative social visions could be attacked or defended became more valuable, and because accident reporting already tended to focus on the social elements of disasters, its cultural currency increased dramatically. This was especially true for the single accident article, which, unconfined by the spatial limitations of multiple accident articles, provided reporters with the opportunity to present people from distinct social backgrounds acting as rational heroes or irrational cowards in the face of danger or imminent death. London dailies whose editorial line and readership gave them a stake in this social imagining thus began to increase their coverage of accidents and consolidated their accident reporting around the single accident article.

The focus on London is for three reasons: first, because London's newspaper industry was the most developed and competitive in Britain; second, because the unequalled size and mobility of London's population, as well as London's centrality to national politics, made questions of prescriptive social imagining particularly poignant; and, finally, because the small scale of London's industrialization problematizes the technological forces that risk society theorists associate with the growth of accident discourse.[8] The analysis presented in this chapter focuses principally on the three most widely circulated London dailies: the *Morning Post*, the *Morning Chronicle* and *The Times*. These papers have been chosen not only because of their large circulation, but also because of their readerships and political positions. By the first decade of the nineteenth century, the *Morning Post* had a circulation of approximately 4500; it was the most staunchly Tory of the

[8] On the importance of prescriptive social imagining for societies with large mobile populations, see J. Vernon, *Distant Strangers: How Britain Became Modern* (Berkeley, CA, 2014).

major London dailies and also the most obsequious to the aristocracy.[9] *The Times* was easily the most widely read of the London daily papers, having a circulation in the early 1820s of 15,000; it was also the most politically independent and targeted at the middle class.[10] The *Morning Chronicle* had been the most widely circulated of the London dailies during the first decade of the nineteenth century, with a circulation of 7000 in 1810, before its readership dropped significantly in the 1820s, as it began to face increased competition from *The Times*; politically it was anti-Tory and socially it was a champion of the middle classes.[11] The editorial line and target readership of these three papers meant that they each had a significant stake in the debates over Britain's social order. Moreover, because the London daily press had a large influence over the development of newspapers nationally, the changes that occurred to the volume and style of accident reporting within these papers provide an opportunity to excavate the origins of an important form of accident discourse in Britain. Indeed, as this chapter will show, the style of accident reporting that first emerged in the London dailies during the 1820s would later be echoed throughout the country, when some of the essential features of this style of reporting became an integral aspect of industrial modernity.

Changes to Accident Reporting in the London Dailies, 1800–30

Between 1800 and 1810, the *Morning Post* published 155 articles that reported a violent disaster under a headline that used the word 'accident'. *The Times* published 76 articles of this type over the same period and the *Morning Chronicle* published only four. Between 1820 and 1830, however, the *Morning Post* published 330 of these articles, *The Times* published 274 and the *Morning Chronicle* published 74.[12] Over no more than two decades, the number of accident articles published in these three

[9] W. Hindle, *The Morning Post, 1772–1937: Portrait of a Newspaper* (Westport, CT, 1937), pp. 65–148; L. Brake and M. Demoor, *Dictionary of Nineteenth-Century Journalism* (Ghent, 2009), p. 427.

[10] S. Morison, *The History of the Times: 'The Thunderer' in the Making, 1785–1841* (London, 1935), p. 243; Brake and Demoor, *Dictionary*, pp. 627–8.

[11] Brake and Demoor, *Dictionary*, p. 426.

[12] Figures based on author's count. For the *Morning Chronicle* and the *Morning Post*, these figures were tallied from the 19th Century British Library Newspapers digital database, and for *The Times*, the author used the Times Digital Archive, 1785–2006.

nationally circulated, London-based daily newspapers increased by proportions ranging from 113 to 1750 %. This significant growth, however, was not the only change that occurred in accident reporting during this decade. Concomitant to the rising number of accident articles was an increasing tendency for reporters to structure their writing around single accidents. While articles that focused on multiple accidents accounted for 74 % of all those published by the *Morning Post* and 50 % of all those published by the *Morning Chronicle* between 1800 and 1810, 20 years later, these multiple accident articles accounted for only 9 % and 3 % of the total number of accident articles published, respectively, by these two papers.

Given the simultaneity of these two changes, one might seek to account for the quantitative change by citing the qualitative one—in other words, to argue that the overall increase in the number of accident articles was the result of a disaggregation of accident reports. The problem with this explanation, however, is that during the first decade of the century, *The Times* was already focusing more than 90 % of its accident articles on single disasters.[13] Since the number of accident articles published in *The Times* during the 1820s also rose at an impressive rate, arguments that centre on disaggregation are untenable. Moreover, it is important to note that none of these three papers increased drastically in size over this period and therefore that the reporting of accidents was always in competition with other forms of news. This being the case, the principal driver behind the growth of accident reporting must have been either an upsurge in the newsworthiness of individual accident events or a rise in the perceived value of the single accident article as a form of reporting.

The validity of the first form of explanation can be assessed by a quick statistical measure. If it were the newsworthiness of individual accident events that was on the upswing, it would be reasonable to assume that there would be an observable change in the types of accidents reported. This change could be driven by either an increased public interest in a particular type of accident—such as was the case during the 1830s, when debates over the regulation of factory safety contributed to increased media attention being given to workplace accidents—or by the emergence

[13] Of the 71 accident articles printed in this paper between 1800 and 1810, 65 centred on single accidents, while only six were based either on reports of multiple accident occurrences or on discussions of how numerous accidents of one sort or another could be prevented in the future. Based on the author's count from the Times Digital Archive, 1785–2006.

of new forms of danger, as occurred during the 1840s, when Britain's first railway boom resulted in a large increase in the number of railway accidents. The available data on the 1820s, however, does not bear out either of these scenarios; on the contrary, it demonstrates a remarkable similarity in the types of accidents reported over the entirety of the first 30 years of the century. Of all the articles which centred on individual accidents published by the *Morning Post* between 1800 and 1820, the most common types were horse and coach accidents and shipwrecks.[14] After these two categories, the next largest were accidents involving a collapsing building, a fire, a gun or drowning.[15] During the 1820s, these sorts of disasters remained the stock and trade of accident reporters and the proportions shifted only to a very minor extent.[16] As such, it would be difficult to suggest that the increased number of articles focusing on single accidents was driven either by novel dangers or increased political or cultural attention being given to a specific category of danger. This quantitative measure, however, does not speak to the other form of potential explanation, according to which it is not the newsworthiness of the accident itself that increases, but rather the value of the single accident article as a medium for conveying interpretation and inscribing meanings on events. The validity of this sort of explanation can only be assessed by a qualitative examination of the similarities and differences between articles that centred on single accidents and those which grouped multiple accidents together under a single headline, before and during the 1820s.

Explaining the Changes: The Social Meaning of Accidents

Throughout this period, regardless of whether accident articles focused on single or multiple disasters, they invariably constructed the disaster(s) through an understanding of the accidental that was uncharacteristic of modernity. In other words, the calamity was treated as lacking any structural causality, predictability or preventability, and issues of risk and liability were rarely discussed. It is important to point out here that it was

[14] The former represented 19 % of all such articles and the latter accounted for 15 %.

[15] Collapsing buildings accounted for 12 %, fires accounted for 8 %, accidents involving guns accounted for 6 % and individuals accidentally drowned accounted for 3 %.

[16] For instance, individuals accidentally drowned increased from 3 % to 9 % and gun accidents fell from 8 % to 6 %.

not as though these more modern ways of thinking about accidents were culturally unavailable. Since the late eighteenth century, discourses and techniques of accident prevention had been actively circulated by organizations such as the Royal Humane Society, members of a developing medical profession, and entrepreneurs involved in a small but growing safety industry.[17] Moreover, as Thomas Laqueur has shown, British culture during these years was also flooded with new 'humanitarian narratives' that emphasized the possibility and importance of preventing violent accidents.[18] Connected with the move towards thinking of accidents as preventable was a growing understanding of risk and practices of risk management. Indeed, during precisely the same decade that accident reporting was expanding, Britain's insurance industry was also experiencing a period of significant growth. In the first 40 years of the century, the volume of life insurance business increased 15-fold and the first significant spurt in this trend came in the 1820s. The stock market boom of 1824–5 and the emergence of new actuarial tables, lower premiums and new offices courting the clerical, medical and military professions all worked to make insurance products both more appealing and accessible.[19] Given these wider social, cultural and intellectual movements, the absence of modern understandings of danger in the newspaper coverage of early nineteenth-century accidents is striking.

Equally, however, the way in which the accidental was conceptualized in the newspaper reporting of these years was not characteristically premodern either. Most notably absent from this period's accident reporting is the idea of providence. This is not to say that accident reporting existed outside of or apart from the dominant religious and principally Christian cosmology of the day. Quite naturally, the hand of God did sometimes feature in accident articles, but its appearance was rare and usually it was employed by reporters as a trope to stylize someone's escape from danger. When, for instance, the clothing of a Mrs Walker caught fire one autumn evening in 1822, causing her to rush out of her house, the *Morning Post* reported that she was only saved by Mr Dewse, who 'providentially' arrived

[17] R. Porter, 'Accidents in the Eighteenth Century', in R. Cooter and B. Luckin (eds), *Accidents in History: Injuries, Fatalities and Social Relations* (Atlanta, GA, 1997), pp. 90–107.

[18] T. Laqueur, 'Bodies, Details and the Humanitarian Narrative', in L. Hunt (ed.), *The New Cultural History* (Berkeley, CA, 1989), pp. 176–204.

[19] T. Alborn, *Regulated Lives: Life Insurance and British Society, 1800–1914* (Toronto, 2009).

on the scene and extinguished the flames.[20] Similarly, in June 1823, when a boulder fell from a cliff at Hastings and, upon shattering, one of its pieces struck the house of an old woman, the *Morning Post* described her survival as 'miraculous'.[21] These sorts of descriptions use providence less as an explanatory device than as a sort of rhetorical embellishment. Moreover, they are clearly a far cry from the atonement narratives—prevalent as a causal explanation for catastrophe elsewhere in English culture—that employed providence as a means of explaining why tragedy befell a particular individual or group.[22] Indeed, when reporters made reference to these more grim representations of providence, they usually did so in the form of ridicule. When a Birmingham coach overturned in August 1823, resulting in the death of Mr Atterbury, the *Morning Post* told its readers that only in a 'less enlightened age' could such an event be interpreted as the warnings of providence.[23]

Neither straightforwardly modern nor pre-modern, then, accident reporting in the major London dailies throughout the first three decades of the nineteenth century typically focused on the victims and social circumstances of the disaster. Accident reporters, for instance, paid great attention to the gender and age of the victims, the number of loved ones they left behind, the efforts of rescuers and victims both during and after the accident, and the ways in which the accident maimed and disfigured the victim's body. This was true both of the multiple accident articles, which dominated accident reporting in the *Morning Post* and the *Morning Chronicle* during the first two decades of the century, and the single accident article, which became the standard mode of accident reporting during the 1820s. The chief difference between these forms of reporting was the number of column inches they gave to individual accidents. Though an obvious difference, it was highly important. As the unwilled outcome of an earlier discoverable cause, accidents by their nature tend to be thought of and retold in a narrative form.[24] As the space available to each accident grew, reporters were afforded more opportunities to introduce

[20] 'Shocking Accident in York', *Morning Post*, 31 October 1822.

[21] 'Accident at Hastings', *Morning Post*, 11 June 1823.

[22] For a discussion of the use of providence to explain the causality of catastrophes during this period, see B. Hilton, *The Age of Atonement: The Influence of Evangelicalism on Social and Economic Thought, 1785–1865* (Oxford, 1986).

[23] 'Late Unfortunate Accident', *Morning Post*, 4 August 1823.

[24] The relationship between accidents and narrative is a central feature of the body of historiography that analyses the historical development of the accident as a concept. See

more thoroughly styled stories. In single accident articles, reporters were able not only to discuss who was affected by a particular disaster, but also to colour in greater detail how gender, class and age structured individual behaviour and social interaction during a moment of tremendous duress. This greater potential for narration thus turned accident reporting into a space of social description where readers could be engaged at an emotive level and where power relations could be imagined and contested. This difference is demonstrated effectively by two examples.

On 22 September 1806, the *Morning Chronicle* ran an article that consisted of three accidents.[25] The first of these recounted the collapse of two houses in Camden, which resulted in 22 individuals being either injured or killed. The report describes how, prior to the disaster, all of the inhabitants of the building were sleeping, how the collapse of the building buried everyone in the ruins, how the efforts of local men resulted in the rescue of all but four and how a coroner's inquest was held the following Saturday.[26] The story is also punctuated by tropes that played on the imagined readers' presumed emotional responsiveness to gender and familial relations. The article details, for instance, how the accident resulted in the death of an infant child and its mother. Finally, the story describes briefly and matter-of-factly the physical injuries suffered by the victims. Beyond this, however, there is very little to the account provided by the reporter. The article simply moves on to the story of another building that collapsed and then finally to the story of a shipwreck. Almost 16 years later, on 26 April 1822, the *Morning Post* ran a single accident article that also centred on the collapse of two houses. Like the earlier story in the *Morning Chronicle*, this accident narrative also proceeds through the same tripartite structure and is punctuated by appeals to the readers' presumed sensibilities to class, age and gender. The central difference is the extent to which these tropes colour the narrative. In the 1822 account, readers are introduced to a Mr Parry, who remembered dressing at the moment of the accident and, upon rationally perceiving the danger of his situation, exited the premises before the building collapsed entirely. In the next sentence, they encounter Mrs Bowles, who only 'miraculously escaped', but cannot remember how she reached the street. In the next paragraph, readers are introduced

R. Vieira, 'The Epistemology and Politics of the Accidental: Connecting the Accident's Intellectual and Cultural Historiography', *History Compass* 11 (2013), pp. 227–34.

[25] 'Accidents & c.', *Morning Chronicle*, 22 September 1806.

[26] 'Dreadful Accident', *Morning Post*, 26 April 1822.

to Mrs Bowles' husband, who, after being saved by the workmen, exits the rubble and is reintroduced to his wife, who is 'extremely ill from fright'. Then, in the final three sentences, the reader is provided with a thorough and affecting discussion of the injuries endured by the accident's victims. In the 1806 article we have a brief description; in the 1822 article we have an emotionally affecting story where gendered subjects, in the face of danger, are fractured according to binaries of rationality/irrationality. By allowing reporters to put rhetorical flesh on narrative bones, the single accident article transformed accident reporting into a poignant space where social imaginaries could be constructed and contested.

This qualitative transformation in accident reporting helps to explain the massive quantitative increase in the number of single accident articles during the 1820s. As British historians have long observed, the period following the conclusion of the Napoleonic Wars in 1815 was defined in large measure by a heightening of social divisions as the post-war economic slump coupled with massive population growth and urbanization significantly intensified the social impact of industrialization.[27] It is for these reasons that British social historians once saw this period as the birth moment of the class system in England.[28] Although the cultural turn has long since disposed of such reifying arguments about ontologically extant classes, there still remains a historiographical consensus that this period represented a moment when the social imaginary became increasingly destabilized, politicized and contested.[29] The 1820s, in particular, can be seen as representing a period of escalation in this process. It opened with the Queen Caroline Affair and the Peterloo Massacre putting the moral legitimacy of the established elites on trial, while the remainder of the decade saw debates over constitutional reform fundamentally transform the way in which Britons thought and talked about their middle class. As Dror Wahrman has demonstrated, the debates over constitutional reform that occurred during the 1820s widely circulated a vision of the middle class as a new, powerful and rapidly growing *social* constituency.[30] While the middle class had long figured as a trope in British political discourse, it had almost invariably been represented as a timeless entity defined by

[27] N. Gash, *Aristocracy and People: Britain, 1815–1865* (Cambridge, MA, 1979).

[28] Most notably E.P. Thompson, *The Making of the English Working Class* (London, 1963).

[29] D. Cannadine, *The Rise and Fall of Class in Britain* (New York, 1993), pp. 61–91.

[30] D. Wahrman, *Imagining the Middle Class: The Political Representation of Class in Britain, c. 1780–1840* (Cambridge, 1995), pp. 243–72.

moral virtues and, if anything, declining in the face of modernity.[31] The third decade of the nineteenth century thus saw both a significant intensification of anti-aristocratic sentiment and the emergence of a new way of envisioning society as structured around the middle class. This destabilization of the social imaginary had an important gender component, as the relative moral vigour of the aristocracy and the middle class was largely contingent on how the virtues and vices of their class-specific forms of masculinity were imagined.[32] This social and cultural context provides a rationale for why the longer narrative accounts of the single accident article became more newsworthy. As established social hierarchies fell into question, the news value of stories which spoke to the legitimacy or illegitimacy of those hierarchies increased. For newspapers that wished to reassert the vitality of the social order inherited from the *ancien régime*, accident narratives provided an ideal discursive space for affirming the vigour of the status quo: if aristocratic men demonstrated selflessness, courage and reason in even the direst of circumstances, then surely their place atop the social order could be vindicated.[33] Meanwhile, for papers that were tied to a social imaginary that stressed the importance of the middle class, accident reporting offered an opportunity to prescriptively reconstruct society around that social constituency.

The social visions promoted by our three papers broke down according to the spectrum described above. The tendency of the *Morning Post* to fawn over the aristocratic elite during this period is well known. As

[31] *Ibid.*, pp. 41–67, 235–43.

[32] A. Clark, 'Gender, Class, and the Nation: Franchise Reform in England, 1832–1928', in J. Vernon (ed.), *Re-reading the Constitution: New Narratives in the Political History of England's Long Nineteenth Century* (Cambridge, 1996), pp. 239–53; L. Davidoff and C. Hall, *Family Fortunes: Men and Women of the English Middle Class, 1780–1850* (Chicago, 1987); D. Wahrman, 'Middle-Class Domesticity Goes Public: Gender, Class and Politics from Queen Caroline to Queen Victoria', *Journal of British Studies* 32 (1993), pp. 396–432.

[33] This account accords with the findings of historians who have studied the cultural and political function of accident discourse in later periods. Steven Biel's cultural history of the *Titanic* disaster, for instance, documented how, immediately following the sinking, narratives emerged in the press and elsewhere of white upper-class men sacrificing themselves in order to save women and children, while racialized workers from the steerage fled the ship like rats with no concern for anyone but themselves. Such narratives, Biel argues, were symptoms of a desire amongst America's elite to legitimate and reinforce culturally the existing social hierarchies in the face of growing racial and gender tensions. See S. Biel, *A Cultural History of the Titanic Disaster* (New York, 1996).

one of the paper's historians has put it: 'Majesty of every kind and from every clime was grist to the *Morning Post*'s sycophantic mill.'[34] Though the paper's opinions on the French Revolution had once garnered it a reputation for independence, it quickly lost that reputation after it was sold by Daniel Stuart in 1803 and its columns began to swell with news on the monarchy and aristocracy. By 1820, it had adopted a clearly reactionary character that was more than evident in its editorial decision to support the magistrates over the radicals in its coverage of the Peterloo Massacre.[35] While certainly not radical papers, the editorial lines of the *Morning Chronicle* and *The Times* differed significantly from that of the *Morning Post*. Far from fawning over the nobility, these papers were both fervent supporters of the parliamentary opposition and champions of a social vision that placed significant weight on the middle class. The *Morning Chronicle* had long acted as a voice of the middle class and, after 1817, when Thomas Barnes assumed the editorship of *The Times*, it too became a champion for the virtues of that section of British society.[36] The differing social imaginaries of the *Morning Post*, the *Morning Chronicle* and *The Times* led to differences in how they reported accidents. This point can be illustrated by an examination of the contrasting ways in which these papers covered accidents involving the aristocratic elite.

The *Morning Post*, in stark contrast to *The Times* and the *Morning Chronicle*, regularly published articles that centred on accidents that caused even minor injuries to members of the aristocracy. On 14 May 1825, the Duke of York fell from his horse and suffered a small bruise to his forehead. Two days later, the *Morning Post* ran an article of about 200 words on the subject, while *The Times* and the *Morning Chronicle* ignored the event completely.[37] In part, this distinction between the three papers was driven by the *Morning Post*'s tendency, noted above, to report on the fashionable world of the nobility. Yet a quick examination of how aristocrats, and particularly aristocratic men, were represented in these accident articles reveals that there was more going on here than the *Morning Post*'s penchant for publishing on matters of aristocratic celebrity. The vast majority of the *Morning Post*'s articles on accidents involving the nobility

[34] W.H. Hindle, *The Morning Post: Portrait of a Newspaper, 1772–1937* (Westport, CT, 1974), p. 115.

[35] *Ibid.*

[36] G. Phillips, 'Barnes, Thomas (1785–1841)', *Oxford Dictionary of National Biography* (Oxford, 2004).

[37] 'The Duke of York—Accidents', *Morning Post*, 16 May 1825.

focused on disasters which placed aristocratic men in physical danger and, invariably, the reporters tended to present these figures as maintaining the highest dignity even when encountering imminent death. When, for instance, Lord Robert Manners fell through the ice while skating in early January 1822, the *Morning Post* depicted his immediate reaction as a rational and masculine attempt to pull himself from danger. 'Lord R. is a strong muscular man', wrote the reporter, 'and with the confidence of a good swimmer he made several attempts to gain the surface of the ice, but unfortunately it only broke to sink him in each effort.'[38] The article then went on to describe how, even with the spectre of death looming, the nobleman's reaction was a selfless concern for the others on the ice. Rather than screaming for help, Manners is reported to have advised his fellows to leave him, as they would only endanger themselves through any attempt at rescue. Narrating the accident in this way not only presented the nobleman in a favourable light, it also provided an implicit justification for the elite position of the aristocracy in the established social hierarchy.

While *The Times* and the *Morning Chronicle* did not often run accident articles that focused on individual members of the nobility, they did report on accident stories where aristocrats were among the victims. Moreover, the fact that these stories were also often covered by the *Morning Post* makes it possible to draw some direct comparisons. On 6 May 1823, for instance, *The Times* and the *Morning Post* ran articles on the subject of a fatal accident at the groundbreaking ceremony for a new orphanage in London.[39] The ceremony was attended by approximately 3000 people, including the Duke of York and Prince Leopold. According to the narratives presented in each paper, the accident unfolded something like this. A carriage procession of orphans, the Lord Mayor and Lord Bishop of London, a number of 'eminent clergymen' and the two nobles listed above entered the outdoor space where the ceremony was to take place. The space consisted of a large platform that was built over the location where the building's foundation was to be laid and a series of benches that had been constructed to provide the female section of the audience with a place to sit. Under the stage was a labourer who operated a machine designed to lower the building's foundation stone. When the procession entered the outdoor space, the benches were already full. The members

[38] 'Accident to Lord Manners', *Morning Post*, 4 January 1822.

[39] 'Frightful Accident', *The Times*, 6 May 1823; 'Interesting Ceremony and Lamentable Accident', *Morning Post*, 6 May 1823.

of the procession were then led on to the stage and the labourer began lowering the foundation stone. At this point, disaster struck. The pulley holding the stone snapped and the platform collapsed, killing the labourer below and injuring a number of the children. In terms of this basic narrative, the report in each paper is generally the same.

The chief difference between the two reports is to be found in their points of emphasis and their descriptions of the social aspects of the event. Whereas the report by the *Morning Post* emphasized the centrality of the aristocratic elite to the organization of the ceremony, the report in *The Times* paid very little attention to the role of the attending aristocrats and instead emphasized the importance of gender and age differentiation to the ceremony's organization. Thus, while the *Morning Post* reported that the ceremony began with the Duke of York being placed at the centre of the stage surrounded by an undifferentiated group of children, *The Times* reported that the children on the stage were divided between boys and girls, that they were placed in a circle around the foundation stone, and that the nobles and other notables were positioned outside of the circle on the left side of the stage. The reports, however, differed not only in terms of their account of the ceremony's organization, but also in terms of how they represented the moment of the accident. When the platform began to teeter, reported the *Morning Post*, the Duke of York rationally observed his danger, moved to a safe part of the stage and escaped the collapsing platform. While everyone else on the stage fell, the Duke's unique intelligence allowed him escape danger. Among those who fell, the *Morning Post* reported that Prince Leopold experienced no injury at all and that only minor injuries were sustained by the Lord Mayor, Lord Bishop, the clergymen and the children. The only serious injury, according to the *Morning Post*, was sustained by the workman below the platform who was crushed to death and whose body was 'horribly mangled'. *The Times* presented a significantly different account of the disaster. Here, the Duke of York is not presented as the only figure who calmly and rationally extricated himself from danger, but rather as one among several people who quickly jumped off the boards while they were falling. Among the others who also jumped to safety was Prince Leopold. Unlike the article in the *Morning Post*, then, *The Times*' report does not present the Duke of York as having some unique ability to brave danger, but instead presents him as one of several people who sought to save only themselves. This implied selfishness is reinforced by the way in which *The Times* represented the victims. Like the *Morning Post*, *The Times* reported that the workman was the only person who suffered a fatal injury and it employed an affecting language to do so: 'the wretched victim was borne away in a dreadfully mangled state'. Unlike the *Morning Post*, however, *The Times* reported that, while not sustaining serious injury, several of the young girls on the stage were plunged below during the accident. Thus, *The Times* created a context where the Duke of York appeared to be motivated not only by a frenzied desire for self-preservation but also a desire which overrode any expectations of chivalric masculinity. Representing the same accident in different ways, the *Morning Post* and *The Times* were able to implicitly advance their respective positions on the legitimacy of aristocratic authority.

The same point can be illustrated by examining how these papers reported on accidents involving the middle class. In the summer of 1827, two accidents involving the construction of the Thames Tunnel received coverage in both *The Times* and the *Morning Post*. The first of these accidents was the flooding of 18 May. In its coverage of this event, the *Morning Post* emphasizes the hubris of the civil engineer, Marc Isambard Brunel, in thinking that his tunnelling shield could withstand the power of the Thames. The paper notes that while it had previously hoped that Brunel would be successful, it now fears that 'Father Thames will ultimately be found too strong'.[40] *The Times* presents the flooding and Brunel in very different terms. Here, the lines of causality for the flood are more carefully sketched out: the accident results from the especially thin soil under that particular part of the river, not from the weaknesses of the engineer and the strength of nature. Moreover, *The Times* stresses that the accident had done little to erode Brunel's confidence. The engineer, the article explains, 'remained as sanguine as ever as to the success of the endeavour' and, most importantly, his 'confidence inspired a similar spirit into the minds of the workmen'.[41] Whereas the *Morning Post* provides a story of the dangers of upsetting the natural order, *The Times* presents a story in which a middle-class man overcomes nature in the name of progress and whose masculine resolve betters men from the lower orders.

The second accident occurred a month later on 27 June. On this occasion, two members of the management Board visited the Tunnel in order to determine if and when its construction could be opened for public observation. The Tunnel at this time still contained, in some areas, approximately nine feet of water, which meant that a small boat had to be used.

[40] 'The Thames Tunnel. Most Alarming Accident', *Morning Post*, 19 May 1827.
[41] 'Accident at the Thames Tunnel', *The Times*, 21 May 1827.

On this occasion, the boat sank and one of its occupants drowned. In its report on this accident, the *Morning Post* lays the blame on Mr Martin, one of the Board members, who was reported to have 'hastily rose' from his seat, causing the boat to overturn. When this happened, the *Morning Post* report continues, Mr Martin and a youth accompanying the party saved themselves by grabbing on to the Tunnel's brickwork, whilst everyone else was hurled into the water. When help arrived, everyone was saved except for a man named Samuel Richardson, who was later dragged from the water drowned. Richardson, the *Morning Post* relays, had been a man of very 'sober and industrious habits' whose wife, upon hearing the news, went down to the Tunnel in a 'most frantic state'.[42] In this story, the stupidity of a man who, the *Morning Post* indicates, was 'well known in the commercial world' leads directly to the death of a respectable worker. In this context, the use of Mrs Richardson functions to enhance the emotional impact of the story and intensify the egregiousness of Mr Martin's thoughtlessness. Unsurprisingly, the narrative spun by *The Times* is starkly different. Here, Mr Martin is not blamed for the accident at all; indeed, he and the other Board member are never even mentioned in the report. Instead, the 'whole cause of the accident' is presented as being 'attributable to an absence of light in the arches'. Moreover, while *The Times*' article mentions the death of Mr Richardson, also describing him as a respectable fellow, it makes no mention of the impact of his death upon his wife. Rather than attempting to affect the audience by describing the human impact of the accident, *The Times* reporter instead focuses on how the company has limited the possibility of a similar accident in the future. The 'recurrence of such an accident ... has now been safely guarded against', *The Times*' readers are told, because an order had been put in for additional gas lights.[43] Whereas the story in the *Morning Post* presents middle-class men endangering workers, the story in *The Times* presents the middle class as the agents of progress.

The above comparisons illustrate how reporters in the *Morning Post* and *The Times* used accident articles as a discursive space within which to construct and contest social imaginaries, and this, in turn, helps to explain the consolidation of accident reporting around the single accident article and the remarkable overall increase in the number of accident articles in the London daily press during these years.

[42] 'Thames Tunnel. Serious Accident', *Morning Post*, 29 June 1827.

[43] 'Thames Tunnel', *The Times*, 29 June 1827.

An important caveat, however, is necessary at this point. The argument is not that the editors of these papers decided to increase the number of column inches they devoted to accident reporting because they consciously wanted to use accident narratives in the service of a wider social agenda. Rather, it is more productive to see this process as being driven by a confluence between the structural operation of what media scholars call 'news values' and a wider cultural need—specific to the 1820s—to reimagine the social. The argument, then, is that the increased politicization of Britain's social structure during the 1820s raised the newsworthiness of stories that could be seen as in line with either the editor's actual or the imagined audience's presumed understanding of how British society is or should be structured.[44] Accident stories were particularly affected by this process for two reasons: first, because of their ability to show how classed and gendered subjects acted under extreme duress; and, second, because of their pre-existing tendency to provide details on the victims of the disaster. Combined, these two aspects of accident reporting allowed the single accident article to demonstrate with great effect the legitimacy or illegitimacy of a specific understanding of the social order.

The Single Accident Article and Industrial Modernity

The argument so far has been directed at elucidating aspects of accident reporting in the 1820s. But we can also situate these quantitative and qualitative changes in accident reporting within a broader historical trajectory and ask how significant they were in the wider history of danger and risk in nineteenth-century Britain. The first point is that the statistical jump in the number of accident articles during the 1820s was not an

[44] My thinking here is guided by Johan Galtung and Mari Ruge's definition of news values. Galtung and Ruge identify 11 structural features that, they argue, determine the perceived newsworthiness of a story. Among these features are 'cultural proximity' and 'consonance', that is, the degree to which the story is believed to be meaningful to the audience of the news organization and the extent to which the event appears to be in accordance with the frameworks of understanding of the imagined audience. I would suggest that the operations of these particular 'news values' were intensified with regard to the social aspects of accident stories during the 1820s. See J. Galtung and M. Ruge, 'The Structure of Foreign News: The Presentation of the Congo, Cuba, and Cyprus Crises in Four Norwegian Newspapers', *Journal of Peace Research* 2 (1965), pp. 64–90.

anomaly—that is, significant only to that decade—but rather the beginning of a consistent trend throughout the century towards greater public interest in accidental disasters. By the 1840s, for instance, the number of accident articles in the *Morning Post* numbered more than 800; a decade later, it was closer to 900.[45] In *The Times*, too, a similar trend was apparent, with more than 1300 accident articles appearing in the 1840s.[46] Also, by this point, accident articles were becoming a staple form of reporting in the rapidly expanding provincial press.[47] The *York Herald*, a weekly paper from the north of England, showed very little interest in accidents during the century's early decades, but by the 1840s it ran more than 100 accident articles and, during the 1850s, it printed more than 300.[48] Similarly, the *Derby Mercury*, also a weekly but from the East Midlands, published very few accident articles during the 1820s, but by the 1840s it printed close to 100 and, during the 1850s, that number tripled.[49]

The trend towards increasing public interest in accidents during these later decades was driven in large measure by the emergence and politicization of new forms of danger. Industrial and factory accidents figured more heavily in these years than they had during the 1820s. To be sure, the danger that most forcefully captured the reporter's eye was the railway accident. Railway accidents accounted for between approximately 25 % and 60 % of all the accident articles during the 1840s and 1850s in the newspapers cited above and, between 1850 and 1880, as Ralph Harrington has argued, 'the violence, destruction, terror and slaughter of the railway accident ... dominated the headlines, commanded public attention and pervaded the contemporary imagination'.[50] But while the types of accidents reported on increasingly came to include different forms of danger, the tremendous rise in the newsworthiness of accident articles and the narrative practices of accident reporting that were established during

[45] Figures based on author's count from the 19th Century British Library Newspapers digital database.

[46] Figures based on author's count from the Times Digital Archive, 1785–2006.

[47] In 1820, there were 100 provincial papers; by 1847, there were 230; by 1877, there were 938; and by 1907, there were 1338. Vernon, *Distant Strangers*, p. 87.

[48] Figures based on author's count from the 19th Century British Library Newspapers digital database.

[49] Figures based on author's count from the 19th Century British Library Newspapers digital database.

[50] R. Harrington, 'Railway Safety and Railway Slaughter: Railway Accidents, Government and Public in Victorian Britain', *Journal of Victorian Culture* 8 (2003), p. 192.

the 1820s formed an important part of the communicative framework through which the Victorians would later engage culturally with the more modern dangers of the industrial world.

Over the past two decades, scholars of risk in disciplines across the social sciences and humanities have begun to stress the importance of the media and the linguistic mechanisms by which understandings of danger are circulated and made sense of culturally.[51] This scholarly discourse has helped to add greater nuance and sophistication to a field of study that has otherwise been dominated by overly deterministic theoretical frameworks, such as Beck's 'risk society' thesis.[52] Among these scholars are a small group of historians of Britain's nineteenth century who have made much of the role played by narrative in accident discourse during the mid- to late nineteenth century, arguing that it came to function as a mechanism for culturally managing the moral discomforts, fears and anxieties that occupied the minds of the Victorians as they grappled with the dangers of industrial life. Elaine Freedgood's recent book on this subject, for instance, shows how reading and writing stories about danger in the world beyond Britain's shores provided the early to mid-Victorians with a cultural strategy of risk management, essentially making industrial Britain seem safe by comparison.[53] Similarly, the work of scholars like Jamie Bronstein, Mike Sanders, Peter Sinnema and Bernhard Rieger demonstrates how, throughout the mid- to late Victorian period, narratives about accidents provided a means of

[51] S. Cottle, 'Ulrich Beck, Risk Society and the Media: A Catastrophic View?', *European Journal of Communication* 13 (1998), pp. 5–32; J. Kitzinger and J. Reilly, 'The Rise and Fall of Risk Reporting: Media Coverage of Human Genetics Research, False Memory Syndrome and Mad Cow Disease', *European Journal of Communication* 12 (1997), pp. 319–50; U. Heise, *Sense of Place, Sense of Planet: The Environmental Imagination of the Global* (Oxford, 2008); Vieira, 'The Epistemology and Politics of the Accidental'; N. Goodman, *Shifting the Blame: Literature, Law and the Theory of Accidents in Nineteenth-Century America* (Princeton, NJ, 1998); J. Go III, 'Inventing Industrial Accidents and their Insurance: Discourse and Workers' Compensation in the United States, 1880s–1910s', *Social Science History* 20 (1996), pp. 401–38.

[52] U. Beck, *Risk Society: Towards a New Modernity*, trans. M. Ritter (New York, 1992); A. Giddens, 'Risk and Responsibility', *Modern Law Review* 62 (1999), pp. 1–10; K. Figlio, 'What is an Accident?', in P. Weindling (ed.), *The Social History of Occupational Health* (London, 1985), pp. 180–208; L.M. Friedman and J. Ladinsky, 'Social Change and the Law of Industrial Accidents', *Columbia Law Review* 67 (1967), pp. 50–82; P.W.J. Bartrip and S.B. Burman, *The Wounded Soldiers of Industry: Industrial Compensation Policy, 1833–1897* (Oxford, 1983).

[53] Freedgood, *Victorian Writing about Risk*.

easing the anxieties that modern technological disasters produced.[54] This group of historians, however, have yet to trace the historical lineage of the narrative techniques which they see as so integral to the functioning and perpetuation of technological modernity. If such a genealogy were conducted, the 1820s would figure as an important decade.

In her study of the newspaper reporting on nineteenth-century British factory and mining disasters, Bronstein argues that reporters writing about accidents for middle-class audiences served a crucial cultural function in Britain's budding industrial society. By narrating industrial accidents as individual stories of bad luck rather than as the result of dangers systemic to processes of industrial production, these reporters allowed their readers to feel sympathy for working-class victims whilst simultaneously absolving them of any guilt and distracting them from wider structural issues. Avoiding questions of causality and culpability, Bronstein demonstrates how reporters instead constructed tragic narratives that focused on the victims, their age and gender, and the number of dependents they left behind. Engaging middle-class readers emotively through evocations of pity, she argues that this type of narrative allowed the Victorian middle class to see itself as moral, while simultaneously allowing it to avoid questions about safety and culpability. 'The narratives of workplace accidents and their social devastation, which littered nineteenth-century newspapers', she writes, 'enabled readers to exercise their Christian feeling toward the less fortunate without really thinking about inequalities of wealth distribution or unsafe work practices.'[55] For our purposes, Bronstein's research suggests that the causeless, human-centred, single accident narrative, first established as the primary form of accident reporting by the London dailies during the 1820s, had by the early to mid-Victorian period become an integral hermeneutic to the functioning of industrial society.

Conclusion

Within the historical teleology of risk society theory, the 1820s represents something of a puzzle. On the one hand, massive changes to how accidents were reported on by an important section of the press seem to mark

[54] See footnote 7 above.

[55] J. Bronstein, 'Caught in the Machinery: The Cultural Meanings of Workplace Accidents in Victorian Britain and the United States', *Maryland Historical Magazine* 96 (2001), p. 166.

the decade as a crucial moment in the transition to a first modernity. Not only did the 1820s see a significant rise in the number of accidents that were reported on by the papers examined here, it also witnessed the consolidation of accident reporting around a particular type of article which would later function as an important cultural means of containing anxieties over the dangers of the industrial world. Furthermore, the causal forces that led to the major quantitative and qualitative changes in accident reporting during this period stemmed largely, though indirectly, from the effects of industrialisation. Yet, on the other hand, an examination of the types of accidents reported and the way in which these accidents were represented suggests clear lines of continuity with the pre-industrial and pre-modern world. It was not the large-scale dangers of the industrial world that most often captivated the attention of accident reporters, but rather the day-to-day dangers of the pre-industrial world. Moreover, it was not the modern discourses of risk and risk management—which were clearly emerging in other areas of British culture—that structured accident reporting in these years, but rather the more human-centred stories that had been the stock and trade of accident reporting in earlier decades.

Within the context of risk society theory, then, the 1820s would appear to constitute a liminal moment, somewhere between the death of a pre-modern culture of danger and the consolidation of the risk regime of a first modernity. Captivated primarily by how danger and risk are engaged with at particular historical stages (pre-modern, modern and late-modern), scholars operating in the risk society framework tend to exaggerate the abruptness and epochal nature of change. As this chapter has suggested, locating research at the joints of historical transition can provide an important corrective to this tendency. While the transformations in accident reporting that took place during the 1820s were part of a wider transition to a modern culture of danger and risk, their peculiarities demonstrate that this broader transition was neither as epochal nor as straightforward as risk society theory presumes.

PART II

Environmental Risks

CHAPTER 4

Artificial Britain: Risk, Systems and Synthetics Since 1800

Chris Otter

'The history of civilization', mused Thomas Huxley in 1893, 'details the steps by which man has succeeded in building up an artificial world within the cosmos.'[1] Huxley suggested that the evolution of *homo sapiens* was inseparable from the creation of a largely artificial physico-moral environment, which he pointedly juxtaposed with 'the state of nature' persisting until at least the Roman invasion of Britain.[2] In contemporary parlance, the human species, at least in Britain, had undertaken a vast act of 'niche construction.'[3] The transformation of human niches would have been perfectly apparent to Huxley, whose world was on the cusp of electrification and automobilization: powered flight was a mere decade away. History seemed to have a particular eco-technological directionality: human beings were being slowly drawn into the orbit of the artificial.

[1] T. Huxley, 'Evolution and Ethics', [1893] in T. Huxley, *Evolution and Ethics: Science and Morals* (Amherst, NY, 2004), p. 83.

[2] T. Huxley, 'Evolution and Ethics: Prologomena', [1894] in Huxley, *Evolution and Ethics*, pp. 1–2.

[3] F.J. Odling-Smee, K. Laland and M. Feldman, *Niche Construction: The Neglected Process in Evolution* (Princeton, NJ, 2003).

C. Otter
Department of History, Ohio State University, 263 Dulles Hall, Columbus, OH 43210, USA

T. Crook, M. Esbester (eds), *Governing Risks in Modern Britain*,
DOI 10.1057/978-1-137-46745-4_4

The 'artificial world' is, in turn, the location of Ulrich Beck's 'risk society'.[4] As human life increasingly unfolded in human-built spaces, the conditions under which populations lived were concomitantly transformed, as were the reflexive relationships people experienced with their own fates.[5] The consequences were contradictory. While life expectancies grew and causes of death shifted from the infectious to non-infectious, new threats and morbidities emerged. 'Risk society' thus developed alongside a more thoroughly 'technological society'.[6] The concept of risk itself has, of course, never been purely reducible to material systems and their effects. It is a polyvalent term, referring to risks themselves, and the perception and government of risk. Indeed, much of the literature on risk society addresses these issues of perception and governance. This chapter, by contrast, focuses primarily on the material dimensions of risk, without suggesting that their apprehension and regulation are insignificant. Since these three dimensions are often inseparable, this is a question of emphasis. The argument, simply put, is that an increasingly artificial human environment underpins and shapes risk society, even if it does not absolutely determine the way risks are comprehended, experienced and managed.

Contemporaries understood these transformations. In 1882, the historian Frederic Harrison argued that Britain had undergone an 'unparalleled change in material life' over the previous 100 years, both absolutely and in comparison to other European nations.[7] In *The Condition of England*, published in 1909, Charles Masterman described mass urbanization as 'the largest secular change of a thousand years: from the life of the field to the life of the city'.[8] The gravitation from field to city was a spatial movement towards an increasingly artificialized life. This shift stimulated fantasies (some dystopian, some utopian), but it also entailed a tangible transformation in risk environments: urbanization meant greater population density, higher levels of airborne pollution, more crime, and numerous psychological and physical afflictions (the 'urban penalty'). Generalized urbanization was a radical act of human niche construction, producing an ecology 'totally different from that in which the human

[4] U. Beck, *Risk Society: Towards a New Modernity*, trans. M. Ritter (London, 1992).

[5] S. Lash and B. Wynne, 'Introduction', in Beck, *Risk Society*, p. 4.

[6] J. Ellul, *The Technological Society*, trans. J. Wilkinson (New York, 1964).

[7] F. Harrison, 'A Few Words about the Nineteenth Century', *Fortnightly Review* 31 (1882), p. 416.

[8] C.F.G. Masterman, *The Condition of England* (London, 1909), p. 96.

race was evolved'.[9] To regard risks as purely 'social constructions' or to ridicule the idea of 'risk-in-itself' downplays the physical reality of such transitions.[10] Human encounters with technology were not only 'mystified modes of social self-encounter, twisted outwards and reified', to quote Beck,[11] they were also bodily encounters with novel environments, with poisons, dusts and machinery: such encounters might be altogether unreflexive and non-cognitive.[12]

The material focus adopted here has three major consequences, relating to *space*, *time* and *the body*. First, space. For Beck, risks 'possess an *inherent tendency towards globalization*'.[13] They 'endanger *all* forms of life on this planet' and possess an irreversible quality.[14] Beck's primary examples are nuclear war and climate change. However, these often stand as proxies for risk in general and occlude more local, unspectacular patterns of technological risk. This chapter argues for the continued and even enhanced significance of the local in the 'artificial world', a significance which cannot be comprehended merely by utilizing the ambiguous portmanteau term 'glocal'.[15] This does not, however, undermine Beck's basic argument about the growing menace of global risks. Risk is not a zero-sum game: local *and* global risks can grow simultaneously.

Addressing risk's spatial localization also has consequences for comprehending its historicity and temporality. Beck argued that risk society proper only emerged in the 1970s.[16] Numerous scholars have, entirely persuasively, argued that complex technological systems, with unpredictable effects,

[9] H. Campbell, *The Causation of Disease: An Exposition of the Ultimate Factors which Induce It* (London, 1889), cited in R. Russell, *Strength and Diet: A Practical Treatise with Special Regard to the Life of Nations* (London, 1905), p. 36.

[10] S. Lash, 'Risk Culture', in B. Adam, U. Beck and J. van Loon (eds), *The Risk Society and Beyond: Critical Issues for Social Theory* (London, 2000), p. 51; B. Adam and J. van Loon, 'Introduction: Repositioning Risk; the Challenge for Social Theory', in Adam, Beck and van Loon (eds), *Risk Society*, p. 10.

[11] U. Beck, *Ecological Politics in an Age of Risk*, trans. A. Weisz (Cambridge, 1995), pp. 158–9.

[12] This critique is not, of course, a novel one. See T. Cooper and S. Bulmer, 'Refuse and the "Risk Society": The Political Ecology of Risk in Inter-War Britain', *Social History of Medicine* 26 (2013), p. 250.

[13] Beck, *Risk Society*, p. 36, emphasis in original.

[14] *Ibid.*, pp. 13, 22, emphasis in original.

[15] U. Beck, 'Risk Society Revisited: Theory, Politics and Research Programmes', in Adam, Beck and van Loon (eds), *Risk Society*, p. 218.

[16] S. Boudia and N. Jas, 'Introduction: Risk and "Risk Society" in Historical Perspective', *History and Technology* 23 (2007), p. 317.

date back to at least the origins of the Industrial Revolution.[17] Indeed, reflexive awareness of the risks of new technologies clearly pre-dates industrialization. Vaccination, for example, generated anxieties about the intermingling of the human and the natural: in 1722, the Reverend Edmund Massey preached a sermon against variolation, calling it a 'Diabolical Operation' that 'banish[ed] Providence out of the World'.[18] To posit a single break dividing risk society from previous periods is to introduce a misleading analytical bifurcation into history.[19] No simple, stadial model of risk, applicable everywhere simultaneously, is empirically sustainable. Further, risks arguably exist in the absence of reflexive apprehension of them. The asteroid strike known as the Cretaceous-Paleogene extinction event (c. 66,000,000 BCE) and the Toba super-eruption (c. 75,000 BCE) are probably the most catastrophic events in planetary history: the former eradicated the dinosaurs and the latter reduced the human population to approximately 4000 individuals. Although dinosaurs and Paleolithic humans lacked the discursive and governmental apparatus associated with 'modern' risk, such events complicate the idea of a single stadial model oriented towards an entirely human modernity.

Finally, a more material analysis involves slightly reorienting our understanding of the bodily experience of risk. The psychological aspects of risk society are clearly significant. Risks are often indiscernible, even as they are permeating our bodies: they generate anxiety, unease and dread.[20] The experience of risk is not, however, entirely or even primarily psychological: risks affect the body in manifold ways. First, new technological systems brought new forms of pain and death into the world: electric shocks, silicosis, chemical burns and many novel forms of cancer. They also led to increased levels of scalding, asphyxiation and violent accidents. Second, the comfortable, disinfected, sedentary, indoor existence characteristic of the twentieth century provided the technological a priori for the epidemiological transition from infectious to non-infectious forms of death. Heart disease, cancer and diabetes replaced infectious diseases as major killers in the West. As Beck noted, chronic illnesses now predominate in the West.[21]

[17] *Ibid.*, p. 319.

[18] Cited in H. Bazin, *Vaccination: A History from Lady Montagu to Genetic Engineering* (Esher, 2011), p. 34.

[19] On Beck's stadial model of risk's historicity, see Lash and Wynne, 'Introduction', p. 3.

[20] Beck, *Risk Society*, p. 49; Adam and van Loon, 'Introduction', in Adam, Beck and van Loon (eds), *Risk Society*, p. 3.

[21] Beck, *Risk Society*, p. 204.

We live longer, but suffer and worry more. Risk society is about haemorrhoids, depression, angina and backache as much as the existential dread of nuclear holocaust.

Living in a more technologically complex society, then, clearly exposed humans to new risks. However, it also transformed human health in undeniably positive ways. Systems of clean water provision have probably done more to increase human life expectancy than any other human invention, for example. Switching from horses to cars might seem ecologically disastrous, but it removed a vast amount of dung from cities, and hence reduced ecologies of flies responsible for persistently high late nineteenth- and early twentieth-century infant mortality rates.[22] Today, British people live to an average of 81.5 years old; this is 30 years more than in 1900.[23] The 'artificial world' thus changed the physical parameters within which life unfolded in ways irreducible to stadial, linear, declensionist, catastrophist or Whiggish historical models. The remainder of this chapter offers a preliminary investigation of this phenomenon by exploring the form and composition of an increasingly artificial world. First, it examines technological systems and the novel risks they created. Second, it explores the material transitions accompanying technological change, and particularly the advent of new synthetic substances and the dangers to human health they unleashed.

Systems and Accidents

System building exploded with the Industrial Revolutions. The first Industrial Revolution (c. 1750–1830) was initially built on water power, but the tapping of mineral energy had epochal consequences for the British economy and ultimately for planetary ecologies. W.S. Jevons noted that the exploitation of coal reserves made Britain 'independent of the limited agricultural area of these islands, and apparently take[s] us out of the scope of Malthus's doctrine'.[24] This shift, from an organic to mineral economy, enabled basic human activities—transportation, communication, sleep, illumination and eating—to be slowly but significantly divorced from

[22] H. Ashby, *Infant Mortality* (Cambridge, 1915), p. 202.

[23] R. Fogel, *The Escape from Hunger and Premature Death, 1700–2100: Europe, America, and the Third World* (Cambridge, 2004), p. 1.

[24] W.S. Jevons, *The Coal Question: An Inquiry Concerning the Progress of the Nation, and the Probable Exhaustion of our Coal-mines*, 3rd edn (New York, 1965), pp. 199–200.

pre-existing 'natural' parameters.[25] Darkness, ice, wind and snow ceased to slow or immobilize economies and determine human activities, which were increasingly shaped not by geography and climate, but by the capacity of steam to override what were previously firm parameters. In Fernand Braudel's *Mediterranean*, all human practices (trade, politics and war) are framed by an ecology which relied on wind, water and animal power: this world slowly (but not entirely) disintegrated after 1800.[26] The second Industrial Revolution (c. 1880–1930) witnessed manifold technological innovations—the internal combustion engine, electricity, flight and cinema—which Vaclav Smil has called an 'unprecedented saltation' in the history of technology.[27] These innovations, crucially, involved the formation of massive, integrated technological systems and the widespread adoption of new and synthetic materials, from light metals to plastics. Taken together, the two Industrial Revolutions mark an unprecedented, if spatially differentiated and temporally distended, age of human-driven material transition.

Technological systems have numerous dimensions: physical, organizational, legal and economic.[28] This chapter largely addresses their physical aspects. A technological system is composed of many interlocking parts, which interact to form a functioning whole, and which then might acquire the type of momentum to make it appear autonomous.[29] Throughout the nineteenth and twentieth centuries, British people found various aspects of their everyday lives slowly systematized in this sense, in particular transportation, communication and energy provision. Water, previously provided by streams, ponds and rainfall, was captured and delivered by large-scale hydraulic systems. The British landscape became traversed by railways, canals, roads, wires, mains and pipes. Human beings slowly retreated into an artificial eco-technological milieu, which became the space where risk was experienced, calculated and managed. By the early

[25] E.A. Wrigley, *Continuity, Chance and Change: The Character of the Industrial Revolution in England* (Cambridge, 1988), p. 80.

[26] F. Braudel, *The Mediterranean and the Mediterranean World in the Age of Philip II*, trans. S. Reynolds (Berkeley, CA, 1995).

[27] V. Smil, *Transforming the Twentieth Century: Technical Innovations and their Consequences* (Oxford, 2006), p. 12.

[28] T. Hughes, 'The Evolution of Large Technological Systems', in W.E. Bijker, T.P. Hughes and T. Pinch (eds), *The Social Construction of Technological Systems: New Directions in the Sociology and History of Technology* (Cambridge, MA, 1987), p. 51.

[29] *Ibid.*, p. 76.

twenty-first century, Northern Europeans were spending around 90–95 % of their time indoors, encapsulated within houses, cars, offices and malls.[30]

Technological systems had several defining features. First, they greatly expanded in terms of scale. Manchester's expansion, for example, necessitated the collection of water from reservoirs built at increasingly greater distances from the city: Gorton (1825–6), Longendale (1851), Thirlmere (1894), Haweswater (1923) and Ullswater and Windermere (1965).[31] In Scotland, 380 drinking-water reservoirs and lochs were being used for water supply by 1971.[32] Second, they included a greater number of specialized, interconnected components. Water supply systems required reservoirs, dams, mains, aqueducts, sluices and filtration technologies. Third, these systems became reliant on coal for pumping and metals for piping: they were industrialized. Fourth, they provided significantly more fresh water than earlier regimes of water provision: Manchester's water use rose from 4.8 to 32.6 gallons per head daily between 1841 and 1875.[33] Fifth, although these changes were dramatic and significant, the process was very uneven. In 1951, 6 % of British houses still entirely lacked piped water.[34] Sixth, these systems produced an increasingly artificial landscape: bodies of water, like Thirlmere, became parts of large urban assemblages. The distinction between the natural environment and the technological environment became increasingly hard to establish, as indeed did the boundary between the urban and the non-urban.

Systematization extended into the domestic realm. Houses became machines powered by coal stocked in bunkers, gas entered through service mains, and later electrical energy flowed through the National Grid, which began operating in 1933. The home was punctured by mains, wires and pipes, becoming 'a nexus of in and out conduits'.[35] Gradually, domestic interiors became barnacled with equipment powered by fossil fuels.

[30] R. Duarte-Davidson, C. Courage, L. Rushton and L. Levy, 'Benzene in the Environment: An Assessment of the Potential Risks to the Health of the Population', *Occupational and Environmental Medicine* 58 (2001), p. 7.

[31] On Thirlmere, see Harriet Ritvo, *The Dawn of Green: Manchester, Thirlmere and Modern Environmentalism* (Chicago, 2009).

[32] T.C. Smout, *Nature Contested: Environmental History in Scotland and Northern England since 1600* (Edinburgh, 2000), p. 107.

[33] J. Burnett, *Liquid Pleasures: A Social History of Drinks in Modern Britain* (London, 1999), p. 22.

[34] A. Ravetz with R. Turkington, *The Place of Home: English Domestic Environments, 1914–2000* (London, 1995), p. 133.

[35] H. Lefebvre, *The Production of Space*, trans. D. Nicholson-Smith (Oxford, 1991), p. 93.

By 1939, three-quarters of British families cooked by gas.[36] During the 1980s, the proportion of homes with domestic freezers rose from 49 to 79 % and those with tumble driers from 23 to 45 %.[37] Slowly, domestic atmospheres became liberated and insulated from climatic vagaries: central heating allowed predictable, unchanging heat in winter, while fans and even air-conditioning provided protection from occasional summer heatwaves.[38] This process was, again, uneven. Many still struggle to pay winter fuel bills, others measure their energy use anxiously through prepayment meters, and a small but significant minority have no home at all.

From their very inception, industrial systems underwent breakdowns and failures: the 'normal accident', in Charles Perrow's famous phrase, is as old as normal functioning.[39] As systems incorporated increasing numbers of tightly coupled components, the scope for unpredictable, non-linear material interactions grew. For example, the first industrial system, gaslight, involved generating, storing, distributing and burning coal gas, a flammable and poisonous substance. Gas networks were assembled from various specialized components, including retorts, scrubbers, condensers, gasholders, mains, meters, governors and burners. The early decades of gas lighting saw many fires, explosions, leaks and asphyxiations, and fire insurance companies immediately opposed the introduction of the new technology.[40] Gas leaked from 'faulty joints, cracked seams, and pinholes in the pipes'.[41] Nine men died when the Nine Elms Gasworks in London exploded in 1865. Shortly afterwards, Thomas Bartlett Simpson, the former owner of Cremorne Gardens in Chelsea, depicted London as an industrial dystopia overtaken by mechanical systems. 'We now find ourselves encircled by about 20 of these dreadful magazines of discomfort, sickness and peril', he noted, 'and an "unavoidable accident", at any one of which may, in the busy hours of day, or in the stillness of night, lay a neighbourhood in ruins, and bury its inhabitants beneath them.'[42] Smaller

[36] C. Davidson, *A Woman's Work is Never Done: A History of Homework in the British Isles, 1650–1950* (London, 1982), pp. 67–8.

[37] Ravetz, *Place of Home*, p. 141.

[38] *Ibid.*, p. 138.

[39] C. Perrow, *Normal Accidents: Living with High-Risk Technologies* (New York, 1984).

[40] W. Webber, *Town Gas and its Uses for the Production of Light, Heat, and Motive Power* (London, 1907), p. 27.

[41] 'Gas Explosions', *British Medical Journal*, 16 October 1886, p. 730.

[42] T. Bartlett Simpson, *Gas-Works: The Evils Inseparable from their Existence in Populous Places, and the Necessity of Removing Them from the Metropolis* (London, 1866), p. 9.

explosions were more frequent; 30,000 cubic feet of gas escaped when a Congleton gasholder erupted in 1879.[43] Less spectacular, but more insidious, were the distant effects of pollution on waterways and the glacial, if momentous, accumulation of particulate matter and greenhouse gases in the atmosphere.

This phenomenon was evident in all technological systems. As the British water supply system grew larger and more technologically complex, new types of disaster emerged. In March 1864, the Dale Dyke Dam in Sheffield burst, releasing a torrent of water and killing nearly 250 people.[44] The accident was caused when a fracture developed in the dam's clay core wall; as material poured through the crack, a cavity formed and moved vertically upwards, producing a sinkhole, which led to the dam being breached. In the absence of smell or sound, accidents in early electricity systems generated considerable unease. 'We are endowed with no special senses, by which we can detect the presence of electricity or magnetism', observed *The Builder* in 1890. 'There is, then, no cause for wonderment that most approach the subject as one of a shadowy nature, if not altogether shrouded in mystery.'[45] Electricity *shocked*, just like the train crash, which produced psychological trauma as well as physical injury and death. The early twentieth-century rise of automotive transportation, meanwhile, caused a sharp rise in fatalities on British roads: from 4856 in 1926 to 6700 just 3 years later.[46]

Accidents ramified across the technological landscape, but they were particularly common in the workplace itself. 'One of the immediate effects of the industrial revolution with its mechanization of industry was a tremendous increase in the number of health and accident hazards faced by the worker, and the subsequent evolution of industry has facilitated a cumulative increase in such hazards', noted the economist Earl Muntz in 1932.[47] Novel industrial processes meant that 'the variety and severity of factory accidents bear close comparison with those of modern warfare'.[48]

[43] *British Architect*, 5 September 1879, p. 95.

[44] G.M. Binnie, 'The Collapse of the Dale Dyke Dam in Retrospect', *Quarterly Journal of Engineering Geology and Hydrogeology* 11 (1978), p. 305.

[45] *The Builder*, 28 June 1890.

[46] P. Bagwell and P. Lyth, *Transport in Britain: From Canal Lock to Gridlock* (London, 2002), p. 95.

[47] E. Muntz, 'Industrial Accidents and Safety Work', *Journal of Educational Sociology* 5 (1932), p. 397.

[48] J. Kerr, 'The Treatment of Industrial Accidents', *British Medical Journal*, 26 August 1922, p. 379.

Bodies were burned, crushed, lacerated and scalded; eyes and limbs were lost. New technologies required awkward postures, bodily contortions and repetitive actions, generating their own specific afflictions, such as telegraphist's cramp and, ultimately, a collection of conditions known as repetitive strain injuries.[49] Working with compressed-air drills produced Raynaud's disease ('dead' fingers).[50] Pounding-up machines in the boot and shoe trades damaged the hands.[51] The coal heaver's spine became 'converted into a rigid shelf and the chest becomes more or less immobilized'.[52]

Mining had long exposed workers to altogether less passive risks than most professions. In the nineteenth century, steam-powered machinery allowed mines to extend far deeper into the earth. As mines became large, complex systems, they became increasingly dangerous places. Between 1846 and 1852, 90 major colliery explosions killed 1084 people.[53] At an 1862 accident at the single-mineshaft Hartley colliery in north-eastern England, 204 people died when the beam of the pumping engine cracked, trapping miners inside the mine.[54] Mining accidents declined slowly thereafter, but coal mine explosions still caused 2953 deaths between 1900 and 1933.[55] Meanwhile, the less spectacular but ultimately more deadly carcinogenic effects of working with coal were becoming more apparent, as cases of black lung (pneumoconiosis) spiked.[56] The mechanization of Scottish mining, for example, triggered escalating disease rates: between 1951 and 1971, over 17,000 British miners died of pneumoconiosis.[57]

The material circumstances of factory life also became more complicated and potentially more deadly. Dusts became objects of concern: 'the dangers of dust explosions were not fully recognized until the present

[49] T. Legge, *Industrial Maladies* (London, 1934), p. 198; P.C. Amadio, 'History of Carpal Tunnel Syndrome', in R. Luchetti and P. Amadio (eds), *Carpal Tunnel Syndrome* (New York, 2007), pp. 3–8.

[50] Legge, *Industrial Maladies*, p. 208.

[51] *Ibid.*, p. 210.

[52] W.A. Lane, *The Prevention of the Diseases Peculiar to Civilization* (London, 1929), p. 12.

[53] J. Bronstein, *Caught in the Machinery: Workplace Accidents and Injured Workers in Nineteenth-Century Britain* (Stanford, CA, 2008), p. 11.

[54] *Ibid.*, p. 41.

[55] R.C. Smart, *The Technology of Industrial Fire and Explosion Hazards* (2 vols, London, 1947), I, p. 176.

[56] A. Lockwood, *The Silent Epidemic: Coal and the Hidden Threat to Human Health* (Cambridge, MA, 2012), p. 52.

[57] R. Johnston and A. McIvor, 'Oral History, Subjectivity, and Environmental Reality: Occupational Health Histories in Twentieth-Century Scotland', *Osiris* 19 (2004), p. 236.

century or that materials in a finely divided form when in suspension in air as a cloud of dust were highly inflammable and would ultimately lead to powerful explosions'.[58] Industrial spaces were zones of complicated equipment, dangerous substances and unpredictable material interactions. The more tightly connected and materially variegated such spaces became, the greater the possibility of unforeseen accidents. Factories handling explosives were particularly vulnerable: in 1917, 50 tons of TNT exploded during a fire at the Silvertown munitions factory in West Ham, killing 73 people and damaging 70,000 houses. Apparently, the blast was audible in Norfolk.[59] Many minor accidents were caused by strange interactions of machines, devices and materials. In July 1944, for example, two people were killed in an explosion and fire at the dispensary at Hallam Hospital, West Bromwich, when a bottle of ether-meth broke and exploded as a result of a spark released from the thermostatic control on an electric sterilizer.[60]

By this date, the fatalistic response to early Victorian mining disasters was dissipating. Prayers and charity had ceased to be the sole or even primary responses to technological calamity. Employers could no longer accuse workers of individual negligence or claim that they knowingly bore responsibility for the risks they ran. Industrial accidents were increasingly seen as part of the normal fabric of technological society. They might be ultimately unavoidable, but various governmental, medical and technological strategies had been introduced to minimize their possibility and mitigate their effects. Mines were subject to inspection from 1850. More significantly, the Employers' Liability Act of 1880 gave injured workers the opportunity to sue for damages.[61] Workers' insurance was consolidated in 1897. Meanwhile, medical advances—antiseptics, anaesthesia and effective blood transfusions, for instance—began to offer the seriously wounded a better chance of survival. Hospitals were equipped with electric quilts to keep patients warm, while orthopaedic surgery was improving. After-treatment might include 'movements, active and passive, possibly massage and faradic stimulation, re-education of muscle, and graduated exercises'.[62]

[58] Smart, *Technology*, I, p. 175.
[59] G. Hill and H. Bloch, *The Silvertown Explosion* (Stroud, 2003).
[60] Smart, *Technology*, II, pp. 20–1.
[61] Bronstein, *Caught in the Machinery*, p. 167.
[62] Kerr, 'Treatment', p. 378.

In addition to these legal and medical developments, factory space became increasingly engineered to reduce the risk of accident. One simple solution was to increase illumination levels: accident rates were generally higher at night and in the darker months of the year.[63] Workers were encouraged to protect their eyes with protective goggles. Inspections grew more regular and detailed. Flammable materials were closely regulated: 'the fire hazard is almost abolished by eliminating every scrap of combustible material'.[64] Governors and cybernetic devices facilitated the automatic regulation of machinery. Self-closing burners which shut off the gas supply in the event of the accidental extinguishing of lights were soon introduced.[65] Accidents involving early refrigerating devices prompted J. and E. Hall, the largest late nineteenth-century manufacturer of British refrigeration equipment, to pioneer automatic safety valves which shut systems down if pressure reached potentially explosive levels.[66] Sprinkler systems were developed over the course of the nineteenth century. In flour mills, where interconnections of multiple machines created many fire risks, automatic sprinklers 'dominate[d] ... the entire field of flour mill insurance' by the late nineteenth century.[67] Ultimately, robotization would further reduce worker injury levels.[68]

Christopher Sellers and Joseph Melling have used the phrase 'industrial hazard regime' to refer to the composite techniques by which risks are perceived and managed. The particular industrial hazard regime sketched here involved various discrete elements: the insurance principle, legal apparatuses, inspection, medical technologies, worker discipline and numerous devices, such as goggles, valves and sprinkler systems. This regime was dynamic and evolving, always responding to the emergence of new risks. It attempted to capture and fix industrial processes and systemic practices in order to insulate them from the aleatory and accidental. Technological systems, however, displayed emergent qualities of their own and their behaviour was never entirely predictable. Instead, material environments

[63] L. Gaster, 'Industrial Lighting and the Prevention of Accidents', *Journal of the Royal Society of Arts* 71 (1923), p. 614.

[64] S. Williams, *The Manual of Industrial Safety* (Chicago, 1927), p. 134.

[65] Webber, *Town Gas*, p. 28.

[66] J. Rees, *Refrigeration Nation: A History of Ice, Appliances and Enterprise in America* (Baltimore, MD, 2013), p. 43.

[67] William Voller, *Modern Flour Milling: A Text-Book for Millers and others Interested in the Wheat and Flour Trades*, 3rd edn (Gloucester, 1897), p. 440.

[68] Smil, *Transforming*, p. 185.

and the humans seeking to control or interact with them partook of the '*dialectic of resistance and accommodation*' which Andrew Pickering sees as defining all human–machine interactions.[69] Technologies often resisted attempts to make them work as humans wished, leading to various accommodations, from reconfigurations of technology to transformations of human practice. The course of this dialectic is never completely known in advance.

A second major source of such emergent risks was purely material, as we shall now see. The systems and artefacts composing and cluttering new human niches were often made of novel or entirely synthetic materials. As one observer noted in 1947, 'new materials and processes are being introduced at an accelerated pace into industry, whilst the employment of chemical reagents with toxic properties and synthetic substances in large numbers is a relatively new phenomenon'.[70] As they circulated from factories to public and domestic space, they transformed the chemistry of risk.

Materials and Risks

In their 1973 textbook *Industrial Chemistry*, Thomas and Farago depicted a world transformed by synthetic materials:

> A look around any home illustrates how the products of the chemical industry form part of our way of life. In the kitchen, we see laminated plastic working surfaces, polyethylene washing-up bowls, detergents for washing dishes and clothes, and sundry kitchen equipment which incorporates chemical materials, from rubber pipes, silicone washers and electrical insulation to stove enamel. We can go all around the house, seeing all manner of chemical products from nylon carpets to thixotropic paint, from the noble gas in the light-bulbs to the television set packed with transistors. These are all the obvious marks of chemistry, but perhaps the more important ones are in places we never see: in factories where chemical products keep machinery turning longer, better and with less maintenance, in medicine where not only are drugs chemical products, but even new fields of surgery—the artificial limb, the kidney machine—depend on chemicals.[71]

[69] A. Pickering, *The Mangle of Practice: Time, Agency, and Science* (Chicago, 1995), p. 22, emphasis in original.

[70] Smart, *Technology*, I, p. 13.

[71] R.W. Thomas and P.J. Farago, *Industrial Chemistry* (London, 1973), p. 1.

The twentieth century was, according to some, the 'age of plastics. For plastics, made of synthetic giant molecules, have become a dominating influence on modern industrial society'.[72] These novel substances increased the 'ease of living for groups of people who previously could not afford the products made from conventional materials'.[73] Our wired, computerized world relies upon synthetic materials and artefacts composed of many different chemical elements. However, exposing bodies and ecosystems to such materials was in many ways a giant environmental experiment, entailing an ongoing and emergent reconfiguring of the human and the physical worlds. The long-term impact of such interactions was inherently unpredictable, as P.R. Peacock of Glasgow's Royal Cancer Hospital explained in 1969: 'Today, chemists have produced hundreds of substances that never existed before, and it may take thousands more years of evolution to learn how our bodies will react to these new synthetic substances.'[74]

The creation and dissemination of entirely new materials was only one dimension of a multi-faceted material transition wrought by both Industrial Revolutions. The synthesis of naturally occurring materials, like ammonia, sodium carbonate and sulphuric acid, was essential to the development of the British chemical industry, especially in Lancashire, Cheshire and Tyneside.[75] These locations became marked by these chemical processes. One official report published in 1877 noted that people must enter Widnes 'with a certain awe and horror, at least on calm, damp days, and wonder if life can be sustained there'.[76] In addition, naturally occurring but relatively rare elements, such as lithium, cadmium, rhenium and radium, were used in unprecedented quantities. These had unpredictable effects: the first serious radium health warning was raised just before the First World War by the Radium Institute of London. Links between jaw cancer and workers who painted clock faces with luminescent paint containing radium were made in the 1920s.[77]

[72] Giulio Natta, cited in F. McMillan, *The Chain Straighteners: Fruitful Innovation: The Discovery of Linear and Stereoregular Synthetic Polymers* (London, 1979), p. 3.

[73] Thomas and Farago, *Industrial Chemistry*, p. 5.

[74] Quoted in Dick Gregory, 'Food Hazard', *Daily Illini*, 5 December 1969, p. 10.

[75] J.R. Partington, *The Alkali Industry*, 2nd edn (London, 1925), p. 2.

[76] *Alkali Acts, 1863 and 1874: Twelfth and Thirteenth Annual Reports by the Inspector of the Proceedings during the years 1875 and 1876* (Parl. Papers 1877 [C.2199]), p. 11.

[77] W. Campbell, 'General and Fine Inorganic Chemicals', in Colin Russell (ed.), *Chemistry, Society and Environment: A New History of the British Chemical Industry* (Cambridge, 2000), p. 193; S. Boudia, 'Global Regulation: Controlling and Accepting Radioactivity Risks', *History and Technology* 23 (2007), p. 391.

Ancient materials, however, remained important. Lead poisoning was 'the most frequent and important chronic industrial poisoning; the symptoms are very varied, and associated with the most different groups of organs', affecting, for example, the brain, the kidneys and the peripheral nervous system, as well as causing eclampsia in pregnant women.[78] In the nineteenth century, lead was widely used for water mains because of its durability.[79] Werner Troesken estimates that up to eight million people were affected by water plumbism in northern England in the 1880s and suggests that infant mortality rates might have increased by as much as 9 % as a result.[80] Lead poisoning was chronic, developing over periods of years. It was not limited to those using water delivered in lead pipes: house-painting, for example, was the most common trade to suffer from lead poisoning.[81]

Occupational lead poisoning became a reportable disease under the 1895 Factory and Workshop Act, and poisoning rates dropped thereafter.[82] But risks from lead did not disappear. Although lead piping was slowly removed, a 1975–6 survey revealed that 7.8 % of household water supplies in England and Wales had lead concentrations over the World Health Organization limit; in Scotland, the figure was 34.4 %.[83] Lead was, moreover, increasingly added to petroleum to boost engine performance. A 1929 Ministry of Health Expert Committee reported that leaded petrol was safe because it was rapidly diluted in exhaust gases.[84] Leaded petrol was only phased out in Britain after 1999. Lead batteries were hazardous, particularly when absorbed into unregulated recycling economies: in 1954, two children were killed and over 24 people were hospitalized in Canklow, Rotherham, when families burned discarded car battery cases purchased from a junk dealer.[85]

Parallel narratives can be told for arsenic, asbestos, silicon and phosphorus. In the nineteenth century, arsenic appeared in wallpapers, rat poison, sheep dip, paints, cigarettes and even medicine. In 1869, *The*

[78] J. Rambousek, *Industrial Poisoning from Fumes, Gases and Poisons of Manufacturing Processes*, trans. T. Legge (London, 1913), p. 177; W. Troesken, *The Great Lead Water Pipe Disaster* (Cambridge, MA, 2006), pp. 30 and 38; C. Warren, *Brush with Death: A Social History of Lead Poisoning* (Baltimore, MD, 2000), p. 13.

[79] Troesken, *Great Lead Water Pipe Disaster*, pp. 10, 18.

[80] *Ibid.*, pp. 21, 238.

[81] Legge, *Industrial Maladies*, p. 52.

[82] Warren, *Brush with Death*, pp. 70–1.

[83] Troesken, *Great Lead Water Pipe Disaster*, p. 196.

[84] Legge, *Industrial Maladies*, p. 51.

[85] Warren, *Brush with Death*, p. 143.

Times warned readers that 'there are so many forms of accidental poisoning ... lying in ambush on all sides of us'.[86] A 1930 study found that 66 % of those working in the asbestos industry for 20 years developed asbestosis, leading to the first asbestos dust control regulations, though they were largely unenforced.[87] The connections between asbestos and mesothelioma (cancer of the lining of the chest) were slowly made over the following three decades, and three South African pathologists published evidence demonstrating a causal connection in 1960. Activism and media exposure played a significant role here, with Britain finally banning all forms of asbestos in 1998.[88] The British public was growing more aware of, and more sceptical towards, the introduction of new chemicals, something vividly demonstrated by the opposition to fluoridation in the 1950s. A 1955 writer to the *British Medical Journal* complained that the fluoridation of Anglesey's water amounted to 'compulsory medical treatment with a toxic substance' and 'mass-dosing without consent'.[89] The most basic materials of life—air and water—were being chemically modified by human activity.

The extraction and utilization of specific materials was a spatially circumscribed process. Lead poisoning and mesothelioma were acquired in many places, but their threats were not 'global' in the same way as those posed by nuclear weapons. Their pathological consequences tended to develop in individuals handling them intimately, who then suffered very particular and extremely painful consequences. More diffuse patterns of exposure were evident with petrol-based lead pollution, however. The regulation of industrial toxins was a protracted and messy process, involving new regimes of factory management and inspection, and the retrofitting and reconstruction of housing and water supply systems. Industrial poisoning became an increasingly prominent issue, with factories equipping themselves with fans, ventilators and sanitary appliances, and their workers with safety helmets and respirators.[90] This suggests a disjuncture

[86] Cited in J. Whorton, *The Arsenic Century: How Victorian Britain was Poisoned at Home, Work and Play* (Oxford, 2010), p. 183.

[87] D. Gee and M. Greenberg, 'Asbestos: From "Magic" to Malevolent Mineral', in P. Harremoës et al. (eds), *The Precautionary Principle in the Twentieth Century: Late Lessons from Early Warnings* (London, 2002), p. 52.

[88] *Ibid.*, pp. 54–7.

[89] C. Dobbs, 'Fluoridation of Public Water Supplies', *British Medical Journal*, 8 January 1955, pp. 105–6.

[90] Rambousek, *Industrial Poisoning*, pp. 229, 237, 244.

between risk's psychological-imaginary and physical experience. While the risks of industrial poisoning undoubtedly became part of shared consciousness, its actual physical experience was limited to specific jobs and spaces.

In contrast to the history of lead and arsenic, the history of synthetic substances dates only to the early nineteenth century and centres on a particularly paleotechnic substance: coal tar, a thick, viscid byproduct of coal combustion. Coal tar was the 'scrap-heap of the vegetable kingdom', a complex cocktail of ammoniacal liquor, naphthas, oils and pitch, which was reduced to ten so-called crudes (including benzene, toluene and xylene). These were then used to produce a cascade of other materials: dyestuffs, pigments, perfumes, medicines, explosives and photographic materials, as well as disinfectant products such as carbolic, examined by Rebecca Whyte in this volume.[91] Crude derivatives of benzene and toluene made the great mid-nineteenth-century European dyestuff industries materially possible.[92] The production of saccharin from coal tar seemed particularly miraculous: 'a teaspoonful will make a barrel of water as savoury as syrup, and a trifling portion will quell the bitterness of quinine'.[93] Coal tar 'is like the magic purse of Fortunatus from which anything wished for could be drawn', gushed the chemist and journalist Edwin Slosson in 1920.[94] It was also, unfortunately, carcinogenic: the surgeon Percivall Pott had demonstrated extensive scrotal epithelioma in chimney sweeps in 1775, a condition later described by another surgeon, Henry Earle, in 1832.[95] Working with coal tar produced an inflammatory skin condition called 'tar eczema', which occasionally assumed a cancerous form 'similar to chimney-sweep's cancer'.[96] Coal tar was simultaneously mundane, miraculous and deadly.

Benzene was the most important coal tar derivative and the most dangerous. First isolated by Michael Faraday in 1825 from coal tar naphtha, it has been industrially produced since around 1849 and is now largely

[91] E. Slosson, *Creative Chemistry: Descriptive of Recent Achievements in the Chemical Industries* (New York, 1920), pp. 62, 64.

[92] L.F. Haber, *The Chemical Industry during the Nineteenth Century: A Study of the Economic Aspect of Applied Chemistry in Europe and North America* (Oxford, 1958), p. 83.

[93] 'Coal Tar Sugar', *Northern Echo*, 16 August 1886.

[94] Slosson, *Creative Chemistry*, p. 61.

[95] H.A. Waldron, 'A Brief History of Scrotal Cancer', *British Journal of Industrial Medicine* 40 (1983), pp. 390–1.

[96] Rambousek, *Industrial Poisoning*, p. 101.

produced from petroleum.[97] It was widely used as a solvent, added to petrol for its anti-knocking properties and used as an intermediary for a vast range of chemical products. It became 'a general component of our chemical era ... even present in miniscule amounts in food and vegetation'.[98] However, following observations of pathologies in factory workers, Carl Santesson in 1897 and Walter Snelling in 1910 established that benzene, in sufficient quantities, began to affect bone marrow. It destroyed platelets and then granular leucocytes, 'finally producing the complete picture of aplastic anaemia', a serious bone marrow disease.[99] Later studies showed a connection between occupational exposure to benzene and the development of leukaemia.[100] Benzene was thus haematotoxic and carcinogenic.

In large concentrations, benzene was also an acute poison. Of 15 fatal cases recorded by the Home Office between 1908 and 1937, practically all involved workmen entering tanks which had been insufficiently emptied of the liquid.[101] In two fatal cases in 1918, the concentration was 16,800 parts per million (ppm), an astonishingly high figure.[102] One 1934 case of fatal benzene poisoning converted the bone marrow into a 'brownish pasty mass'.[103] Chronic cases, meanwhile, developed more slowly. To take one example, a man beginning work in 1937 supervising machines spreading cellulose resin on to cotton textiles became ill in 1944 and died of bone marrow hyperplasia in 1946.[104]

Regulation developed slowly. The India Rubber Regulations of 1922, for example, stated that for all fume processes (involving benzene), there

[97] N.K. Weaver, R.L. Gibson and C.W. Smith, 'Occupational Exposure to Benzene in the Petroleum and Petrochemical Industries', in M.A. Mehlman (ed.), *Carcinogenicity and Toxicity of Benzene* (Princeton, NJ, 1983), p. 63; C. Maltoni, 'Myths and Facts in the History of Benzene Carcinogenicity', in Mehlman (ed.), *Carcinogenicity and Toxicity of Benzene*, p. 1.

[98] B. Goldstein, 'Clinical Hematoxicity of Benzene', in Mehlman (ed.), *Carcinogenicity and Toxicity of Benzene*, p. 51.

[99] 'Benzene', *British Journal of Industrial Medicine* 1 (1944), p. 254.

[100] A. Yardley-Jones, D. Anderson and D.V. Parke, 'The Toxicity of Benzene and its Metabolism and Molecular Pathology in Human Risk Assessment', *British Journal of Industrial Medicine* 48 (1991), p. 438.

[101] *Toxicity of Industrial Organic Solvents: Summaries of Published Work Compiled by Ethel Browning under the Direction of the Committee on the Toxicity of Industrial Solvents* (London, 1937), p. 32.

[102] *Ibid.*, p. 10.

[103] Home Office Report, 1934, cited in *Toxicity of Industrial Organic Solvents*, p. 46.

[104] V.H. Bowers, 'Reaction of Human Blood-Forming Tissues to Chronic Benzene Exposure', *British Journal of Industrial Medicine* 4 (1947), pp. 88–92.

should be efficient exhaust draughts and inlets of air.[105] Preventive techniques mirrored those in other toxic industries, including 'the protection of workers entering enclosed spaces liable to contain benzol fumes by the use of positive-pressure air helmets of hose masks, and the conduct of all such work by means of two or more men familiar with the dangers'.[106] Workers should be educated about benzene risks and constantly reminded of them by labels and posters.[107] More significant was the establishment of (contested) thresholds beyond which concentrations were illegal. Between the 1930s and the 1990s, the legal threshold for atmospheric benzene fell from 100 ppm to 5 ppm.[108] These developments, coupled with more efficient processing in petrochemical factories, have reduced the incidence of benzene poisoning in Britain significantly, even if benzene emissions rose with heavy automobile use from the 1960s.[109] Benzene in outdoor air has been routinely monitored since 1991 as part of the automatic hydrocarbon monitoring network of the Department of the Environment, Transport and the Regions. These tests have demonstrated highest exposures along kerbsides, in garages, around petrol pumps and in smokers' homes. Estimated benzene intake varied by location and habit: a rural non-smoker might inhale 75 μg per day, while an urban worker smoking alongside a busy road for 8 hours would breathe in over ten times this amount.[110] Benzene has become a 'ubiquitous pollutant' in a hydrocarbon society.[111]

Polychlorinated biphenyls (PCBs), first synthesized in 1881 and mass produced since 1929, are composed of two connected benzene rings plus chlorine atoms. They were first used in electrical equipment (in particular, transformers and capacitors) because of their resistance to high temperatures and their insulating properties; later uses included plastics,

[105] Occupational Safety and Health Branch of the International Labour Organization, 'Survey of Laws and Regulations Concerning the Use of Benzene in Industry', in *Benzene: Uses, Toxic Effects, Substitutes* (Geneva, 1968), p. 212.

[106] Legge, *Industrial Maladies*, p. 113.

[107] R. Truhart, 'Measurement of the Concentration of Benzene in the Working Environment and in Industrial Products with other Technical Control Methods', in *Benzene: Uses, Toxic Effects, Substitutes*, pp. 148–9.

[108] *Toxicity of Industrial Organic Solvents*, p. 11. Yardley-Jones, Anderson and Parke, 'Toxicity', p. 442.

[109] Duarte-Davidson, Courage, Rushton and Levy, 'Benzene in the Environment', p. 3.

[110] *Ibid.*, pp. 4, 5, 9.

[111] L. Perbellini, G. Faccini, F. Pasini, F. Cazzoli, S. Pistoia, R. Rosellini, M. Valsecchi and F. Brugnone, 'Environmental and Occupational Exposure to Benzene by Analysis of Breath and Blood', *British Journal of Industrial Medicine* 45 (1988), p. 350.

lubricants and adhesives. Those producing the material soon suffered skin and eye complaints, but later in the twentieth century it became clear that the effects of PCBs were more disturbing. They induced miscarriages in women and damaged foetuses.[112] They bio-accumulated in ecosystems and were then detected in fish, seals and birds.[113] PCBs, like other signature pollutants of the twentieth century, endangered animals and ecosystems, not just individual humans. This was followed in 1968 by the PCB contamination of rice oil in Japan, which poisoned 1800 people, producing serious long-term health problems.[114] Production of PCBs ceased in Britain in 1978, but its ecological effects, it seems, will linger much longer, leaving a world permeated with toxins.[115]

Each new synthetic substance brought peculiar and molecularly specific risks. Various techniques to manufacture artificial silks, for example, were developed in the later nineteenth century, with the viscose process, pioneered by Cross and Bevan, proving most successful.[116] Clothing, furniture, lacing, wigs and insulating material could all be manufactured cheaply and effectively, and by the mid-1920s, such artificial silks were being referred to as rayon.[117] 'We seem to be on the eve of a revolution in textiles that is the same as that taking place in building materials', enthused the relentlessly optimistic Slosson.[118] Rayon manufacture, however, necessitated the use of carbon disulphide, a largely human-made compound which is also 'a severe chronic general nerve poison', causing mania, nerve poisoning and atherosclerosis.[119] Carbon disulphide

[112] N. Langston, *Toxic Bodies: Hormone Disruptors and the Legacy of DES* (New Haven, CT, 2010), p. vii.

[113] R. Risebrough and B. de Lappe, 'Accumulation of Polychlorinated Biphenyls in Ecosystems', *Environmental Health Perspectives* 1 (1972), p. 39.

[114] J. Koppe and J. Keys, 'PCBs and the Precautionary Principle', in Harremoës et al. (eds), *The Precautionary Principle in the Twentieth Century*, p. 65.

[115] *Ibid.*, p. 70.

[116] V. Hottenroth, *Artificial Silk: A Complete Treatise on the Theory, Manufacture and Manipulation of all the Known Types of Artificial Silk*, trans. E. Fyleman (London, 1928), p. 258.

[117] P. Blanc, 'Rayon, Carbon Disulfide, and the Emergence of the Multinational Corporation in Occupational Disease', in C. Sellers and J. Melling (eds), *Dangerous Trade: Histories of Industrial Hazard across a Globalizing World* (Philadelphia, PA, 2012), p. 80.

[118] Slosson, *Creative Chemistry*, p. 121.

[119] *Toxicity of Industrial Organic Solvents*, pp. 361, 363; M. Tolonen, S. Hernberg, M. Nurminen and K. Tiitola, 'A Follow-up Study of Coronary Heart Disease in Viscose Rayon Workers Exposed to Carbon Disulphide', *British Journal of Industrial Medicine* 32 (1975), p. 9.

poisoning, along with aniline and chronic benzene poisoning, became notifiable on 31 December 1924.[120]

Nylon, 'an absolutely new material', began replacing rayon after 1940.[121] It was one of manifold *plastic* substances artificializing the material landscape of Britain in the mid-twentieth century. 'Plastics are to be regarded as *new* materials, rather than as substitutes for *old* materials', declared Charles Stine, vice-president of the chemical manufacturer DuPont. 'Look about your automobile and your home and you will find a variety of fabricated articles made from plastics.'[122] The earliest nineteenth-century plastics, such as Parkesine, used cellulose as a feedstock; twentieth-century plastics used coal tar and oil. Today's most important plastics are polyethylene, polypropylene and PVC.[123] Polyethylene is one of the most ubiquitous substances imaginable and is used for bags, sheets, bottles, containers, rubbish bins and toys, while PVC produces insulation, pipes, tiles, wrapping, shower curtains, garden furniture and credit cards.[124] Like benzene and PCBs, plastic is ubiquitous: it has been found drifting across the Southern Ocean, entombed in Arctic ice and lining the intestines of sea creatures. This dusting of the planet with traces of artificial substances clearly demonstrates that human beings have created an 'artificial world.'

Conclusion

> Everywhere one looks, henceforth, the everyday objects and habits of one's life ripple off into widening circles of causes and effects, linking them to the larger orders of the biosphere: long-lost origins, future ramifications, reverberations coming in and going out, enveloping unfamiliar places and strange creatures.[125]

[120] Legge, *Industrial Maladies*, p. 4.

[121] W. Haynes, *This Chemical Age: The Miracle of Man-Made Materials* (New York, 1942), p. 309.

[122] Charles Stine, cited in S. Fenichell, *Plastic: The Making of a Synthetic Century* (New York, 1996), p. 135.

[123] V. Smil, *Making the Modern World: Materials and Dematerialization* (Chichester, 2014), p. 62.

[124] *Ibid.*, p. 63; Smil, *Transforming*, p. 131.

[125] M. Bess, *The Light-Green Society: Ecology and Technological Modernity in France, 1960–2000* (Chicago, 2003), p. 276.

As Michael Bess suggests in the quote above, to inhabit an artificialized world is to be entangled in a boundless web of connections that blur any straightforward distinction between the local and the global. The technological systems which support us are immediate and intimate, yet simultaneously vast and largely invisible: the better they function, the less we notice. The analysis here suggests six conclusions.

First, it points to the persistence of the local. While the local-global polarity has become somewhat cloudy, it should not be abandoned. The technologically systematized nature of existence, and the undeniable material diversification of our physical milieu, means that many risks remain extremely localized. Industrial accidents, from the Nine Elms tragedy in 1865 noted above to the explosion at Flixborough chemical plant in 1974, affected relatively small populations, almost always in working-class neighbourhoods. Class, then, matters rather more than Beck allows: local industrial risks rarely have a 'boomerang effect' on their perpetrators.[126] Globalization amplifies this phenomenon: Warren Anderson, the CEO of Union Carbide, never faced trial over the Bhopal disaster. Likewise, the distribution of toxic materials over physical space is extremely uneven. The classic experience of industrial poisoning was choking to death in an incompletely ventilated tank without a respirator, a highly bounded, indeed profoundly claustrophobic, event. The physical reconstruction of domestic space created new, local material risks. While pollutants like sulphur dioxide and lead accumulated in the atmosphere, formaldehyde, nitrogen oxides, carbon monoxide and tobacco became concentrated in encapsulated and increasingly sealed domestic spaces.[127] Indoor air pollution has probably increased over the past few decades.[128] The landscape of risk is probably more materially variegated and localized than at any time in human history. There has been no straightforward, linear shift from local to global risk.

Second, the enduring significance of local risk should not, however, disguise the emergence of less spatially bounded chemical dangers. The idea that risks are outsourced from the domestic to the planetary level, advanced by Smith and Ezzati and sometimes called the 'environmental risk transition',

[126] Beck, *Risk Society*, p. 37.

[127] P. Brimblecombe and G. Bentham, 'The Air that We Breathe: Smogs, Smoke and Health', in M. Hulme and E. Barrow (eds), *Climates of the British Isles: Present, Past and Future* (London, 1997), pp. 253–5.

[128] *Ibid.*, pp. 255–6.

retains some merit.[129] The dispersal of lead, benzene, PCBs and plastics operates across diffuse spaces which are not 'local'. PBCs and plastics, for example, have accumulated in oceanic ecologies around Antarctica. The environment is now indelibly marked by human activity; it is not for nothing that 'modernity' is often being reperiodized as 'the Anthropocene'. Similarly, fossil fuel use has added immense quantities of greenhouse gases, sulphur dioxide and fine particulate matter to the earth's atmosphere, producing climate change and an invisible global epidemic of air pollution deaths. Coal-fired power stations generate nearly 60 % of all CO_2 released by global stationary sources.[130] Predictions suggest that for each terawatt-hour of electricity produced from coal, there are 24.5 deaths, plus 225 serious illnesses and 13,288 minor ones.[131] Fossil fuels, as Jevons predicted long ago, catapulted the British economy beyond its 'natural' limits and towards a deeper, more ineluctable thermodynamic threshold.[132] Our industrial way of life, Dipesh Chakrabarty concludes, 'forces on us a recognition of some of the parametric (that is, boundary) conditions for the existence of institutions central to our idea of modernity and the meanings we derive from them'.[133]

Third, risk operates at multiple temporalities and speeds. Searching for a threshold dividing a 'modern' risk society from a 'non-modern' one is almost certainly a fruitless endeavour.[134] Systems spread unevenly: as Graham and Marvin have argued, systems have increasingly splintered, producing 'enclaves' and 'premium network spaces' in which the wealthy protect themselves from risks which persist and grow in areas whose networks are older, more dispersed and less well-maintained.[135] Furthermore, particular material risks have their own distinct and even plural temporalities—a point also made by Timothy Cooper in this volume. Benzene, for example, could act as an acute poison, killing quickly, or a chronic poison, slowly rotting bone marrow over years. Industrial

[129] K. Smith and M. Ezzati, 'How Environmental Health Risks Change with Development: The Epidemiologic and Environmental Risk Transitions Revisited', *Annual Review of Environment and Resources* 30 (2005), p. 295.

[130] Lockwood, *The Silent Epidemic*, p. 71.

[131] *Ibid.*, p. 3. A terawatt is 10^{12} W.

[132] Jevons, *Coal Question*.

[133] D. Chakrabarty, 'The Climate of History: Four Theses', *Critical Inquiry* 35 (2009), p. 217.

[134] For a more developed argument along these lines, see D.L. Smail and A. Shryock, 'History and the "Pre"', *American Historical Review* 118 (2013), pp. 709–37.

[135] S. Graham and S. Marvin, *Splintering Urbanism: Networked Infrastructures, Technological Mobilities and the Urban Condition* (London, 2001).

accidents happen in a split second, but their emotional, physical and economic fallout lasts decades. To inhabit our systemic world is to experience risk operating at different speeds, from the fast and immediate to the almost incomprehensibly slow and dreadful.

Fourth, we can make some highly speculative observations about the ways in which human experience changed along with new systems and materials. Industrial society transformed economies of pain, perhaps most obviously through novel forms of war, but also through historically unusual technological accidents, which subjected the body to brutal forms of burning, scalding, electrocution, asphyxiation, laceration and dismemberment. More common and more chronic has been both the long-term exposure to toxins and the emerging 'mismatch' diseases of technological society: osteoporosis, arthritis, type-2 diabetes and obesity. The term 'mismatch' suggests that while humans biologically evolved to inhabit a wide variety of environments, they have never experienced such rapid environmental change as over the past two centuries.[136] These threats of acute and chronic conditions structure many contemporary anxieties, typified by the emergence of 'stress', which was first used in a biological rather than a purely technological context by Hans Selye in the 1930s.[137] Advanced technological systems, however, also produce a hitherto unprecedented level of material comfort: temperature regulation, soft beds, clothing, clean water, abundant food and machines doing almost every conceivable act for us, from opening canned food to keeping us alive. These comfort levels are, in turn, sources of anxiety (during blackouts, for example) and morbidity (by physically weakening us). This particular fourfold existential structure—pain, morbidity, stress and anxiety, and comfort—is historically novel, at least in its generalized and democratized form.

Fifth, issues of governance and epistemology remain significant. Various techniques have been mobilized to prevent, regulate and manage the multiplying risks of a technologically complex society. Legislation has been regularly passed and revised to manage workplace conditions, for example, and ensure that industrial spaces are dotted with respirators, fire extinguishers, sprinkler systems and sanitary facilities. Systems are regulated (by norms and laws defining, say, maximum voltage or pressure) and designed to be self-regulating (through feedback technologies, valves, governors and so forth). This requires an immense apparatus of measuring equipment, calculation

[136] D. Lieberman, *The Story of the Human Body* (New York, 2013), p. 349.

[137] N. Talley, 'Dyspepsia and Non-ulcer Dyspepsia: An Historical Perspective', in T.S. Chen and P.S. Chen (eds), *The History of Gastroenterology* (London, 1995), p. 127.

devices and, most recently, computerized modelling to translate systems into endless sequences of data. The sheer volume of data then allows multiple versions of reality to be constructed, as is evident with almost every pollutant imaginable and, ultimately, with climate change itself. Acceptable levels of, for example, benzene or lead have been routinely revised, lowered and, in turn, contested, as the open-ended process of resistance and accommodation unfolds. Risk society is a world of ramifying and fractured knowledge, of endless truth-production and truth-destruction. These truths are not, however, epistemologically or epidemiologically equal. Historians have laboured to demonstrate the ways in which corporate interests have conspired not only to produce truths but also to actively obscure, demolish and distort truths which threaten their economic interests.[138] The very materiality of risk society thus demonstrates the paralysing political dangers of postmodern relativism, as Bruno Latour has argued.[139]

Finally, Britain is now a largely artificial place. 'In nature', states Beck, 'we are concerned today with a highly synthetic product everywhere, an artificial "nature". Not a hair or a crumb of it is still "natural", if "natural" means nature being left to itself.'[140] This might be slightly hyperbolic, but the connection between 'risk society', 'technological society' and 'artificial society' is tight, as Jacques Ellul noted: 'we can survive neither in natural environments nor in a social environment without our technical instruments. Our gadgets are as necessary to us as food'.[141] Britain has become artificialized. 'Natural' spaces are simply holes that happen to be left between networks. Life and death take place not in 'Britain', but in an interlocking technological megasystem arranged on the obscured and partially obliterated geography of the British Isles. Huxley was right: we have truly created 'an artificial world within the cosmos' and this world has reshaped the parameters of risk. It is a very comfortable, but profoundly unsettling, place to live.

[138] The literature here is large, spectacular and endlessly depressing. See, for example, G. Markowitz and D. Rosner, *Deceit and Denial: The Deadly Politics of Industrial Pollution* (Berkeley, CA, 2002); N. Oreskes and E. Conway, *Merchants of Doubt: How a Handful of Scientists Obscured the Truth on Issues from Tobacco Smoke to Global Warming* (New York, 2010); and R. Proctor, *Golden Holocaust: Origins of the Cigarette Catastrophe and the Case for Abolition* (Berkeley, CA, 2011).

[139] B. Latour, 'Why Has Critique Run Out of Steam? From Matters of Fact to Matters of Concern', *Critical Inquiry* 30 (2004), pp. 224–48.

[140] Beck, *Risk Society*, p. 81.

[141] J. Ellul, *What I Believe* (Grand Rapids, MI, 1989), p. 133, cited in Smil, *Transforming*, p. 256.

CHAPTER 5

Danger in the Drains: Sewer Gas, Sewerage Systems and the Home, 1850–1900

Tom Crook

'There are "a thousand gates to death"!' declared S. Stevens Hellyer in the preface to his *Plumber and Sanitary Houses*, first published in 1877, quoting a play by Seneca: 'Few are wider, or open more readily, than those in our own homes, when unlocked by noxious gases or bad air from drains.' The portals of death were many: 'a polluted water-tank, a brick cesspool, a foul drain, a bottled-up soil pipe, a sink "*bell*" trap!' Switching to the literal, Hellyer noted how rail passengers were urged to lock the doors of their carriages in the interests of safety, and his own book, so he claimed, switching back to the metaphorical, was designed to help homeowners and tenants do the same with respect to their domestic sanitary arrangements. The aim of his 'little treatise' was to empower every 'home-maker' to put a 'padlock' on the 'gates of death'.[1]

Hellyer was dramatizing for commercial effect. He had a book to sell, he was keen to promote the services of plumbers and he was a sanitary-ware manufacturer. He was by no means a disinterested observer. The

[1] S.S. Hellyer, *The Plumber and Sanitary Houses: A Practical Treatise on the Principles of Internal Plumbing Work, or the Best Means for Effectually Excluding Noxious Gases from our Houses* (London, 1877), p. v.

T. Crook
Department of History, Philosophy and Religion, Oxford Brookes University, Tonge Building, Headington Campus, Gipsy Lane, Oxford OX3 0BP, UK

T. Crook, M. Esbester (eds), *Governing Risks in Modern Britain*,
DOI 10.1057/978-1-137-46745-4_5

history of governing risks is made up of many things, however, and one of these is the pursuit of profit. Most notably, the insurance business is just that, and it was a business that assumed increasingly aggressive and diverse forms during the Victorian period.[2] Hellyer's trade was in generating technological solutions to environmental dangers rather than actuarial probabilities and premiums. He must surely have been pleased. His book was in its fourth edition by 1887, by which point he was dwelling on the virtues of his own patent, prize-winning Optimus toilet, an improved variant of the valve-closets that had been marketed in England since the late eighteenth century.[3]

Yet, however much they might be mediated by financial self-interest, risks and dangers are above all historical, embedded in shifting material-technological configurations as much as those of a cultural sort. As Chapter 1 of this volume has suggested, they are a product both of changing ideas and assumptions about how the world operates, and of changes in how the world is organized physically. Historians have been critical of the work of Ulrich Beck and rightly so, but his broad point—which he shares with other risk theorists—that risks are compound phenomena, at once historical, material and discursive, is surely a good one. Hellyer's book on plumbing is a case in point. It was one of many that emerged in the 1870s offering advice on how best to govern the danger of 'sewer gas', a product of the complex water-borne sewerage systems that began to appear in British towns from the 1850s. The assumption he made was that these hazards were man-made and therefore might be managed and eradicated with further resort to human agency. Likewise, he was confronting a novel dynamic born of reforming the physical fabric of homes and cities, whereby technological 'progress' also made for problems. To adopt Beck's theoretical idiom, his book was part of the 'reflexive' interrogation not just of the environmental hazards created by urbanization—crudely, in this case, dirt and disease—but of the *solutions* as well. Hellyer may have been a businessman, but he was also grappling with issues that defined the advent of urban modernity in Victorian Britain.

In the grand scheme of environmental hazards created by the Victorians, sewer gas might be placed on the margins. Factories, for instance, created unprecedented problems of air and river pollution, and burgeoning urban

[2] T. Alborn, *Regulated Lives: Life Insurance and British Society, 1800–1914* (Toronto, 2009).

[3] R. Palmer, *The Water-Closet: A New History* (Newton Abbot, 1973), pp. 46–8.

gas networks periodically generated deadly explosions.[4] Sewer gas was not even the biggest problem caused by large-scale sewerage systems, which also led to the conundrum of how to deal with the novel substance of 'sewage', a term which dates from the 1830s. Quite what to do with tons of human excrement mixed with tons more of rainwater and domestic slops proved a decidedly tricky issue and was not resolved until the Edwardian period.[5] Remarkably, between the 1840s and 1890s, sewage disposal was the subject of no fewer than six select committee and seven royal commission reports.[6]

Even so, sewer gas was no more or less complex than these other hazards and it was managed in much the same regulatory fashion. Standards were set and revised, inspectors were called in, and technological solutions were implemented and reviewed. But sewer gas deserves our attention for two further reasons. First, whereas sewage caused problems at the outfalls, which were normally located on or near a river, sewer gas targeted the home, the very space that was supposed to be 'sweet', morally as much as physically. At the popular level, the risk it posed is thus difficult to dissociate from the *fear* it aroused on account of its ability to infiltrate what was supposed to be an inviolable sphere of intimacy and safety. What kind of danger, then, did it really pose? The second reason is that although there was broad agreement that sewer gas was injurious to health and a nuisance, public health professionals were unable to reach any consensus regarding its precise pathogenic agency. Indeed, as we shall see, bacteriological research only made matters worse by suggesting that sewer air was no more or less harmful than normal household air. To put it another way, it was a danger that was defined as much by fear and dispute as expert 'rationality' and technical know-how. We shall return to this issue in the

[4] A.S. Wohl, *Endangered Lives: Public Health in Victorian Britain* (London, 1984), Chapters 8–9; B. Luckin, *Pollution and Control: A Social History of the Thames in the Nineteenth Century* (Bristol, 1986); S. Mosley, *The Chimney of the World: A History of Smoke Pollution in Victorian and Edwardian Manchester* (Cambridge, 2001); C. Otter, *The Victorian Eye: A Political History of Light and Vision in Britain, 1800–1910* (Chicago, 2008), Chapters 4–6; M. Whitehead, *State, Science and the Skies: Governmentalities of the British Atmosphere* (Chichester, 2009).

[5] C. Hamlin, 'William Dibdin and the Idea of Biological Sewage Treatment', *Technology and Culture* 29 (1988), pp. 189–218; and D. Schneider, *Hybrid Nature: Sewage Treatment and the Contradictions of the Industrial Ecosystem* (Cambridge, MA, 2011).

[6] This excludes some reports on the related subject of metropolitan water supplies and sewers. See P. Cockton, *Subject Catalogue of the House of Commons Parliamentary Papers, 1801–1900: Volume IV* (Cambridge, 1988), pp. 31–3.

conclusion. The chapter begins with the gas itself: what was it and where did it come from?

The Danger of Sewer Gas

Sewer gas was the product of a new order of technologically ambitious, water-borne sewerage systems. The old order was encapsulated in a single technology dating back to the medieval period: the cesspool, where effluence was allowed to stagnate before it was collected by nightmen. The new order, by contrast, was distinguished by circulatory speed and technological connectivity—at least in theory. Edwin Chadwick offered the most seductive vision. Promoted via his Towns Improvement Company set up in 1844 and later from his official fiefdom, the General Board of Health (GBH, 1848–58), it received its most eloquent expression in 1852, when his ally F.O. Ward spoke before the first International Congress of Hygiene held in Brussels. Its 'fundamental principle' was 'circulation instead of stagnation', which in practice amounted to an all-embracing, steam-powered complex of pipes. In 'one great movement' it transferred excreta to outlying fields while bringing back rainwater from distant hills. There were no cesspools collecting waste, or even standpipes providing drinking water. Instead, a 'self-acting' network of tubes linked homes and the countryside, simulating as it did so the natural efficiency of the body. Small-bore pipes formed the 'veins' and 'arteries', water the 'blood' and a liquid-pumping steam engine 'the heart'.[7]

Such was the initial technological dream. No foul gases escaped into homes or streets; water and waste remained in perpetual motion. The reality was otherwise: fractious, contested and characterized by an array of alternatives to water-borne systems and water-closets. In general, as Christopher Hamlin has detailed, sanitary engineers preferred a more pragmatic combination of pipes and larger, egg-shaped brick sewers to Chadwick's fixation with small-bore tubular designs.[8] In a similar spirit of pragmatism, local authorities opted to deal with the question of water supplies separately and with good reason: water supply systems were just

[7] The address was subsequently reissued in 1880, along with embellishments by Chadwick and others, as 'Circulation or Stagnation; Being the Translation of a Paper by F.O. Ward on the Arterial and Venous System for the Sanitation of Towns', *Transactions of the Sanitary Institute of Great Britain* 2 (1880), pp. 267–71.

[8] C. Hamlin, *Public Health and Social Justice in the Age of Chadwick: Britain, 1800–1854* (Cambridge, 1998), Chapter 10.

as technologically demanding as sewerage systems and were embroiled in debates about the merits of public and private ownership.[9] Take London, for example. Joseph Bazalgette's monumental scheme for the Metropolitan Board of Works (1855–88) relied on pipes for immediate house drainage and oval, brick-lined sewers of varying dimensions elsewhere. Meanwhile, London's water supplies remained in the hands of seven private companies.[10] The so-called Pipe-and-Brick Sewers War of the 1850s then gave way to a still deeper cleavage between advocates of water-carriage systems and various 'dry' or 'conservancy systems'. The most notable instance of the latter was the introduction of pail-closets in cities such as Birmingham, Manchester and Nottingham, where excreta was collected in tubs subject to weekly removal.[11]

The profusion of alternative systems is partly explained by considerations of financial cost and the local availability of sufficient water supplies, but it is also explained by the novel risks and dangers generated by water-carriage systems, among them sewer gas. For critics, one kind of pollution—a stagnating, cesspool-based variant—had been replaced by another: a technologized, water-borne variant. The problem was not wholly new. The brick-built, flat-bottomed sewers that had begun to emerge during the early nineteenth century were criticized for failing to relieve residents of noxious gases on account of blockages. In 1847, flat-bottomed sewers were condemned by the engineer John Roe as 'elongated cesspools'.[12] Egg-shaped sewers were designed to avoid filthy accumulations and they were certainly an improvement on the old, but they were hardly perfect. Blockages and accumulations persisted, meaning that all water-borne systems relied on flushing mechanisms and even the use of manual hoses. Small wonder Roe's term stuck: as late as 1902, an editorial in the journal *Public Health Engineer* used it to describe the majority of egg-shaped sew-

[9] On the politics of water supply, see, among other accounts, D. Fraser, *Urban Politics in Victorian England: The Structure of Politics in Victorian Cities* (London, 1979), Chapter 7; and J. Broich, *London: Water and the Making of the Modern City* (Pittsburgh, PA, 2013). On the technical-engineering aspect, see G.M. Binnie, *Early Victorian Water Engineers* (London, 1981); and Luckin, *Pollution and Control*, Chapter 2.

[10] S. Halliday, *The Great Stink of London: Sir Joseph Bazalgette and the Cleansing of the Victorian Metropolis* (Stroud, 2001).

[11] A useful overview is provided in M.J. Daunton, *House and Home in the Victorian City: Working-Class Housing, 1850–1914* (London, 1983), Chapter 10.

[12] *Metropolitan Sanitary Commission: First Report of the Commissioners Appointed to Inquire Whether any and what Special Means may be Requisite for the Improvement of the Health of the Metropolis* (Parl. Papers 1847–8 [888]), p. 31.

ers, claiming they were merely 'underground retorts for the manufacture of sewer gas'.[13]

More importantly, the sheer scale and intricacy of the new sewerage systems raised the stakes considerably. Of particular importance was the fact that sewered houses were connected to expansive networks that carried the waste of thousands of other dwellings. Only a soil pipe stood between the interior of a house and a continual flow of other people's water-borne waste. And these houses were on the increase: by the mid-1870s, there were over 700,000 water-closets in London and some 8000 in Birmingham. Wealthy towns in particular might be well connected by this point: in Cheltenham, for instance, there were 8725 houses and 8500 water-closets.[14] Yet, quite whether or not all this building and connecting amounted to progress depended on the technical integrity of the systems. 'You may abolish cesspits ... from the neighbourhood of your houses by proper sewerage', noted the author of *A Lay Lecture on Sanitary Matters*, 'but unless you are guarded against the return into your dwellings of the gases of decomposition from the sewers, you may be worse off than before.'[15]

Analogies might be made with railway and gas supply systems, where the growth of technological complexity also led to a proliferation of potentially troublesome points and details. The safety of these large-scale systems turned on just this: the effective functioning of multiple micro-mechanisms. A misaligned rail, a perforated gas main: the consequences could be fatal. No doubt sewers, including natural ones based in small watercourses, had long generated unwholesome gases, but the distinctiveness of the sewer gas danger partly lies here, in its circulation within increasingly ramified, complex subterranean networks.

It is no surprise that the problem was put on the professional agenda during the 1850s, just as some of Chadwick's GBH-sponsored schemes were built and the question of an integrated system for London stumbled towards resolution. The problem first reared its head in a set of reports concerning an outbreak of 'fever' during the winter of 1852 in Croydon, which had recently been sewered under the superintendence of the

[13] 'The Sanitation of London', *Public Health Engineer*, 3 May 1902, p. 341.

[14] Figures provided in W.M. Egglestone, *House Drainage and Sanitary Catalogue* (Stanhope, 1889), p. 18.

[15] S.S. Brown, *A Lay Lecture on Sanitary Matters, with a Paper on Sewer Ventilation* (London, 1873), p. 31.

GBH. One cause among others, so the GBH's investigations suggested, was a lack of ventilation in the sewer pipes, which meant that there was no escape for foul gases other than through the syphon traps that opened into houses via water-closets. It was also noted how the use of domestic fires and chimneys—and thus accompanying changes in domestic air currents—only made the matter worse, effectively sucking gases into homes.[16]

The GBH's terms of choice were 'noxious gases' and 'effluvia'. It was only in 1858 when 'sewer gas' featured in the title of a sanitary text, constituting the first sustained investigation of the problem: Henry Letheby's *Report ... on Sewage and Sewer Gases, and on the Ventilation of Sewers.*[17] Letheby was Medical Officer of Health (MOH) for the City of London, where he would remain until 1874, as well as Professor of Chemistry at the London Hospital. The report accordingly detailed the chemical composition of sewer gas. It was here where there developed some kind of consensus. Recognition certainly increased of the multiple variables that affected its precise composition, including the size and air-flow of any given sewer and the nature of the sewage it contained. Still, in broad terms, what Letheby had first detailed in 1858 was still being endorsed in the late Victorian period: namely, that sewer gas might contain sufficient sulphureted hydrogen, carbonic acid, methane and ammonia to induce some kind of poisoning or asphyxia.[18] Letheby dramatized the matter: 'acute poisoning' meant those affected 'fall powerless, as if shot; the lips become livid; the face turgid ... the breathing difficult and spasmodic'; some fell into a coma and died. Later texts simply affirmed the possibility: an 1892 survey of waste disposal technologies stated that if inhaled in sufficient quantities, it could cause death by poisoning or asphyxiation, citing evidence from France.[19]

[16] *Reports by Neil Arnott, Esq., M.D. and Thomas Page, Esq., C.E. on an inquiry ordered by the Secretary of State, relative to the prevalence of disease at Croydon, and to the plan of sewerage, together with an abstract of evidence accompanying the reports* (Parl. Papers 1852–3 [1648]), pp. 8–10, 33–5; and *Statement of the preliminary inquiry by T. Southwood Smith, Esq., M.D., and John Sutherland, Esq., M.D. on the epidemic at Croydon; together with reports by R.D. Grainger, Esq. and Henry Austin, Esq. to the General Board of Health, on the circumstances connected with the epidemic attack of fever at Croydon* (Parl. Papers 1852–3 [1683]), pp. 43–4.

[17] H. Letheby, *Report to the Honourable Commissioners of Sewers of the City of London, on Sewage and Sewer Gases, and on the Ventilation of Sewers* (London, 1858).

[18] *Ibid.*, pp. 23–48.

[19] W.H. Corfield and L.C. Parkes, 'The Disposal of Refuse', in T. Stevenson and S.F. Murphy (eds), *A Treatise on Hygiene and Public Health: Volume I* (London, 1892), pp. 841–2.

Another danger that Letheby highlighted was the explosive potential of sewer gas. This too continued to be acknowledged amid occasional instances of exploding sewers. In 1875, a blast at a sewer grate in Leicester's Market Place hurled a kerbstone into the air and uprooted, 'as if by an earthquake', nearby flagstones.[20] In 1896, a bricklayer in Burton-on-Trent narrowly avoided death when he lit a candle in a sewer; the explosion that followed shook adjacent houses whilst uprooting three or four manhole covers.[21] Letheby, however, also quoted the GBH's Croydon investigations and it was here, in relation to the more important question of sewer gas as a means of generating disease, where professionals disagreed most. Fatal explosions and poisonous inhalations were one thing, but they were mercifully rare.

The infective associations multiplied during the 1870s, as sanitary and medical professionals drew variously on anecdotal experience, epidemiological evidence and the authority of evolving 'germ theories'.[22] In his *Diseases of Modern Life*, published in 1876, the revered sanitary reformer Benjamin Ward Richardson suggested that sewer air caused typhus fever, scarlet fever and smallpox.[23] Other so-called zymotic diseases associated with sewer gas included cholera, diarrhoea and especially diphtheria among the young.[24] The principal association, however, was with typhoid, the etiological intricacies of which were now better understood, if not resolved, thanks to the work of William Budd and Charles Murchison in the 1850s and 1860s.

It was the epidemiological labours of George Buchanan in particular that helped to forge the association, first for the Medical Department of the Privy Council (MDPC, 1858–71) and then the Local Government Board (LGB, 1871–1919). In the *Ninth Report* of the MDPC, Buchanan speculated that an epidemic of typhoid (or enteric fever) in Worthing in 1865 had been caused by foul gases 'bubbling up through the traps of sinks and water-closets'. Sewerage systems were a good thing, he noted,

[20] 'A New Danger from Sewer Gas', *British Medical Journal*, 8 May 1875, p. 617.

[21] 'Sewer Gas Explosion at Burton', *Berrow's Worcester Journal*, 14 November 1896, p. 6.

[22] M. Worboys, *Spreading Germs: Disease Theories and Medical Practice in Britain, 1865–1900* (Cambridge, 2000).

[23] B.W. Richardson, *Diseases of Modern Life* (London, 1876), pp. 388–91.

[24] Reviews of the relevant literature were produced at the time. See especially P.H. Bird, *Hints on Drains, Traps, Closets, Sewer Gas, and Sewage Disposal* (Blackpool, 1877), pp. 6-22, and *Sewer Gas and its Effects: Extracts from the Work of the Leading Sanitary Authorities* (Liverpool, 1879).

but they had their 'drawbacks', adding that the epidemic had principally affected 'well-to-do houses'.[25] Buchanan's bubbling traps featured again in the 1870s, this time in two detailed investigations into outbreaks of typhoid fever in Caius College, Cambridge in 1874 and in Croydon in 1875.[26] In the former, faulty plumbing had enabled sewer air to infect the water supplies of the College's Tree Court section; in the latter, 'infection was delivered from sewers directly into the air of houses'. Sewer gas 'is, as it were, "laid-on" to houses', he noted.[27]

Infected food, milk and water supplies were among the other factors credited with causing typhoid, but the role of sewer gas continued to be affirmed by subsequent LGB investigations, including of epidemics at Melton Mowbray (in 1881), Sherborne (1882) and York (1884). Likewise, epidemiological work undertaken by MOsH in Bristol, Nottingham and Leeds during the 1890s confirmed the link between defective house drainage and typhoid, as well as diphtheria.[28]

At the very least, then, there was some kind of correlation between the existence of sewer gas, faulty traps and infectious diseases. Yet, correlation does not make for necessary causation and the interpretive problems were many. For one thing, there was the conundrum of the rude health enjoyed by the nightmen that emptied cesspools. As early as the 1840s, the physician William Guy had provided statistical evidence attesting to the superior health of nightmen compared to bricklayers and brick makers, and yet nightmen spent their working hours engulfed in foul miasmas.[29] Still in the 1890s, public health professionals were noting what appeared to be an anomaly.[30] Crucially, bacteriological investigations complicated matters, demonstrating that the inner life of sewers was more complex and, in atmospheric terms at least, more salubrious than had hitherto been recog-

[25] *Public Health: Ninth Report of the Medical Officer of the Privy Council, with Appendix* (Parl. Papers 1867 [3949]), pp. 194–5.

[26] 'Enteric Fever at Caius College, Cambridge', *Public Health: Reports of the Medical Officer of the Privy Council and Local Government Board. New Series, no. II* (Parl. Papers 1874 [C. 1066]), pp. 63–78; 'On Enteric Fever at Croydon, by Dr Buchanan', *Public Health: Reports of the Medical Officer of the Privy Council and Local Government Board. New Series, no. VII* (Parl. Papers 1876 [C. 1508]), pp. 40–71.

[27] 'On Enteric Fever at Croydon, by Dr Buchanan', *Public Health*, p. 48.

[28] A useful overview is L.C. Parkes, 'Review of Books: "Is Sewer Air a Source of Disease?"', *Journal of the Sanitary Institute* 16 (1896), pp. 142–52.

[29] W.A. Guy, 'On the Health of Nightmen, Scavengers and Dustmen', *Journal of the Statistical Society of London* 11 (1848), pp. 72–81.

[30] Corfield and Parkes, 'The Disposal of Refuse', pp. 841–2.

nized. It was a more nuanced appreciation that paralleled broader developments in the study of typhoid, which was then in the process of assuming a fully developed microbiological dimension: in 1880, the typhoid bacillus was identified by two German bacteriologists, Carl Eberth and Edwin Klebs, and in 1884 it was cultured for the first time by Georg Gaffky.

In the British context, two sets of experiments framed what in 1888 was judged an emerging 'controversy' among professionals: those by Thomas Carnelley and J.S. Haldane conducted at Westminster Palace and Dundee in 1886, and those by J. Parry Laws conducted in 1892 and in 1893 (with F.W. Andrewes) for the London County Council's (LCC) Main Drainage Committee.[31] In each case, air was collected from sections of selected sewers and then put to laboratory analysis in order to determine its organic and inorganic composition. The conclusions reached by the two reports were broadly the same: that the micro-organisms in sewer air came entirely or nearly so from the air outside rather than from sewage (not unless there was considerable splashing); that these micro-organisms were mostly moulds and micrococci, whereas sewage was mostly composed of bacilli; and that there were fewer micro-organisms in sewer air compared to the air of houses and streets. Laws concluded his second report of 1893 as follows:

> Although one is led almost irresistibly to the conclusion that the organisms found in sewer air probably do not constitute any source of danger, it is impossible to ignore the evidence, though it is only circumstantial, that sewer air in some instances has had some causal relation to zymotic disease.

There was, he added, certainly the danger of poisoning, given its chemical composition, but it was 'quite conceivable … that the danger of sewer air causing disease is an indirect one'.[32]

Did any of this really matter? In some respects it did. Professionally, it constituted another point of tension between epidemiological approaches

[31] T. Rowan, *Disease and Putrescent Air: Some Principles which Must Govern the Efficient Ventilation of Sewers and the Effective Hygienic Treatment of 'Sewer Gas'* (London, 1888), p. 11. The experiments are detailed in T. Carnelly and J.S. Haldane, 'The Air of Sewers', *Proceedings of the Royal Society of London* 42 (1887), pp. 501–22; J.P. Laws, *London County Council: Reports and Sewer Air Investigations* (London, 1893); and J.P. Laws and F.W. Andrewes, *London County Council: Report on the Result of Investigations on the Micro-organisms of Sewage* (London, 1894).

[32] Laws, *London County Council: Reports and Sewer Air Investigations*, p. 11.

and those of a bacteriological sort. Certainly some professionals felt affronted by the work of Laws. MOsH published articles defending a causal link between sewer gas and infectious disease, as did sanitary engineers.[33] One of the leading professionals of the late Victorian period, Louis C. Parkes, questioned not so much the findings of Laws as their significance. In 1896, he published a review of Laws' reports, which besides noting that the experiments were conducted only on a limited number of sewers—and no two sewers were the same—cited the abundant epidemiological evidence which suggested that there was indeed a link between faulty drainage and outbreaks of typhoid and diphtheria. Parkes concluded on a combative note: 'The bacillary theory of the origins of infectious disease is not yet in a position to command universal support, when opposed in toto to the teachings founded upon the laboriously acquired facts of epidemiological investigation.'[34]

But in other respects, it did not matter much at all. As a number of historians have demonstrated, a kind of methodological eclecticism emerged at the institutional level of the LGB and local MOsH, where interested professionals mixed and matched different approaches and the insights they yielded.[35] More importantly, for all its micro-biological intricacies, sewer gas still constituted a danger, as Laws himself admitted, just as it had earlier for those of a miasmatic inclination. Indeed, those at the time were keen to encourage a balanced view. In 1898, the engineer H. Alfred Roechling presented a synthesis of the research that had been undertaken in Britain, Germany and Italy. His conclusion represented the consensus at the end of the century: namely, that sewer gas had the power of 'predisposing' the body to attacks of typhoid fever, and possibly other diseases too, even if it was not clear that it was a direct cause.[36] It was a moderate conclusion, self-consciously steering clear of 'extremes', and it was the one that seems to have been shared by most MOsH, sanitary inspectors, architects and engineers.

[33] R.H. Reeves, *Reports and Investigations on Sewer Air and Sewer Ventilation* (London, 1894); 'Diseases Occasioned by Emanations from Sewer-Drained Cesspools and other Organic Refuse', *The Sanitary Record*, 8 September 1894, pp. 1003–6; and 'Bacteriology of Sewer Air', *The Sanitary Record*, 10 November 1894, pp. 1160–2.

[34] Parkes, 'Review of Books', p. 152.

[35] See especially C. Hamlin, *A Science of Impurity: Water Analysis in Nineteenth-Century Britain* (Berkeley, CA, 1990); and A. Hardy, 'On the Cusp: Epidemiology and Bacteriology at the Local Government Board, 1890–1905', *Medical History* 42 (1998), pp. 328–46.

[36] H.A. Roechling, *Sewer Gas and its Influence upon Health* (London, 1898), pp. 84–5.

Equally, all could agree that sewer gas was a nuisance, something which statute law defined in suitably flexible terms: a 'nuisance', that is, was both a general annoyance and something that was 'injurious to health', or indeed *might* be injurious to health.[37] Either way, there were good reasons for taking action. At the very least, sewer gas made for a foetid annoyance and it was surely best to play it safe and ensure that all the technological details were accounted for and functioning as best they could. This, at any rate, seems to have been the dominant ethos when it came to reforming drainage and sewerage systems. Safety first; amenity and comfort a close second; causal intricacies third: such was the general order of considerations that helped to define the sewer gas danger. There was, however, a further facet: public alarm, or at the very least alarm on the part of the middle and upper classes whose homes were much more likely to contain water-closets.

'Home Sweet Home'

By mid-century, the wealthy public was accustomed to reading about cesspools and privy-middens, and especially those situated in the back-to-back courts of the urban poor. Foetid, filth-ridden and morally and physically corrupting—such was the dominant image of working-class slums that was popularized by journalists and social investigators. Evidently, on one level, sewer gas was a class issue, as Michelle Allen has argued.[38] It was alarming precisely because noxious gases and miasmatic atmospheres were supposed to distinguish the homes and streets of 'the Great Unwashed', not those of the middle and upper classes, and certainly not when they had embraced state-of-the-art technology. It was this class dimension that did most to raise the profile of the problem. Public attention had arisen occasionally at the local level during the 1860s, normally in relation to foul-smelling streets, but it assumed national proportions in late 1871, when the Prince of Wales

[37] C. Hamlin, 'Public Sphere to Public Health: The Transformation of "Nuisance"', in S. Sturdy (ed.), *Medicine, Health and the Public Sphere in Britain, 1600–2000* (London, 2002), pp. 189–204; J.G. Hanley, 'Parliament, Physicians and Nuisances: The Demedicalization of Nuisance Law, 1831–1855', *Bulletin of the History of Medicine* 80 (2006), pp. 702–32; and T. Crook, 'Sanitary Inspection and the Public Sphere in Late-Victorian and Edwardian Britain: A Case Study in Liberal Governance', *Social History* 32 (2007), pp. 369–93.

[38] M. Allen, *Cleansing the City: Sanitary Geographies in Victorian London* (Athens, OH, 2008), pp. 42–53.

contracted typhoid fever at Londesborough Lodge in Scarborough, owing, so a subsequent investigation suggested, to defective drainage and exposure to sewer gas.[39] The intense press coverage that surrounded the Prince's affliction perhaps made for a moment of national unity. 'We are today but one household in which the QUEEN is the revered head', noted a lead article in the *Standard*, 'and her suffering son the centre and object of our hopes and prayers.'[40] But it also was a moment when the middle classes in particular confronted their vulnerability. Sanitary reform was a matter for all classes, noted an editorial in the *Liverpool Mercury* entitled 'The Sewerage Panic'. The overcrowded poor had 'the most to fear; but the perverseness of builders and architects renders the position of the middle-class householder also one of considerable danger'.[41]

The period of December 1871 to January 1872 represents the high-point of national alarm regarding the sewer gas danger, fuelled by the daily drama of the Prince's condition (he survived in the end), but sewer air was now established as a matter of periodic comment in the press and as a key point of reference for all those like Hellyer who sought to sell advice on matters of domestic plumbing. The class dimension was crucial and one theme was the need to avoid complacency: Hellyer, for instance, could not resist noting the case of the Prince in the preface quoted at the start of this chapter. Above all, however, it was the technological ironies and inversions that did most to nurture public alarm. One of these was that the domestic water-closet doubled as a technology of privacy and detachment *and* as a technology of connection and publicity. In 1876, a leader in *The Times* noted this, suggesting that 'the universal extension of a general and public system of drainage' demanded more, not less, vigilance on the part of tenants and homeowners:

> Formerly, when every house more or less disposed of its own drainage, though matters were bad enough, the extent of the mischief could generally be measured. Now, however, each house, unless specially protected, is exposed to the attacks of the whole town, and yet, as a rule, no greater precautions are taken than heretofore to keep the enemy at bay.[42]

[39] For a useful summary of the various investigations, see 'The Illness of H.R.H., The Prince of Wales', *British Medical Journal*, 9 December 1871, pp. 671–3.

[40] *The Standard*, 11 December 1871, p. 4.

[41] 'The Sewerage Panic', *Liverpool Mercury*, 15 December 1871, p. 6.

[42] 'Health and Sewage of Towns', *The Times*, 21 September 1876, p. 5; *The Times*, 22 September 1876, p. 9.

The privacy of the home was now more vulnerable than ever—connected in fact, quite literally, to the anonymous abstraction of 'the whole town' and its sewered excreta. The noxious fumes of a cesspool were bad enough, but still more dangerous were the excremental, water-borne gases generated by people one did not even know. To whom did they belong? It was impossible to say.

The troubling interplay of privacy and publicity, detachment and connectivity mingled with another dynamic: control and loss of control. In broad terms, technology was understood as a sign of man's power over nature, and in this case of man's growing control over the domestic environment and the awkward waste products generated by organic life. Yet it also led to a loss of control—or, more precisely, a loss of accessibility and understanding, as the drainage of the home became a matter of labyrinthine networks of hidden pipes and sewers. 'As to risk of fire, in almost every house there are many elements of danger: they are generally, so to speak, behind the scenes—that is, behind the grate, in the flooring, or in the roof', noted *The Times* in a lead article published in December 1871, at the height of the fuss surrounding the Prince. 'So much for fire', it went on, before turning to sewer gas:

> It [sewer gas] is a more terrible, more constant and far more insidious danger which now occupies the foreground of public anxiety. It is the pestilence that walketh in darkness—that is to say, in the darkness of drains, traps, pipes, close fittings, abstruse mechanisms, out of reach and out of sight altogether.[43]

Technological complexity alienated, then, just as it also empowered and reassured. Metaphor helped to dramatize the insidious agency of sewer gas in this respect: on into the 1880s, it was still being described as 'a lurking danger', 'a loafing intruder' and 'the enemy within'.

And this fear fostered one thing above all: an eye for detail, as the material intricacies of the home were transformed into potential conduits for sewer gas. A final inversion, then, this time of scale: minuscule details made for big consequences—death, ultimately. In 1872, the engineer G. Mather published a pamphlet addressed to 'John Bull' on the subject of sewer gas, where he stressed the dangers that lay in the details. The soil pipe that connected the closet to the drains was of particular importance, he argued,

[43] *The Times*, 7 December 1871, p. 9.

adding 'that should there be a flaw in the pipe, however small the aperture, if even like the scratch of a pin, gas would be drawn through in the course of the night to the closet', and from there to bedroom, 'sufficient to poison a whole family'.[44] Other texts employed visual means to convey the proliferation of pathological possibilities, most notably T. Pridgin Teale's *Dangers to Health: A Pictorial Guide to Domestic Sanitary Defects*, first published in 1878 and in its fourth edition by 1883. He was especially keen to encourage the public 'to ferret out unsuspected sources of illness' and, to this end, his guide contained 55 plates, most of which illustrated specific defects: unsyphoned traps; jerry-built drains; faulty joints; leaky pipes; and rat-infested floors. Heavy black lines illustrated the crucial features in any given diagram, whilst blue lines and arrows indicated the trajectory of sewer gas as it weaved its way from the drains into bedrooms, kitchens and living rooms. There was in fact nowhere it was not capable of infiltrating somehow (see Fig. 5.1).

Governing Details

The underlying premise was sound enough: sewer gas was dangerous. The question was quite how and to what extent. As we have seen, professionals squabbled about causality and method. Meanwhile, the public was put on alert, convinced that all bad smells threatened disease. Still, this potent mixture of fact and fear was not without its uses. 'No doubt this conviction in the public mind of the dangerous character of sewer gas has at times given rise to exaggerated fears', noted Roechling, 'but it has had the good effect, by bringing pressure to bear on our sanitary authorities, of vastly improving the hygienic conditions and surroundings of our houses and towns.'[45] So it did, though it is immensely difficult to generalize about the improvements that took place, given that class mattered so much. By and large, working-class houses remained much less salubrious than those of a middle- and upper-class sort. Furthermore, even by the Edwardian period, not all working-class houses were equipped with water-closets. Pail-closets and even rudimentary ashpits (essentially cesspits) remained common in major cities such as Manchester and Newcastle.

[44] G. Mather, *Sewer Gas, Ventilation of the Sewers, Drainage and Ventilation of Buildings on an Improved Principle* (London, 1872), p. 5.

[45] Roechling, *Sewer Gas and its Influence upon Health*, p. 5.

Fig. 5.1 'Water-closet with arrangements all faulty, compared with w.c. with the faults remedied.' Plate XVI in T. Pridgin Teale, *Dangers to Health: A Pictorial Guide to Domestic Sanitary Defects* (London, 1878). Published with the kind permission of the Bodleian Library, Oxford

Nonetheless, the regulatory response to the uneven, class-specific diffusion of sewerage systems and water-closets extended far beyond the powers of a state, proto-collectivist, liberal or otherwise. Water-borne sewerage systems, perhaps, were a very material manifestation of a growing sense of communal responsibility for public health, to the extent that they were funded from the ratepayer purse and were the product of guidance from central offices. What mattered most, however, was governing the details of systemic design and functioning, and this was the work of multiple agents, including those of a commercial sort. Foucault wrote of the way disciplinary forms of power were based upon a 'political anatomy of detail' and the training and specification of minor bodily gestures and movements. These were crucial, he argued, to the making of docile, predictable subjects.[46] An analogous investment in detail is evident in the case of managing infrastructural systems, where it meant attending to minute technological components so that they might combine and function in ways that were safe and predictable: a case of taming technological rather than human complexity. The voluminous technical literature that emerged within the railway and gas—and later electricity—industries provides abundant evidence of this. A similar descent into detail is apparent in the case of sewerage and domestic drainage systems and the management of sewer gas. Three aspects might be highlighted.

One is the setting and refinement of construction standards. Bylaws played a role here. Certainly earlier measures, such as London's Building Act of 1774, had provided a degree of regulation, especially in relation to construction materials in order to mitigate the risk of fire, but it was only during the 1840s when acts of this sort began to drill down into domestic sanitary details.[47] The 1844 Metropolitan Buildings Act, for instance, specified minimum room dimensions (seven feet in height) and the correct fall of drains (at least half-an-inch per ten feet).[48] The LGB followed suit in 1877 with a set of its own model bylaws, which for the first time prescribed two arrangements designed to protect against sewer gas: the use of siphon traps at the point where the house drains connected with the main sewers; and the installation of ventilation mechanisms, one at

[46] M. Foucault, *Discipline and Punish: The Birth of the Prison*, trans. A. Sheridan (London, 1991), pp. 136–41.

[47] S.M. Gaskell, *Building Control: National Legislation and the Introduction of Local Bye-Laws in Victorian England* (London, 1983), pp. 3–20.

[48] D. Gibbons, *The Metropolitan Buildings Act. 7th & 8th. Vict. Cap. 84; with Notes and an Index* (London, 1844), pp. 146–9.

the point where the drains met the sewer (in the form of a disconnection chamber or grated opening) and another where it joined the house (in the form of a shaft or pipe leading up the side of the house to the gable).[49] The LGB's bylaws quickly became the key point of reference. By 1882, over 1500 local authorities had laws of their own, as approved by bureaucrats in Whitehall.[50]

Implementing these standards was another matter. In particular, the work of local authorities was frustrated by a variety of commercial and private agents. Connections had to be made between house drains and sewer mains, and this could prove sluggish owing to the opposition of landlords: it took Reading Corporation over 6 years (1876–82) to enforce the connection of roughly 6000 houses.[51] Legal challenges by householders further stalled the process, amid disputes regarding the precise meaning of 'public sewers' and 'private drains', and who should pay for improvements.[52] The interests of private and commercial agents, however, were not necessarily opposed to those of public health. Slipshod 'jerry-building' may have continued, but it is also clear that competition for trade spurred greater technical refinement. The 1870s and 1880s, for instance, witnessed a profusion of handbooks pitched at the building and plumbing trades. Hellyer's *The Plumber and Sanitary Houses*, quoted at the start of this chapter, was but one of many: others included William Eassie's *Healthy Houses* and W.H. Corfield's *Dwelling Houses*, which also went through multiple editions. All dwelled on the minutiae of house drains and how they should be combined in order to secure durability: pipes, falls, glazes, traps, grates and sockets. Meanwhile, sanitaryware companies provided an abundance of alternatives, catering for various budgets. If the LGB prescribed general standards—for example, that all drains should be 'suitably trapped'—entrepreneurial manufacturers filled out the details. A pamphlet on the subject of sewer gas published in 1877 detailed four

[49] [Local Government Board], *Model Bye-Laws for Sanitary Authorities* (London, 1886), Part 4.

[50] G.E. Cherry, *Cities and Plans: The Shaping of Urban Britain in the Nineteenth and Twentieth Centuries* (London, 1988), p. 41.

[51] A.W. Parry, 'The Separate System of Sewerage as Carried Out at Reading', in *Proceedings of the Association of Municipal and Sanitary Engineers and Surveyors: Volume IX, 1882–83* (London, 1883), pp. 105–6.

[52] H.P. Boulnois, *The Municipal and Sanitary Engineers' Handbook*, 3rd edn (London, 1898), pp. 317–22; E.C.S. Moore, *Sanitary Engineering: A Practical Treatise on the Collection, Removal and Final Disposal of Sewage*, 2nd edn (London, 1901), pp. 16–20.

water trapping technologies: Weaver's Ventilating Trap; Bavin's Dip Trap; the Red Hill Trap; and the Registered Interceptor Sewer-Air Trap.[53]

A second aspect is inspecting and testing. The practices themselves are exemplary of the new ethos of infrastructural risk management and its two guiding assumptions: first, that it was a matter of identifying problems *before* they caused sickness, injury and death; and, second, that even the best technologies were liable to deteriorate or malfunction. The most important development was the advent of official forms of local sanitary inspection. The first sanitary inspectors were appointed in cities such as London, Liverpool and Birmingham in the 1840s, and by the 1880s they could be found in all urban and most rural areas. Their duties were many and by the late Victorian period, cities were home to specialist food and slaughterhouse inspectors, normally under the charge of a chief inspector. But however elaborate any given system of local inspection, dwellings featured high on the list of priorities. By the 1890s, for instance, Manchester Council was employing 28 inspectors to patrol the city's residential districts and in 1896 alone they visited more than 46,000 houses.[54] This did not, however, preclude the involvement of commercial agents, albeit almost exclusively in relation to middle- and upper-class dwellings. From the 1870s, private surveyors and engineers placed adverts in the press publicizing their services. In 1880, a duo of London-based engineers sought to exploit fears regarding sewer gas—their advert began by noting the case of a recent typhoid victim in Holland Park—charging one guinea for a full check and accompanying certification.[55] Alternatively, middle- and upper-class householders could subscribe to self-organized voluntary associations, such as the London Sanitary Protection Association, which charged an annual premium in return for routine inspections and a contribution towards the cost of any repairs.[56]

Either way, official or private, inspections proceeded in the same fashion. Questions were asked of the householders or tenants; toilets were examined and flushed. Inspections were also aided by a variety of design features and technologies that enhanced access to now-hidden networks of pipes and drains. On the one hand, the very likelihood of malfunction

[53] Bird, *Hints on Drains, Traps, Closets, Sewer Gas, and Sewage Disposal*, pp. 33–9.

[54] [J. Niven], *Health Officer Report: 1896* (Manchester, 1897), pp. 148–9.

[55] C. Innes and W.K. Burton, *Sanitary Inspection of Dwelling Houses, with Special Reference to London Houses* (London, 1880).

[56] 'Sanitary Assurance', *The Sanitary Record*, 15 June 1881, pp. 478–9; 'London Sanitary Protection Association', *The Sanitary Record*, 15 March 1882, p. 383.

and the need for maintenance was factored into the design equation. Crucial here was the introduction from the 1870s of inspection chambers and manholes, which enabled convenient access to junction points receiving the branch drains of premises before they entered the main sewer.[57] On the other hand, inspectors came equipped with miniature mobile testing devices for assessing the plumbing. A basic test consisted of placing a strong-smelling liquid into a water-closet or sink, followed by a pail of hot water. Should the smell become apparent, it was sure evidence of a defective drain or fractured soil pipe. The 'scent test' might be performed using drops of peppermint, or even a Banner Drain Grenade, essentially a phial containing pungent gas.[58] Other tests included the use of smoke, but the most reliable, so it was claimed, was the 'hydraulic test', which involved stopping up a pipe and then monitoring the level of water. If the level dropped, it normally meant joints were 'sweating' or a pipe had cracked.[59]

The final aspect is technological experimentation and critique, and the gradual emergence of safer, more reliable components and arrangements. Once more, both commercial and official-professional agents played a role. Most notably, perhaps, it was commercial manufacturers that pioneered the relatively simple and sanitary 'wash-down closet' that would triumph in the twentieth century, which combined a basin and a trap in a single piece of glazed earthenware, leading to an 'S'-shaped curve. Early variants included Humpherson and Co.'s Beaufort model and Twyford's Deluge, both patented in the 1880s. Professional involvement was most pronounced beyond the home, where it centred on the question of sewer mains and in particular their means of ventilation as they coursed beneath streets. The principle was sound enough: ventilation would allow for the introduction of fresh air, as well as relieve pressure on a local system as a whole, so that domestic mechanisms such as gable shafts were not the only means of diffusing sewer gas. The practical problem was how to ventilate sewers without polluting the streets and houses above. As one borough engineer put it in 1882, 'as a means for securing that every person

[57] T.E. Coleman, *Sanitary House Drainage, its Principles and Practice* (London, 1896), pp. 55–60, 71–4.

[58] L.C. Parkes, 'The Testing of Drains', *Public Health* 15 (1902–3), pp. 272–8.

[59] Useful overviews of testing include Coleman, *Sanitary House Drainage*, pp. 161–77; and G.J.G. Jensen, *Modern Drainage Inspection and Sanitary Surveys* (London, 1899), pp. 76–88.

passing by shall breathe the greatest possible amount of poisonous gas, this arrangement [sewer ventilation] is almost perfect'.[60]

Ventilation assumed various forms as borough engineers wrestled with this conundrum. The surveys undertaken at the time highlighted three principal methods.[61] One was the installation of shafts leading upwards from a sewer to the surface of a roadway, otherwise known as 'open' or 'surface ventilation'. Another option, first trialled by Bazalgette in the mid-1850s, was to install pipes linking the crown of a sewer to nearby factory chimneys. The third was ventilation via street lighting. The most elaborate mechanism here was the Holman-Keeling Sewer Gas Destructor, first marketed in 1886, which involved the installation of miniature gas burners at the base of similarly gas-powered lamps. Certainly the most popular method was surface ventilation. It had the approval of the LGB and it was also the cheapest and most straightforward; however, it was also the most problematic. As early as the 1870s, engineers had begun abandoning the method owing to public complaints of nuisances, and the practice of closing open ventilators on these grounds gathered pace around the turn of the century.[62] In 1902, Grimsby's borough engineer sent questionnaires to 51 local authorities on the subject, and of these some 35 had abandoned, or were in the process of abandoning, surface ventilation.[63] Instead, attention shifted back to two other points in any local system: better flushing mechanisms within sewers and the improvement of chimney and gable shafts running up the sides of houses—shafts in fact that can still be seen today running up the sides of British houses.

Conclusion

Popular ignorance of health-related risks was a common complaint in the Victorian era. 'The risks that people run every day, without knowing of their existence, are often much greater than those which give them the greatest uneasiness', noted the social investigator and editor of the *Builder*, George Godwin, in *Another Blow for Life,* published in 1864: 'They are frightened by a squib that cannot hurt them and sit contentedly

[60] Quoted in Boulnois, *The Municipal and Sanitary Engineers' Handbook*, p. 340.

[61] Useful overviews include 'Cleansing and Ventilating Sewers', *The Surveyor*, 13 October 1892, pp. 211–14; and Boulnois, *The Municipal and Sanitary Engineers' Handbook*, pp. 340–7.

[62] E.B. Ellice-Clark, 'Ventilation of Sewers', *Proceedings of the Association of Municipal and Sanitary Engineers and Surveyors: Volume I, 1873–74* (London, 1875), p. 55.

[63] 'The Ventilation of Sewers', *Public Health Engineer*, 14 May 1904, pp. 487–8.

week after week on a barrel of gunpowder with a lighted fuse within an inch of the bung-hole, not believing in the danger till they find themselves blown into the air.'[64] The examples of this might be multiplied. Roger Cooter has noted the obsession with railway accidents during the early Victorian period, despite the fact that on average twice as many people were killed in horse-related accidents and six times as many drowned.[65]

Was not the perception of the danger of sewer gas much greater than the actual danger—was it one of Godwin's 'squibs'? Perhaps so, but this is to ask the wrong kind of question. Crucially, experts could not agree on the danger it posed. Indeed, just as professional enquiry began to converge on its relation to typhoid (and to a lesser extent diphtheria), so did bacteriological research point to all manner of micro-biological complications. All could agree that sewer gas was dangerous, but the precise threat it posed remained unclear. Ultimately, considerations of this sort did not matter much, for besides the broad agreement that sewer gas was dangerous *somehow*, all could agree that it was deeply unpleasant.

The 'facts' of the matter were thus mutable, as were the fears of the public. But even if there had been expert consensus on the danger posed by sewer gas, it would be wrong to dismiss the input of the public. Public health professionals were supposed to serve the public, and both were grappling with the (unintended) consequences of a new technological environment in the form of large-scale sewerage systems. The public did so as those who lived with this infrastructure on a daily basis, professionals as those who helped to design it, but no one pretended it was perfect, only that it was a step in the right direction, a work in progress. Finding the solutions was undertaken in much the same spirit: a spirit of trial-and-error, whereby experimentation, testing and the need for inspection were taken for granted.

To put it another way, the sewer gas danger and its management was made up of many elements, among them fears and facts, expert, commercial and public agency, not to mention a new subterranean world of pipes, drains and sewers. Sociological theorists such as Ulrich Beck write of the way in which 'science' has lost its 'monopolization' on defining risks and dangers in an era of late modernity. The case of sewer gas suggests that this has long been the case.

[64] G. Godwin, *Another Blow for Life* (London, 1864), p. 23.

[65] R. Cooter, 'The Moment of the Accident: Culture, Militarism and Modernity in Late-Victorian Britain', in R. Cooter and B. Luckin (eds), *Accidents in History: Injuries, Fatalities and Social Relations* (Amsterdam, 1997), p. 112.

CHAPTER 6

Public Health and Public Safety: Disinfection, Carbolic and the Plurality of Risk, 1870–1914

Rebecca Whyte

The nineteenth century is still regarded as the time when public health became modern. The mechanisms underpinning the causation and transmission of disease were grasped with growing levels of precision; public health policy assumed a national dimension under the direction of various central offices, beginning with the General Board of Health in 1848, and mortality gradually declined, heralding the start of an 'epidemiological transition' towards more chronic, non-infectious diseases.[1] To be sure, historians no longer write in terms of the 'origins' of a welfare state that was still to come: the emphasis in recent work has been on the contingent and contested nature of how public health policies were devised, implemented

[1] An excellent summary of this transition is S. Szreter and A. Hardy, 'Urban Fertility and Mortality Patterns', in M. Daunton (ed.), *The Cambridge Urban History of Britain: Volume III, 1840–1950* (Cambridge, 2000), pp. 629–72.

R. Whyte
The Scottish Government, St Andrew's House, Regent Road,
Edinburgh EH1 3DG, UK

T. Crook, M. Esbester (eds), *Governing Risks in Modern Britain*,
DOI 10.1057/978-1-137-46745-4_6

and practised.[2] Nonetheless, the importance of nineteenth-century public health initiatives in tackling some of the most egregious failings of an emergent urban-industrial society retains prominence.

This remarkable transformation, however, involved confronting *and* creating problems. This is evident in Tom Crook's contribution to this volume, which examines how the advent of large-scale, water-borne sewerage systems generated the novel danger of sewer gas. This chapter examines another fraught arena of public health reform: the practice and promotion of chemical disinfection.[3] Disinfection per se was nothing new, but it became a prominent and pervasive tactic during the second half of the century. On the one hand, it became part of localized disease prevention strategies. From the 1870s in particular, local authorities undertook increasingly ambitious disinfection programmes, principally as a response to outbreaks of infectious disease. On the other hand, a wide range of disinfectant preparations was marketed to the public for use on a routine, preventive basis in and around the home. Put simply, as a matter of both public and private practice, disinfection emerged as a crucial means of managing the risks and dangers of infectious diseases. Yet, as we shall see, disinfection also created risks and dangers of its own, for these new and more widely available substances were, by design, supposed to be deadly, and quite how they were then used by those in their possession was intrinsically difficult to regulate—some, evidently, used them for altogether self-destructive purposes. The chapter explores this decidedly difficult arena of reform and regulation through a case study of the troubling trajectory of carbolic acid. It begins with the rise of disinfection as a means of preventing and managing the spread of disease.

[2] Notable works in this respect include J.M. Eyler, *Sir Arthur Newsholme and State Medicine, 1885–1935* (Cambridge, 1997); C. Hamlin, *Public Health and Social Justice in the Age of Chadwick: Britain, 1800–1854* (Cambridge, 1998); R. Woods, *The Demography of Victorian England and Wales* (Cambridge, 2000); and N. Durbach, *Bodily Matters: The Anti-Vaccination Movement in England, 1853–1907* (Durham, NC, 2005).

[3] For a fuller discussion of disinfection in all its forms during this time, a subject that has been neglected by historians as a particular field of practice, see R. Whyte, 'Changing Approaches to Disinfection in England, c. 1848–1914' (PhD thesis, University of Cambridge, 2012).

The Uses and Significance of Disinfection

Disinfection was an established prophylactic technique by the mid-nineteenth century. The inland responses to Britain's four cholera epidemics (1831–2, 1848–9, 1853–4 and 1866), for instance, involved the use of a variety of disinfectant techniques, recalling practices deployed against plague in earlier centuries. Sulphur and coal tar were burned in order to purify the atmosphere; streets were hosed down and accumulations of filth were removed; houses were fumigated with chlorine gas and limewashed.[4] All of these practices were understood as 'disinfection', if also as 'purification', 'cleansing' and 'sanitation': a jumble of terms that covered a jumble of practices designed to manage the risk of further infection.

The development of germ theories in the latter half of the nineteenth century changed the way in which disinfection was defined and understood.[5] This did not transform all uses of the word: still at the end of the century, the term 'disinfection' possessed what sometimes was described as a 'loose' or 'generic' meaning, where it referred to any practice that rendered the spread of infection less likely.[6] Yet, that some definitions might be regarded as 'loose' and 'generic' reflected the growing equation of disinfection with killing germs. This began during the 1870s, when some professionals began speaking of a 'science of disinfection' and, by the 1890s, both popular and professional texts were offering at least two kinds of distinction in a field of practice that was now more specialized and varied.[7] One was between deodorization, antisepsis and disinfection, where the latter specifically and exclusively meant 'germicide' or 'bactericide'. The other was between disinfection by heat and chemical disinfection. As one primer on hygiene and public health put it in 1894: 'True disinfection, that is destruction of germs, may be effected by heat or by chemical methods.'[8]

[4] P. Baldwin, *Contagion and the State in Europe, 1830–1930* (Cambridge, 1999), pp. 136–9, 147–55; C. Hamlin, *Cholera: The Biography* (Oxford, 2009), Chapter 3.

[5] M. Worboys, *Spreading Germs: Disease Theories and Medical Practice in Britain, 1865–1900* (Cambridge, 2000).

[6] W.N. Twelvetrees, 'Disinfection: Physical, Chemical and Mechanical', *Sanitary Inspectors Journal* 3 (1897), pp. 22, 28.

[7] John Dougall seems to have been the first to promote it as such in an address to the National Association for the Promotion of Social Science in 1874. 'The Science of Disinfection', *British Medical Journal* (hereinafter *BMJ*), 24 October 1874, pp. 530–1.

[8] B.A. Whitelegge and G. Newman, *Hygiene and Public Health*, 4th edn (London, 1894), p. 244.

At the same time, disinfection became more important as a tactic employed by local authorities. Along with tactics of compulsory notification and the immediate isolation of the sick, it was one of three promoted by Medical Officers of Health (MOsH) by way of 'stamping out' cases and outbreaks of infectious disease, among them smallpox, scarlet fever, diphtheria, typhoid and measles. Stamping out systems coalesced only slowly and in fits and starts across Britain, beginning with a handful of local authorities in the mid-1870s, but by the mid-1890s, the majority of authorities had implemented compulsory notification schemes and had access to new or improved isolation hospital facilities.[9] The power to compel the disinfection of homes, persons and items of property was among a number of measures provided for in a series of statutes—in particular, the 1866 Sanitary Act, the 1875 Public Health Act and the 1890 Infectious Disease (Prevention) Act—designed, so it was stated, to 'prevent the risk of communicating any infectious diseases or of spreading infection'.[10] Others included the power to remove persons to hospital and to fine cab drivers for knowingly accepting the custom of infected individuals.

Quite how often these powers were used depended on the incidence of cases and outbreaks of disease. Yet, besides the relative regularity of outbreaks, the voluminous literature that emerged on stamping out suggests that disinfection practices had become an established part of municipal sanitation by the 1890s. The rigour was unprecedented. Although practices might be tailored according to the nature of the affliction—typhoid normally meant increased attention to disinfecting drains and destroying foodstuffs—the general ethos was to disinfect all possible means of transmission, in all cases, in all circumstances; or what amounted to a risk-averse attention to detail and the varied surfaces, objects and spaces that comprised the environment where a case had been discovered. Items in close contact such as clothes were a particular danger, but walls, carpets and even cutlery and books were rendered suspect. Ideally, nothing would escape some form of disinfection.

[9]On stamping out, see A. Hardy, *The Epidemic Streets: Infectious Disease and the Rise of Preventive Medicine, 1856–1900* (Oxford, 1993), pp. 6–7, 116–28; G. Mooney 'Public Health versus Private Practice: The Contested Development of Compulsory Infectious Disease Notification in Late Nineteenth-Century Britain', *Bulletin of the History of Medicine* 73 (1999), pp. 238–67; and Baldwin, *Contagion and the State in Europe, 1830–1930*, pp. 149–55, 319–23.

[10]A useful overview of these immensely complex provisions is L.C. Parkes, *Infectious Diseases: Notification and Prevention* (London, 1894).

The process began once a case of infection had been notified to a MOH or discovered by a sanitary inspector. Basic practices such as opening windows persisted, thereby allowing for the introduction of sunlight and fresh air, or what some referred to as 'natural disinfectants'.[11] Likewise, carpets and rugs were beaten; floors were brushed and swept. Otherwise it was a question of practising disinfection by heat or by the application of chemicals. Mattresses, bedding and clothes were normally taken from the home and treated by heat, whether in the form of boil-washing, steaming or baking in dry heat. It seems that practices gravitated towards the use of steam, partly because it did less damage to fabrics (there was some concern for the value of private property). Commercial agents and manufacturers played a crucial role in this respect. An abundance of specialist technologies emerged from the 1870s, which were variously located at refuse works, isolation hospitals or in purpose-built municipal disinfection stations. The most popular models were Lyon's Steam Disinfector, the Equifex Saturated Steam Disinfector and Reck's Disinfecting Machine.[12] They were readily used: in just one quarter of 1898, for instance, Manchester Corporation disinfected over 4000 textile items using municipal machinery.[13]

Municipal agents such as sanitary inspectors might also apply chemical disinfectants in situ, at the location where a case had been discovered or reported. Houses were emptied of inhabitants and then fumigated, normally using sulphur burned in iron receptacles; chlorine gas and later formalin were also used. Whitewashers would then follow, cleansing surfaces with substances such as caustic soda; wallpaper might be stripped and removed.[14] Yet, as with other forms of managing risk examined in this volume, this was not solely about mobilizing the agency of officials; the public also had an important role to play. This was especially the case in relation to the 'sick room', the place where the afflicted—should they have

[11] H.C. O'Neill and E.A. Barnett, *Our Nurses and the Work they Have to Do* (London, 1888), p. 130; R. Roose, *Infection and Disinfection* (London, 1888), p. 36.

[12] J. Priestley, 'Disinfectors and Disinfectants, 1874–95: A Contrast', *The Sanitary Record*, 5 July 1895, pp. 18–21.

[13] [J. Niven], *Health Officer Report: Second Quarterly Report, 1898* (Manchester, 1898), p. 15.

[14] J. Robinson, *Sanitary Inspectors' Practical Guide*, 2nd edn (London, 1884), pp. 104–9; E.F. Willoughby, *The Health Officer's Pocket-book: A Guide to Sanitary Practice and Law for Medical Officers of Health, Sanitary Inspectors, Members of Sanitary Authorities, etc.* (London, 1893), pp. 111–26; and A. Taylor, *The Sanitary Inspector's Handbook* (London, 1893), pp. 123–47.

been permitted to stay at home rather than sent to a hospital facility—were looked after and nursed. Given their enjoyment of more spacious homes, it was the middle and upper classes that were the principal practitioners of domestic sick nursing. The location was normally an upstairs bedroom, suitably divested of any objects that might harbour germs, such as rugs or carpets and any superfluous furniture. It was then a question of enacting the kinds of measures employed by municipal authorities. Once the room had been vacated, for instance, rooms were fumigated, walls were white-washed and repapered, and floors and furniture scrubbed with disinfectant solutions.[15]

Domestic sick nursing was only occasional—a matter of acting and improvising only when an infection had struck. Members of the public, however, including the working classes, were also enlisted as agents of more regular, preventive practices of disinfection. This was partly encouraged via the work of voluntary societies and official agents, and a profusion of popular advice texts on the subject of domestic economy. Disinfection advice usually took a standard form, detailing the objects and surfaces that needed attention, various disinfecting methods and the need for routine, timetabled practices. It was also encouraged by a growing number of commercial manufacturers keen to sell their disinfectant products, which in turn entailed the use of adverts that featured in popular newspapers and magazines.[16] Mid-nineteenth-century products such as Burnett's Fluid (derived from zinc chloride) and Condy's Fluid (potassium permanganate) remained popular. The most notable development, which began during the 1870s, was the promotion of carbolic acid (phenol) and related products involving cresols such as Jeyes' Fluid, Izal and Lysol.[17] Quite how and to what extent these products were used is difficult to discern. Class and the size of household budgets mattered enormously, even if it is clear that cleansing was a gendered activity, for it was principally housewives and (female) domestic servants who applied the substances in

[15] On sick nursing, see, among other accounts, T. Billroth, *The Care of the Sick at Home and in the Hospital: A Handbook for Families and Nurses* (London, 1890); A. Schofield, *Manual of Personal and Domestic Hygiene* (London, 1894); and A. Newsholme, *Hygiene: A Manual of Personal and Public Health* (London, 1902).

[16] L. Loeb, *Consuming Angels: Advertising and Victorian Women* (Oxford, 1993), p. 7; D. Vincent, *Literacy and Popular Culture: England, 1750–1914* (Cambridge, 1989), p. 169.

[17] On the multiple products available, see J. Gay, *Disinfection and Disinfectants* (London, 1895), pp. 6–10; and G. Newman, *Bacteriology and the Public Health*, 3rd edn (London, 1904), pp. 439–44.

practice. Nonetheless, recent work suggests that cleansing rituals changed among women of all classes, including the more regular and intense use of disinfectant products.[18]

Professionals and officials were acutely aware of the need for public co-operation of this sort: as was so often affirmed, improvements in public health were best secured through the voluntary efforts of members of the public rather than through recourse to official hectoring and legal compulsion.[19] Professionals, however, were equally concerned about the choices the public made in the context of a commercialization of disinfection products and their variable chemical composition and efficacy. The recommendation of apparently useless disinfectants was a source of concern throughout the period 1870–1914. Professional authors dismissed popular disinfectants as 'parlour disinfectants' and 'placebos' or, again, as 'useless' and 'a mockery to those who do know [about disinfection] and a mischievous delusion to those who do not'.[20] The more restrained critics commented that the composition of many commercial disinfectants was unknown and thus their effectiveness was unverified. Many commentators attributed this to the wily ways of manufacturers. Marketing methods were seen as 'dubious at best'.[21] Other authors claimed that advertisers knew the extent of public ignorance and actively exploited it.[22]

We should perhaps expect as much: commercial operators were concerned to maximize revenue, while professionals were concerned to enhance the health of the public. Criticisms of a burgeoning market of commercial disinfectants, however, were part of a wider debate: could the public be relied upon to undertake effective disinfection at all? This too

[18] See especially V. Kelley, *Soap and Water: Cleanliness, Dirt and the Working Classes in Victorian and Edwardian Britain* (London, 2010).

[19] Hardy, *The Epidemic Streets*, pp. 267–80; T. Crook, 'Sanitary Inspection and the Public Sphere in Late-Victorian and Edwardian Britain: A Case Study in Liberal Governance', *Social History* 32 (2007), pp. 384–9.

[20] 'Disinfectants', *Medical Times and Gazette*, 1 November 1873, p. 488; 'Improvements in Pharmacy', *BMJ*, 13 February 1886, p. 312; Roose, *Infection and Disinfection*, p. 55; C.G. Moor and T.H. Pearmain [with R.H. Tanner], *Applied Bacteriology*, 3rd edn (London, 1906), p. 373; H.M. Richards, 'The Cleansing of Schoolrooms', *Public Health* 22 (1908–9), p. 461; and T.W. Naylor Barlow, 'Disinfectants: Their Scientific Uses, their Quack Uses and their Dangers', *Public Health* 23 (1909–10), p. 230.

[21] E. Crisp, *Smallpox and its Prevention* (London, 1871), p. 5; Richards, 'The Cleansing of Schoolrooms', p. 461; and Naylor Barlow, 'Disinfectants', p. 230.

[22] H. Kenwood, 'The Unbridled Practice of Medical Quackery', *Public Health* 13 (1900–1), p. 102.

might be expected, given the difficulties of regulating practices that took place in private homes, but the verdict was generally negative, and the consensus among medical and public health professionals was that the public was poorly informed about disease prevention. In 1893, Birmingham's MOH, Dr Alfred Bostock Hill, noted that people were altogether ignorant about the nature of *materies morbi* and that there was a 'hopeless fog' in their minds as to the differences between antiseptics, disinfectants and deodorants, and the correct uses of these agents, meaning that public efforts often did more harm than good.[23] Just as despairingly, another MOH, T.W. Naylor Barlow, stated that 'the man in the street [thinks] that you just have to show a microbe a disinfectant and it would immediately succumb'.[24] It reflected a deeper administrative problem: whereas some kind of control might be exercised over disinfection measures undertaken by local authorities—the substances used and the rigour of their application, for example—this was not true of those undertaken by members of the public, and especially women, in homes. And yet, these were just as essential to securing a safe, germ-free environment and closing down the risk of the generation and transmission of infectious diseases. It was against this backdrop that discussions about the safety of chemical disinfectants in the home played out.

Disinfectants, Poisons and Safety

Poisons were part of everyday life before more or less toxic disinfectants were introduced. Notably, given its wide array of uses—from killing rats and dyeing wallpaper to preserving dead animals (taxidermy)—arsenic was freely available to purchase before the 1851 Arsenic Act, which sought, however unsuccessfully, to limit its use to industrial and agricultural practices.[25] Other poisonous materials that found their way into the home included lead (in pipes), alum (in bread) and boracic acid (in milk). Marketed to the public for widespread use as part of day-to-day cleanliness rituals, disinfectants added to the number of harmful substances that

[23] 'Proceedings of the Birmingham Branch', *Public Health* 6 (1893–4), p. 49.

[24] Naylor Barlow, 'Disinfectants', p. 230.

[25] P. Bartrip, '"A Pennurth of Arsenic for Rat Poison": The Arsenic Act 1851 and the Prevention of Secret Poisoning', *Medical History* 36 (1992), pp. 53–69; J.C. Whorton, *The Arsenic Century: How Victorian Britain was Poisoned at Home, Work and Play* (Oxford, 2011), pp. 133–8.

could be found in the home.[26] This was recognized at the time and the issue of the safety of disinfectants was debated from the 1860s onwards. It is especially evident in discussions about the hypothetically 'perfect' disinfectant. Many professional authors set out a list of characteristics which the ideal disinfectant should possess, specifying that it was desirable it should be non-poisonous and non-irritant.[27] It is clear that safety, both in terms of non-toxicity when ingested and to a lesser extent in terms of damage to the skin or wounds, was a crucial consideration when contemplating the ideal disinfectant.

Commentators did not always elaborate on why safety was so important, but judging by the other qualities often detailed, it seems safety served a dual purpose: it protected the health of those using the disinfectant and it ensured that disinfection was undertaken properly and thoroughly. Indeed, at the most basic level, safety was necessary to ensure that chemical disinfectants saved lives rather than took them away; and although those recommending their use would not have been liable for any deadly consequences, any deaths would have undermined the willingness to practise disinfection. Crucially, safety featured in the promotion of disinfectants. Popular advice texts, as well as adverts in the press, singled out non-toxicity and harmless action on human tissue as significant features.[28] During the 1880s and 1890s, adverts for Jeyes' Fluid described it as the 'Best, Safest and Cheapest' disinfectant, noting that it was non-toxic and did not burn the skin.[29] Similarly, Izal was promoted as the 'New Non-Poisonous Disinfectant' and as 'the most effective and safest Disinfectant'.[30] Manufacturers, it might be argued, would hardly have claimed anything else, but that these considerations featured so prominently suggests a wider public concern with safety, and that non-toxicity was a quality demanded by at least some sections of the public.

[26] J.H. Timins, *On Artificial Disinfectants* (London, 1878), p. 16; G.H. Giffen, *Students' Manual of Medical Jurisprudence and Public Health*, 2nd edn (London, 1906), p. 170.

[27] [Anon.], *The Disinfectant Question* (London, 1869), p. 31; G. Nuttall, *Hygienic Measures in Relation to Infectious Diseases* (London, 1893), p. 16; W.W. Beveridge and C.F. Wanhill, *The Sanitary Officer's Handbook* (London, 1912), p. 186.

[28] In terms of advice texts, see Roose, *Infection and Disinfection*, pp. 42–3, and S. Rideal, *Disinfection and the Preservation of Food* (London, 1903), p. 221.

[29] See, for instance, *The Sporting Times*, 11 June 1887; p. 8; *The County Gentleman*, 22 October 1887; p. 1431; *Pall Mall Gazette*, 31 July 1895, p. 1; *Daily News*, 4 September 1900, p. 1.

[30] See, for instance, *Hearth and Home*, 6 July 1893, p 287; *The Graphic*, 19 August 1893, p. 3; and *Nottinghamshire Guardian*, 12 January 1895, p. 1.

There was, however, an opposing viewpoint that challenged the idea that safety should be privileged and prioritized. Put simply, 'safety' was worthless if the disinfectant was either ineffective or needed to be used in large and expensive quantities. Tellingly, lists of the characteristics of a perfect disinfectant always listed effectiveness, but not always safety. It was not uncommon to subordinate safety to effectiveness. C.G. Moor and T.H. Pearmain, for instance, in their professional handbook *Applied Bacteriology*, first published in 1897, stated that while it was 'indispensable' for any disinfectant to be effective, it was only 'desirable' that it was non-poisonous and non-caustic (though they did grant that disinfectants that were lethal by limited contact were unusable).[31] Others made the point that combining efficacy and non-toxicity was intrinsically difficult. As early as 1869, the leading Scottish chemist Robert Angus Smith stated that 'all disinfectants are poisonous in sufficient quantity', further explaining that disinfectants were 'safe' only because the amount needed to kill germs was less than the amount that would kill an animal.[32] For Smith, a wholly non-poisonous disinfectant was a contradiction in terms. The problem of reconciling these qualities was a common point of reference, including among local officials, for they too had to make choices about which disinfectants to employ. 'In selecting a disinfectant for general use, cheapness in comparison with their disinfecting power, and freedom from poisonous qualities seem to be leading indications', noted one metropolitan MOH before an audience of sanitary inspectors in 1885. 'Unfortunately, however, most of those which are cheap and non-poisonous are not sufficiently active for general use', he added, singling out the chemicals alum and chloral.[33]

Bacteriology played a crucial role in sapping professional confidence in non-poisonous disinfectants, in particular research during the 1890s and early 1900s that demonstrated the relative hardiness of germs compared to human cells. Writing in 1903, F.W. Andrewes, then a lecturer at St Bartholomew's Hospital, London, set out a typical opinion that disinfectants intended for common use 'must not produce too injurious an effect on the human tissue with which it comes into contact'. Nevertheless, he also stated that it was unrealistic to expect a disinfectant to be non-toxic, as this would compromise its effectiveness: 'It is too much to ask',

[31] Moor and Pearmain, *Applied Bacteriology*, pp. 363–4.

[32] R.A. Smith, *Disinfection and Disinfectants* (Edinburgh, 1869), p. 126.

[33] J.W. Tripe, 'Disinfectants and their Uses', *The Sanitary Record*, 15 April 1885, p. 438.

he went on, that any practical disinfectant 'should be non-poisonous to man'.[34] Others again, though stopping short of ruling out the idea that a non-poisonous disinfectant might exist, were sceptical that any might be found.[35] It is telling that these statements were made for the most part by medical practitioners and bacteriologists, whose primary concern was setting out professional standards rather than providing popular instruction. There was evidently a divide between professional and public opinion. The divide was not absolute: bacteriologists might be positive about some popular disinfectants, in particular those derived from coal tar. Yet these same bacteriologists were often sceptical that these substances were, as some sought to claim, truly 'non-poisonous'.[36] For professionals and experts at least, toxicity was a crucial quality of any 'true' disinfectant, and safety was subordinate, within reason, to germicidal effectiveness. Some degree of danger was a necessary part of any effective form of domestic disinfection—a practice, as we have seen, that was also judged crucial to reducing the risk of infection.

Carbolic Acid and Suicide: Balancing Public Health and Public Safety

The tension between these different—if complementary and necessarily interlinked—risks is amply apparent in debates that emerged during the 1890s regarding the safety of carbolic acid. Also known as phenol, carbolic acid was (and remains) a moderately strong caustic poison and ingesting the substance can cause a painful and lingering death. Carbolic as a disinfectant achieved widespread popularity among both the public and public health professionals from the 1870s, becoming the second most popular disinfectant after sulphur by 1880.[37] Its use was not without injury, however. Carbolic acid is recorded as having caused deaths from 1866, and as the number of cases rose during the 1870s and 1880s,

[34] F.W. Andrewes, *Lessons in Disinfection and Sterilisation: An Elementary Course of Bacteriology, Together with a Scheme of Practical Experiments Illustrating the Subject-Matter* (London, 1903), p. 90.

[35] W. Partridge, *Bacteriological Examination of Disinfectants* (London, 1907), p. 9.

[36] G. Newman, *Bacteria, especially as they are related to the Economy of Nature, to Industrial Processes and to the Public Health* (London, 1899), p. 333; Andrewes, *Lessons in Disinfection and Sterilisation*, p. 90; and Rideal, *Disinfection and the Preservation of Food*, pp. 220–1.

[37] J. Spottiswoode Cameron, 'Sanitary Progress During the Last Twenty Five Years and in the Next', *Public Health* 15 (1902–3), pp. 69–70.

greater attention was paid to the problem, prompting discussion as to how to reduce the death toll.[38] These included reforming the labelling and design of the bottles in which it was commonly sold, as well as attempts to extend control via either new regulations or for carbolic to be included under the 1868 Pharmacy and Poisons Act (see below).[39] At this point, discussion was limited: the comparatively low death tolls made this primarily an issue for toxicology and clinical practice rather than the media and the government.

This was to change as the death toll from carbolic increased. In 1889, significant rises in carbolic-related fatalities raised concerns, receiving expression in a number of medical journals.[40] In 1891, the surgeon J. Brendon Curgenven claimed that the Registrar-General's reports showed that carbolic was 'a highly dangerous poison in the hands of the public'.[41] The issue came to the fore in 1893, when the Tory MP John Macdona compiled mortality figures using the Registrar-General's statistics, revealing a shockingly rapid increase in the number of deaths, most of which were suicides. He submitted these to Parliament for discussion and attempted to get the figures publicized by the Home Office.[42] The 'scandal' of carbolic deaths was now brought to widespread medical attention. *The Lancet* and the *British Medical Journal* (*BMJ*), as well as *The Times*, supported Macdona's campaign and called for regulation in order to reduce deaths.[43] For the medical profession and for some sections of the press, it seemed obvious that the suicide death toll from carbolic poisoning was rising rapidly and required action.

It is instructive to consider the trends in carbolic deaths in order to see what exactly this concern was based upon. Peter Bartrip has illustrated the way in which the arsenic panic of the 1840s was whipped up by the media and used to advantage by the medical profession (something that partly explains the passage of the 1851 Act noted above).[44] Was the carbolic

[38] *The Times*, 15 July 1869, p. 4; *The Times*, 7 August 1878, p. 10.

[39] G.W. Harrison, 'Case of Suicide by Carbolic Acid', *The Lancet*, 25 July 1868, p. 133.

[40] See especially 'Preventable Poisoning', *BMJ*, 23 February 1889, pp. 424–5.

[41] J.B. Curgenven, *The Disinfection of Scarlet Fever and other Infectious Diseases by Antiseptic Inunction* (London, 1891), p. 6.

[42] 'Parliamentary Intelligence', *The Lancet*, 9 December 1893, pp. 1482–3.

[43] A.E. Harris, 'The Fatal Record of Carbolic Acid', *The Lancet*, 28 November 1896, pp. 1519–20; *The Times*, 25 June 1898, p. 10; 'Carbolic Acid and the Pharmacy Acts', *BMJ*, 24 February 1894, p. 427.

[44] Bartrip, '"A Pennurth of arsenic for Rat Poison"'.

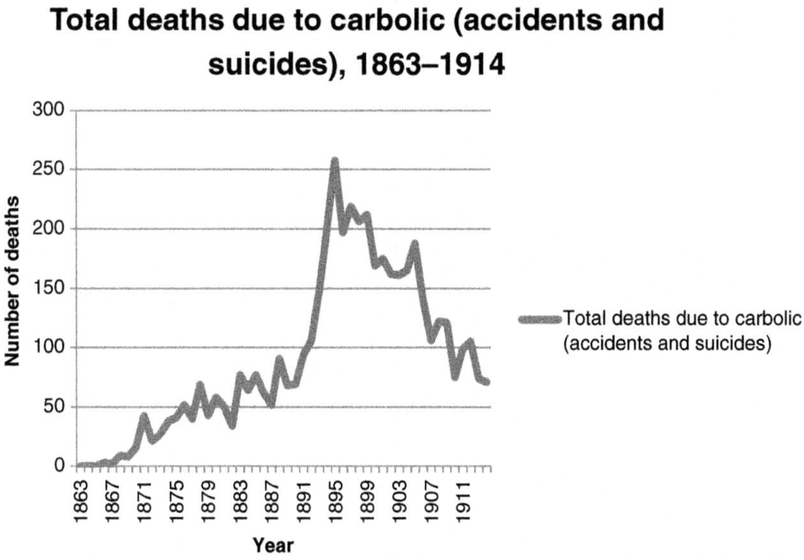

Fig. 6.1 Total deaths due to carbolic (accidents and suicides), 1863–1914. Figures derived from the *Annual Reports of the Registrar-General of Births, Deaths and Marriages* for England and Wales

panic of the mid-1890s also more to do with media attention than an actual rise in carbolic-related deaths? Figure 6.1 shows the total number of deaths between 1863 and 1914. Deaths increased moderately throughout the 1870s and 1880s, but leapt in the 1890s, making it—as the revered chemist and MOH A.W. Blyth was later to comment—'the most prolific poison' of the decade.[45] There was then a decline towards the end of the period. These statistics can be broken down into accidents and suicides. Some suicides were probably returned as accidents, so the two categories were not completely separate. They do, however, show differing trends, as figure 6.2 demonstrates. Clearly, the greatest number of carbolic deaths throughout the period was due to suicides, which peaked in the mid-1890s. The cause of this is difficult to explain, as with all suicides, but it is

[45] A.W. Blyth and M.W. Blyth, *Poisons: Their Effects and Detection*, 4th edn (London, 1906), p. 32.

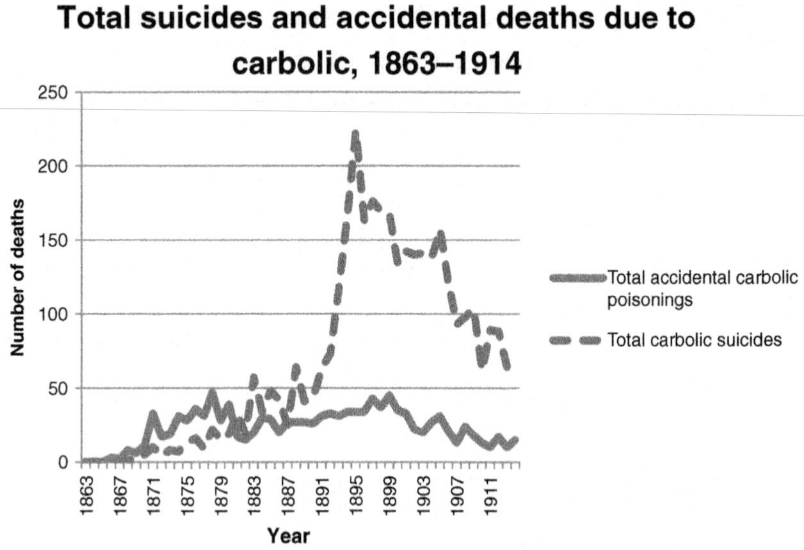

Fig. 6.2 Total suicides and accidental deaths due to carbolic, 1863–1914. Figures derived from the *Annual Reports of the Registrar-General of Births, Deaths and Marriages* for England and Wales

likely to be only partially answered by the wider availability of the chemical as a disinfectant.

Nonetheless, though the question of causality remains unclear, the result was intensified calls for regulatory action, which initially concentrated on slotting carbolic into existing frameworks. As it stood, substances classified as 'poisons' were regulated under the 1868 Pharmacy and Poisons Act, which set out two schedules.[46] Schedule 1 listed the most dangerous substances, among them arsenic, prussic acid, cyanide and emetic tartar, which were accordingly subject to more stringent control. Pharmacists were to sell these only to known individuals or people introduced by someone known. The name of the poison, quantity and purpose for which it was to be used, as well as the name of the purchaser and the date of sale were to be entered in a special 'poison book', signed by the purchaser and dispenser. The bottle had to be labelled 'poison' and

[46] H.H.L. Bellot, *The Pharmacy Acts, 1851–1908* (London, 1908), Chapter 3.

carry the name and address of the seller. Schedule 2, on the other hand, listed what were considered less active and less dangerous poisons, which included opiates and oxalic acid, and patent medicines containing morphine and mercury. There was no requirement to register any transactions, but it was stipulated that the substances had to be sold labelled with the chemical's name, the word 'poison' and the name and address of the seller. Both schedules limited sale to licensed retailers and registered chemists, and imposed penalties for infringement.

It was supposed that including carbolic within the 1868 Act would enforce safer retailing practices. Registered chemists were thought to be safer, as they already followed reasonable precautions in terms of labelling.[47] But not all retailers were voluntarily following safe practices. Unregistered oil shops and grocers came under fire for selling carbolic in unlabelled teacups, bottles and jars, ignoring even the most basic safety precautions. Some commentators even suggested that having carbolic in a grocer's shop alongside household products made it appear safe, thereby encouraging complacency. The 'unsafe' availability of carbolic from such outlets meant that even when other retailers refused to sell carbolic, customers could simply go elsewhere. Regulation, it was argued, was needed to control the behaviour of these people or exclude them from selling carbolic entirely.[48]

The campaign involved the mobilization of various professional groups, including the Pharmaceutical Society, founded in 1841 to represent chemists and pharmaceutical retailers, which had an established consultative role in relation to legislation. Medical journals and the British Medical Association were active in promoting regulation throughout the 1890s, frequently calling upon the Pharmaceutical Society to take action.[49] Coroners repeatedly recommended that carbolic be added to the poisons schedule to help prevent accidents and suicides.[50] The *Chemist and Druggist*, a journal representing professional chemists,

[47] 'Poisoning by Misadventure: Opinions of the Press', *BMJ*, 27 January 1894, pp. 208–9.

[48] 'Poisoning by Misadventure', *BMJ*, 9 July 1892, p. 91; 'Poisoning by Carbolic Acid', *BMJ*, 16 December 1893, pp. 1341–2; 'Poisoning by Carbolic Acid', *BMJ*, 6 October 1894, p. 774.

[49] 'Preventable Poisoning', *BMJ*, 23 February 1889, pp. 424–5; J.H. Davies, 'Two Cases of Fatal Poisoning by Carbolic Acid', *The Lancet*, 8 March 1890, p. 539.

[50] *The Times*, 13 April 1891, p. 4; 'The Sale of Poisons', *BMJ*, 13 November 1897, p. 1441; *Chemist and Druggist*, 25 June 1898, p. 1009.

supported this campaign.[51] Official agents also played a part: in 1893, the Local Government Board (LGB) acted on Macdona's parliamentary efforts by writing to the Pharmaceutical Society to recommend that it start the process of adding carbolic to the schedules contained in the 1868 statute. With this effort ending in failure, the LGB then made a 'strong representation' to the Privy Council, which had the power to amend legislation in a swift fashion (in particular via Orders in Council) and introduce bills of its own.[52]

These efforts were not without consequence, if also not without frustration. Earlier, in 1892, the Pharmaceutical Society had decided to recommend the inclusion of carbolic within the Poisons Act and made a formal request to the Privy Council for this to be done. After this was rebuffed, the Society made two more requests in 1894 and 1895, which were once again unsuccessful. The Privy Council acknowledged the calls for regulation, but refused to heed them.[53] The reasons the Privy Council gave for denying the addition of carbolic to the 1868 Act were telling. It doubted whether regulation would decrease the number of deaths, given that most carbolic deaths were suicides that would have occurred anyway. More importantly, carbolic was felt to be too valuable to allow any restriction. Regulation would limit the public's ability to get hold of a necessary chemical and would have a negative impact on trade, thus threatening both public health and general economic well-being.[54] Unsurprisingly, this view was shared by the carbolic industry. In 1893, Mr Calvert, the owner of a company that produced a range of carbolic-based disinfectants (generally under the name of Calvert's), claimed that the increase in deaths was much smaller than increases in poisoning due to other scheduled substances and rejected the idea that suicides could be prevented by regulation.[55] All in all, so

[51] *Chemist and Druggist*, 25 May 1889, p. 730; *Chemist and Druggist*, 1 November 1890, p. 623; *Chemist and Druggist*, 2 February 1895, p. 188.

[52] 'Poisoning by Carbolic Acid', *BMJ*, 16 December 1893; 'Carbolic Acid and the Pharmacy Acts', *BMJ*, 24 February 1894, p. 427.

[53] 'Poisoning by Carbolic Acid', *BMJ*, 6 January 1894, p. 34; *Chemist and Druggist*, 19 October 1895, p. 591; 'Poisoning by Carbolic Acid', *BMJ*, 26 September 1896, pp. 871–2.

[54] *The Times*, 25 June 1898, p 10; 'Parliamentary Intelligence', *The Lancet*, 2 July 1898, pp. 62–6.

[55] 'Poisoning by Carbolic Acid', *BMJ*, 30 December 1893, p. 1446.

it was suggested, regulation would cause myriad problems and provide few benefits.

The pros and cons were much debated and further comment ensued for and against intervention. The *BMJ*, for instance, writing in 1894, continued to urge that existing legislation was perfectly suitable and that the only obstacle was the agreement of the Privy Council.[56] Another editorial in 1896 suggested that the continuing high number of deaths meant that concerns about the public availability of disinfectants and placing restrictions on trade should be put to one side.[57] It was not, however, a truly popular debate: although the question of regulation attracted occasional comment in the daily press, discussion was largely limited to professional journals such as the *BMJ*, *The Lancet* and *Chemist and Druggist*. This was perhaps because carbolic was linked to the altogether sensitive issue of suicide: the public might have feared arsenic hidden in sweets, but could be—or at least were supposed to be—confident that they were not at risk of committing suicide, whatever the poisons to hand.

Eventually, the Privy Council succumbed and in 1896 it agreed to consider a general revision of the Poisons Act. In keeping with other reforming initiatives of the period, such as those relating to tort law and the regulation of dangerous trades, this proved a slow process and was not without expressions of frustration on the part of professionals. Indeed, the breakthrough had to wait until 1900, when the Privy Council ordered that preparations containing over 3 % of carbolic acid or its homologues had to be added to the list of the less dangerous 'scheduled poisons', which in practice meant they had to be sold only by approved retailers and supplied in bottles clearly labelled as 'poison'.[58] The 1900 Order thus upheld the role of chemists in managing the risks posed by saleable poisons, and it was largely welcomed by doctors and chemists, though misgivings were expressed about the extent to which the measure was publicized. A blow had been struck for safety over and against the dangers of indiscriminate commercial availability and unregulated consumption.

Unsurprisingly, complaints were made by retailers, who were opposed to their trade being, as they saw it, unfairly damaged for what was little public benefit, and this in turn prompted medical and chemical journals

[56] 'Carbolic Acid and the Pharmacy Acts', *BMJ*, 24 February 1894, p. 427.

[57] 'Poisoning by Carbolic Acid', *BMJ*, 26 September 1896.

[58] 'The Scheduling of Carbolic Acid', *The Lancet*, 8 September 1900, p. 752; 'The Regulation of the Sale of Carbolic', *The Lancet*, 19 January 1901, pp. 200–1.

to suggest that this was merely irresponsible retailers attempting to defend their unsafe trade.[59] Equally, however, not all professionals toed this pro-regulation line, or at least not without pointing to the pitfalls. The argument was twofold: first, regulation had restricted the supply of what, in the hands of most people, was a useful substance for preserving health and preventing the spread of disease and sickness; and, second, it had encouraged the manufacture and supply of weaker, less effective disinfectants. In 1902, an editorial in the *Public Health Engineer* argued that regulation had limited the sale of carbolic for public health purposes. Noting how disinfection was especially useful when it came to preventing the spread of smallpox, it stated:

> They [the Government] have virtually, by prohibiting the general trade from selling it, withdrawn what is regarded as one of the strongest disinfectants from the market. Under the poisons schedule of the Pharmacy Act of 1868, the sale of carbolic acid ... is restricted to duly registered chemists and druggists, with the result that the public have foisted on them by unscrupulous purveyors so-called disinfectants that do not disinfect at all, because they do not contain more than three per cent of the 'poison'.

It went on to add that although carbolic might have been the cause of death of 'one or two suicidal maniacs', it was also capable of saving 'the lives of thousands'. What it called 'grandmotherly interference' had deprived the public of a crucial means of sanitary self-protection and of banishing the danger of infectious diseases. 'We are fearfully and wonderfully governed!', it concluded, ironically.[60]

This was not a lone voice. Medical commentators suggested that regulation would merely encourage manufacturers to downgrade the carbolic content of disinfectant preparations, making them less effective. Regulation had 'placed a premium on inefficiency'.[61] The concern was not baseless: manufacturers themselves claimed they had done just this to avoid their

[59] 'The Carbolic Worry', *Chemist and Druggist*, 8 September 1900, p. 414; 'The Sale of Carbolic Acid', *Chemist and Druggist*, 29 September 1900, p. 549.

[60] 'The Sale of Disinfectants', *Public Health Engineer*, 1 February 1902, pp. 81–2.

[61] 'Medical Notes in Parliament', *BMJ*, 1 May 1909, p. 1085; S. Rideal, 'Disinfection', *Journal of the Royal Sanitary Institute* 28 (1907), p. 374; 'Regulation of Carbolic Acid', *Chemist and Druggist*, 8 June 1907, p. 875.

products being restricted.[62] There were repeated calls from the medical and chemical journals for the LGB to rectify the problem, though it was not clear what might be done, save for encouraging MOsH to educate the public about the matter.[63] Others posited a shift in consumer preferences, pointing towards the growing popularity of safer creolin and other weaker coal tar preparations.[64] In 1909, R. Tanner Hewlett, delivering the annual Milroy Lecture organized by the Royal College of Physicians, claimed that regulations had flooded the market with 'less than 3 % carbolic' preparations.[65] It seems that, however unintentionally, regulation did indeed promote the use of ineffective disinfectants.

Equally, it is not entirely clear whether such measures actually diminished death tolls. As figures 6.1 and 6.2 suggest, given the overall decline that took place during the Edwardian period, it could be that regulation helped to encourage greater safety and responsibility. Yet the decline in carbolic-related deaths was uneven and, in any case, it started during the mid-1890s, some years before regulation began, which suggests that regulation was merely one of many factors at work. Further regulations would ensue, however, before the Edwardian period was out. Most notably, in 1913, the Privy Council enacted a measure that reflected the difficulties involved in managing what was a useful if dangerous substance.[66] On the one hand, amid ongoing concerns about carbolic-related deaths, it extended existing regulations to all carbolic preparations, of whatever strength or form; on the other hand, in order to ensure easy availability to the public, it lifted restrictions on where these products could be sold. Carbolic products were once more freely available, so long as they were properly labelled with the word 'poison' and the name and address of the vendor. The Privy Council intended this to settle the problems that had arisen since its Order of 1900 and to sidestep calls for the further regulation of the strength of disinfectants. The repeated calls for increased safety

[62] *Committee on Poisons: Minutes of Evidence taken before the Departmental Committee Appointed by the Lord President of the Council to Consider Schedule A to the Pharmacy Act, 1868. Part II* (Parl. Papers 1903 [Cd. 1443]), pp. 58–9.

[63] 'Medical Notes in Parliament', *BMJ*, 1 May 1909, p. 1085; *Chemist and Druggist*, 22 June 1907, p. 948; *Chemist and Druggist*, 24 April 1909, p. 632.

[64] 'The Standardisation of Disinfectants', *The Lancet*, 13 November 1909, p. 1454.

[65] R.T. Hewlett, 'The Milroy Lectures on Disinfection and Disinfectants', *The Lancet*, 27 March 1909, p. 894.

[66] 'The Sale of Carbolic Acid', *The Times*, 21 October 1912, p. 19; 'Medical News', *BMJ*, 26 April 1913, p. 919.

in the sale and use of carbolic disinfection had paid off, albeit not without some concessions to its effectiveness as a popular sanitary technology.

Conclusion: The Dilemmas of Disinfection

Carbolic acid, it should be emphasized, was not the only disinfectant substance embroiled in regulatory debates and difficult choices: mercury chloride, also referred to as corrosive sublimate, was another that attracted the attention of the press and professionals, if not to the same extent as carbolic.[67] Nor were humans and matters of disease prevention the only sources of anxiety during the 1870–1914 period. In 1901, for instance, the Privy Council appointed a committee to look into the revision of the 1868 Poisons Act, but, on the evidence that the committee received, it was forced to conclude that matters of agriculture (in particular the use of disinfectants in sheep-dips) and horticulture (the use of disinfectant to protect crops from weeds, parasitical insects and fungoid growths) were just as important as those of what it dubbed 'sanitation'.[68]

Nonetheless, the rise and popularity of carbolic serves as a useful case study of the dilemmas of disinfection. On the one hand, disinfectants had to be both effective and germicidal, and popular and accessible. Although local authorities carried out disinfection in response to outbreaks of infection, the ongoing work of the public—and women especially—in the domestic sphere was required in order to prevent outbreaks from happening in the first place. On the other hand, however, these very requirements, all of which were crucial to managing the risk of infection, also introduced risks of their own, not least that carbolic might be mishandled or even used as a means of suicide. Despite extensive attempts to make carbolic safer by presenting it in distinctive bottles, fully labelled and sold by responsible retailers, the continued number of deaths indicate that at least some consumers could not be relied upon to use disinfectants responsibly, even where extensive information had been provided. The risks at stake were many and varied, extending beyond the risk of infection.

[67] For a fuller discussion, see Whyte, 'Changing Approaches to Disinfection in England, c. 1848–1914', Chapter 6.

[68] *Committee on Poisons: Report, Supplementary Report and Minority Report, of the Departmental Committee Appointed by the Lord President of the Council to Consider Schedule A to the Pharmacy Act, 1868. Part I* (Parl. Papers 1903 [Cd. 1442]), pp. v–ix.

Regulation was accordingly difficult. Legislation was needed to regulate poisonous disinfectant substances and ensure, at the very least, that they were labelled as such—as 'poisonous', that is, which in the case of carbolic preparations meant those that contained 3 % or more carbolic acid. Yet there was also a countervailing argument to this. As we have seen, there was significant concern about the use of ineffective disinfectants. Many 'safe' disinfectants were reckoned to be useless at killing bacteria. It was also suggested that members of the public did not truly understand the importance or proper applications of disinfection and were thus misled by slickly marketed commercial preparations that were simply not strong enough. Certainly the debates on safety demonstrate ambivalence regarding the role of the public. Whilst public co-operation was needed, members of the public were often characterized as likely to poison themselves with effective disinfectants, or else lull themselves into a false sense of security by using 'safe' but ineffective preparations. Safety regulation was a double-edged sword: although regulation might protect the public, helping to secure more responsible patterns of consumption and use, it could also threaten public health by undermining effective disinfection. Somehow a balance had to be struck between public safety and public health.

CHAPTER 7

Risk, Time and Everyday Environmentalism in Modern Britain

Timothy Cooper

This chapter uses Marxist categories of analysis to investigate the relationship between ideas of risk, time and what radical geography has termed 'everyday environmentalism' in modern Britain.[1] The concept of everyday environmentalism offers an explicit counterpoint to traditional historical approaches to environmental risk, which have, either implicitly or explicitly, given primacy to ecological ideas, state activity and scientific expertise in the formation of modern environmental consciousness.[2] By contrast, the concept of an everyday environmentalism claims that the real work of making environmental politics is often done elsewhere, specifically in the sphere of everyday life, which is central to social reproduction.

[1] A. Loftus, *Everyday Environmentalism: Creating an Urban Political Ecology* (Minneapolis, MN, 2012); N. Heynen, M. Kaika and E. Swyngedouw (eds), *In the Nature of Cities: Urban Political Ecology and the Politics of Urban Metabolism* (London, 2005).

[2] M. Veldman, *Fantasy, the Bomb and the Greening of Britain: Romantic Protest, 1945–1980* (Cambridge, 1994); R.H. Grove, *Green Imperialism: Colonial Expansion, Tropical Island Edens and the Origins of Environmentalism, 1600–1860* (Cambridge, 1995); J. Radkau, *Nature and Power: A Global History of the Environment* (Cambridge, 2008).

T. Cooper
College of Humanities, University of Exeter, Penryn Campus,
Cornwall TR10 9FE, UK

T. Crook, M. Esbester (eds), *Governing Risks in Modern Britain*,
DOI 10.1057/978-1-137-46745-4_7

In the everyday realm, an environmental politics is produced in antagonism to the right of the 'expert' or the state to determine acceptable risk. Moreover, this chapter builds on previous attempts to introduce political ecology into historical accounts of risk.[3] It does so by giving analytic priority to quotidian forms of environmental knowledge and politics that are often effaced or erased from analyses of environmental risk that adopt a governmental or state perspective.

However, the idea of everyday environmentalism cannot necessarily be neatly mapped on to the categories of class, gender or race in the manner of classic studies of environmental justice (although those categories invariably arise in its analysis).[4] Rather, the analysis of everyday environmentalism places attention on the range of possible environmental practices that emerge from the contradictions between the requirements of the capitalist accumulation process and the needs of everyday life. As Alex Loftus, for instance, has shown in the case of struggles over water supply in contemporary South Africa, the antagonisms between these two spheres of social reproduction are an important locus of environmental politics.[5]

Environmental hazards and risks offer excellent opportunities for such analysis as they commonly embody just these contradictions. Indeed, the capitalist historical dimension of risk is often underplayed in studies of risk or the risk society—including the studies of Ulrich Beck—which assume that the 'reflexive' critique of risks is characterized by an individuated,

[3] T. Cooper and S. Bulmer, 'Refuse and the "Risk Society": The Political Ecology of Risk in Inter-War Britain', *Social History of Medicine* 26 (2013), pp. 246–66.

[4] R. Bullard, *Dumping in Dixie: Race, Class and Environmental Quality*, 3rd edn (Boulder, CO, 2000); R.D. Bullard and G.S. Johnson, 'Environmentalism and Public Policy: Environmental Justice: Grassroots Activism and its Impact on Public Policy Decision Making', *Journal of Social Issues* 56 (2000), pp. 555–78; G. Massard-Guilbaud and R. Rodger, *Environmental and Social Justice in the City: Historical Perspectives* (Cambridge, 2011); M. McLaughlin, 'The Pied Piper of the Ghetto: Lyndon Johnson, Environmental Justice, and the Politics of Rat Control', *Journal of Urban History* 37 (2011), pp. 541–61; C. Montrie, *A People's History of Environmentalism in the United States* (London, 2011); E.D. Blum, *Love Canal Revisited: Race, Class and Gender in Environmental Activism* (Lawrence, KS, 2011).

[5] A. Loftus, 'Reification and the Dictatorship of the Water Meter', *Antipode* 38 (2006), pp. 1023–45; V. Taylor and F. Trentmann, 'Liquid Politics: Water and the Politics of Everyday Life in the Modern City', *Past & Present* 211 (2011), pp. 199–241; M. Ekers and A. Loftus, 'Revitalizing the Production of Nature Thesis: A Gramscian Turn?', *Progress in Human Geography* 37 (2013), pp. 234–52.

as opposed to a social and collective, culture of politics.[6] Even those who have emphasized the social construction of risk have tended to view society through a cultural lens, where perceptions of risk generate bordering practices for communities, allowing them to patrol a sense of identity.[7] Yet there are other ways to view the production of environmental hazards. In modern societies, environmental risks are often the result of the transformations of nature demanded by the forces of capital.[8] Such risks embody the antinomies between the socio-natural environments required for the accumulation of capital and the often conflicting needs and desires of everyday life.

Here it will be argued that political analysis of antagonisms over nature, health and risk suggests the existence of a subaltern or everyday environmentalism that emerges across, as well as within, the cleavages of class and gender. Such conflicts embody the temporal dimensions and antinomies of social reproduction in capitalist societies. In particular, they reveal some of the tensions between the socio-natures of capital, dedicated to the unceasing accumulation of value, and the social ecologies of everyday life. One consequence of this is that the politics that resist manufactured environmental risks can arise in a wide variety of potential forms, sometimes apparently quite conservative, and often among people who may explicitly reject being labelled as 'environmentalists'.

This chapter adapts Henri Lefebvre's approach to the everyday as a level of the social totality that is composed of overlapping temporalities.[9] For Lefebvre, the everyday can be read musically, as an emergent quality of the interaction of different temporal dimensions or motifs. In the everyday, linear time, the time par excellence of capitalist logics of production and progress, meets cyclical time, the time of biological repetition and social reproduction. Many historical studies of everyday life underplay these

[6] U. Beck, *Risk Society: Towards a New Modernity*, trans. M. Ritter (London, 1992); A. Giddens, *Modernity and Self-Identity: Self and Society in the Late Modern Age* (Cambridge, 1991).

[7] M. Douglas and A. Wildavsky, *Risk and Culture: An Essay on the Selection of Technological and Environmental Dangers* (Berkeley, CA, 1983).

[8] N. Smith, *Uneven Development: Nature, Capital and the Production of Space* (Athens, GA, 2008); N. Castree, 'Marxism and the Production of Nature', *Capital & Class* 24 (2000), pp. 5–36.

[9] H. Lefebvre, *Critique of Everyday Life, Volume 2: Foundations for a Sociology of the Everyday*, trans. J. Moore (London, 2002); H. Lefebvre, *Rhythmanalysis: Space, Time and Everyday Life*, trans. S. Elden and G. Moore (London, 2004).

relationships between materialist concerns with temporality and social reproduction in favour of questions of knowledge, ideas and language.[10] Yet, in everyday life, risk is inherently temporal. Time is the medium of social reproduction. Under capitalist logics, linear time is dedicated to the unending accumulation of value. On the other hand, repetitive time is the locus of the reproduction of everyday life, of biological needs and of what appears to us as 'normality'.[11] The antagonism between these temporalities does not, of course, exhaust the complex temporalities of risk in modernity, but it provides a vital heuristic in understanding how perceptions of environmental risk function politically in everyday life.

This analysis, by placing its focus on risk in the context of social reproduction and the everyday, distinguishes itself from the prevailing idealism of much of the current cultural and political historiography of science. As Jo Guldi has convincingly argued, the history of modernity has come to focus on accounts of governmental, disciplinary or bio-political power enacted through the discursive powers of the state (at various levels) and the expert. Such accounts suggest a determination of everyday life by systems of knowledge and their associated technologies.[12] As Guldi notes, this understanding of the relationship between history, technology and everyday life is partly a consequence of the kinds of archives on which historians have come to rely. As Richard Hölzl recognizes, when one's textual resources are mainly scientific and technical treatises, then even critical historical engagement with scientific knowledge can silently reproduce the dominance of the expert gaze.[13]

This can be seen in recent critics of the notion of disciplinary power and the 'panoptic gaze'. Chris Otter's excellent scholarly critique of Foucauldian approaches to the history of technology, *The Victorian Eye*, rightly stresses the failures and limits of panopticism when applied as an analytic to the nineteenth century.[14] Yet the players in this story remain

[10] F. Trentmann, 'The Politics of Everyday Life', in F. Trentmann (ed.), *The Oxford Handbook of the History of Consumption* (Oxford, 2012), pp. 521–47.

[11] Lefebvre, *Rhythmanalysis*, pp. 51–6.

[12] Jo Guldi, 'The Other Side of the Panopticon: Technology, Archives, and the Difficulty of Seeing Victorian Heterotopias', *Journal of the Chicago Colloquium on Digital Humanities and Computer Science* 1 (2011). Available at: https://letterpress.uchicago.edu/index.php/jdhcs/article/view/79 (date accessed 17 November 2015).

[13] R. Hölzl, 'Historicizing Sustainability: German Scientific Forestry in the Eighteenth and Nineteenth Centuries', *Science as Culture* 19 (2010), pp. 431–60.

[14] C. Otter, *The Victorian Eye: A Political History of Light and Vision in Britain, 1800–1910* (Chicago, 2008).

mainly bureaucratic experts, local and national state apparatuses and their associated textual practices.[15] Shane Ewen's important work on socio-technical disasters in the nineteenth century also places most of its focus on the interactions of experts and the state.[16]

The concept of an 'everyday environmentalism' challenges the dominant archival gaze through a willingness to excavate those critical perspectives on science, technology and risk that emerge in the semantic field of everyday life.[17] Unfortunately, recent theoretical tendencies in the history of science and technology, especially the so-called new materialism, have done little to challenge this state of affairs.[18] With some key exceptions, it remains rare to find among historians of the environment or technology a focus on explicitly subaltern counter-narratives of technology or risk.[19] It is perhaps indicative that exceptions to this rule tend to emerge from disciplines such as geography and anthropology where qualitative techniques to capture the subaltern gaze, including interviewing, have greater currency.[20]

These themes are illustrated here through two case studies. The first, a study of the politics of refuse disposal in twentieth-century Britain, draws on historical and contemporary examples of resistance to imposed risks. It provides an examination of long-term exposure to unquantifiable risk imposed by the requirements of urban reproduction. The second, a study of the *Torrey Canyon* oil disaster in 1967 and its aftermath, is an example of

[15] C. Otter, 'Cleansing and Clarifying: Technology and Perception in Nineteenth-Century London', *Journal of British Studies* 43 (2004), pp. 40–64.

[16] S. Ewen, 'Sheffield's Great Flood of 1864: Engineering Failure and the Municipalisation of Water', *Environment and History* 20 (2014), pp. 177–207; S. Ewen, 'Socio-technological Disasters and Engineering Expertise in Victorian Britain: The Holmfirth and Sheffield Floods of 1852 and 1864', *Journal of Historical Geography* 46 (2014), pp. 13–25.

[17] Lefebvre, *Critique of Everyday Life, Volume 2*, pp. 276–315.

[18] Z. Gille, *From the Cult of Waste to the Trash Heap of History: The Politics of Waste in Socialist and Postsocialist Hungary* (Bloomington, IN, 2007); Z. Gille, 'Actor Networks, Modes of Production and Waste Regimes: Reassembling the Macro-Social', *Environment and Planning (A)* 42 (2010), pp. 1049–64; D.H. Coole and S. Frost (eds), *New Materialisms: Ontology, Agency and Politics* (Durham NC, 2010).

[19] Montrie, *A People's History of Environmentalism in the United States*; M. Armiero and L. Sedrez (eds), *A History of Environmentalism: Local Struggles, Global Histories* (London, 2014).

[20] See, for instance, M. Allen, *Cleansing the City: Sanitary Geographies in Victorian London* (Athens, OH, 2008); S. Foote and E. Mazzolini, *Histories of the Dustheap: Waste, Material Cultures, Social Justice* (Cambridge, MA, 2012); J.R. Fleming and A. Johnson (eds), *Toxic Airs: Body, Place, Planet in Historical Perspective* (Pittsburgh, PA, 2014).

an apparently dramatic rupture and of the risks imposed by the changing energy requirements of an increasingly global capitalism. Yet it also reveals some contradictory consequences, in particular the limits of an environmentalist response to the risks of oil spills, which can be explained by the social reproduction needs of everyday life and their temporal dynamics. It draws upon oral interview material, as well as more traditional archival materials, to explore some of the antagonisms that analysis of the expert gaze would overlook.

Risk and Resistance

During the nineteenth and twentieth centuries, the problem of urban waste disposal was a significant political question in everyday life.[21] We still live with the consequences of the construction of complex networked technical apparatuses designed to ensure the continuous, repeated cleansing of our cities, a process that also ensures their reproduction as sites for the accumulation of capital and the reproduction of labour power.[22] Without the regular and systematic disposal of refuse, urban life would quickly become untenable and the reproduction of urban capitalism impossible.[23] Today this conundrum is often referred to as a problem of 'sustainability'.[24] In Marxist terms, the same problematic reflects the antinomies of social reproduction under the rule of capital.[25] Capital accumulation occurs in urban spaces that are assemblages of material and biological flows that require

[21] M. Gandy, *Recycling and the Politics of Urban Waste* (Basingstoke, 1994); T. Cooper, 'Challenging the "Refuse Revolution": War, Waste and the Rediscovery of Recycling, 1900–50', *Historical Research* 81 (2008), pp. 710–31; T. Cooper, 'Burying the "Refuse Revolution": The Rise of Controlled Tipping in Britain, 1920–1960', *Environment and Planning (A)* 42 (2010), pp. 1033–48; R.G. Stokes, R. Köster and S.C. Sambrook, *The Business of Waste: Great Britain and Germany, 1945 to the Present* (Cambridge 2013).

[22] J.A. Tarr and G. Dupuy (eds), *Technology and the Rise of the Networked City in Europe and America* (Philadelphia, PA, 1988); J.A. Tarr, *The Search for the Ultimate Sink: Urban Pollution in Historical Perspective* (Akron, OH, 1996).

[23] Cooper and Bulmer, 'Refuse and the "Risk Society"'; D. Harvey, *Justice, Nature and the Geography of Difference* (Oxford, 1996).

[24] P. McManus, 'Contested Terrains: Politics, Stories and Discourses of Sustainability', *Environmental Politics* 5 (1996), pp. 48–73; P. Marcuse, 'Sustainability is Not Enough', *Environment and Urbanization* 10 (1998), pp. 103–12; P. Desrochers, 'Victorian Pioneers of Corporate Sustainability', *Business History Review* 83 (2009), pp. 703–29; P. Warde, 'The Invention of Sustainability', *Modern Intellectual History* 8 (2011), pp. 153–70.

[25] R. Luxemburg, *The Accumulation of Capital*, trans. A. Schwarzschild (London, 2003).

constant management and maintenance in order to ensure their reproduction. Waste poses a key hazard to the temporal reproduction of urban space. Its disposal ensures the continuance of material flows through the 'urban metabolism' and the ongoing biological health and cultural well-being of city dwellers.[26] It is therefore unsurprising that waste has become a key political and cultural question in urban life. Wherever waste disposal breaks down, the legitimacy ('sustainability') of the social and economic order comes into question. This is one reason, perhaps, why uncollected refuse became an enduring image of the industrial struggles of the 1970s and 1980s.[27]

A key conundrum of the modern system of waste disposal is what to do with the refuse collected. Whereas waste collection and removal is a continuous cyclical process, disposal is, or more accurately should be, final. Yet, in reality, such finality is a myth, for waste persists or lasts in its final place of disposal.[28] Even incinerators produce a toxic ash that requires dumping. Different technologies of disposal produce different ecological consequences and different culturally contingent political effects. It can seem obvious that people would oppose the dumping or incineration of waste in their areas, the corollary of the selfish individualism—or 'nimbyism'—that contemporary ideology expects to find everywhere.[29] But as a number of analysts have shown, this fails to explain either why opposition to refuse disposal emerges or why it persists.[30] Experts made efforts throughout the twentieth century to allay fears regarding the environmental and health risks of waste disposal sites—to prove that they could be managed and their biological and toxic risks eliminated.[31] The transition from crude tipping and incineration to controlled tipping or sanitary

[26] Heynen, Kaika and Swyngedouw (eds), *In the Nature of Cities.*

[27] P. Hounsell, *London's Rubbish: Two Centuries of Dirt, Dust and Disease in the Metropolis* (Stroud, 2013), pp. 139–50.

[28] J. Scanlan, 'In Deadly Time: The Lasting on of Waste in Mayhew's London', *Time & Society* 16 (2007), pp. 189–206.

[29] I. Welsh, 'The NIMBY Syndrome: Its Significance in the History of the Nuclear Debate in Britain', *British Journal for the History of Science* 26 (1993), pp. 15–32.

[30] P. Devine-Wright, 'Beyond NIMBYism: Towards an Integrated Framework for Understanding Public Perceptions of Wind Energy', *Wind Energy* 8 (2005), pp. 125–39; J. Cope, 'When is a NIMBY Not a NIMBY? The Case of the St Dennis Anti-Incinerator Group', *Cornish Studies* 18 (2010), pp. 58–69.

[31] J.F.M. Clark, '"The Incineration of Refuse is Beautiful": Torquay and the Introduction of Municipal Refuse Destructors', *Urban History* 34 (2007), pp. 255–77; Cooper, 'Burying the "Refuse Revolution"'.

landfill during the mid-twentieth century was part of a bid to allay public anxieties over the proximity of waste treatment sites to new housing estates through a technological fix.[32]

Yet such fixes commonly demanded the sacrifice of some spaces to the overall needs of the modern hygienic project. There is a long history of resistance to different types of refuse disposal that rendered certain spaces final 'sinks' for urban waste, a history which dates back to the late nineteenth century and the advent of refuse or dust 'destruction' (incineration). One telling example is the blackly humorous remark of a working-class woman in Edwardian Aberdeen, speaking out against a dust destructor proposed for her neighbourhood. She suggested that the local council should 'have houses erected all-round the destructor, and compel the councilors to live in them, in order that they might have the first and best samples of what they were to give to those who resided in the district'.[33] Her frustration reflects questions of both political and class power at the heart of decisions as to who would be exposed to the consequences of refuse disposal, which in the case of destructors meant air pollution by smoke and dust, as well as the smell of refuse. However, it also reflects the temporal politics at stake in such projects. The final site of disposal for her is also a lasting site of dwelling for working-class residents, and it is one that those empowered to decide on the production of certain risks should be invited to join permanently. Her remarks reveal, quite precisely, the temporal dimension of resistance to imposed risks.

Both expert discourses of risk and technological fixes were typically appropriated by bureaucratic forces to contest the temporalities of risk production. During the 1930s, for instance, the fears of local residents regarding the future sanitary effects of Salford's controlled tips at Wallness were subject to emphatic denials by the city's Cleansing Committee, which relied on the evidence of the Medical Officer of Health to assert that there was no ongoing nuisance or danger to health; local experience suggested otherwise, however.[34] Such instances of antagonism, in which everyday life clashed with expert opinion, are widely evidenced and reveal powerful tensions over time and dwelling in contesting the legitimacy of particular risks. For instance, a Medical Officer of Health only experienced a tip at irregular intervals, however often and however objectively

[32] Cooper, 'Burying the "Refuse Revolution"'.

[33] *Aberdeen Daily Journal*, 6 July 1910, p. 8.

[34] *Salford City Reporter and Salford Chronicle*, 22 September 1933, p. 9.

he might inspect the site. Residents, on the other hand, were asked to live with a tip every day. Their permanent gaze critiqued the passing bureaucratic perspective precisely because it saw what was permanent and what was experienced as 'normal'.[35] Its authority drew from the temporal, embodied experience of dwelling in place rather than from abstract knowledge or passing analysis. Letters to the *Salford City Reporter* reflect this. Residents troubled the discourse of scientific progress that legitimated landfill, equating it with practices of the past that should be superseded by more healthful methods, perhaps even by incineration.[36] They challenged discourses of modernity that underpinned defences of particular technologies precisely by appropriating the claim to modernity and progress. At stake in these conflicting temporal gazes was the very question of what it meant to be modern.[37] When residents attacked controlled tipping as anti-modern, as a permanent derangement of a local ecology, they claimed for themselves, as *permanent* dwellers in place, the right to affirm what modernity and safety might mean from within their temporal domain, that is, a continually healthful environment, free of the apparatuses and insanitary effects of urban cleansing.

Resistance to bureaucratic logics of disposal might itself be contradictory and antagonistic in nature. Two letters that appeared on the subject of dumping in a suburban metropolitan paper, the *West Drayton and Yiewsley Weekly Journal*, in August 1935 demonstrate the complexities. The first is a letter from a housewife complaining of the problems of refuse collection in the district.[38] The second, under the title 'Rubbish Shot Here', attacked the dumping of the demolished remains of central London's old Waterloo Bridge in the district, complaining that it was 'a pity we cannot retaliate by dumping into the middle of Hyde Park'.[39] Side-by-side, the correspondence performs a contradiction, one a demand for the improvement of the suburban system of domestic refuse collection and the other decrying the use of the area as a dump for others' refuse. It is insufficient to describe this kind of contradiction as the unconscious consequence of the invisibility of urban networks to an ignorant urban public, as some

[35] F. Trentmann, 'Disruption is Normal: Blackouts, Breakdowns and the Elasticity of Everyday Life', in E. Shove, F. Trentmann and R. Wilk (eds), *Time, Consumption and Everyday Life: Practice, Materiality and Culture* (Oxford, 2009), pp. 67–84.

[36] *Salford City Reporter*, 15 December 1933, p. 7.

[37] B. Latour, *We Have Never Been Modern*, trans. C. Porter (Cambridge, MA, 1993).

[38] *West Drayton and Yiewsley Weekly Journal*, August 1935, p. 4.

[39] *Ibid.*

have done.[40] Such contradictions were a necessary consequence of modern urban metabolisms. In the same year, Yiewsley experienced agitation over such phenomena as '14 days accumulation of rubbish festering in back yards'.[41] Such problems were increasingly normal in growing suburban areas.

Temporal struggles of this sort have persisted into the present, constituting an uncanny repetition of the social relations embodied in processes of refuse disposal. In the early twenty-first century, a combination of European regulation and the privatization of refuse disposal services has come together in a new ensemble of technologies and social relations embodied in the waste-to-energy-incinerator, commonly, though misleadingly, represented as a 'green' alternative to landfill.[42] According to a report in *The Guardian*, up to 39 new incinerator plants were planned or under construction in the UK in 2013.[43] This expansion is occurring despite acknowledged overcapacity for incineration in continental Europe.[44]

The rise of the waste-to-energy incinerator, supported by a combination of European and national environmental policy, such as the landfill tax, and local councils keen to outsource the problem of refuse disposal, has been fiercely resisted by residents whose localities have been chosen as the sites for new incinerators. The districts of St Dennis, Cornwall and Devonport, Plymouth, for example, have both had incinerator plants imposed on them in the face of strong local opposition.[45] Both are poorer districts, and opposition grounded in the environmental and health impacts

[40] R.F. Hirsh and B.K. Sovacool, 'Wind Turbines and Invisible Technology: Unarticulated Reasons for Local Opposition to Wind Energy', *Technology and Culture* 54 (2013), pp. 705–34.

[41] *West Drayton and Yiewsley Weekly Journal*, 18 January 1935, p. 2.

[42] J. Reno, 'Motivated Markets: Instruments and Ideologies of Clean Energy in the United Kingdom', *Cultural Anthropology* 26 (2011), pp. 389–413; J. Reno, 'Managing the Experience of Evidence: England's Experimental Waste Technologies and their Immodest Witnesses', *Science, Technology & Human Values* 36 (2011), pp. 842–63; C. Alexander and J. Reno, 'From Biopower to Energopolitics in England's Modern Waste Technology', *Anthropological Quarterly* 87 (2014), pp. 335–58.

[43] J. Doward and T. Burke, '"March of the Incinerators" Threatens Drive to Recycle More Rubbish', *The Guardian*, 18 August 2013. Available at: www.theguardian.com/environment/2013/aug/18/march-of-the-incinerators-recycling (date accessed 17 November 2015).

[44] 'Continental Drift—How Much Might UK Waste Exports Grow?', *Isonomia*. Available at: www.isonomia.co.uk/?p=1894 (date accessed 17 November 2015).

[45] 'Plymouth Incinerator Row Rumbles on—Despite Building Nearing Completion', *Plymouth Herald*, 17 September 2014. Available at: www.plymouthherald.co.uk/Plymouth-incinerator-row-rumbles-despite-building/story-22935837-detail/story (date accessed 17 November 2015).

of incineration has been rebuffed by government and business alike. For residents, there is a class politics in play in the selection of sites: as one opponent has succinctly put it, 'you wouldn't dare see this in Plymstock or any other Tory supporting area'.[46]

Where corporations make profits and councils see a solution to their waste disposal woes, residents experience a profound sense of powerlessness. The environmental risks of refuse incineration are well known: government reports acknowledge an impact. They include the escape of highly toxic dioxins through exhaust flues, and the tremendous difficulties of disposing of toxic bottom- and fly-ash, the end products of incineration.[47] However, in such cases, scientific knowledge is often deployed politically to minimize the risks such chemicals pose and to legitimate incineration. Bizarrely, from a scientific perspective, expertise can even be used to argue against the need for local studies of any incinerator's specific impacts on the basis that potential impacts are already 'known' to be low. For example, the South West Devon Waste Partnership quoted the then Health Protection Agency's summary of existing national knowledge to argue that: 'The evidence suggests that any potential damage to health of those living close to incinerators is likely to be very small, if detectable. The Agency therefore does not believe that studies of public health around individual incinerators are scientifically justifiable.'[48] This review of current evidence was, however, based heavily on research first conducted in 2004; the Plymouth incinerator was completed in 2014.[49]

For residents, of course, arguments about *national* concentrations of particulate emissions miss the point that their problem is with the *local* concentrations from a particular source. From a resident's perspective, they are being told that their health is expendable as the price of maintaining wider urban amenity. As one Devonport resident wrote bitterly: 'I can't wait for it [the incinerator] to start working, pollouting [sic] where I live

[46] Anonymous Facebook posting, https://www.facebook.com/theplymouthherald/posts/10152302788001902 (date accessed 17 November 2015).

[47] D.N. Pellow, *Resisting Global Toxics: Transnational Movements for Environmental Justice* (Cambridge, MA, 2007); P. Connett, *The Zero Waste Solution: Untrashing the Planet One Community at a Time* (White River Junction, VT, 2013).

[48] Plymouth City Council, www.plymouth.gov.uk/swdwpnewsevents (date accessed 17 November 2015).

[49] UK Health Protection Agency, *The Impact on Health of Emissions to Air from Municipal Waste Incinerators* (London, 2009), pp. 1, 3–4.

and killing me! Yet, I have no say in this.'[50] Yet, this sense of powerlessness can, paradoxically, invigorate local opposition, and the organized response to incineration over the past decade has been more powerful than anything seen before. There are now over 40 active local opposition groups fighting the erection of such facilities in the UK.

Incinerators, like other waste treatment technologies, intervene in places and transform the local environment. They enact a change that is permanent, but whose long-term consequences are uncertain, unseen and perhaps unknowable. If subaltern groups lack the organization to make the health impacts of waste disposal sites visible through political campaigning, they may never be taken into account at all. Clusters of cancers or other diseases can always be dismissed as random or statistically insignificant by 'boffins'. 'Low-level' and longer-term impacts are hard to discern and inherently difficult to calculate. One of the characteristics of the risks posed by waste treatment sites, then, is that they are enduring and ever present in the everyday (perhaps even literally visible outside the window). The fear they inspire lurks in the background, both as a threat to health and as a social judgment on the value of a place and the people who live there. The temporal dimension of waste disposal is, in this particular context, iterative: it is repeated daily in innumerable small acts of the production and disposal of refuse across a cityscape whose total impact on the health and well-being of workers and residents is uncertain or unaccounted for. It is precisely this enduring, invisible quality that renders the risks of waste disposal so problematic to those asked to live with them and that so poignantly invokes the democratic question of who has the right to decide what risks are endured, by whom, for how long, and with what consequences.[51]

Catastrophe and Resilience

In the case of waste disposal, the everyday experience of risk reflected a temporality of endurance and repetitious dwelling through time and place. But what about the case of more immediate threats presented by catastrophic failures? In catastrophes, the temporal dimensions of risk emerge from the radical and immediate disruption of repetitive time or

[50] Anonymous Facebook posting, https://www.facebook.com/groups/291924978341/ (date accessed 21 April 2015).

[51] Beck, *Risk Society*, p. 57.

what passes for 'normality'. When the supertanker *Torrey Canyon* ran aground off the coast of Cornwall in March 1967, an invisible, potential hazard became a very real and immediate disaster.[52] Catastrophes dramatize threats in different ways compared to enduring and persistent forms of risk.[53] Their 'riskiness' is immediate and tangible, even where it may be invisible: an oil slick lying off-shore and out of sight. They demand an immediate policy response rather than scientific or medical justification for future action.

The *Torrey Canyon* grounding was the first catastrophic loss of a supertanker and it marked something new. It was the first of a series of supertanker disasters that would stretch into the present. It was followed by the *Sea Star*, *Amoco Cadiz*, *Atlantic Empress*, *Odyssey* and *Exxon Valdez*, all ship-based spills of over 100,000 tons.[54] Yet, as Timothy Mitchell has shown, the transformation of the global energy regime that created the conditions for such an accident had its roots in the nineteenth century with the growth of global oil companies and the invention of the modern oil tanker.[55] During the twentieth century, the size, number and distribution of oil tankers progressively increased with new 'jumbo-ized' tankers emerging in the 1960s carrying six-figure loads. However, the *Torrey Canyon* emergency was not defined simply by scale; indeed, the response to the spill was defined as much by a temporality of urgency and requires its own explanation.

For Hilary Rose, the *Torrey Canyon* disaster marks the end of a period of trust in scientific and technical expertise to resolve catastrophic failures.[56] Yet, one might as easily argue that the spill marks the apotheosis of public trust in technological fixes to catastrophic problems. Indeed, the 'catastrophic' character of the *Torrey Canyon* lay less in the oil it carried, or the scale of the spill, than in the results of the response that followed.

[52] P. Burrows, C. Rowley and D. Owen, '*Torrey Canyon*: A Case Study in Accidental Pollution', *Scottish Journal of Political Economy* 21 (1974), pp. 237–58.

[53] G. Bankoff, 'Constructing Vulnerability: The Historical, Natural and Social Generation of Flooding in Metropolitan Manila', *Disasters* 27 (2003), pp. 224–38; G. Bankoff, *Cultures of Disaster: Society and Natural Hazards in the Philippines* (London, 2003).

[54] E. Nalder, *Tankers Full of Trouble : The Perilous Journey of Alaskan Crude* (New York, 1994).

[55] T. Mitchell, *Carbon Democracy: Political Power in the Age of Oil*, 2nd edn (London, 2013); T. Mitchell, 'Carbon Democracy', *Economy and Society* 38 (2009), pp. 399–432.

[56] H. Rose, 'Risk, Trust and Scepticism in the Age of the New Genetics', in B. Adam, U. Beck and J. van Loon (eds), *The Risk Society and Beyond: Critical Issues for Social Theory* (London, 2000), pp. 63–77.

This reflected recognition at every level of government, and society more widely, that the oil washing ashore represented a dire threat in need of an immediate technological solution: the extensive use of highly toxic 'detergents' as part of the 'clean-up operation'.[57] And yet these chemical emulsifiers proved devastating to marine life across Cornwall's shoreline.

This emergency response was contingent upon the temporal anxiety generated by the oil in terms of immediate socio-economic impact rather than longer-term considerations of health and environmental well-being.[58] One resident, Tony Issacs, remembered local people being 'very afeared' of the oil coming ashore and affecting the all-important summer holiday season.[59] Numerous interviewees recalled the sense of anxiety among the local community as the oil washed ashore. Marion Caldwell, who was working in Penzance in 1967, spoke of the grounding as one of the worst events to affect Cornwall as a whole, recalling that it touched nearly everyone in her local community.[60]

The example of *Torrey Canyon* demonstrates the ways in which certain risks become legitimated by the state, set into a hierarchy of threats to be addressed, leaving others to be ignored. Here the economic risks to livelihood and income presented by the oil were accepted as the immediate and legitimate objects of a state response. This was the difference between the vast resources that the British government and local authorities were willing to pour into the clean-up operation in the wake of the *Torrey Canyon*'s grounding, and the manner of the responses to concerns with waste disposal. The spilling of oil along the holiday beaches of Cornwall was an immediate threat to a core part of the Cornish economy, and highly expensive and damaging chemical cleansing of the beaches was the result. It is notable that in northern France, where the shellfish industry was important, the application of toxic detergents in large amounts was avoided.[61]

Thus, the very nature of the emergency and the understanding of the kind of risks it presented was determined by economic factors and the social reproduction needs of dominant social groups in a particular locale. To this extent,

[57] C. Gill, F. Booker and T. Soper, *The Wreck of the 'Torrey Canyon'* (Newton Abbot, 1967).

[58] See A. Green and T. Cooper, 'Community and Exclusion: The *Torrey Canyon* Disaster of 1967', *Journal of Social History* 48 (2015), pp. 892–909.

[59] Tony Issacs, interviewed by A. Green, 11 June 2012, 05:00–10:00.

[60] Marion Caldwell, interviewed by A. Green, 17 July 2012, 15:00–20-00.

[61] R. Petrow, *The Black Tide: In the Wake of Torrey Canyon* (London, 1968).

a catastrophe like an oil spill exposes the hidden ideological character of 'risk'. What might appear to be a contingent problem for individuals or a community suddenly becomes a question of the mode of social reproduction in the affected locality as a whole, as well as of the social and political relations that sustain it. Catastrophe, through its immediate temporal disruption of everyday social and economic reproduction, demonstrates that the production and legitimation of risk, far from being individuated, is always at a base level inherently social.[62]

As suggested above, the way in which the risks of the spill were produced as immediate lay in the character of the political response.[63] As one respondent noted, politicians were keen to be seen to be doing something, even where their understanding of local ecological conditions was thin or non-existent. The clean-up operation became a 'real PR exercise for the politicians', to quote another resident.[64] The politics of this 'emergency period' therefore also inhabited its own particular temporality, one very different from that experienced by communities exposed to refuse disposal sites. It was sped up: a moment of intervention in which everyone apparently pulled together in what was seen as a common project. Interviewees remembering the *Torrey Canyon* disaster repeatedly commented on the 'excitement' of the immediate aftermath, where the normality of everyday life gave way to a flood of emergency workers and soldiers, and even the military bombing of the stricken vessel in an effort to burn the remaining oil.

However, in the aftermath of an emergency, the effects of environmental catastrophe linger; the repetitive dimension of the everyday returns to produce a new 'normal' that recomposes the experience of everyday life. While for the official gaze the emergency ended with the beaches cleaned, the tourists returning and an official report, the community's own memories of the disaster were more deeply engrained and conflicted, even some 45 years after the event. They present a longer-term experience of remembering (and forgetting) the enduring impact of the event, both environmental and emotional. Memories of the smell of the oil, and the fate of the sea birds caught up in it, were particularly strong. For Alison Stuckey, 'the smell was incredible; we lived 10 minutes away, a walk from

[62] Beck, *Risk Society*; Cooper and Bulmer, 'Refuse and the "Risk Society"', p. 23.

[63] J. Sheail, '*Torrey Canyon*: The Political Dimension', *Journal of Contemporary History* 42 (2007), pp. 485–504; Petrow, *The Black Tide*.

[64] Stuart Charles, interviewed by A. Green, 18 July 2012, 50:00–55:00.

the beach; the smell of the oil was something I'll never forget'.[65] It was not forgotten that the community lived in a permanently transformed environment. Some remembered that the detergent applied in the clean-up had done more damage than the oil itself, highlighting the ways in which the effects of the disaster were multiplied, rather than mitigated, by the nature of the official response.[66] Robert Cook remembered it taking up to 5 years for seaweed and limpets to recover from the operation. As he put it, 'every trace of sea life in rockpools went completely'.[67] 'Government boffins' and outside experts, who determined how the shoreline was cleansed, excluded quotidian knowledge both of maritime conditions and the environment.[68] Their determination of the 'risk' to be addressed, and the means through which it was mitigated, produced feelings of alienation from the dictates of a distant central power.[69]

Rescue from the economic threat of the *Torrey Canyon*'s oil was thus purchased at the price of widespread ecological devastation to Cornwall's seashore. Short-term disaster was traded for another medium- to long-term catastrophe that did not register as strongly to the official gaze. Nonetheless, in the memories of those living in Cornwall in the wake of the incident, the disaster lived on in manifold everyday ways. These continuing 'risks' were often of a small, irritating, domestic variety, but they symbolized a permanently transformed environment. Marion Caldwell, for example, remembered the way in which oil from the beaches would be walked into houses by children after they had played on the beaches and that it was always around 'for a long, long time'.[70] The incident also lived in unknowable fears and risks. Stuart Charles told a story of people carrying on swimming during the holiday season, even though a thin film of oil covered bodies. He suggested that the fact he carried on surfing on polluted beaches might have been 'foolish' in terms of its unknowable effects on health: a fear that the oil may have invisible, continuing effects even as people returned to the normal routines of everyday life.[71]

This return to the routine or the normal also explains one of the more curious effects of the grounding. Environmental historians are used to

[65] Alison Stuckley, interviewed by A. Green, 29 May 2012, 00:00–05:00.

[66] Vivian Stratton, interviewed by A. Green, 29 May 2012, 35:00–40:00.

[67] Robert Cook, interviewed by A. Green, 17 July 2012, 05:00–10:00.

[68] David Stevens, interviewed by T. Cooper, 26 July 2012, 00:00–05:00.

[69] A. Green and T. Cooper, 'Community and Exclusion'.

[70] Caldwell, 15:00–20:00.

[71] Charles, 40:00–45:00.

studying pollution incidents as sources of environmental politics. The toxic pollution incident at Love Canal, New York, in the 1970s, for example, offers a paradigmatic instance of the post-war construction of environmental activism from the realization of a hidden toxic risk—in that case, the risk to health posed by landfilled dioxins and other chemicals, and the class, gender and race dynamics that influenced the subsequent politicization of the response.[72] In the case of the *Torrey Canyon*, there was no environmentalist response. Although interviewees generally agreed that the incident contributed to the emergence of environmental consciousness, few had been members of environmental organizations, and several rejected the label 'environmentalist' altogether. When Eric Busby was asked if the event had had an effect on people's environmental awareness, he stated that 'it probably did to a certain extent. Although I was probably influenced much, much more when I came out of the fire service, and saw some of the needless pollution that goes on around the place'.[73] Environmentalists were, on the other hand, 'a bit of a pain in many ways', tending to be extreme or obsessive in their focus on nature and to be ignorant of technical expertise.[74]

In many respects there was a less overtly political response to the *Torrey Canyon* than we have seen in the case of waste disposal, with its lingering, yet difficult to discern effects. A long-lasting, often invisible threat appears to have generated more clearly political responses than a major disaster. How can we account for this? The answer to this may in part reside in the temporal dimensions that have been under scrutiny in this chapter. In the case of the *Torrey Canyon* disaster, the risks of the oil spill were clearly and strongly mediated by the immediate economic impact. Waste disposal, on the other hand, commonly did not threaten economic sustainability; indeed, it was vital to maintaining the economic functioning of the city. It was rather more unambiguously parasitic on the rhythms of everyday life, inserting a permanent and repeated daily threat to health and happiness. To some extent, then, in terms of an everyday environmental politics, it was this smaller-scale but more enduring and discounted form of risk that appears to have had more purchase.

[72] R. Newman, 'Making Environmental Politics: Women and Love Canal Activism', *Women's Studies Quarterly* 29 (2001), pp. 65–84; A.M. Hay, 'A New Earthly Vision: Religious Community Activism in the Love Canal Chemical Disaster', *Environmental History* 14 (2009), pp. 502–27; Blum, *Love Canal Revisited*.

[73] Eric Busby, interviewed by A. Green, 20 May 2012, 55:00–60:00.

[74] *Ibid.*

Risk, Time and the Everyday in the 'Anthropocene'

What do these two case studies of the everyday temporalities of risk demonstrate? Risk society theorists have investigated the tensions between knowable and unknowable risks, and between small-scale risks and catastrophic global disasters.[75] These offer important insights into the changing historicity of risk. However, the politics of risk and fear do not originate from questions of scale alone. Alongside questions of scale and knowledge, risk also expresses the clash of the various temporal dimensions of social reproduction in everyday life.[76] The temporality of risk is therefore critical to understanding the vexed relationship between environmental hazards and environmental politics.

Moreover, discourses of risk in everyday life clearly recombine the languages of scientific expertise with expressions of the needs and desires of everyday experience in complex and antagonistic ways. Seen from an everyday perspective, risks take on a far more contested and authentically political quality than is sometimes apparent in analyses building on Foucauldian assumptions and methods. These discourses are themselves dependent upon various temporal antinomies. The two case studies here have shown that risks can be radically *present*, as in the form of catastrophic disasters that disrupt normal social life and demand immediate action, or they can be *enduring*, repetitive, lived-with through time, an ever-present, unmeasurable threat to a potential future collective self. More than this, even an apparently catastrophic disaster can be re-incorporated into the everyday, such that life goes on as if nothing had happened. The temporal dimensions of risk are therefore continually shifting and are contested by social, economic and political forces playing out in various ways through antagonistic experiences of time. Capitalist, bureaucratic time is not the same as everyday time, with which it often conflicts. Claiming that a refuse dump can be made safe to live alongside, or an oiled beach cleaned and returned to normal, is ultimately an attempt to legitimate or efface disruptions to everyday time in the service of particular interests. Discourses of risk are therefore inherently ideological, and everyday environmentalisms are formed wherever counter-forces seek to contest such attempts at legitimation. Sometimes those counter-forces can be expressed explicitly,

[75] Beck, *Risk Society*; B. Luckin, 'Nuclear Meltdown and the Culture of Risk', *Technology and Culture* 46 (2005), pp. 393–9.

[76] B. Massumi (ed.), *The Politics of Everyday Fear* (Minneapolis, MN, 1993).

but are often to be found in the structure of community memory itself, a memory that refuses to forget a hidden history of underlying ecological disruptions.

What does all this mean now, in the so-called anthropocene, when capitalism has apparently taken on the capacity to re-order geological space and time with an attendant multiplication of the scale of risks posed to organic life?[77] World historian Jason Moore has critiqued the idea of the anthropocene as a distinct historical epoch, doing so from a Marxist perspective and pointing to the ways in which current environmental change and anthropogenic global warming are of a piece with the wider history of capitalism's relationship to nature.[78] There is much to agree with in this criticism; however, approaching the problem from a macro-level can also make it difficult to discern a possible point of popular political intervention. Environmental historians must also suggest ways in which people can again actively intervene in determining the future evolution of socio-ecological systems. The interrelationship between risk and everyday life offers one such possible point of intervention. In everyday environmentalisms, quotidian resistances to imposed risks generate fertile moments of critical reflection on environmental possibilities. They form a temporal politics, a struggle between the time of capitalist production and that of human reproduction. In the anthropocene, these temporal antinomies are reaching the status of absolute contradictions. With the onset of anthropogenic global warming, capital ceases to fuel itself purely from past accumulation (especially the deep past represented by fossil fuels) and it comes to rely upon consuming future time. The struggle to shift social production in such a way as to bring global warming under control is also a temporal struggle—a struggle for the future.

This focus on the temporal dimensions of social reproduction complicates a presentation of risk as increasingly individuated. If such individuation may be visible at the level of environments and bodies, then the introduction of time upsets these factors. Time connects risks and hazards through space and memory, joining individuals and communities through

[77] W. Steffen, P.J. Crutzen and J.R. McNeill, 'The Anthropocene: Are Humans Now Overwhelming the Great Forces of Nature?', *AMBIO: A Journal of the Human Environment* 36 (2007), pp. 614–21.

[78] J. Moore, 'Anthropocene or Capitalocene?', http://jasonwmoore.wordpress.com/2013/05/13/anthropocene-or-capitalocene (date accessed 17 November 2015); A. Malm and A. Hornborg, 'The Geology of Mankind? A Critique of the Anthropocene Narrative', *The Anthropocene Review* 1 (2014), pp. 62–9.

collective processes of resilience, repetition and remembering. In a single moment, risks are simultaneously past, present and future, and therefore *social* in the widest historical sense of the term. Risks are lived with, and remembered by, individuals and communities even when they are invisible to, or forgotten by, the state or capital. Memories of risk disrupt normality, haunting it with the remembrance that the normal is the consequence of a catastrophe. We see this in the moment a refuse treatment plant poses the question of a community's ecological future. It is similarly dramatized in the disruption to normal social life of a sudden environmental disaster.

What hope there is that we might avoid the worst consequences of global warming may lie in moments that mobilize everyday temporal contradictions. Perhaps such moments are now emerging in protests against fracking or the attempts of permaculturists to chart a way towards a more sustainable agriculture.[79] Such everyday environmentalisms seek a time beyond the exhausted, accumulative and linear momentum of the capitalist present—a time that will transform social reproduction and everyday life.[80]

[79] P. Cole, M. Worsdale and G. Gold, *Fracking Capitalism: Action Plans for the Eco-Social Crisis* (London, 2013).

[80] A. Negri, *Time for Revolution*, trans. Matteo Mandarini (London, 2013).

PART III

Mobility and Leisure Risks

CHAPTER 8

Drunk Driving, Drink Driving: Britain, c. 1800–1920

Bill Luckin

Why drink driving? What can an exploration of this elusive offence reveal about the social relations of mobility in nineteenth- and twentieth-century Britain? Drunk and 'furious' riding and driving had threatened life and limb from the first irrecoverable moment at which men and women—few of them abstemious—began to make journeys from hamlet to village and village to town.[1] Little is known about patterns of accidental death and injury in the medieval and early modern periods, let alone casualties attributable to drunk driving and riding.[2] However, the ancient rules of the road held that a 'furiously' intoxicated individual who ran down and

[1] For background to the continuingly high levels of consumption for most of the nineteenth century, see J. Greenaway, *Drink and the British: A Study in Policy-Making* (Basingstoke, 2003); and J. Nicholls, *The Politics of Alcohol: A History of the Drink Question in England* (Manchester, 2009).

[2] See B. Hanawalt, *The Ties that Bound: Peasant Families in Medieval England* (Bloomington, IN, 1986), pp. 271–4. For other sources and a chronological framework for the exploration of different kinds of urban calamity, see B. Luckin, 'Accidents, Disasters and Cities', *Urban History* 20 (1993), pp. 5–18. An ESRC project under the leadership of Dr Steven Gunn entitled 'Everyday Life and Accidental Death in Sixteenth Century England' promises to yield important results.

B. Luckin
University of Bolton, Deane Road, Bolton BL3 5AB, UK

T. Crook, M. Esbester (eds), *Governing Risks in Modern Britain*,
DOI 10.1057/978-1-137-46745-4_8

killed a man, woman or child should—if testimony stood up in court—be found guilty of criminal negligence and severely punished under the law of manslaughter.[3] Yet, if evidence from the early nineteenth century is anything to go by, very large numbers of those who had drunk too much, and who killed or injured other road users, went unpunished in a cultural environment still shaped by a collective belief in providence and the non-preventable nature of the majority of accidents.[4]

In a small country with a relatively small population, the traditional rules of the road may have worked moderately well. But from the mid-eighteenth century onwards, the explosion in regional industrialization and the rapid growth of towns and cities made Britain's urban thoroughfares increasingly dangerous. With a population close to one million, late eighteenth-century London was regularly paralysed by traffic jams. Deaths increased and medical men pondered the problem of a shortage of emergency hospital beds and lay ignorance of the basics of first aid.[5] In the 1830s, London recorded around 100 street deaths a year and about ten times that number of injuries. By the 1870s and 1880s, fatalities had greatly increased: in 1881, the capital registered a death toll of over 350, a figure that rose to nearly 600 in 1891.[6] This was not only a British phenomenon. Fatalities and injuries in Paris, a much smaller city, were lower. Nevertheless, in 1879, the French capital recorded 75 street deaths, double the annual average in the 1830s.[7] Urban America experienced similar kinds of increase. By the 1880s, traffic jams had become commonplace in New York.[8] In 1885, Boston recorded 18 horse-tram-associated deaths and 50 injuries from the same cause.[9]

[3] On the complexities of criminal negligence and manslaughter—'a crime against the state'—see J.W. Thatcher and D.J.H. Hartley, *The Law of the Road* (London, 1909), p. 23; and M.J. Allen, *Textbook on Criminal Law*, 8th edn (Oxford, 2005), p. 303.

[4] For a classic theoretical-cum-historical overview, see K. Figlio, 'What is an Accident?', in P. Weindling (ed.), *The Social History of Occupational Health* (London, 1985), pp. 180–206. See also R. Campbell, 'Philosophy and the Accident', in R. Cooter and B. Luckin (eds), *Accidents in History: Injuries, Fatalities and Social Relations* (Amsterdam, 1997), pp. 17–34.

[5] R. Porter, 'Accidents in the Eighteenth Century', in Cooter and Luckin (eds), *Accidents in History*, pp. 90–106.

[6] A. Causton, *A Comprehensive Scheme for Street Improvements in London, Accompanied by Maps and Sketches* (London, 1893), p. 7. See also J. Winter, *London's Teeming Streets, 1830–1914* (London, 1993), pp. 48–9, 203–4.

[7] *Morning Post*, 8 July 1879, p. 7.

[8] C. McShane and J.A. Tarr, *The Horse in the City: Living Machines in the Nineteenth Century* (Baltimore, 2007), p. 167. See also the pioneering C. McShane, *Down the Asphalt Road: The Automobile and the American City* (New York, 1994).

[9] McShane and Tarr, *Horse in the City*, p. 168.

Scrutiny of big city transport and driver–pedestrian relations between 1860 and 1900 confirms that when the first motor vehicles chugged on to the streets of London, Paris and New York, they arrived in a proto-automotive environment.[10] Ideology reflected technological transformation. Pro-motorism—the assumption that pedestrians must dodge traffic rather than motors and horse-drawn vehicles adjust to the needs of non-drivers—long pre-dated the triumph of the automobile. Pro-motorism was based on the assumption that the vast majority of drivers, whether on horses or behind the wheels of cars, could be confidently expected to behave in a safe and responsible manner. Unwitting pedestrians, on the other hand, were likely to flout the informal etiquette of the road. Pro-motorist pressure-groups—notably the Royal Automobile Club (RAC) and the Automobile Association (AA)—played a central role in the framing of road traffic law and insisted that successive governments should commit themselves to under- rather than over-regulation. Relationships with the police must remain cordially non-antagonistic.[11] Congenial rather than adversarial negotiation over infringements would prove much more beneficial to all categories of road user than draconian government measures designed, so it was argued, to 'restrict' the new form of transport.[12]

In the far distant 1960s, drink driving in Britain would develop into the Achilles' heel of pro-motorism. In 1936, Norway began to make use of special traffic courts to track down a new breed of offender: a driver impaired but not necessarily intoxicated by alcohol. In the 1960s, other nations, including Britain and the USA, followed the Scandinavian lead. Tense interchanges in the House of Commons and the House of Lords in the 1960s revealed more about the day-to-day conduct of the vast majority of British drivers than at any time in the preceding 70 years. Two major academic reports—by the University College London researcher G.C. Drew in Britain and the American Robert Borkenstein, who worked at Indiana University—convinced a clear majority of MPs that exceptionally large numbers of 'non-drunk' but drinking, and hence dangerously impaired,

[10] D. Miller, 'Driven Societies', in D. Miller (ed.), *Car Cultures* (London, 2000), p. 6. See also for an imaginative context C.G. Pooley, 'Landscapes without the Car: A Counterfactual Historical Geography of Twentieth-Century Britain', *Journal of Historical Geography* 36 (2010), pp. 266–75.

[11] W. Plowden, *The Motor Car and Politics, 1896–1970* (London, 1971), Part 1.

[12] See C. Emsley, '"Mother, What *Did* Policemen Do When There Weren't Any Motors"? The Law, the Police and the Regulation of Traffic in England, 1900–1939', *Historical Journal* 36 (1993), pp. 357–81; and J. Moran, 'Crossing the Road in Britain, 1931–1976', *Historical Journal* 49 (2006), pp. 477–96.

drivers were placing the lives of other road users at risk on a regular basis.[13] Motoring libertarians hit back, but were outgunned by committed Labour reformers and liberal-minded Conservatives. Pro-motorist spokesmen and lobbyists, especially those associated with the AA and the RAC, beat a strategic retreat. Within a generation, the social relations of mobility in Britain entered a phase in which unreconstructed libertarianism suffered a series of life-threatening body blows.

Other issues played key supporting roles, notably the responsibility of car manufacturers to produce safe and less accident-prone vehicles, and the use of safety-belts.[14] But the passionate arguments surrounding Barbara Castle's 1967 Road Safety Act set the ball rolling. During this action-filled period, motoring libertarianism fought its own variant of Custer's Last Stand. In so doing, it made explicit what had hitherto remained cloudily implicit. The anti-drinking debate, and the measures that it generated, demystified and undermined the taken-for-granted verities of pro-motorist ideology in twentieth-century Britain.[15]

This chapter reaches back to an era long pre-dating the invention of the internal combustion engine. Examining the detail of newspaper reports and legal documentation, it focuses on the dynamics of accidents and the impassioned debates about what constituted 'drunk' and 'furious' driving. It interrogates attitudes adopted by coroners, magistrates and judges, as well as the fate of the countless men, women and children who were killed or disabled as a result of the uncontrolled behaviour of what would now be recognized as unambiguously intoxicated or impaired drivers and riders. Towards the end of the chapter, the focus

[13] G.C. Drew, W.P. Colquhoun and H.A. Long, *Effect of Small Doses of Alcohol on a Skill Resembling Driving (Medical Research Council Memorandum, No. 38)* (London, 1959); R.F. Borkenstein et al., *The Role of the Drinking Driver in Traffic Accidents* (Bloomington, IN, 1964).

[14] R. Irwin, *Risk and the Control of Technology: Public Policies for Road Traffic Safety in Britain and the United States* (Manchester, 1985).

[15] For an overview of the British position in a comparative context, see B. Luckin, 'A Never-Ending Passing of the Buck? The Failure of Drink Driving Reform in Interwar Britain', *Contemporary British History* 24 (2010), pp. 363–84; and B. Luckin, 'A Degree of Consensus on the Roads: Drink Driving Policy in Britain, 1945–70', *Twentieth Century British History* 21 (2010), pp. 350–74. See also the excellent account in B.H. Lerner, *One for the Road: Drunk Driving since 1900* (Baltimore, MD, 2011). Lerner focuses on the USA, but there is revealing comparative material in the early chapters of his book. See also J. Burnham, *Accident Prone: A History of Technology, Psychology and Misfits of the Machine Age* (Chicago, 2009), pp. 67–86.

shifts to an interim period in which larger numbers of motors chugged on to Britain's already-crowded streets and began radically to change traffic flows. Accidents associated with the consumption of alcohol now involved motors ploughing into horse-drawn vehicles and terrified horses colliding with motor cars. Speeds were higher than they had been in the period between the 1850s and the 1890s. But throughout the period between the early nineteenth century and the arrival of the motor car and beyond, offending riders and drivers were just as likely to receive a moral warning as pay a fine or be sentenced to imprisonment. This occurred in a cultural environment in which pedestrians were implicitly typecast as obstructions, and in a society devoted to ever more rapid circulation, both in London and in clusters of towns in the Midlands and the north moving towards large-scale industrialization.

Alcohol, Accidents, Testimony and 'Character'

When did it begin? A series of acts passed in the late eighteenth and early nineteenth centuries sought to reduce accidents attributable to the drunken behaviour of coach and cabmen. The first measure entered the statute book in 1788. In 1820, road users' 'outside vehicles' gained minimal protection from coachmen who began a journey when already drunk. This measure was reinforced by the Stage Coach Act 1832 and the Police Clauses Act 1847: the latter made specific mention of 'those [who in general drive] when intoxicated'.[16] For the next 20 years, being drunk while in charge attracted minimal reformist attention. Then, in 1872, a Licensing Act, mainly concerned with the management and control of pubs and beer houses, incorporated amendments designating driving when drunk a separate offence and punishing those who behaved 'furiously' while under the influence with a fine of 40s or a month in prison, 'with or without hard labour'.[17] In 1903, the Motor Car Act contained clauses on the problems of reckless and dangerous motoring, and the failure of drivers to stop following an accident. However, Parliament refused to revisit the problem of rigorously defining 'drunk'. It would be 50 years before the topic

[16] R. Light, *Criminalizing the Drink Driver* (Aldershot, 1994), pp. 11–14: N. Ley, *Drink Driving Law and Practice* (London, 1993), pp. 1–2; T.C. Willett, *Criminal on the Road: A Study of Serious Motoring Offences* (London, 1962), pp. 64–72, 92–4.

[17] Willett, *Criminal on the Road*, pp. 92–3.

re-emerged.[18] Throughout the nineteenth century and on into the early twentieth century, successive governments refused to dirty their hands with regulations designed to save lives on the road.[19]

Between 1800 and the mid-1920s, a loose and structurally ambiguous body of anti-accident law was pragmatically interpreted by coroners, magistrates, judges and juries. Senior members of the judiciary pondered and on some occasions appear to have mimicked popular beliefs about the meaning of drunkenness in order to settle a complex question: at what point did a driver or rider become a threat to himself and other road users? As we shall see, there appears to have been widespread agreement at every social and cultural level on the major signs of what an inebriated individual *looked* like when he (or she) staggered down the street. But there were numerous overlapping perceptions of the point at which an individual became so drunk that he constituted a threat to himself and others. From the 1870s, sobriety tests were more widely used. Approaches varied, but in most places suspects were asked to state and write their name, touch a small mark on the wall, pick a pin off the floor and clearly enunciate a tongue-tying phrase like 'Peter picked a peck of pickled peppers'. Since the end of the eighteenth century, traffic-besieged London had drawn on the services of district part-time police-surgeons to administer these tests. Much later, in 1888, a professional metropolitan body was established and, over time, an increasing number of provincial practitioners joined this organization. Only in 1949, however, did police-surgeons establish a fully national association of their own.[20]

Two cases, one in the early 1820s and the other in the 1860s, demonstrate the ways in which alcohol-associated road and street accidents were perceived, differentiated in law and punished. In September 1822, a gentleman of very 'respectable appearance' drove his trap 'furiously' on to the pavement near Regent's Park, London. The horse stumbled, ran into a bystander and killed him. Eye-witnesses protested that the trap-driver was drunk, but the gentleman stood his ground and insisted that he was sober. His horse's belly-band had broken and it was this, he claimed, that

[18] Light, *Criminalizing the Drink Driver*, p. 13.

[19] Emsley, '"Mother, What *Did* Policemen Do When There Weren't Any Motors"?'; and Plowden, *Motor Car and Politics*.

[20] The narrative is related in outline in R.D. Summers, *History of the Police Surgeon* (London, 1988). See also A.D. Matthews, *Crime Doctor: The Memoirs of a Police Surgeon* (London, 1959); and H. de la Haye Davies, *In Suspicious Circumstances: Memories of a Northamptonshire Police Surgeon* (Newbury, 1998).

had caused the animal to panic: he had become involved in an unavoidable accident. At the coroner's hearing, street eye-witness details of the episode were replayed. Testimony and counter-testimony played a crucial role in confirming the presence or absence of drunk and 'furious' driving. Argument raged over rival presentations of the classic signs of intoxication: the look of the eyes and pupils, the smell of the breath, steady or unsteady balance, clear or slurred verbal articulation.

Initially in the Regent's Park case, the question of drunkenness or sobriety dominated the hearing. Several witnesses repeated their conviction that the gentlemanly trap-driver had displayed all the classic signs of drunk and 'furious' behaviour. Others were less certain. For his part, the trap-driver knew that if he were adjudged responsible for killing a pedestrian when drunk, he could be charged with manslaughter and sentenced to anything between 3 months' and a year's hard labour. He therefore made a direct appeal to the jury, begging them to accept that he was a sober-living member of the community who always rode and drove with care. He may, he admitted, have drunk a 'little' on the day in question, but not enough to lose control. Finally, he 'shed tears' of remorse and pleaded for forgiveness. He also called a character witness, a doctor from Islington, whom he had known for 30 years. The doctor told the court that his friend was a man of 'humanity', 'steady conduct' and 'benevolence of disposition'. This did the trick. The jury softened, withdrew and found him not guilty. The decision elicited 'satisfaction' in 'an exceedingly crowded court'. Theatricality and pathos had replaced attempts to reconstruct what had happened outside the gates of Regent's Park. The trap-driver's remorse and the doctor's character statement convinced the jury that they were dealing with a man who was unlikely ever again to become involved in a serious street accident. The coroner returned a verdict of accidental death.[21]

In 1864, an exceptionally serious street incident threatened to destroy communal cohesion in the Birkenhead village of Norton. Several eye-witnesses claimed that a local farmer—something of a pillar of the community—had been intoxicated to the point of allowing his horses to bolt, trample and kill an elderly woman. At an initial hearing, he was declared innocent of causing the woman's death and escaped a manslaughter charge. Then an unsalaried Church of England Bible reader, a member of the original jury, claimed that the farmer had in fact been

[21] 'Charge of Manslaughter', *Morning Post*, 17 September 1822, p. 1.

'stupefied' with drink. A second hearing revealed wide divergences in eye-witness testimony. (Second hearings were extremely rare.) Several villagers said that the farmer had been drinking heavily. A doctor who had been called to a cottage to save the woman's life said that he had smelled alcohol on the suspect's breath. However, like many other medical men, he refused to commit himself to stating that the farmer had been culpably drunk. Suspicion of guilt was further undermined by a compelling character statement by a neighbour and friend, who told the coroner that he had visited the farmer 'more than a thousand times', but never found him 'in drink'. This testimony was strengthened by a handful of witnesses who insisted that the Bible reader had acted out of malice and organized a vendetta against the farmer because the latter had only rarely attended church or communion. During the subsequent trial in Chester, feelings ran high, both in the city and in Norton. The judge informed the jury that 'if the death of the woman was caused by the prisoner getting drunk and attempting to drive when he was not capable, then he would be guilty of manslaughter'. But—and this was the case in countless drunk-driving cases—there was too little evidence to proceed: eye-witness accounts had been profoundly contradictory. The judge also hinted that the Bible reader had indeed given prejudiced and unreliable evidence, and had been motivated by an obsession with the suspect's repeated failure to attend Sunday service. The farmer walked free.[22]

Each of these cases centred on members of the well-to-do and 'respectable' classes. In proceedings involving the working classes, court officials invariably and sententiously warned of the temptations of the bottle, lecturing cab drivers and carters on how to mend their ways and develop into dependable and fully moralized members of the caste-bound society to which they belonged. If found guilty of manslaughter—the fatality had to be shown to have flowed directly from criminal negligence—a 'non-respectable' member of the community fared far worse than his social superior. A drunken stage-coach driver who ran over and killed a child might find himself sentenced to a year's penal servitude. Aristocratic, middle-class and 'respectable' Victorians invariably escaped with 3 months' hard labour—a punishment much less destructive of soul and body. In non-fatal cases, however, coroners' juries, magistrates and judges worked on

[22] 'Committal of Farmer for Manslaughter at Neston', *Liverpool Mercury*, 1 June 1864, p. 5. See also *Liverpool Mercury*, 13 August 1864.

the assumption that little could be done to stem the unending stream of drink-related problems that flowed into the courts. Consumption of large amounts of alcohol was quite simply a routine part of everyday life.

A minority of editorial writers disagreed. In 1802, a Hampshire newspaper told its readers that coachmen should be prevented from calling at 'public houses situated between the port-towns'. The habit rendered them 'intoxicated ... and incapable of driving'. They should be educated into behaving less irresponsibly.[23] But such warnings had little effect on drivers, who continued to drink as they had always drunk. In 1837, an intoxicated London cabbie fell asleep and meandered along King William Street with his whip hanging limply by his side. When he was apprehended, he could scarcely 'put one foot in front of the other'. The Lord Mayor issued the usual moral reprimand, but let him free.[24] Two years later, another cabman accepted brandy from a passenger before racing crazily through the 'most populous streets', ricocheting off other vehicles and terrifying bystanders. The Lord Mayor pondered imprisonment, but opted for another and, perhaps from the point of view of the accused, less desirable punishment. He marked his licence with the single condemnatory word: 'drunkenness'.[25] This might mean the end of a job.

In 1849, an intoxicated hearse-driver made his wobbling way from Fleet Street to Temple Bar in London. Slipping from his seat, he was trampled by his horses and suffered 'serious injuries on his body and legs'. The magistrate decided that the hearse-driver had received punishment enough and dismissed the case.[26] Lenient treatment was also handed down to a drunk cabman who was said to have lashed his horse with unforgivable ferocity: a recurrent and suspicion-rousing offence. He had also been driving his vehicle 'at a most furious rate'. Begging for mercy, the cabman told the court that he had a wife and three children. He vowed that, if he were found innocent, he would 'take the pledge'. The errant cabman was fined ten shillings, a lenient pittance for a magistrate but as much as three-quarters of a week's pay for a cabman.[27]

[23] 'Travelling by Mail Coaches', *Hampshire Daily Telegraph*, 16 August 1802, p. 4. See also J. Tilling, *Kings of the Highway* (London, 1957), p. 21.

[24] 'Mansion House London', *Leeds Times*, 4 November 1837, p. 21.

[25] *London Standard*, 10 January 1839, p. 4.

[26] 'Accident in Fleet Street', *Lloyd's Weekly Newspaper*, 29 December 1849, p. 25.

[27] *The Times*, 14 November 1865, p. 11.

Those accused of killing or maiming other road users when in a state of near-intoxication were sometimes allowed to pay or informally negotiate damages, either as individuals or employees of coach or cab companies. In 1805 in York, a plaintiff claimed that a drunk coach driver had knocked him down and broken his leg. The driver was reprimanded, but the injured party was subsequently awarded the astonishingly large sum of £600—paid, we must assume, by his employer.[28] A dozen or so years later, another intoxicated driver raced round Piccadilly Gardens in Manchester, overturned his vehicle and smashed a passenger's thigh. The bones failed to knit and the victim was crippled. The driver received a caution, but the coach company found itself liable for the barely credible sum of £2000.[29] In 1849, a respectable Londoner, a chaise driver, admitted to having drunk himself into a near-stupor before knocking down and seriously injuring two pedestrians. The magistrate warmed to the accused and offered him an escape route. Would he retire 'with his victims' and find a way of 'compensating them for the injuries they had received'? The medical bills were settled. The chaise driver went free.[30]

Increased coverage in newspapers in the 1860s suggests that road accidents were becoming more frequent in urban areas—and not only in Britain. In *Crime and Punishment*, Fyodor Dostoevsky spares us nothing in a reconstruction of a typical and alcohol-related fatality in St Petersburg in the mid-1860s. Each of the details corresponds to an uncanny degree to the typical course of events during a street crisis in later nineteenth-century London or Manchester. In Dostoevsky's account, Raskolnikov sets off on yet another of his interminable, guilt-ridden rambles round St Petersburg. He comes across a crowd milling round a stationary coach and realizes that the gory body on the pavement is that of his friend, the loquacious, once respectable and esteemed but now ne'er-do-well alcoholic Marmelodov: 'Blood was flowing from his face, from his head. His face was all battered, scraped, and mangled.' The crowd shows little sympathy for the victim and cheers the coach-driver on when he shouts: 'I saw him crossing the street, reeling, nearly falling over.' The driver had yelled a warning, but Marmelodov either failed to hear or deliberately threw himself—as many alcoholics were believed to do—under the

[28] *York Herald*, 15 June 1805, p. 11.
[29] 'Furious Driving', *Manchester Mercury*, 15 July 1817, p. 3.
[30] 'Police', *London Standard*, 26 December 1849, p. 4.

wheels of the coach.[31] Raskolnikov gets his friend home and calls for a doctor. But when the victim's shirt is removed, his family wish it had been left where it was:

> His whole chest was torn, mangled, mutilated; several ribs on the right side were broken. On the left side, just over the heart, there was a large, ominous yellow-blackish spot, the cruel blow of a hoof ... The policeman [said that] the injured man had been caught in a wheel and dragged, turning, about thirty paces along the pavement.[32]

In a speech in 1873, the Liberal Home Secretary H.A. Bruce adopted a surprisingly pessimistic position in the Commons. In London, he implied, Dostoevyskian scenes were everyday events. 'Agents of death' lurked round every corner. Vans competed with light and heavy carts and wagons and drays struggled for space with carriages, 'ridden horses', omnibuses and cabs. (Between 1869 and 1872, according to Bruce, the number of cabs in London had increased from 5500 to 7000.) Street accidents, he stated, were surprisingly rare in crowded areas which possessed formal crossings. But serious incidents were becoming more frequent in less effectively 'guarded' back-streets. According to official statistics, more lives were lost on the suburban streets and roads of leafy Highgate than any other part of the Metropolitan Police District.[33]

In 1876, vehicular confusion in Sheffield, leading to the death of an elderly woman who was trying to cross the road in the path of a tram, confirmed several of Bruce's points. The suspect was a cart-driving publican who had failed to make allowance for a tram and, swerving unpredictably, struck the pedestrian and killed her. Street witnesses believed that the suspect displayed the classic signs of being 'furiously' drunk. In the coroner's court, a similar picture emerged: the publican had been out of control and failed to slow down as the tram approached. The coroner struggled to make sense of the testimony and counter-testimony. He also tried to set out the prevailing—and confusing—position at law.

[31] F. Dostoevsky, *Crime and Punishment*, trans. R. Pevear and L. Volokhonsky (London, 2007), pp. 175–6.

[32] *Ibid.*, p. 182.

[33] *Hansard (House of Commons)*, 3rd ser., vol. 216, cols 994–7 (16 June 1873). On slightly improved levels of traffic control in some places in the capital at this time, see Winter, *London's Teeming Streets*, p. 48.

The accused, he said, possessed an inalienable right to drive along any thoroughfare legally open to him. At the same time, nobody should be allowed to prevent an unfortunate person like the deceased from 'going about her business'. A driver must take every care not to 'run people over'; equally, a pedestrian had a duty to 'take precautions not to be run over'. The coroner also said that if a horseman were seen to be over-using the whip (as the publican had been) and in a manner that might be intuitively connected to 'furious' intoxication or irresponsibility, he should be found guilty of a serious offence. On the other hand, the jury might decide that although an individual like the publican had been driving too fast, he may not have been involved in a legally culpable act.

In other words, the publican may have become involved in a street accident—like many thousands of others—'to which no blame attached'. Struggling to sustain legal coherence, the coroner had gradually marginalized and neutralized the issue of alcohol—the aspect of the incident that had originally triggered anger, argument and counter-argument in the street. The question of responsibility had been simplified—accidental or non-accidental, blameworthy or blame-free. Did the jury understand what the coroner had said? Possibly not: in Essex in the early 1860s, a jury concluded that a 'deceased came by his death accidently, through the dangerous driving of the accused'. The coroner sent them back to reconsider their verdict.[34] In the Sheffield case, the publican was declared innocent.[35]

During the 1870s, a handful of reformers—including the short-lived Society for the Prevention of Street Accidents and Dangerous Driving—claimed that the law had failed to adjust to a radically different kind of transport environment.[36] At the same time, magistrates and judges continued to adopt a lenient attitude towards both 'respectable' and working-class members of the community who drank to excess, drove or rode 'furiously', and knocked down and killed or seriously injured tram and omnibus passengers, pedestrians and bystanders. Children seemed more vulnerable than they had been. Playing and running in the street or cadging a fun-filled lift from a carter or drayman too often ended in disaster.

[34] 'Committed for Manslaughter', *Essex Standard*, 3 May 1861, p. 3.

[35] 'The Fatal Street Accident in the Wicker', *Sheffield Independent*, 25 October 1876, p. 4.

[36] On this elusive organization, see 'Street Accident and Dangerous Driving', *Morning Post*, 8 July 1879, p. 7; *Huddersfield Chronicle*, 11 October 1879, p. 7; and R. Cooter, 'The Moment of the Accident: Culture, Militarism and Modernity in Late-Victorian Britain', in Cooter and Luckin (eds), *Accidents in History*, pp. 108, 123–4.

Writing about the capital, James Winter confirms the trend: during the final third of the nineteenth century, conditions became more 'harrowing' for anyone crossing a street with a child in tow.[37] Those responsible for killing or maiming the young frequently escaped with light sentences. In 1877, in Belfast a court erupted into near-violence after a 5-year-old died as a result of being mangled by a 'heavy-wheeled float'. The driver, who said that he had consumed a 'little drink', was judged sober and released.[38] A year later, an intoxicated drayman ran down and killed a child of 10. The girl 'lingered' for a few days, but then died. The legal record fades at the point at which the drayman entered the plea that unavoidable 'skidding' on tram lines, rather than drunkenness, had made it impossible for him to avoid the accident.[39] In the early 1880s, a 'stupefied' London cabdriver was sent to prison for seriously injuring a child, but only for 3 weeks.[40]

Glimpsing a Vision of 'Safety'?

The final 30 years of the century witnessed the beginnings of a kind of anti-accident movement. The London-based Society for the Prevention of Street Accidents and Dangerous Driving, mentioned above, made little headway. In Manchester, the *Evening News* welcomed the formation of the new body. In that city, an editorial stated, 'thousands of vehicles' were still passing along streets that were 'no wider' or 'more commodious' than they had been a century earlier. In those days, the population had been 'low' and 'omnibuses, cabs, lorries, railway vans, tradesmen's carts, tram-cars, and carriages of all kinds' were almost wholly unknown. In more recent times, drivers and riders had become insufferably arrogant. Nevertheless, the editorial continued, some pedestrians were deaf, 'others wholly or partly blind' and yet others 'hesitant and nervous'. 'Not a few' must be counted 'downright fools'. But the assumption that pedestrians should be blamed for the misery that accompanied street fatalities and injuries must be vigorously refuted. 'No justification ... [could be found] for running over them.'[41] Little of this made sense to the powerful Metropolitan Amalgamated Cabdrivers' Association. Scattered appeals for

[37] Winter, *London's Teeming Streets*, p. 49.
[38] 'Fatal Accident Inquest', *Belfast Newsletter*, 7 July 1877, p. 3.
[39] 'Fatal Accident', *The Observer*, 31 August 1879, p. 6.
[40] *Morning Post*, 13 September 1881, p. 4.
[41] *Manchester Evening News*, 17 July 1879, p. 2.

reform convinced the cabmen that a conspiracy was afoot. It had clearly been mounted by a 'number of crotchety, fussy busybodies [who] would be likely to prove a great nuisance to the public and ... society in general'.[42]

Those who sympathized with accident victims faced an uphill battle. As early as 1845, a woman spoke out movingly during an investigation into the death of a young man in open country near Oxford, who had fallen from his horse. The victim, who had been on a day-long binge, lost control of his reins, fell forwards on to the ground and died when a heavy wheel passed directly 'over the full length of his body'. The woman told the court that 'it [was] high time some step was taken to prevent such furious and dangerous driving'.[43] In the same year at Stepney Green, a witness evoked sympathy for an elderly pedestrian who had been knocked down by an intoxicated carman. It had, he said, been his 'duty to interfere, and the duty of everyone to do so. If people would interfere when they see furious and reckless driving in the public streets, there would not be so many of these dreadful occurrences'. Accidents, he concluded, involved 'loss of valuable lives, and maiming of men, women and children'.[44]

None of this had a noticeable effect on daily life and movement in late Victorian roads and countless offenders continued to walk free. The intoxicated driver of a break in Eltham, who crashed into and overturned another vehicle, which then tumbled over and killed a female pedestrian, found himself judged guilty of appalling behaviour, but not in a sufficiently strong form to render him guilty of criminal negligence. This was despite the fact that several witnesses stated that they had seen him wobble drunkenly before falling flat on his face on the road.[45] The difficulties of forcing home a charge of criminal negligence were as prevalent as they had ever been. This was demonstrated in 1883 in a notorious fatality near Towcester. On a dark country road, an allegedly drunk hawker drove his cart into the trap of an elderly woman—a member of the social elite—who had been staying at a grand country house. The lady was thrown out of her carriage. She 'lingered on' with gangrene, but then died. The coroner's jury concluded that the hawker had been 'very much the worse for wear' and must therefore be adjudged fully responsible for the lady's death. In the upper court, however, the charge was dismissed. As the *Northampton Mercury*

[42] 'Street Accidents', *The Times*, 15 January 1880, p. 10.

[43] 'Fatal Accident from Furious Driving', *Sheffield Independent*, 9 September 1845, p. 8.

[44] 'Killed in the Streets', *East London Observer*, 11 September 1869, p. 7.

[45] 'Summary of the Morning's News', *Pall Mall Gazette*, 6 September 1880, p. 1.

rather wearily put it, the decision 'should not surprise [readers] ... seeing how difficult it is to prove criminal negligence'.[46] At the inquest hearing, the coroner had emphasized—in a familiar theme—that in cases of this kind, there would always be contradictory testimony.[47]

That the arrival of the internal combustion engine exacerbated dangers already associated with an ever-wider range of vehicles jostling for space on urban streets is well known.[48] Writing in the late 1930s, Virginia Woolf, an obsessive and accurate observer of urban change, described in fictional form the visual shock of encountering a radically modified and now increasingly heavily motor-influenced traffic flow in a socially exclusive sector of the West End in 1910: 'Down Park Lane and Piccadilly vans, cars, omnibuses ran along the streets as if the streets were slots; stopped and jerked; as if a puzzle were solved, and then broken, for it was the season and the streets were crowded.'[49] Nevertheless, in the early years of the automotive revolution, the vast majority of accidents—including those involving indisputably intoxicated drivers—continued to involve horses and horse-drawn vehicles. (There were only about 9000 cars in Britain in 1904.)[50] In 1895 in Bromley, Kent, a jobmaster hurtled down a hill in a trap and killed a woman. He told the coroner's jury that he had had a 'drop to drink', but no more than that. A witness and a police-surgeon at the station where the suspect was examined—this was now an increasingly widespread procedure—supported his claim, but the jury disagreed. At the point at which the jobmaster fades from the historical record, he was about to be remanded on suspicion of manslaughter.[51]

Now, as earlier, the intermixing of public and private modes of travel exacerbated the dangers of the street. In an exceptionally well-documented case in Manchester in 1895, a pedestrian was killed when she tried to cross the road in front of an oncoming tram. The driver, John Dale, was charged with causing the death of Elizabeth Madden, aged 60. Madden had tried to cross the road when the vehicle was only four yards away. A witness stated that as soon as the victim had been knocked down, Dale shouted 'Let the horses go' and 'whipped them up'. He had clearly hoped to get

[46] 'Towcester: Notes on the News', *Northampton Mercury*, 26 January 1884, p. 4.

[47] 'The Case of Alleged Manslaughter', *Northampton Mercury*, 19 January 1884, p. 8.

[48] Plowden, *Motor Car and Politics*, pp. 60–83; and S. O'Connell, *The Car and British Society: Class, Gender and Motoring, 1896–1939* (Manchester, 1998), pp. 119–21.

[49] V. Woolf, *The Years* (London, 1937), p. 139.

[50] Plowden, *Motor Car and Politics*, Appendix B, p. 456.

[51] 'The Charge against the Jobmaster', *Pall Mall Gazette*, 4 October 1895, p. 7.

away before the law lumbered into action. Eventually a policeman was summoned and Dale was stopped. At the station, the suspect admitted he had been drinking and then added gloomily: 'This is hard cheese for me.'

The hearing at Salford Police Court was dominated by the usual kind of conflicting on-the-spot testimony. Witnesses used radically different criteria to substantiate claims about Dale's mental and behavioural state. The suspect was defended by a solicitor employed by the Manchester Carriage and Tramways Company. The solicitor used three arguments. First, Dale had not exceeded the eight miles per hour speed limit laid down by the Board of Trade. Second, he could not have been drunk because—despite the death of Madden—he had in fact (or so it was claimed) completed a full day's work. Finally, four yards' 'notice' had been insufficient to prevent a fatal collision. Madden had behaved irresponsibly, not Dale. During the trial, the question of drunkenness gradually became marginalized. The bench concluded that the evidence was insufficient to remand the suspect on a charge of manslaughter, indicating yet again how difficult it was to find an offender guilty of criminal negligence. The bench also agreed with the defence argument that the driver had completed a full daily contractual obligation. Elizabeth Madden's rush across the road had been self-destructively life-threatening: the elderly pedestrian, not Dale, must take the posthumous blame.[52]

Nevertheless, and despite the dominant role of horses and horse power in town and country, Britons now found themselves having to confront increasing numbers of incidents exclusively associated with or caused by motor vehicles. Town dwellers had partially adjusted to radical changes in traffic flows from the 1850s onwards. Had they failed to do so, surely many more would have been killed or seriously injured than was in fact the case. But those living in both urban and rural areas found the new 'mechanical marauder' deeply disorienting. In a Leicestershire village in 1896, a 'bewildered' woman stepped out in front of a car. She was knocked down and seriously injured. 'There were', the magistrate was told, 'no notice-boards up cautioning people to look out for cars.' Eye-witnesses differed about the speed of the car, with estimates varying between the pace of a bicycle, a fire-engine and a fast gallop. The motorist had 'rung his bell', but this had seemed to 'bewilder' the woman: she panicked and stepped into the road.[53] Town officials protested against

[52] 'The Charge against a Tramcar Driver', *Manchester Evening News*, 2 October 1895, p. 3.
[53] 'Fatal Motor Car Accident', *Stamford Mercury*, 28 August 1896, p. 3.

the dangers of the new motor age. In 1898, a coroner in Scarborough complained that 'we do not like the idea of motor cars coming into the town, and knocking people over. We ought to satisfy ourselves as to the safety of such machines'.[54]

Two years later in Derby, a joy-riding motorist dumbfounded the local community by driving his machine repeatedly round the Corn Market: 'twelve persons ... were compelled to jump out of his way'. The car was traveling at 12 miles per hour.[55] In the same year, Dundee, a city that had relatively few motor cars, experienced a rash of 'furious' driving cases, including an incident that led to the death of a child. Perhaps, some argued, the new cult of speed had been transmitted by the revolutionary arrival of the internal combustion engine, which, in the manner of a deadly disease, infected cabmen, carters and gentlemanly riders.[56] Motorists drank as heavily as cabmen and tram drivers, but on countless occasions, this played a triggering role in increasing speed and either killing or injuring victims more grievously than in the period that had been wholly dominated by horse power. On a road near Lancaster in 1899, an intoxicated driver, travelling at 18 miles per hour, ran up and over a footpath and knocked down a woman. She survived, but her baby was 'thrown out of a bassinette', with horrific consequences.[57]

By the beginning of the new century, national and local newspaper readers were being bombarded with details of a spate of exceptionally serious incidents on the roads, including many involving the excesses of fast-driving metropolitan party-goers. At two o'clock in the morning in Paddington in May 1904, a driver careered down a street at between 25 and 30 miles per hour. He collided with a hansom cab, killing a female passenger. Two other people in the car were intoxicated. The motorist claimed that 'he had had something to drink, but was not drunk'. He escaped with a £10 fine.[58]

As serious injuries and fatalities attributable to motors appeared to be on the increase, alcohol—and the quest to understand the impact of drinking on drivers' competence—preoccupied the courts to a greater

[54] 'The Fatal Motor Car Accident at Scarborough', *Sheffield Daily Telegraph*, 21 April 1898, p. 6.

[55] 'County Police Court', *Derby Mercury*, 28 December 1898, p. 7.

[56] 'Child Fatally Injured', *Dundee Courier*, 29 April 1898, p. 6.

[57] 'Motor Car Driver Fined', *Coventry Evening Telegraph*, 15 May 1899, p. 4.

[58] 'Serious Motor Accidents', *Manchester Courier and Lancashire General Advertiser*, 21 May 1904, p. 8.

degree than in the pre-motor period. Increasingly, coroners, magistrates, judges and juries asked whether there was any evidence to imply that a driver or rider had visited a tavern or hotel on the day of an accident. How much had been drunk? Did the evidence suggest that a suspect had become heavily intoxicated? What invariably remained obscure, however, was precisely how much may have been consumed—bar-room reminiscences provided astonishingly confusing testimony for judges and jurors—and what kind of effect a given number of drinks may have had on a driver's ability to control his vehicle. During a debate on the report stage of the Motor Car Bill in 1903, a small number of members circled round the problem. A.H. Allhusen, Conservative MP for Hackney Central, argued that the motor industry must protect itself by supporting a measure to 'purge' drivers 'addicted' to alcohol.[59] W.L.A.B. Burdett-Coutts, Conservative MP for Westminster, seconded the idea of introducing a deterrent clause because he feared that only a very small number of people understood the 'delicate and dangerous nature of motor car driving'.[60] But the vast majority agreed with the President of the Local Government Board, Walter Long. A problem existed, but it would surely be very 'hard' to take away a man's licence 'if he was found drunk on one occasion.'[61] Motor drivers and chauffeurs were privileged species.

A small number of coroners and judges were beginning to have doubts about the reliance on traditional definitions of drunkenness. What precisely was it? How could it be measured and evaluated? In 1905, a judge at Warwick Assizes sentenced an intoxicated motorist, responsible for running down and killing a pedestrian, to 2 months' imprisonment. In his summary, he asked whether road users could ever feel 'comfortable' about hearing a 'motor-car coming at night [and] not knowing if the driver [was] sober or not?'[62] A year later, the report of the Royal Commission on Motor Cars recommended a measure to sentence first offenders to a £10 fine or a month's imprisonment. To this would be added an endorsement. A second offence would involve 'deprivation of the license for such period as the Court may think fit in addition to the other penalties prescribed

[59] *Hansard (House of Commons)*, 4th ser., vol. 127, col. 480 (7 August 1903).
[60] *Ibid*., col. 482.
[61] *Ibid*., col. 480.
[62] 'The Motor Fiend', *Leamington Spa Courier*, 3 February 1905, p. 5.

by the [proposed] Act'.[63] Parliament failed to act not least because, as a spokesman for the militantly pro-car Motor Union insisted, drunk driving constituted a much less pressing problem in most people's minds than speed, 'dust and recklessness'.[64] He may have been right. Speed—and the 'cult of speed'—rather than the dangers of starting a journey under the influence of alcohol (and hence invariably travelling much faster and less safely than someone who was sober) lay at the heart of pro-pedestrian agendas seeking to delay the now widely predicted dominance of the internal combustion engine.

Speaking for the Road Union, an organization that campaigned for the rights of the non-driving public, the Duke of Northumberland hoped that motor owners, 'intoxicated, as it were, by the power of speed, suddenly put in their hands', would, as the new machine became 'more familiar' to them, 'use it in a more becoming manner'.[65] Few shared Northumberland's muted optimism, not least since intoxicated drivers were now using increasingly subtle ploys to evade prosecution. In 1909, a motor engineer's joyride to Southend ended in the death of a 14-year-old boy. Was it a sign of slightly changing times that the driver, who had been stopping off at pubs for most of the day, tried to protect himself by nobbling a passing labourer who had seen the accident and said: 'You don't want to get me into trouble', and to a bystander, 'You know I've only had a glass or two'?[66] Northumberland's choice of words may have been deliberate—'intoxicated by speed'—but the dangers of drink driving failed to feature on Road Union agendas. However, more judges now made their anxieties known. In 1913 in Manchester, a private owner had his appeal for clemency rejected. The judge told him that drunk driving had become disastrously frequent. Manchester must clamp down on blatant irresponsibility on the part of intoxicated and speeding motorists. Sentencing the man to 12 months' hard labour, he warned the community that 'things [had become] bad'. Something must be done.[67]

[63] *Royal Commission on Motor Cars, Volume I: Report of the Royal Commission on Motor Cars* (Parl. Papers 1906 [Cd. 3080]), p. 36.

[64] *Royal Commission on Motor Cars, Volume II: Minutes of Evidence taken by the Royal Commission on Motor Cars with Appendices and Index* (Parl. Papers 1906 [Cd. 3081]). Qs. 11, pp. 469–73. Evidence of George Langridge.

[65] 'A Duke Speaks Out', *Hull Daily Mail*, 28 October 1908, p. 4.

[66] 'The Hadleigh Motor Fatality', *Chelmsford Chronicle*, 26 February 1909, p. 6.

[67] 'Sentence on Stubbs: Twelve Months', *Manchester Courier and General Advertiser*, 22 February 1913, p. 12.

Drink and Accidents in the Motor Age

The problem came into full focus during evidence given to the Select Committee on Motor Traffic in 1913. The Commissioner of Police for the City of London, Sir William Nott-Bower, presented a census of traffic flow in the Golden Square Mile between seven in the morning and seven at night. This had been taken on a single day in April 1911. Nott-Bower divided vehicle categories into 'mechanically propelled' and 'horse drawn'. Unsurprisingly, the internal combustion engine had made massive strides: over 10,000 cabs and cars and 5500 omnibuses had entered, left or travelled within the confines of the City on the day in question. Nevertheless, the total of 'horse propelled' still massively outnumbered motor-powered vehicles: when the census was taken, there were 45,000 vans, carts and 'others' in that category. In addition to motor cars and vans and horse-drawn omnibuses, pedestrians in the City had to watch out for nearly 3000 'carrier' and 9500 pedal cycles.[68]

Little had changed by the end of the First World War: in 1918, British railway companies still relied on 32,500 horse-drawn vehicles as opposed to about 250 motor conveyances.[69] Nevertheless, in every urban area, the struggle for space between traditional and novel forms of transport had become increasingly risk-ridden (though the terms 'risk' and 'safety' were seldom heard in court hearings during this period). Traffic control remained underdeveloped; so did the working reality of an accepted etiquette on the road. Drunk or sober, more drivers were crashing into horses and horse-drawn vans, carts and omnibuses, and more panicked horses were now colliding with cars and bicycles. Many drivers and riders were horribly mangled, but many more pedestrians almost certainly became the victims of death and injury on the street. Little wonder that in 1912, an editorial writer at *The Times* rather helplessly concluded that the 'truth about accidents seems hidden in a pretty deep well'.[70]

Meanwhile, newspapers carried stories detailing tragic aspects of fatal car (and horse-associated) accidents. In May 1913 near Leicester, two men and a 'lady passenger' set off for home following a day's drinking in

[68] *Report from the Select Committee on Motor Traffic, with Proceedings, Evidence, Appendices, and Index* (Parl. Papers 1913 (278)). Q. 1, p. 243. Evidence of Sir William Nott-Bower. For a London census undertaken in 1904, see also J.F.J. Reynolds, *General Notes on the Problem of London Traffic* (London, 1904), p. 37.

[69] P.S. Bagwell, *The Transport Revolution, 1770–1885* (London, 1974), pp. 210–11.

[70] 'Automobilism', *The Times*, 9 April 1912, p. 11.

pubs and hotels. The owner of the car was a well-to-do industrialist. He had bought champagne and a 'small bottle of port' for the journey. His companion, who was also his chauffeur, heard a dull bump: he had run over a female pedestrian. The chauffeur tried to stop, but the industrialist shouted out: 'Drive on for the sake of the girl', referring to his lady friend in the back. The pedestrian was left on the road to die. In his comments to the jury, the coroner spoke of 'disgrace', but the fatality was officially recorded as an accident.[71]

When he gave evidence to the Select Committee on Motor Traffic in 1913, Sir Edward Henry, the Commissioner of the Metropolitan Police, argued that whenever a motorist was suspected of being 'drunk', he should be charged under a new and separate act. Current procedures had failed. Henry stated that when a London motorist was believed to be intoxicated, he was taken to a station and 'watched'. By the time a sub-divisional surgeon had arrived, the time lapse allowed too many drivers to 'pull round'. Too often, motorists (and riders) who had been 'drunk' two hours earlier were adjudged to be within the margin of safety.[72] Sir William Nott-Bower made a complementary point. The police were not seeking 'arbitrary powers', but with the law as it stood, constables faced an impossible task. Amid the hubbub that accompanied a street accident, it was impossible for an officer to 'make a calm and deliberate inquiry'. Surely it would be better if the suspect were taken back to the station to ensure a degree of 'calmness', something 'notoriously absent in the hustle and bustle of the street'?[73]

Thirty years before the gloomy editorial in *The Times* in 1912, the *Edinburgh Evening News* drew attention to the 'Southport experiment'. The town's police had decided to replace impressionistic, eye-witness (and, very often, also courtroom) terms—'drunk as a lord', 'fuddled', 'sober as a judge'—with a single test: could a suspect walk steadily along a six-inch-wide board?[74] Sobriety tests changed slowly, and each locality had its own means of telling whether a driver was unambiguously intoxicated. At the end of the First World War, a Lambeth police-surgeon claimed that he swore by a method that required a suspect to write his or her name,

[71] 'Motor Tragedy', *Manchester Courier and Lancashire General Advertiser*, 9 May 1913, p. 15.

[72] *Report from the Select Committee on Motor Traffic*. Q. 2795. Evidence of Sir Edward Henry.

[73] *Ibid*. Qs. 1371–5. Evidence of Sir William Nott-Bower.

[74] 'A Test of Drunkenness', *Edinburgh Evening News*, 18 January 1882, p. 3.

pick up a pin from a desk and say 'provisional artillery'.[75] In the same year, a sheriff in Fife—half-playfully, possibly not—told the jury that if a man 'could count his change he was not drunk'.[76] In 1922 at the Old Bailey, a doctor told a judge that he had flashed a light in the eyes of a driver suspected of being intoxicated following a serious accident. He wanted to know whether the man's pupils had contracted and 'at what speed'. The judge responded: 'You don't use the chalk line test?' Pedantically, the doctor responded that, in his opinion, this was the 'unfairest test in the world—enough to make a man drunk'. The defence lawyer joined in the fun: 'You did not try the prisoner with "ragged rascals run", or something of that kind?'[77]

The role of the historian is to explain why people thought about an issue in the way they did rather than the ways in which they should have thought, according to early twenty-first-century standards. In Britain in the early 1920s, very few specialists believed that drunk driving accounted for large numbers of fatalities or injuries, or that the government should support radical road traffic reform. But by the mid-1930s—when the nation found itself engulfed in an accident crisis of unprecedented proportions—growing numbers believed that ministers and civil servants should take the 'Scandinavian' road. A small international road safety movement had come into being and in terms of legislative change, the Ministry of Transport (MoT) knew just about everything that it needed to know about the differences between drunkenness and impairment. A small group of scientists, including the prolific 'accident specialist' H.M. Vernon, the public health supremo Sir Arthur Newsholme and the eminent statistician Major Greenwood, were strongly attracted to elements of the 'Scandinavian model'. They made their views known to the MoT, but to little effect.[78]

A generation or so earlier, in the 1890s, a small number of coroners, judges and politicians came to the conclusion that there might be all the difference in the world between being intoxicated and alcoholically impaired. These were two different conditions, but the latter, 'invisible' one could evidently be as dangerous as full drunkenness, as identified by the 'signs' ritually recited in eye-witness accounts of accidents. A driver who had consumed a 'reasonable' amount might make a mistake that could lead to bloody and tragic consequences.

[75] *Derby Daily Telegraph*, 19 May 1920, p. 3.

[76] 'Reckless Driving in Fife', *Dundee Courier*, 4 August 1920, p. 4.

[77] 'Sobriety Test', *Evening Telegraph*, 23 November 1922, p. 3.

[78] Luckin, 'A Never-Ending Passing of the Buck'.

Between the early nineteenth century and the 1890s, changes in the rate of circulation gave birth to wide-ranging repercussions for non-riders and, to a lesser extent, riders and drivers. Problems, particularly in relation to the severity of injuries, intensified with the arrival of the internal combustion engine. Throughout the period as a whole, walking down a city street became an increasingly dangerous activity.[79] At a remarkably early date, the onus fell on non-drivers, who were implicitly expected to adjust to a new phase in the transport needs of what many believed to be the greatest material civilization the world had ever seen, and in which speed had become inseparable from large-scale regional industrialization and a massive increase in the movement of people and goods.[80] Drivers and riders were asked by judges and coroners to proceed 'cautiously'. Both groups had to steer clear of pedestrians who failed to take due care when crossing the road. However, in court summaries, the vast majority of judges and coroners adhered to a well-worn watchword: vehicles first, pedestrians second.

Conclusion

Between the early nineteenth century and the 1890s, coaches, carts, buses and trams dominated the social relations of mobility and laid the basis for the full emergence of pro-motorism in the early twentieth century. If a driver or rider from any social class killed or maimed a pedestrian, he might, if he were unlucky, find himself tried for criminal manslaughter. But between 1800 and 1920, this proved an exceptionally difficult charge to sustain. Only a paltry proportion of individuals out of many thousands of annual offenders found it necessary to defend themselves in an upper court for criminal negligence. Most suspects received a moral dressing down and/or a fine and 'returned', stigma-free, to the society and class to which they belonged. Since punishment normally took the form of a reprimand, lessons were unlikely to be learnt.[81] Only in the very recent

[79] Winter, *London's Teeming Streets*, p. 49.

[80] The classic interpretation remains W. Shivelbusch, *The Railway Journey: The Industrialization of Space and Time in the Nineteenth Century* (Leamington Spa, 1986). See also C. Studeny, *L'invention de la vitesse: France XVIIIe–XXe siècle* (Paris, 1995); and S. Kern, *The Culture of Time and Space, 1880–1918* (London, 1983).

[81] J. Braithwaite, *Crime, Shame and Reintegration* (Cambridge, 1988).

past have road traffic accidents involving drunk and/or dangerous driving become fully moralized *and* criminalized.[82]

What, then, changed with the arrival of cars, vans and motor cycles at the end of the nineteenth century? Many things, of course, but one above all others. Since horses continued to play a major role in Britain's expanding transport system until the beginning of the 1920s, increasing numbers of drivers and non-drivers suffered injuries that were more severe than in the period between the beginning of the nineteenth century and the 1890s. When terrified horses ran into motors and motors ploughed into horse-drawn vehicles, a new world came into being. Countless drivers died or suffered grievously, but the historical record strongly suggests that many more pedestrians bore the brunt of accidental death and injury on the road.[83]

[82] In the early 1960s, when T.C. Willett completed the research for his *Criminal on the Road*, full criminalization and 'shaming' remained a distant reformist goal.

[83] Quantification for our period is, of course, thin on the ground. But see the retrospective analysis for the interwar period in G.O. Jeffcoate, 'The Importance of Alcohol in Road Accidents', *British Journal of Addiction* 54 (1958), pp. 37–50. This throws light back on to the pre-motor era.

CHAPTER 9

Risk on the Roads: Police, Motor Traffic and the Management of Space, c. 1900–50

Chris A. Williams

Policing does not merely respond to an outside world of people, practices and technologies; it actively helps to shape and constitute this world. Nowhere is this more apparent than in the ways in which the British police became, and remain, experts in the field of regulating motor traffic risks. They now expect and enjoy the right to be consulted on policy initiatives and legislation relating to traffic, and to serve on planning committees—an authority that builds on the day-to-day work of officers as agents of traffic management. The existing historiography on the police response to the rise of motorized traffic in the twentieth century can be usefully analysed through the threefold classification offered in Keith Laybourn's recent study: enforcement, education and engineering.[1] Previous work has tended to focus on the issue of *enforcement*: should the police have been the scourge or the champion of the motorist? Sean O'Connell has pointed to the extent to which the police were complicit in a rebalancing of law enforcement that favoured the private motorist; Clive Emsley

[1] K. Laybourn, *The Battle for Britain's Roads, c. 1890s to c. 1970s: Police, Motorists and the Law* (Basingstoke, 2015).

C.A. Williams
Arts Faculty, Open University, Walton Hall, Milton Keynes MK7 6AA, UK

T. Crook, M. Esbester (eds), *Governing Risks in Modern Britain*,
DOI 10.1057/978-1-137-46745-4_9

has noted that, even so, relationships between police officers and motorists remained a significant source of friction before 1939.[2] Laybourn and David Taylor have disputed O'Connell's characterization of the police as essentially on the side of the motorist, arguing that many police interventions were intended to maintain a balance between motorists, pedestrians and cyclists.[3] Mathew Thomson has written about *education*, particularly of children, and the role that it played over the course of the century in shifting British childhood indoors.[4] O'Connell sees the focus on education rather than enforcement as one way in which the motor lobby's interests were dominant.[5] Meanwhile, David Sheen and Bill Luckin have moved towards identifying a timescale over which these regulatory changes took place. They identify an experimental phase before 1920, followed by one characterized by the triumph of the motor lobby, which lasted until the 1960s, when the state took a stronger approach to enforcement.[6]

This chapter seeks to restore the importance of *engineering*, and the place and function of spatial-environmental solutions relating to the design of streets and roads. The use of these solutions was not necessarily to the detriment of tactics of enforcement and education, but it became the option that the police tended to prefer, certainly as a long-term solution. Two men in particular, Arthur Bassom (1865–1926) and Herbert Alker Tripp (1883–1954), played key roles throughout this period as traffic experts in the Metropolitan Police (hereinafter 'the Met'), and exemplify the growing authority of police officers in terms of determining policy and the management of traffic-related risks. Both men feature in the account that follows.

The broad aim, however, is twofold: first, to recover the professional and institutional milieu in which different strategies—and especially the engineering one—were developed, discussed and prioritized in order to

[2] S. O'Connell, *The Car in British Society: Class, Gender and Motoring, 1896–1939* (Manchester, 1998); C. Emsley, '"Mother, What *Did* Policemen Do When There Weren't Any Motors"? The Law, the Police and the Regulation of Traffic in England, 1900–1939', *Historical Journal* 36 (1993), pp. 357–81.

[3] K. Laybourn and D. Taylor, *Policing in England and Wales, 1918–39: The Fed, Flying Squads and Forensics* (Basingstoke, 2011), pp. 126–7.

[4] M. Thomson, *The Lost Freedom: The Landscape of the Child and the British Post-War Settlement* (Oxford, 2013), Chapter 5.

[5] O'Connell, *The Car in British Society*, p. 126.

[6] B. Luckin and D. Sheen, 'Defining Early Modern Automobility: The Road Traffic Accident Crisis in Manchester, 1939–45', *Cultural and Social History* 6 (2009), pp. 212–13.

manage risk on the roads; and, second, to examine the ways that claims to expertise on the part of police forces were supported by their ability to deploy knowledge of accidents, by their mastery of statistics, and by their durability and latency as an organization. As other chapters in this volume suggest, governing risks is a complex and composite process. Risks might be generated by the advent of new technologies, material substances and socio-environmental conditions: or crudely, in this case, the advent of more motor vehicles on Britain's streets. Equally, these risks also have to be defined and documented through different kinds of knowledge and associated forms of authority. Furthermore, choices have to be made about how to regulate them—contingent choices that are shaped by the interests and priorities of professionals and experts just as much as by the interests and priorities of commercial agents and members of the public. It is a composite quality very much in evidence here in the case of policing traffic-related risks amid the birth of a motorized society.

Policing Traffic in the Early Twentieth Century

In early twentieth-century Britain, policing was, among other things, a series of interventions into the public world of policy-making and governance, so that this world might better meet police priorities. Chief among these priorities was the creation of an environment for motorists, cyclists and pedestrians in which day-to-day traffic policing would be cheap and bureaucratically unproblematic. This was not necessarily about resisting a role per se in regulating traffic; rather, it involved ensuring that traffic regulation assumed a form that best suited the institutional interests and needs of the police. It was a pressing issue partly on account of the enormous increase in the number of motor vehicles, which, as Bill Luckin concludes in his contribution to this volume, posed a greater threat to life and limb compared to horse-drawn forms of transport: they were faster, heavier and generally more deadly. In 1905, there were roughly 32,000 motor vehicles on Britain's roads, counting both passenger cars and commercial vehicles; by 1940, this figure had increased to more than two million.[7] Managing traffic-related risks as part of a broad strategy of

[7] Figures cited in Emsley, '"Mother, What *Did* Policemen Do When There Weren't Any Motors"?', p. 358.

accident prevention—as opposed to one of detection and reaction, and labour-intensive law enforcement—was judged to be central to the long-term police mission.

This long-term view of the correct role of the police evolved over the period under consideration here, and it did so in a professional milieu that came into its own in the early twentieth century. Harold Perkin argued that from the late nineteenth century, a professional service class grew more and more powerful, largely at the expense of the owners of capital, but also in a way that tended to head off or co-opt the political challenge of organized labour. This was 'a self-confident, self-regulating, professional class imbued with the idea of public service', which was at the apogee of its power in the 1950s and 1960s.[8] Senior police officers and civil servants were part of this class and collectively were anxious to reproduce its values. Senior officers—many of whom later trained together at Hendon Police College, established in 1934—were members of an occupational world that enabled them to interact easily with their opposite numbers in motorists' pressure groups and local and central government. In particular, police experts in traffic were welcomed into elite circles such as the higher reaches of the Royal Automobile Club (RAC), earlier established in 1897 as a home of pro-motorism, as well as the Institute of Transport, an industrial interest group founded in 1919. Both were patronized by men of high status. Other key agents included local authorities, the Ministry of Transport, established in 1919, the National 'Safety First' Association (NSFA), formed in London in 1916 and largely financed by the motor industry (it later became the Royal Society for the Prevention of Accidents, or RoSPA, in 1941), and the Road Research Laboratory, established in 1933 by the Department of Scientific and Industrial Research.

Professional status, however, was only one component of the authority of the police in relation to traffic and the determination of traffic policies. It was also rooted in practice and the logistical presence of police officers as agents of enforcement: as one member of the Met's civilian staff claimed in 1920 in the *Police Review*, the police were the 'only organisation in the country which possess the necessary machinery for the proper

[8] H. Perkin, *The Third Revolution: Professional Elites in the Modern World* (London, 1996); M. Thompson, review of *The Third Revolution: Professional Elites in the Modern World* in *Reviews in History*. Available at: www.history.ac.uk/reviews/review/29 (date accessed 18 November 2015).

and effective control of the roads'.[9] This was already apparent before the First World War, when police responses to the problem of motor traffic were largely reactive and ad hoc. Crucial here were practices of street-level law enforcement, such as a constable directing traffic, a role the police had exercised since the mid-Victorian period. Motor vehicles joined horse-drawn vehicles as objects of monitoring and occasional prosecution. Other established tactics included the licensing and inspection of cabs and buses.[10] All of these practices continued into the interwar period, when they were joined by a host of further policy initiatives that were variously legal, educational and environmental. The first legislation to target specifically petrol-powered vehicles was the 1903 Motor Car Act, which set a speed limit of 20 miles per hour on public highways and introduced the mandatory registration of vehicles. Further acts followed: the 1930 Road Traffic Act, for instance, imposed new responsibilities on car drivers, making third party insurance obligatory, 'careless driving' an offence and disqualification an ultimate sanction.

These laws, of course, required enforcement, which was ultimately the role of the police. Some relief, however, was afforded by the emergence of targeted educational initiatives, which were largely welcomed by the police. The Highway Code, for instance, was first published in 1931, setting out what the then Minister of Transport, Herbert Morrison, described in the preface as those 'good manners' that 'all courteous and considerate persons' should observe.[11] The BBC and the NSFA began encouraging what was termed 'road sense' in the 1930s, a campaign sponsored by the Ministry of Transport (MoT) that focused on educating all road users as an alternative to greater legal restrictions on drivers. Posters and window bills were used to spread the message, as well as radio adverts and short cinema films. Police themselves played a role: from the mid-1930s, it became common for officers to visit schools and lecture pupils.[12]

Finally—and along with the MoT, NFSA and various expert bodies such as the British Medical Association—the police played a role in recommending and advising on similarly bespoke environmental interventions, which were paid for by local authorities. Established interventions, such

[9] *Police Review*, 9 January 1920, p. 12.

[10] C. Emsley, *The English Police: A Political and Social History*, 2nd edn (London, 1996), pp. 147–8, 229–30.

[11] Ministry of Transport, *The Highway Code* (London, 1931), p. 1.

[12] J. Moran, 'Crossing the Road in Britain, 1931–1976', *Historical Journal* 49 (2006), pp. 481–3.

as subways and 'traffic refuges' (or later 'pedestrian islands'), were more widely used. Other technologies were more novel, including electric-powered traffic lights, which were installed in British towns from 1927 onwards.[13] The most notable development was the attempt to provide designated crossing points. Beginning in London in the mid-1920s, various technologies were introduced, including the use of 'Please cross here' signs and amber globes, popularly called 'Belisha beacons', as well as the laying of two lines of studs to mark a specific area of passage. By the end of the 1940s, there were over 30,000 crossings in Britain. Further innovations stemmed from the work of the Road Research Laboratory. The laboratory was instrumental in the invention of the 'zebra' crossing in the late 1940s, after a series of studies on the conspicuousness of different road markings, and then, following further research in the 1950s, the 'pelican' crossing with a push-button-controlled signal.[14]

At the same time, within local police forces, more manpower and resources were dedicated to traffic responsibilities. Since the Victorian period, large urban forces had operated with special, if sometimes informal, sub-departments or teams dealing with carriages and cabs and securing order on roads. This process now intensified as 'traffic control' and the organization of 'traffic patrols' emerged as a part of police duties. The police themselves were motorized, partly by way of catching criminals on the move, but also by way of securing better traffic management. By the 1920s, for instance, the Met was in possession of a variety of cars, vans and motorcycles, and in 1934 appointed a Traffic Officer to oversee the force's resources in this respect, which amounted to more than 500 vehicles. A year later, a special driving school was established at Hendon Police College.[15] All of this was at the discretion of local forces and was only slowly supplemented by direction and encouragement from the Home Office. In the late 1930s, the Home Office began to fund special traffic patrols for selected police forces, initially as an experiment labelled 'courtesy cops', whereby policemen in cars would politely but firmly point out any minor infringements of the rules of the road. However, it was not

[13] M.M. Ishaque and R.B. Noland, 'Making Roads Safe for Pedestrians or Keeping Them Out of the Way? An Historical Perspective on Pedestrian Policies in Britain', *Journal of Transport History* 27 (2006), pp. 125–31.

[14] *Ibid.*, pp. 126–8.

[15] C.A. Williams, *Police Control Systems in Britain, 1775–1975: From Parish Constable to Control Room* (Manchester, 2014), pp. 148–52; *Report of the Commissioner of Police of the Metropolis for the Year 1934* (Parl. Papers 1934–5 [Cmd. 4866]), pp. 34–5.

until 1959 that special grants for traffic patrols were rolled into the Home Office's annual police grant.[16] At this point, they also became compulsory rather than optional and were henceforth carried out in a more standardized manner.

There were good reasons, perhaps, why the police gained power over traffic-related risks. Britain was home to more and more cars, and a growing body of regulations required enforcing. Most of all, the number of accidents, both fatal and non-fatal, increased. In 1913, the number was roughly 2000 and 40,000, respectively. By the 1930s, the number of road fatalities had risen to around 6000 a year, coupled with an average of roughly 150,000 non-fatal accidents.[17] Indeed, the importance of protecting the public from road traffic accidents evidently informed perceptions of police responsibilities. A policy statement prepared at the end of the Second World War by senior police officers in conjunction with the Home Office argued that, in order to meet the challenge of 'the present grave situation on the roads', police resources 'proportionate to the injury which is being done to the community' should be used. The paper overtly defended this position, in a departure from the usual departmental tone of policy papers: 'Random talk is often heard as to the Police being "withdrawn from their legitimate duties" to deal with traffic. Obviously, however, there can be no duty more legitimate and more essential than the protection of life and limb.'[18]

Nonetheless, we should avoid any Whiggish presumption of necessary progress, whereby problems eventually generate the solutions they deserve and the right agents to carry them out. As we shall see, choices had to be made about the nature and implementation of policies, and who should bear the administrative burden. Two broader points should also be made. The first is that the police had to lobby for power over policy-making: it was not something that was either assumed or taken for granted. To be sure, the police, and in particular high-ranking officers, were always consulted in the multiple royal commissions and select committee inquiries that were conducted from the start of the century, beginning with the Royal Commission on Motor Cars in 1905–6. Yet they were

[16] The National Archives (hereinafter TNA), Home Office (hereinafter HO) 287/163, Motor patrols: enquiry into increasing use of motor patrols; use of motor cycles with radios, 1950–1960.

[17] See figures in Emsley, '"Mother, What *Did* Policemen Do When There Weren't Any Motors"?', p. 359.

[18] TNA Ministry of Transport (hereinafter MT) 34/96, Traffic schemes: Mobile Police Force. n.d. (mid-1945).

consulted alongside multiple others agents, including magistrates, local councillors and car manufacturers (for example, the Society of Motor Manufacturers and Traders), as well as leading members of the RAC and cyclist and pedestrian associations.

Equally, the police often had to jockey for policy-making influence at the upper tiers of government, where they were not always welcome. In 1922, for example, the Central Conference of Chief Constables, the official representative body, had to ask the Home Office for greater involvement in the drawing-up of regulations for transport 'in order to secure, directly or indirectly, more effective control over motor traffic for the better protection of the public'.[19] The request was eventually granted and resulted in a comprehensive official report, published in 1925 and entitled 'Traffic Problems', produced by a committee of police chiefs and representatives of motor manufacturers and drivers.[20] The MoT, by contrast, was less willing than the Home Office to involve police officers in policy-making. The committee that produced its report on 'Taxation and Regulation of Road Vehicles' in 1922 had no police members, although it called upon police of varying ranks, right down to constables, to give evidence.[21] Earlier, in 1919, Frank Elliott, Assistant Commissioner to the Met, had been appointed by the Home Office to sit on a committee discussing matters connected with London traffic.[22] Even so, the MoT's decision to legislate on the issue in 1921 came as a surprise to the Met Commissioner, Sir William Horwood. He asked for more details, given that:

> it appears to me of the highest importance that before any rules and regulations for the control of London traffic are made, the Police, upon whom the onus of carrying out such rules will fall, should be consulted as to the details. I need hardly add that a Bill of this description, unless it has the advantage beforehand of criticism by experts, might very probably necessitate a considerable increase in the establishment of the Police Force if its proposals are to be properly carried out by the Police.[23]

[19] TNA HO 358/2, Home Office: Central Conference of Chief Constables: Minutes and Papers. Minutes of meeting held at the Home Office on 28 June 1922, p. 5.

[20] TNA HO 45/11961, Traffic problems. Police and Road Users' points of view, 1923–5: 'Report of the Committee of Representatives of Police Forces in Great Britain and of Road Users Appointed to Consider and Report on Traffic Problems' (1925).

[21] TNA HO 45/11961, Traffic Problems. 'Second Interim Report of Ministry of Transport Departmental Committee on the Taxation and Regulation of Road Vehicles' (1922).

[22] TNA HO 45/12256, London Traffic Bills, 1923 and 1924 Metropolitan Police Orders 1926. 1919–26: Memo 'Ministry of Transport', 23 July 1923.

[23] TNA HO 45/12256, London Traffic Bill Letter from Commissioner, 16 July 1921.

Following Horwood's intervention, the Home Office expressed doubts about the proper role of the police in this process, supporting more MoT involvement and noting that the Home Office 'has never been equipped with the machinery or the staff for traffic work, and we have had to depend for expert advice on the Commissioner's staff, who are naturally inclined to look at these questions from a police point of view'.[24] Not every civil servant who commented agreed with this position, but it seems that even the Home Office was not completely happy with the degree it had to rely on the input of the police. Skirmishes of this sort were not necessarily endemic. Nonetheless, they attest to the fact that it was never axiomatic that the police should wield influence over the formation of traffic regulations, even if, as Horwood argued, police officers were responsible for enforcing measures on the ground.

The second key point is linked to the first and is evident in Horwood's anxieties: simply that whilst the police were eager to protect the public on the streets and ensure public order, they were also profoundly conscious of their multiple other roles and limited resources. As Emsley has shown, from the start of the century, a common complaint among police officers was the onerous nature of their traffic responsibilities. Some of them seem to have sympathized with pro-motorist depictions of the police as unwelcome agents of regulation, and most officers were conscious of the need to enjoy good relations with the public.[25] Equally, there was the threat of traffic responsibilities unduly distracting from their other roles. As Laybourn has shown, senior officers such as Leonard Dunning, first as Head Constable of Liverpool and then as the Home Office-based Inspector of Constabulary during the period from 1912 to 1930, held a consistent position that the police had become overburdened with administrative duties. Suppressing crime and catching criminals, not harassing motorists, was the 'true' vocation of the police. The likes of Dunning looked to establish a separate force of traffic wardens to regulate cars.[26]

This process created an ongoing argument about what the precise role of the police should be. The growing risks posed by motor traffic meant that few resisted entirely some role in controlling the streets. In fact, the general consensus was that a role should be exercised; the question was

[24] TNA HO 45/12256, London Traffic Bills. Memo 'Ministry of Transport', 23 July 1923.

[25] Emsley, '"Mother, What *Did* Policemen Do When There Weren't Any Motors"?', pp. 371–7.

[26] Laybourn, *The Battle for Britain's Roads, c. 1890s to c. 1970s*, p. 74.

what kind of role and what it amounted to in practice, given other priorities. One instance of this kind of agonizing can be found in the conclusion to a royal commission convened in 1928 to review the powers of the police as a whole. Under a section entitled 'Miscellaneous Duties', it bemoaned the messy variety of functions that had arisen 'quite outside the sphere of the prevention and detection of crime', including in relation to dog licences, diseases of animals, 'aliens' (immigrants) and the sale of food and drugs. In terms of additional burdens, however, the report singled out 'the phenomenal growth of work in connection with road traffic which has resulted from the advent of the motor vehicle'. This had not only 'diverted' resources away from preventing crime, which the report regarded as 'fundamental'; it had brought 'a large number of law-abiding citizens', for the first time, 'into conflict with the law', creating unprecedented 'antagonisms': 'Under present circumstances the Police are in danger of being overburdened with duties, whilst their efficiency is being simultaneously impaired by criticism that is often unfair and undeserved.' And yet, the commission's report went on, the police were undoubtedly the best body for applying new laws and regulations, given 'their training and tradition'. More public money was surely part of the solution, it suggested.[27] Similar arguments can be found throughout the interwar period and they evidently informed more local assessments of the role of the police, as we shall see. But first we should look at the kinds of knowledge the police wielded in the service of demonstrating their authority and organizational advantages.

Information, Practice and Authority

At the heart of this authority was not just the experience and presence of officers on the beat, in and around streets; it was also based on the knowledge that was derived from these institutional and organizational strengths. The police were not the only repository of information about traffic risks and related accidents and fatalities. As Chapter 1 of this volume has noted, the General Register Office was a vital source of information in relation to national aggregates of accidental deaths. In 1863, the office began listing road traffic fatalities as a discrete item and, in 1873, it began to distinguish between the types of vehicle involved, which later included motor cars. Nor were the police the only organization that sought to wield

[27] *Report of the Royal Commission on Police Powers and Procedure Dated 16 March, 1929* (Parl. Papers 1928–9 [Cmd. 3297]) pp. 81–2.

statistical knowledge in the service of bolstering claims about how the regulation of roads ought to be conducted. The NSFA, for instance, collected and deployed statistical information in the course of its efforts to improve road safety. In 1929, a royal commission report on the control of road traffic praised—and quoted—a set of statistics gathered by the NFSA, which 'filled a gap', so it suggested, in 'official information': namely, a table based on information supplied by coroners during the years 1926–8 that detailed the specific causes of fatal accidents, ranging from excessive speed (the most common cause) to 'improperly overtaking' and failure 'to keep to the nearside of the road'.[28]

Nonetheless, the police had an inbuilt advantage over other interested groups. Besides access to relevant sources of official information, they could also generate knowledge about the kinds of problems they dealt with on a day-to-day basis, among them sluggish traffics flows and congestion, unlicensed and unfit vehicles, and the nature and location of accidents. The importance of this kind of cumulative and experiential knowledge is amply evident in the case of Arthur Bassom, whose stellar career in the Met was built on this. Joining in 1886, he transferred to the Public Carriage Branch the next year. In 1901, he was appointed Chief Inspector and given charge of the branch at the time when it was forced to regulate motor vehicles. H.M. Howgrave-Graham, the Commissioner's Secretary in the 1920s and 1930s, had this to say about the office expertise at Scotland Yard, the headquarters of the Met:

> There are a number of small affairs that police have to attend to. Each one of them has its own little group of orders and regulations founded usually on some Act of Parliament. For each one of them there is an 'expert' (or a bunch of experts) at Scotland Yard—someone ready to give the right answer if a conundrum not covered by standing orders arises in one of the 172 Metropolitan police stations. I am thinking of such matters as firearms, explosives, lost dogs, cruelty to animals, foot-and-mouth disease, missing persons, suicides, street musicians, pedlars, beggars, house-to-house collections, flag days, etc. There are plenty more.[29]

This was the backroom world in which Bassom worked at the start of the century. With the motorization of London, however, his mechanical

[28] *Royal Commission on Transport: First Report: The Control of Traffic on Roads* (Parl. Papers 1929–30 [Cmd. 3365]), pp. 5–6, 48–53.

[29] H.M. Howgrave-Graham, *Light and Shade at Scotland Yard* (London, 1947), p. 31.

expertise and ability to direct a growing department tasked with licensing vehicles meant that he became the 'expert' whose involvement in police responses to increased traffic risk was essential. In 1906, he was promoted to Superintendent of Hackney Cabs. In this capacity he served as an expert witness in the case of accidents, assessed the detail of design features, and was the expert who appeared in front of various committees of inquiry, especially in relation to vehicle licensing.[30] He was an early recipient of the King's Police Medal in 1919 and of an OBE in 1920, and was promoted to Chief Constable as he reached the mandatory retirement age for superintendents.[31] In 1924, he was being described in the press as 'the London traffic controller', having been appointed as the Met's Director of Traffic Services just the year before.[32] Among his other achievements was devising the Bassom Scheme for numbering London bus routes, which was introduced following the 1924 London Traffic Act.

Bassom is testament to the kind of authority and prestige that now attended detailed, institutionalized knowledge of traffic. It is also evident in the broader culture of inquiry that surrounded the 'traffic problem'. Beginning in the Edwardian period, the police, and senior officers especially, became increasingly adept at deploying this knowledge to support arguments about how to manage traffic risks. A striking example is the evidence gathered by the Select Committee on Motor Traffic conducted in 1912–13. It contained no fewer than 17 appendices of submitted papers and statements, and of these, by far the largest—and most frequently referenced in the committee report—was Appendix C, submitted by the Met's Commissioner, Sir Edward Henry, which itself comprised 63 separate items of information.[33] These items ranged from the number of road fatalities per square mile of the Met's district and the age and sex of the deceased to the estimated speed of vehicles involved in accidents and whether or not they had skidded before impact. It was using this information that Henry urged the importance of wider streets and the provision of more traffic refuges. Meanwhile, Bassom, who was also called to give evidence, stressed the importance of the relocation and better enforcement

[30] *Daily Express*, 10 October 1906, p. 5; *Daily Express*, 6 September 1911, p. 5.

[31] *London Gazette*, 31 December 1918; *The Times*, 19 January 1926, p. 1.

[32] *Daily Express*, 2 January 1914. p. 4; *Report of the Commissioner of Police of the Metropolis for the Year 1923* (Parl. Papers 1924 [Cmd. 2189]), p. 17.

[33] *Report from the Select Committee on Motor Traffic, Together with the Proceedings of the Committee* (Parl. Papers 1913 [278]), pp. 992–1039.

of stopping places for tramcars—all suggestions that received the endorsement of the committee.

Of course, recommendations and endorsements were one thing, acting on and implementing them another. Even so, attempts by the police to shape the agenda of reform were clearly linked to an ability to exploit knowledge that other agents and institutions either could not obtain at all or could not access quite so readily. The very institutional durability of the police meant they could not only store data; they could also, uniquely, assemble this data as statistical time-series, thereby enabling comparisons to be made over different stretches of time and space, and in relation to different variables. This extended to traffic per se and congestion. In the mid-1920s, when the Home Office was considering once more how best to approach the traffic problem, one civil servant noted that 'Scotland Yard showed me a very elaborate table', which in this case detailed total traffic movements at selected points in London in 1904, 1912, 1919 and 1920–3 in order to demonstrate the changing nature of metropolitan road use.[34] Equally, the police could zoom in on particular aspects and analyse them in detail. In 1924, in a paper to the Institute of Transport, Bassom began by labelling different means of transport in terms of their 'congestive units'.[35] He then used police data to measure the exact length of time in seconds that traffic stopped at particular points in an average day. Multiplying the delay in seconds by the number of vehicles, he was thus able to arrive at the cost of congestion, or what he specified as the '3574 working hours lost to the community every 12 hours' at these points alone.

The real informational trump card held by the police lay in their knowledge of accidents. The police's unique ability to investigate and understand road accidents was sometimes explicitly cited as one of the reasons why local highways departments should be obliged to listen to their expertise when making design decisions, but it was always implicit—a message conveyed in the detail and exactness with which they were able to recall, marshal and mobilize knowledge of road accidents.[36] It was knowledge based on a combination of qualitative and quantitative expertise, which itself was bound up with their logistical presence on the streets: of knowing what happened, when and where, and then categorizing it according

[34] TNA HO 45/12256, London Traffic Bills, 1923 and 1924.

[35] TNA HO 45/11961, Bassam, 'Transport on the Highway', presented to the Institute of Transport, 3 November 1924, pp. 8–15.

[36] TNA MT 34/96, Traffic schemes. 'Committee on Road Safety. The Police Function'.

to reported causal factors. In the address noted above, Bassom detailed that there were 668 fatal and more than 30,000 non-fatal accidents in the Metropolitan district in 1923. Bassom compared these figures to those of the four previous years, dividing them up by vehicle type whilst placing them into one of 25 categories according to how they had happened, such as 'Crossing road' and 'Falling off vehicle in motion'. It was common for other organs of the state to rely on this knowledge, in particular the MoT. In 1929, the MoT published a special report, relying on accident data from the Met, which gave in great detail the various circumstantial categories of how children were killed on London's roads.[37] This categorized risk in terms of location in London, time of day and the nature of the accident. In this case, the disaggregation of the horrific total of child deaths rendered the numbers easier to cope with and held out the prospect that they could be governed by a series of discrete measures, such as the enhanced provision of crossing patrols near schools.

The police often reminded others of their advantages in this respect, in particular the way in which knowledge of accidents was part of their everyday bureaucratic capabilities. Unsurprisingly perhaps, given the volume of traffic it had to contend with, the Met seems to have been especially pioneering. Summoned to give evidence before a select committee on metropolitan traffic in 1919, Assistant Commissioner Elliott described how the Met had begun to keep special maps on which fatalities were marked, with different colours for different types of vehicle. They had 'led to very useful results', he went on, noting how they had prompted further investigations: 'occasionally we find that a refuge might be useful, or occasionally we find that fast driving has grown up in that particular part, and we establish controls and work them'.[38] By the 1930s, work of this sort had become routine, giving rise to the idea of an 'accident black spot'. It seems the term first became common in the mid-1930s, when one regulatory tactic was to erect notices bearing the words 'Accident Black Spot—Take Care' at particularly troublesome junctions or stretches of road. Indeed, so routine had this work become that it was subject to reform. In 1936, the Met introduced Accident Report Books that had to be carried by all constables.

[37] TNA HO 45/16125, Protection of school children from traffic dangers, 1913–32, 'Report on Street Accidents to Children in Greater London' (HMSO, London, July, 1929).

[38] *Report from the Select Committee on Transport (Metropolitan Area), Together with the Proceedings of the Committee, Minutes of Evidence and Appendices* (Parl. Papers 1919 [147]), pp. 27–8.

As the Commissioner explained, besides encouraging uniformity of information collection, these books could be used as the principal record, thus preventing the need for secondary reports and further bureaucratic labours.[39] What began in the Met eventually spread elsewhere, including the use of maps, which constitute, perhaps, the most potent symbol of the spatial-logistical nature of accident knowledge and corresponding attempts to govern risk on the roads. In 1945, for instance, a Home Office committee tasked with setting post-war policing priorities recommended that traffic patrol patterns should be established in conjunction with a standardized 'casualty map' maintained by each force detailing accident black spots. These maps were described as the 'key to police activity' and a 'staple item' of intelligence.[40]

Policing Choices and Responsibilities

What, then, were the solutions that the police preferred, and how were these solutions developed and deployed? In brief, it was a process of ongoing negotiation in which the police privileged engineering and, to a lesser extent, educational solutions, whilst ensuring that any legal and regulatory solutions either worked to their advantage or were limited. This was a complex process, for in some respects the police desired to control the roads: as noted above, public safety was a core concern and ensuring good order on the roads had been part of the police mission since the Victorian era. Indeed, the risk of accident and the risk of congestion went together: in 1914, the Met's response to the Select Committee on Traffic linked the two, based on the premise that 'obstruction begets congestion, and congestion in the streets ... is a source of danger'.[41] Equally, the police were conscious of demands on their time and their multiple other roles, not least fighting crime. They always kept a firm eye on questions of cost and professional convenience.

This can be seen in a variety of scenarios. The main way in which the Met regulated motor vehicles before the First World War was via licensing, in particular of taxis and buses, which at that point comprised

[39] *Report of the Commissioner of Police of the Metropolis for the Year 1936* (Parl. Papers 1936–7 [Cmd. 5457]), pp. 52–4.

[40] TNA MT 34/96, Traffic schemes. 'Committee on Road Safety. The Police Function', p. 3.

[41] *Report from the Select Committee on Motor Traffic*, p. 162.

the majority of motor traffic. Licensing was one of the more important governmental techniques deployed by state authorities on a large scale from the nineteenth century.[42] Under Bassom's tenure as Superintendent of the Public Carriage Office, police were charged with regulating the design of buses and taxis in an attempt to make their size, shape and manoeuvrability suitable for London's streets, testing all drivers at New Scotland Yard and maintaining a vigorous inspection regime. In his evidence to the 1913 select committee noted above, Bassom reported the tests carried out and the number of inspections. These consisted of regular re-certifications as well as random spot-checks: over 25,000 vehicles were reported as unfit in only 9 months during 1912.[43] This was time-consuming work, but the Met assiduously avoided taking on any extra direct administrative responsibilities. In the late 1910s and 1920s, for instance, the Met declined to involve itself in the allocation of bus routes, even though it had the power to determine the siting of bus stops and the lack of bus-route regulation was acknowledged as a source of congestion. Assistant Commissioner Elliott was in favour of police representation on a London-wide transport authority, but he did not want this body to be responsible for allocating omnibus routes. This position was supported by successive commissioners, principally because—to quote Elliott in 1919—'there would be such a lot of wire-pulling to get omnibuses off particular routes. The Commissioner had to live on friendly terms with the public generally and he did not desire to be saddled with the odium of deciding a thing like that'.[44] Vehicle regulation was a standardized process, and the organization of stops and taxi ranks was spatially discrete, but controlling and monitoring routes would have given the police a diffuse responsibility covering their whole area, subject to the desires of thousands of commuters. They preferred to risk congestion than public odium.

These dense processes of negotiation can also be seen in the way in which the police privileged engineering and technological interventions, paid for by local authorities, over those that required additional manpower resources. This was especially evident in the question of who should take responsibility for managing children around schools, which was a consistent source of debate throughout the first half of the century.

[42] M. Valverde, 'Police Science, British Style: Pub Licensing and Knowledges of Urban Disorder', *Economy and Society* 32 (2003), pp. 234–52.

[43] *The Times*, 29 January 1913, p. 13.

[44] 'London Traffic Problems', *The Times*, 13 June 1919, p. 10.

As early as 1914, the Met suggested to the London County Council that it should erect barriers to stop children rushing into the street outside school gates, whilst encouraging teachers to stand watch.[45] The suggestion was accompanied by a detailed list of school sites where the police thought barriers, and perhaps 'motor danger signs', would be useful. In general, the Met accepted a degree of responsibility for protecting children in the immediate vicinity of schools, in conjunction with teachers, but they were careful to limit this, resisting the idea that this was a normal part of their duties.[46] In 1928, the Bishop of Southwark appealed for a report on the deaths of children on London's roads. The Superintendent of the Met's Public Carriage Office replied in a manner designed to minimize the panic and redefine the problem. He began by noting that accidents involving children had remained constant while those involving adults had risen, and he was keen to stress that only a minority of the fatalities among children had occurred during journeys to and from school.[47] The Met provided a defensive appendix to this report, noting how it had accepted in 1913 that the protection of children from traffic was a legitimate part of its duty, but that this did not equate to a promise to be outside every school, particularly if this led to the neglect of its other duties.

The problem of demands on police time to protect school children continued throughout the interwar period. Some 320 men had been assigned to the task in 1913; by 1931, the figure was more than 1000.[48] In 1930, one senior officer claimed that this resulted in higher crime, asserting that 'house-breakers and other evil-doers are very well aware of the times during which the eyes of so many Police officers are concurrently withdrawn from the streets of the locality in general'.[49] The Met repeatedly pressed the London County Council to make more use of barriers and notices, but still MPs and teachers looked towards the police to patrol school crossings to prevent children from being knocked

[45] TNA HO 45/16125, Protection of school children from traffic dangers, 1913–32. London County Council to Commissioner of Police, 21 November 1914.

[46] TNA HO 45/16125, Protection of school children from traffic dangers, 1913–32. 'Street Accidents to Children' (1929), pp. 12–13.

[47] TNA HO 45/16125, Protection of school children from traffic dangers, 1913–32, Memorandum, 11 February 1928.

[48] 'Police Control of Traffic', *The Times*, 29 January 1913, p. 7.

[49] TNA HO 45/16125, Protection of school children from traffic dangers, 1913–32, Tripp to Dixon, 25 April 1930.

down.[50] In this context, changes to the urban environment—particularly those funded by other local bodies—were attractive to a labour-intensive police force, though this did not preclude sponsoring other forms of regulation. The educational efforts of the BBC and the NFSA noted above were welcomed by the police. Later solutions included the organization of 'school crossing patrols' staffed by local residents, which began after the Second World War. Crucially, although these patrols were now organized and trained by the police, local authorities remained legally and financially responsible.[51]

Indeed, there were few areas of motor traffic regulation that the police did not think might be enhanced by some kind of engineering intervention. When the 1919 Select Committee on Traffic asked Elliott if he could establish organized queues for bus stops, he resisted on the grounds that it would require police supervision. He preferred reorganizing and re-siting the stops; capital was cheaper than labour.[52] It was a consultative role the police expected to—and evidently did—enjoy. As one Met policy paper confidently stated in 1928: 'Whenever Police are consulted as to structural improvements, street lighting is one of the items taken into consideration ... In a number of cases quite recently the Commissioner has pressed the Local Authorities for increased lighting. The suggestions put forward by the Police are generally accepted.'[53] Another technical solution promoted by the police was the installation of traffic lights instead of men on the ground directing vehicles and pedestrians. The ambitious Chief Constable of Nottingham, Athelstan Popkess, had by 1931 already replaced every police officer on point duty at simple intersections by traffic lights. He was looking next to using automatic traffic signals to relieve the 40 or so men he had on duty outside schools at their closing time.[54]

[50] TNA HO 45/16125, Protection of school children from traffic dangers, 1913–32, 'Street Accidents to Children' (1929), p. 19; 'Police Supervision over Children Crossing the London-Brighton Road at Kingswood', 24 June 1931.

[51] H. Scott, *Scotland Yard* (London, 1954), pp. 234–7; *Report of the Commissioner of Police of the Metropolis for the Year 1950* (Parl. Papers 1950–1 [Cmd. 8359]), pp. 18–19.

[52] 'London Traffic Problems', *The Times*, 13 June 1919, p. 10.

[53] TNA HO 45/16125, Protection of school children from traffic dangers, 1913–32, Memorandum, 11 February 1928.

[54] TNA HO 45/16125, Traffic: Protection of school children from traffic dangers, 1913–32, 'Children Coming out of School: Relief of Police by Installation of Suitable Signals', Memorandum, 10 February 1931.

Equally, however, the police had to flex their institutional muscles on occasions in order to secure influence at the local level, much as at the national level of policy-making described in the first section. To take one example, in 1932, Kent County Council modified the traffic flow around a war memorial in the town of Orpington, which was part of the Metropolitan Police District. The council did so without consulting the police, prompting local officers to report this to the Met's traffic specialists. A subsequent report by the Met disapproved of the work on the grounds that it had enhanced neither traffic flow nor safety, citing reduced visibility in relation to the latter. The Met also objected to the council's compromise solution of a traffic light-controlled junction. In 1933, the police carried out a comprehensive traffic survey which supported their objections, refusing to let the issue lie and preventing the council from relying on a fait accompli. In 1939, the police eventually obtained the outcome they wanted: a roundabout junction, paid for by the county council.[55]

The Long-Term Police Vision

As a permanent organization with a disciplined workforce, the police possessed formidable advantages in bureaucratic conflict concerning the regulation of motor traffic and the design of streets and roads. During the mid-twentieth century, this authority developed still further. As Laybourn has argued, the police view that their expertise in the reduction of traffic risks was inherent, unique and invaluable flourished like never before with the rise of town planning. Police became involved in advising about the design of roads, automatic traffic lights, town centre development, urban freeways and the new motorways of the 1950s.[56] This development consolidated a shift from a largely responsive and localized perspective, in which the police attempted to ameliorate specific problems of street environments, to one that was more proactive, technocratic and comprehensive, where the police sought a role in advising on technological solutions and the redesign of roads and road networks. Time horizons shifted accordingly: the expectation was that, ultimately, long-term strategies of education and engineering would prove more effective and durable than immediate, site-specific law enforcement.

[55] TNA Metropolitan Police Office (hereinafter MEPO) 2/4760, Roundabout layout at Orpington War Memorial, junction of Station Road and High Street, 1932–9.

[56] Laybourn, *The Battle for Britain's Roads, c. 1890s to c. 1970s*, pp. 156–67.

That the police should focus on long-term engineering solutions was a common point of reference in the mid-twentieth century. The Met's post-war Commissioner, Harold Scott, wrote in 1954 that the 'police must constantly study road conditions which make accidents likely', before detailing the imposition of non-skid surfaces and the removal of traffic refuges—by this point seen as a source of unnecessary danger to motorists—as examples of this. [57] The focus on engineering was also evident in a variety of individual careers. Popkess, noted above, was at the forefront of using and publicizing technological solutions to policing problems.[58] In 1954, he published *Mechanised Police Patrol*, in which he argued that 'mechanizing' police patrols significantly enhanced the capacity for mobility and offensive crime prevention. Operational methods included the employment of 'special mission patrols', or Q-cars (vehicles camouflaged as tradesmen's vans and the like), and the use of radio communication. Another instance is Arthur Young, who in 1944 was appointed Chief Constable of Hertfordshire, from where he advocated the involvement of the Met in the training and licensing of driving instructors, and defended an active role for the police in terms of advising on matters of road engineering and design.[59]

It was most of all evident in the career of H. Alker Tripp, who joined the Met in 1902 as a lowly clerk. Rising through the ranks, by the 1930s he had become the Met's pre-eminent traffic expert, serving as Assistant Commissioner from 1932. A keen motorist and cyclist, he devoted the next 15 years to the study of London's traffic problems, as well as those of other cities throughout Europe and North America. He became the standard-bearer for police authority in relation to matters of traffic regulation and the design of roads, invoking, as others had before him, the organizational advantages of the police. In a paper given to the Institute of Transport in 1933, he wrote that 'the police should be in a better position to gauge the situation than most people, because they are able from daily experience in dealing with accidents, congestion and obstruction to say in what respects in the aggregate the existing accommodation

[57] Scott, *Scotland Yard*, p. 234–7.

[58] N. Hayes, 'Popkess, Athelstan Horn (1893–1967)', *Oxford Dictionary of National Biography*, www.oxforddnb.com.oxfordbrookes.idm.oclc.org/view/article/97916 (date accessed 18 November 2015).

[59] TNA Department of Scientific and Industrial Research (hereinafter DSIR) 12/156, Road Research Board. 'Letter to the Secretary from the Secretary of the Road Research Board Committee on Vehicles', 16 September 1946.

falls short of public needs and desires'.[60] His reputation was sealed with two publications: *Road Traffic and its Control*, published in 1938, and a second study, published in 1942, entitled *Town Planning and Road Traffic*, each of which advanced a more holistic view of road traffic and of the roads not just within towns and cities, but also between them. His aim was to eliminate risk, especially on trunk roads, by a system of total segregation of road traffic.[61] His expertise was quickly recognized: after the Second World War, the Department of Scientific and Industrial Research set up a committee to establish a research agenda for road design, granting Tripp the role of chair. Arthur Young was called upon to submit evidence, toeing the line advanced by Tripp and others that 'the police should be consulted before any major alterations are made to the highway'.[62]

This was not about encroaching on hostile professional territory, for claims to prominence by senior police officers such as Young and Tripp were also backed by planners themselves. Patrick Abercrombie, the internationally revered town planner, wrote the foreword to Tripp's *Town Planning and Road Traffic*, in which he welcomed the police as 'our most progressive positive reformers', and backed Tripp's conclusion that 'it is only by planning that a radical improvement can be found'.[63] Tripp himself felt that although in the short-term traffic had to be made to fit the road, this was only a stopgap measure until the colossal task of making Britain's roads fit for modern traffic had been completed.[64] Tripp defined the police's role as equal to that of the planner, who ought, he suggested, not begin his work until the people who had the 'practical knowledge' had briefed him. These were the police, 'who, being the persons on the spot, have the first-hand knowledge. From their reports and figures, casualty maps and graphs can be worked out by others and statistics can be compiled, but the whole main fund of basic knowledge, as well as of practical

60 TNA MEPO 5/348, Road Transport, 1920–38. H.A. Tripp, 'The Design of the Streets for Traffic Requirements', paper read to the Institute of Transport, 13 November 1933, p. 5.

61 TNA DSIR 12/156, Road Research Board. 'A Review of the Principles Put Forward by Sir Alker Tripp', September 1946.

62 TNA DSIR 12/156, Road Research Board. 'Letter to the Secretary from the Secretary of the Road Research Board Committee on Vehicles', 16 September 1946.

63 P. Abercrombie, 'Foreword' to H.A. Tripp, *Town Planning and Road Traffic* (London, 1942), pp. 7–8.

64 *Ibid.*, p. 18.

experience, remains and can only remain with the Police'.[65] Police knowledge was tacit and inscribed in practice, and for that reason it was inherently powerful: the bedrock upon which reform had to proceed.

The detail of Tripp's prescriptions for the shaping of towns was underpinned by the principle that ends were best attained through engineering rather than regulatory means and that the end goal for main roads was uninterrupted fast traffic, with junctions designed to enhance safety factors. Tripp's work stressed that solving problems by changing the built environment was preferable to using regulations, which could only be a temporary solution. He also deprecated the role of education, assigning this to a 'transitional phase' before the ultimate engineering cure.[66] His vision was of halved 'or even lower' fatalities once the roads had been reshaped to his detailed prescriptions.[67] Within existing towns, his main recommendation involved a redefinition of roads, modelling them according to their specialized function, in which 'every road should have its character and ticket: there must be no nondescripts'.[68] His aim was to replan, wherever possible, for maximum segregation and differentiation as a way of shaping behaviour and minimizing risk. The designated 'precinct' town centre, made famous by Colin Buchanan's report of 1963, *Traffic in Towns*, was already part of Tripp's thinking.[69]

Tripp's work was consistent with the mainstream of mid-twentieth-century policing. Police approaches to traffic had much in common with their approach to other aspects of their role, which turned upon a distinction between the generally law-abiding and those otherwise disposed. In 1945, a committee on road safety formed by the police and Home Office suggested that traffic offenders should be divided up into two categories. The first and larger one was 'the British public', or those who were 'ignorant' and who should primarily be dealt with via advice. This was because 'a system under which fear becomes the controlling factor in obtaining the required reaction among so large a section of the public who, as individuals, are generally law abiding is not, it is urged, likely to produce the most effective results'.[70] The second category consisted

[65] *Ibid.*, p. 21.
[66] *Ibid.*, p. 23.
[67] *Ibid.*, p. 57
[68] *Ibid.*, p. 58.
[69] *Ibid.*, p. 67.
[70] TNA MT 34/96, Mobile Police Force. 'Committee on Road Safety. The Police Function', p. 4.

of the police's 'deadly enemy ... the road hog'. These were people who could not be taught or encouraged to drive in a risk-averse fashion; they were 'merely concerned with not getting caught'. In their case, it was proper to prosecute them for 'technical offences', since only this could bring about the intention of the various highways and road traffic acts, which was to secure safety. Imprudent road users were amenable neither to education nor to admonishment or suggestion by police officers. They were also immune to the effects of increased surveillance.[71] Hence, they were 'deliberate offenders' and catching them with plain-clothes officers in unmarked cars was deemed fair game.[72] This was a more subtle version of the division between 'average motorist' and 'road hog', which had been pushed by the motor lobby in earlier decades.[73] Therefore, as far as the police saw law enforcement, drivers were split into two categories, each of which required different treatment. The honest could be educated to avoid risk; the selfish needed to be compelled.

Tripp's view, however, as set out in *Town Planning*, also served to blur this distinction, making less mention of the 'road hog'. He contended that pedestrians and motorists alike remained too governed by impulse to be controllable by education and enforcement. The pedestrian might in normal times be careful crossing the road, but given the chance to catch a bus, only an obstruction would stop him or her from making a dangerous move. The driver, too, 'will often take risks which he would strongly condemn at any other time' if in a hurry.[74] As such, drivers' choices must be constrained 'to reduce to a minimum the amount of harm which he can do to himself [sic] or others'.[75] Police thinking thus considered that the public were not always rational actors, yet their actions could nevertheless be understood by the police, given their experience: 'town planners, engineers and surveyors have all been known to devise schemes which quite ignore the factor of human nature. The traffic specialist, if he is a police officer, is much less likely to forget that factor, because he has been

[71] For conscious use of this effect by the police at this time, see C.A. Williams, 'Police Surveillance and the Emergence of CCTV in the 1960s', in M. Gill (ed.), *CCTV* (Leicester, 2003), p. 18.

[72] TNA MT 34/96, Mobile Police Force. 'Committee on Road Safety. The Police Function', pp. 4–5.

[73] O'Connell, *The Car in British Society*, pp. 120–1.

[74] Tripp, *Town Planning and Road Traffic*, p. 24.

[75] *Ibid.*, p. 25.

well schooled in human perversity'.[76] It was thus here where spatial and engineering solutions played a crucial role, for they applied to everyone, at all times, regardless of their particular inclination. It made for an abstract form of risk management, to the extent that it sought to target all road uses, and yet it was also a matter of very material, technical interventions into the design and layout of roads.

Conclusion

During the first half of the twentieth century, the British police variously defended, resisted and actively defined a role in the management of motor traffic risks. This was true in relation to both the regulatory practices that were put into place and the processes that formulated these practices. As has been argued, we should not take for granted the role of the police in this respect. It was a contingent process and choices had to be—and were—made. Car manufacturers and motorist groups had their own interests, of course, and so too did the police. Overall, in the 1920s and 1930s, the police opted for power and responsibility over traffic rather than letting it shift to other agencies. Yet they sought to do so on their own terms, something that involved exploiting their position as a permanent, bureaucratic force and the informational strengths that derived from this.

The post-war generation of police chiefs eventually embraced enforcement for car drivers, agitating for tougher penalties for dangerous driving and supporting the introduction of breathalysers following the 1967 Road Safety Act.[77] In the preceding decades, however, they promoted educational and engineering strategies, eventually carving out a position of authority for the police in relation to matters of road design. By the 1940s, the Home Office's view of the proper role of police with regard to traffic included law enforcement, crime prevention, education and accident investigation. But it also included 'the study of the traffic problem; and the development and advancement of the technique of traffic control in all its phases', as well as 'consideration of the need for amendment or extension of the traffic law' and 'consideration of the need for improvement in road conditions … in matters of communications, layout and general planning'. The hope was that 'the complex problem of traffic control'

[76] *Ibid.*, p. 24.

[77] Luckin and Sheen, 'Defining Early Modern Automobility', p. 224; B. Luckin, 'Anti-Drink Driving Reform in Britain, c. 1920–80', *Addiction* 105 (2010), pp. 1538–44.

might be reduced 'to an exact science'.[78] Engineering thus came to occupy a privileged place in the package of measures employed by the police for reducing risk on Britain's roads. This was a long-term vision of reform, but this too fitted their existing institutional strengths. Police forces could collect long-term data, could maintain bureaucratic pressure over time, and could embark upon multi-generational programmes for the remodelling of the nation's roads, towns and psyches.

[78] TNA MT 34/96, Traffic schemes. 'Committee on Road Safety. The Police Function', p. 2.

CHAPTER 10

'Maximum Supervision': Risk, Danger and Public Water in Post-War Britain

Glen O'Hara

The concept of enjoying more 'leisure' often provided a catchphrase and cure-all for twentieth-century Britons—a fact that has helped the topic take its full place among innovative recent histories of free time and play.[1] It was a key part of what the populace thought they had fought for in the Second World War. When Walter Monckton, at that time working for the Ministry of Information, helped to draft *What We are Fighting For* in 1940, he urged that 'for the workers of Great Britain there must be greater security, increased partnership in industry, [and] more fruitful leisure'.[2] The idea was extraordinarily pervasive and expansive. In 1964, Frederick Corfield as the Conservative Joint Parliamentary Secretary at Housing and Local Government informed the House of Commons:

> We have a continually rising standard of living, enormously increased mobility with the increased ownership of the motor-car, new shopping habits and

[1] See T. Collins, 'Work, Rest and Play: Recent Trends in the History of Sport and Leisure', *Journal of Contemporary History* 42 (2007), pp. 397–405.
[2] A. Roberts, *Eminent Churchillians* (London, 1994), p. 248.

G. O'Hara
Department of History, Philosophy and Religion, Oxford Brookes University, Tonge Building, Headington Campus, Gipsy Lane, Oxford OX3 0BP, UK

T. Crook, M. Esbester (eds), *Governing Risks in Modern Britain*,
DOI 10.1057/978-1-137-46745-4_10

> a technological revolution which promises more and more leisure and a different way in which people are encouraged or inclined to use their leisure.[3]

Decision-makers and commentators from across the expert and political spectrum were enthusiastic about the prospects for more free time. 'Recreation and leisure' was one of the nine key areas that the Department of Economic Affairs thought should be central to their 'Very Long Term Economic Planning' exercise in 1966.[4] Long-term statistical projections envisaged a gradual fall in working hours along the lines of those experienced earlier in the century.[5] Harold Wilson's Special Economic Adviser, Thomas Balogh, thought that: 'In the very long run … poverty should be more or less eliminated. By 1985 about 70 % of … adult life (excluding sleeping and eating time) will take the form of leisure.'[6]

These developments were not without their anxieties, however. Commentators such as J.B. Priestley feared the impact of 'greyhound racing and dirt track performances … given at all hours of the day and night, pin table establishments doing a roaring trade … and idiotic films being shown down every street'.[7] Equally, the mounting importance of leisure was thought by economists to be pushing down Britain's Gross Domestic Product figures, since the enjoyment and voluntary 'work' involved was not included in the statistics.[8] It was a sense of foreboding that focused particularly on the lives of young people, who were a site of concern for policy-makers and civic society alike. Apparently aimless, troubled and potentially ungovernable in an age of prosperity and paid holidays, their free time was a constant site of ordering and re-ordering designed to give their lives purpose and point. The Conservatives' whole concept of 'youth' in the early 1960s was designed to appeal to young people via a

[3] *House of Commons Debates* (hereinafter *H. of C. Debs.*), Fifth Series, vol. 687, cols 729–30, New Towns Bill, Second Reading, 20 January 1964.

[4] National Archives of the United Kingdom, London (hereinafter TNA). EW 25/258, Secretary's memorandum to DEA study group on long-term population distribution, 'Interim report', 9 May 1966; see Northern Economic Planning Council, *Challenge of the Changing North: A Preliminary Study* (London, 1966), p. 34.

[5] C. Leicester, *Britain 2001 AD: An Analysis of Economic Activity, Work and Leisure Time at the Turn of the Century* (London, 1972), p. 35.

[6] TNA PREM 13/262, Balogh to Beckerman, 11 January 1965.

[7] The quotation is from Priestley's contribution to *Picture Post*'s 'Plan' for Britain, entitled 'When Work is Over'. See J. Hill, *Sport, Leisure and Culture in Twentieth-Century Britain* (Basingstoke, 2002), p. 7.

[8] TNA CAB 134/1817, Economic Planning Board, minutes, 30 January 1961.

vast network of sports centres, youth clubs and County Colleges, where they would learn the skills to 'take advantage' of the new opportunities for leisure and free time. As the Education Secretary, David Eccles, told the Cabinet in 1960: 'In the next twenty years we shall see a great increase in all kinds of voluntary education and leisure activities ... what we need [to build] is a great variety of opportunities.'[9]

Outward bound activities in remote areas, for instance, were seen as one way of entrenching these 'opportunities' and of avoiding the strains of modern life and stresses demanded by up-to-date educational attainment. But these too were attended by foreboding about young people's ability to stand up to such challenges, as well as the dangers and risks that attended the activities themselves. In a dynamic amply evident in other chapters in this volume, policies aimed at progress also generated novel problems and pitfalls of their own. At a Royal College of Surgeons Convention held to consider 'Accident Prevention and Life Saving' in May 1963, the Duke of Edinburgh started the day by worrying that 'the speed and complication of modern life is such that the ordinary person ... is subject to many more and greater risks than at any time in history ... Mechanical contrivances are beginning to work faster than we can think. More leisure and longer holidays offer opportunities to take part in new activities ... but in a boat or on a mountain we are surrounded by dangers and risks'.[10] At the same event, the German educator Kurt Hahn emphasized 'the need to understand the underlying causes of accidents in adventurous pursuits amongst young people ... [which were] related to the conditioning of individuals [which] should be physical, nervous and spiritual'. Yet, Hahn felt, 'there was an absence of conditioning as a result of the modern way of life'. What the Royal College termed 'the pressures of modern educational systems' and 'the anxieties of the nuclear age' required systematic study and 'treatment' via strenuous activity, but such pursuits might become all the more competitive, the Convention felt, and all the more dangerous, due to just this heightened fretfulness and angst.[11]

[9] TNA CAB 134/1664, Eccles memorandum to Education Policy Committee, 'County Colleges', 8 February 1960.

[10] Duke of Edinburgh, 'Introduction', in J.H. Hunt (ed.), *Accident Prevention and Life Saving: Papers Given at a Convention held at the Royal College of Surgeons of England, May 1963* (Edinburgh, 1965), p. 1.

[11] Royal College of Surgeons, *Report of the Working Party on Accident Prevention and Life Saving* (London, 1963), p. 48.

This chapter focuses on another of those 'different ways' to enjoy leisure that Corfield had optimistically invoked in 1964: playing on or near water. The possibilities were many and varied, and they are examined here in order to recover some of the anxieties about risk that accompanied the idea and practice of 'affluence' in post-Second World War Britain. For British people did indeed enjoy more leisure time during the economic 'golden age' that stretched from the early 1950s to the 1970s, but this also brought with it myriad new concerns: among other things, about the dangerous nature of the semi-derelict industrial landscapes that economic growth had created and then made obsolete; about the presence of children and young people, and especially teenagers, in those areas; and about how both the organs of the state and multiple other policy actors (for example, charities, school and local authorities), as well as parents and the young themselves, should respond.

The chapter attends to all of these elements and begins by examining the nature and perceptions of the new threats that attended the growth of water-borne leisure activities, drowning in particular. It then considers the policy responses, including the types of public information that were deployed to help foster a new type of leisure-oriented, safety-conscious citizen. Finally, it considers the struggle to create an integrated administrative council on water safety that could mediate between all the varied interests and agents involved. In so doing, the aim is to recover something of the dynamics of opportunity and fear, anxiety and progress in the more leisured and affluent society of post-war Britain.

Progress and Fear in the Post-War British Landscape

Water sports thrived in post-Second World War Britain. This was not an entirely new departure. The 1930s had seen a rash of outdoor lidos built—180 in all, concentrated in London, adding to the 50 or so that had existed before that point—and they symbolized fun, youth, the body beautiful and even modernity itself.[12] Indoor pools markedly increased in number too—by some 135 between 1918 and 1940—though the 300 outdoor facilities outstripped this by some way. The numbers of swimmers

[12] J. Gardiner, *The Thirties: An Intimate History* (London, 2010), pp. 519–20; J. Smith, *Liquid Assets: The Lidos and Open Air Swimming Pools of Britain* (Swindon, 2005), pp. 19–23.

soared: in Liverpool from 1.32 to 2.23 million between 1914 and 1932, and in Birmingham from 882,000 to 1.69 million.[13] The numbers of both types of pool mounted in response to public demand, particularly among families with young children. In 1936, Harold Annison, a water polo player and British representative to the Olympic Games in 1920 and 1924, noted that 'during the last few years the numbers patronizing our baths have multiplied to such an extent that those in authority have provided better facilities ... Modern children are brought up to find enjoyment in the water, and grow up into adults who seek enjoyment in that element. This is one of the causes of ... the boom in swimming'.[14]

But in the post-Second World War era, water-borne leisure activities became still more ubiquitous, varied and popular than before. Crucially, they spread out from the more confined and supervised spaces represented by indoor pools and lidos, embracing all sorts of pursuits that were much harder to regulate. Boating in its various forms regularly involved three million Britons by the early 1990s, becoming what the Royal Yachting Association called 'one of the most popular outdoor activities in the United Kingdom'.[15] Holidays at the seaside boomed in an age of high employment, rising wages and paid holidays. The British Travel Association estimated that there was a rise from 25 million domestic holidays being taken in 1951 to about 30 million per year during the 1960s, a figure that was to peak at just under 40 million in 1973–4. Perhaps three-quarters of the main holidays taken every year were at the seaside.[16] Weston-super-Mare hosted some 375,000 visitors in 1949; by the mid-1950s, this figure had reached 430,000. One estimate for 1966 suggested that at least 24 million Britons would spend at least one day that year in an English seaside resort.[17]

The revival of Britain's canal network was another such development. As part of its preparations for the Stockholm Conference on the Environment in the summer of 1972, the Department of the Environment

[13] I. Gordon and S. Inglis, *Great Lengths: The Historic Indoor Swimming Pools of Britain* (Swindon, 2009), pp. 169, 171.

[14] H.A. Annison, *Swimming* (London, 1936), pp. 156–7.

[15] Royal Yachting Association, *Boating Safety on Reservoirs, Lakes and Gravel Pits* (Eastleigh, 1994), p. 6.

[16] J. Walton, *The British Seaside: Holidays and Resorts in the Twentieth Century* (Manchester, 2000), pp. 63–4.

[17] J. Hassan, *The Seaside, Health and the Environment in England and Wales since 1800* (Aldershot, 2003), p. 135.

published a compendium of civil society's views on the environment, *How Do You Want to Live?*, and it was full of praise for water-based amenities. John Humphries, Chairman of the Inland Waterways Association (IWA), opined that 'we have inherited a network of 2000 miles of waterways which pass through the most glorious unspoilt countryside and which intersect almost every major industrial conurbation'.[18] The post-war era saw those arteries in a parlous state, and only 380 of those more than 2000 miles were still being used for freight traffic. This process now went into reverse. The 1968 Transport Act stipulated that 1100 miles of canals should be considered 'cruising waterways', whether or not they were fully open, while another 600 miles of canal were taken over by the British Waterways Board and were supposed to be re-developed for use as amenity sites.[19] By the early twenty-first century, more than 500 miles had been re-opened, mostly with the active co-operation or via the work of the IWA.[20] The IWA's membership rose from 800 in 1949 to 11,000 in 1973. Between 1951 and 1972, the number of licences issued for pleasure craft grew fourfold, with two million people using inland waterways by 1973.[21] These canals sometimes doubled as swimming pools as well, especially for urban populations: in July 2013, one urban swimming safety organizer told BBC Radio 4's *Broadcasting House* that he had learnt to swim in his local canal in Stockport, where he was watched over by his mother, who was constantly on the look-out for rats.[22]

The post-war building boom also saw new gravel pits being excavated and then filled with water as 'amenity' land when they were mined out, particularly once the construction of higher buildings demanded more 'wet' high-gravel aggregates rather than sand.[23] The interwar years between 1923 and 1937 had seen sand and gravel production increase eightfold.[24] That rate of extraction continued to expand rapidly after

[18] Department of the Environment, *How Do You Want to Live?* (London, 1972), p. 145.

[19] P.J.G. Ransom, *Waterways Restored* (London, 1974), p. 20.

[20] For a comprehensive list, see https://www.waterways.org.uk/waterways/restored_waterways (date accessed 20 November 2015).

[21] B. Harrison, *Seeking a Role: The United Kingdom, 1951–1970* (Oxford, 2009), pp. 13–14.

[22] BBC Radio 4, *Broadcasting House*, 14 July 2013.

[23] Conservative Party Archive, Bodleian Library, Oxford, CCO 150/3/3/1, 'Town and Country Planning', Party brief for CPC discussion groups, December 1960.

[24] Quarry Managers' Journal, *The Directory of Quarries, Clayworks, Sand and Gravel Pits* (Birmingham, 1939), p. 390.

the Second World War, if unevenly and not at such breakneck speed: by 162 % between 1950 and 1970, in fact, with nearly half of that production being concentrated in the south-east of England.[25] This left thousands of inundated pits to be reclaimed by local authorities and the public. At the height of the boom, it was estimated that between 4000 and 5000 acres of new works were mined out every year.[26] If we narrow in on Middlesex and Surrey, two of the home counties at the forefront of this production, something of the accelerating effect on land use may be discerned. These two counties between them contained 84 quarries and pits in 1939; 85 even when the post-war economy had only just begun to recover in 1951; and rising to 97 by 1968–9. Only by 1972–3 was there any sign that the sector was maturing, when 86 pits were recorded as being open in those two counties.[27] This was the moment when many were filled in with water as they closed, either partially or completely.

Meanwhile, bird-watching and fishing grew apace around rivers and the edges of new suburban gravel pits, as well as the 'super reservoirs' that sprang up around Britain to keep the country's expanding cities watered.[28] By the early 1960s, the *Angling Times* even felt moved to publish a specialist guide for fishing in gravel pits, while sponsoring a research project on what types of fish might thrive in these new and welcome sites at which to practise the sport. A new edition of the publication's 1950s London fishing guide contained seven pages (out of 64) on sand and gravel pits.[29] They were both activities on which fathers liked to take their older children, in an era when rising incomes and changing social norms saw many more fathers take pride in the organization and subsidy of their offspring's leisure.[30] Angling was the sixth most popular sport in Britain during the

[25] C.G. Down, 'The British Aggregates Industry: Planning and Environmental Issues', *Minerals and the Environment* 1 (1979), pp. 112–14.

[26] T.U. Hartwright, 'Worked-out Gravel Land: A Challenge and an Opportunity', *Environmental Conservation* 1 (1974), pp. 139–43.

[27] Quarry Manager's Journal, *Directory* (1939), pp. 250–2, 283–7; and (1951), pp. 317–21, 282–4; Quarry Managers' Journal, *Directory of Quarries and Pits* (London, 1961–2), pp. 347–9, 392–7; (1968–9), pp. 338–9, 371–3; and (1972–3), pp. 302–3, 329–31.

[28] Graffham Water and Rutland Water are two good examples. J. Lowerson, 'Angling', in T. Mason (ed.), *Sport in Britain: A Social History* (Cambridge, 1989), p. 36.

[29] A. Pearson, *Angling in Gravel Pits* (London, 1961), pp. 5, 15; K. Sutton, *The New Fishing for Londoners: Where to Fish in London's Rivers, Reservoirs, Park Lanes, Canals, Ponds, Lakes and Gravel Pits* (London, 1962), pp. 44–50.

[30] S. Todd and H. Young, 'Baby Boomer to "Beanstalkers": Making the Modern Teenage in Post-War Britain', *Social and Cultural History* 9 (2012), pp. 452, 457–8.

1970s, drawing in a regular 1.4 million participants who fished every month. This amounted to nearly 4 % of the population, almost all of which was male.[31] Altogether, there were some 3.5 million anglers in Britain by the 1970s. It was a marked increase on the half a million to a million regular anglers in the interwar period, years during which the Working Men's Angling Association alone had 600,000 members, but when many local clubs were in desperate economic straits.[32]

The expansion of access to new and more varied watery landscapes, however, also created new hazards and was accompanied by a growing sense of foreboding. The Royal Life Saving Society leader and educationalist Margaret Jarvis was quite clear about this in her *Your Book of Survival Swimming*, first published in 1965: 'today people have more leisure time and there is more travelling to enjoy our rivers, canals, lakes, reservoirs and the sea ... It is not surprising then to learn that there are about 1000 deaths by drowning each year in this country'.[33] The 1963 Royal College of Surgeons' Convention made a similar point when it highlighted the fact that 'in an age when so many more of the population can enjoy leisure time and holidays, it is a major tragedy that so many people risk their lives, particularly on the long coasts of the British Isles ... [and] even in the inland cities and waterways'.[34]

Above all, all types of standing water presented the danger of young people risking their lives as they swam in deep, cold, obstructed or dirty water. The birth rate rose during the late 1950s and 1960s, leading to fears about what such large numbers of children and young people would do, unsupervised, during the summer holidays.[35] In an era before near-universal car ownership, and when there were fewer opportunities for play in the home than would emerge in the 1980s and 1990s, it was common to see children in the streetscape. 'Playing out' was an accepted part of

[31] Sports Council, *A Digest of Sports Statistics* 1 (1983), Table 1, vii.

[32] S.G. Jones, *Sport, Politics and the Working Class: Organised Labour and Sport in Inter-War Britain* (Manchester, 1992), p. 26; M. Huggins and J. Williams, *Sport and the English, 1918–1939* (London, 2006), p. 14; J. Hassan, *A History of Water in Modern England and Wales* (Manchester, 1998), p. 82.

[33] M. Jarvis, *Your Book of Survival Swimming and Lifesaving* (London, 1965), p. 13.

[34] Royal College of Surgeons, *Prevention*, p. 59.

[35] G. O'Hara, '"We are Faced Everywhere with a Growing Population": Demographic Change and the British State, 1955–64', *Twentieth Century British History* 15 (2004), pp. 243–66; C. Ellis, 'No Hammock for the Idle: The Conservative Party, "Youth" and the Welfare State in the 1960s', *Twentieth Century British History* 16 (2005), pp. 441–70.

young people's lives, a social norm that only changed much later in the twenty-first century due to parental anxiety and the growing emphasis on the kinds of close supervision analysed in this chapter. Even so, gathering on or near roads was one source of concern and so too was 'playing out' on or near water.[36] Inland waterways were often clogged with rubble, even if they were coming gradually back into use for canal boats and pleasure cruisers. *How Do You Want to Live?* reported excitedly that:

> there are 2000 miles of inland waterways in Great Britain, and their former use for industry and transportation is giving way to recreation ... there should undoubtedly be special grants to local authorities to clear canals and put locks into working order, so that full use can be made for leisure of this outstanding natural asset.[37]

Yet they also remained neglected in places, often dangerously so: as one key IWA figure put it in a later account, for many years 'local authority officials, not blessed with the IWA's vision of waterway potential, tended to regard disused or little used canals only as places for children to drown, rubbish to accumulate and rats to breed'.[38] A related problem was the absence of the kind of supervision that could be found in swimming pools, where attendants were required to keep a watchful eye over bathers. The Royal Life Saving Society noted in its 1960s *Life Saving and Water Safety* handbook that 'seventy-five percent of drowning accidents occur in places such as canals, rivers, gravel pits, etc., which can never be fully supervised or protected'.[39]

Growing affluence and leisure time therefore put more citizens—and, more especially, children and young people—in danger. Equally, the very novelty of these sources of danger must explain the attention they attracted, for drowning itself remained rather unusual and was in fact in decline. This was not always apparent and there were few detailed studies of the matter during the post-war years. Data on the raw number of drownings had been available from 1839, when the General Register Office (established in 1837) began publishing official statistics according

[36] M. Thomson, *The Lost Freedom: The Landscape of the Child and the British Post-War Settlement* (Oxford, 2013), Chapter 5.

[37] Department of the Environment, *How Do You Want to Live?* p. 156.

[38] Ransom, *Waterways Restored*, p. 25.

[39] Royal Life Saving Society, *Life Saving and Water Safety*, 2nd edn (London, 1969), p. 10.

to a nosology designed by its chief statistician, William Farr. Drowning appeared under the category of 'Violent Deaths', where it featured alongside poisoning, railway accidents and wounding, but both then and on into the early twentieth century, statistics of drowning were seldom examined in detail, even if they might be quoted.[40] One study conducted by the Admiralty in the 1960s showed that drowning seemed to be more prevalent in the north of England than the south, yet even at the Royal College of Surgeons' 1963 Convention, this point was not rigorously examined. The Royal Life Saving Society tentatively raised the figure of 304 deaths during 1961 among under-16s at the same meeting, but it was very unclear how it differentiated this from 'certain occupational hazards and cases of "found drowned"'.[41] But when the Government Statistical Service began to gather more detailed figures about the types and locations of such deaths—taking account of pressure from a well-publicized official Working Party set up by the Home Office, which reported in 1977 (see below)—their relatively rare nature became even clearer. The Working Party report itself could identify 922 drownings in England and Wales between 1 November 1974 and 31 October 1975 and, of these, 170 were under the age of 15.[42]

Certainly there were real risks, and one 1970s study mounted by the Royal Society for the Prevention of Accidents (RoSPA) demonstrated that the number of *near*-drownings probably ran at the same level as actual deaths.[43] Even so, the numbers of deaths were by now on a clearly declining trend. Figures provided by RoSPA show that 657 people drowned in the UK as a whole during 1983, which then declined to 599 in 1985 and 430 in 2001. Only a proportion of these were revealed by RoSPA statistics to have been under 14 years of age: 104 in 1983 and a much lower 33 in 2001. And for all the attention paid to canals and man-made inland waterways, the majority of these people had drowned in rivers

[40] See General Register Office, *Regulations, and a Statistical Nosology, Comprising the Causes of Death, Classified and Alphabetically Arranged* (London, 1843), p. 26.

[41] W. Davies, 'Prevention of Death by Drowning', in Hunt (ed.), *Accident Prevention and Life Saving*, pp. 231–5; E. Hale, 'The Royal Life Saving Society', in Hunt (ed.), *Accident Prevention and Life Saving*, p. 271.

[42] Home Office, *Report of the Working Party on Water Safety* (London, 1977), Figure 1, pp. 165, 179. For the Working Party's recommendations on research, see pp. 122–3.

[43] Royal Society for the Prevention of Accidents (RoSPA), *Drowning: A Cloud over Holiday Fun* (London, 1978), p. 4.

or the sea: 58 % in 1983 and again 58 % in 2001.[44] It had been the same in 1974–5: as the Home Office Working Party report's appendices revealed, that same share stood at 50.3 % of deaths for England and Wales in those years. Much smaller numbers had died in canals (76) or water-filled quarries (29).[45] These numbers also represented a very small number of accidental deaths. By way of comparison, the numbers dying in road traffic accidents in England and Wales were as follows: 6439 in 1974, 4973 in 1985 and 2990 in 2001.[46] So although each drowning represented an enormous personal tragedy, the publicity and the warnings it attracted (not to mention the type of danger highlighted) seem not to have matched the scale of its numerical significance.

Water Safety: The Public Policy Response

Nonetheless, the *perception* of greater risk was evidently very influential in this period—a challenge for policy-makers that forced them to try to mobilize multiple official and non-official actors. In 1971, a National Water Safety Conference was held on this topic, making clear from the start its belief that 'as more and more people become car owners there is the danger of such vast overcrowding ... that accidents and fatalities will occur more frequently'.[47] These risks, it was thought, would have to be countered by the combined action of the multifarious agencies that patrolled the boundaries between the welfare state, local government and the third, or charitable, sector. Such action was clear in a large-scale campaign begun in 1970, backed by organizations as diverse as the British Red Cross, the Dock and Harbour Authorities' Association, the Royal Humane and Royal Life Saving societies, local authorities and teachers' groups. A National Code for Bathers was produced and displayed in many hotels and guest houses; local authorities were provided with an advisory guide on 'Accident Prevention in and on the Water'.[48] But this was only one element in a wider public policy response that focused on formal

[44] RoSPA, *Drownings in the UK* (1983, 1985, 2001). Available at: www.rospa.com/leisuresafety/statistics (date accessed 20 November 2015).

[45] Home Office, *Water Safety*, Table 1, p. 166.

[46] Registrar-General for England and Wales, *Mortality Statistics: Injury and Poisoning* 26 (London, 2003), Tables 3a–3b, pp. 28–31.

[47] Glamorganshire Archives, County Council files (hereinafter Glamorganshire) BB/C/8/337, Water Safety Conference, programme, 10 November 1971.

[48] *Ibid.*, BB/C/8/351, 'National Water Safety Campaign 1970': list of member bodies.

swimming instruction, ambitious public information campaigns and at least the ambition to build a national administrative machinery. It is these efforts to mobilize multiple interest groups, beyond those under the direct influence or control of the state, to which we now turn.

The first element of this response was also the most established: namely, increasing the amount of children and young adults who were taught to swim. Indeed, inhabitants of the British Isles had long been swimming, surrounded by water as they were and still are. Sea bathing, for instance, became fashionable during the reigns of George II and George III, albeit mainly for therapeutic purposes, and the Victorians swam much more than their forebears, doing so also in novel indoor facilities.[49] In 1865, there were some 50 public baths in England, almost all of them built since the 1840s, and by 1901 there were 210.[50] The growing popularity of indoor swimming—evident, for instance, in the establishment of the Amateur Swimming Association in 1869—placed a premium on instruction, as did increasing resort to bathing unsupervised in rivers and canals. In the 1870s, one public health journal labelled canals 'death-traps' during the summer 'drowning season'.[51] The propensity to 'take a "dip" whenever it is possible' certainly created anxiety among swimming experts and enthusiasts, a feeling exemplified in the published works of the (ultimately unsuccessful) cross-Channel swimmer Montague Holbein. Most Britons still could not swim properly, even though they wanted to get into the water as often as possible: as Holbein put it in 1903, 'for one bather who can swim you will find thirty who cannot'.[52]

Lessons were thus introduced in the mid- to late Victorian period to reverse this state of affairs. Swimming was widespread in the prestigious fee-paying public schools surveyed by the Clarendon Commission's investigation of the early 1860s. By contrast, local board and voluntary schools' provision was rare until 1890, when the Education Department began to allow schools administered by the London School Board to build the required facilities; swimming was then placed in the national Code

[49] A. Corbin, *The Lure of the Sea: The Discovery of the Seaside in the Western World, 1750–1840*, trans. J. Phelps (London, 1995), pp. 57–62; P. Langford, *A Polite and Commercial People: England, 1727–1783* (Oxford, 1992), p. 103.

[50] Gordon and Inglis, *Great Lengths*, p. 51.

[51] '"Death-Traps' in the Metropolis', *The Sanitary Record*, 18 September 1875, pp. 200–1; 'The Drowning Season', *The Sanitary Record*, 9 September 1876, pp. 166–7.

[52] M. Holbein, *Swimming* (London, 1903), p. 12.

of Education.[53] But public funding for instruction was still not authorized for elsewhere in the country until the local authority of Newark in Nottinghamshire was allowed to go ahead with swimming lessons in 1904. The growing number of Britons who wanted to swim therefore had to rely on an informal network of trainers and life-saving instructors, partly under the purview of the short-lived Professional Swimming Association that looked after the paid side of the sport during the 1880s.[54] It was precisely this desire to educate young people in the practicalities of swimming that lay behind the foundation of the Life Saving Society in 1891 (later, after 1904, the Royal Life Saving Society noted above), under the patronage of the Duke of York. Its handbook, training drills and competitions were designed to encourage the inclusion of swimming instruction 'in the curriculum of every School, College and Training Ship'.[55]

Anxieties about access to standing water and an insistence on the teaching of swimming continued during the post-Second World War era, when they dovetailed with concerns about aimless youth and national competitive efficiency. The means usually chosen to manage these problems was to build up a more active, responsible and risk-averse citizenry via the efforts of the manifold agencies described above. Provided by the Royal Life Saving Society, life-saving clubs, the Scouts and Girl Guides and by schools and youth groups, life-saving courses became a key component of an attempt to cultivate a self-reliant and able young population. As early as the 1930s, Harold Annison had emphasized that 'it should be the ambition of everyone ... to practise the several methods of life-saving ... it is, without doubt, the duty of every swimmer to learn the methods of rescue, release, and resuscitation'.[56] In 1965, Margaret Jarvis echoed Annison when she argued for the following: 'we should all accept responsibility for our OWN SAFETY in and near water, and train accordingly. Parents with small children should see that they are properly supervised near water. This training in watermanship can start at an early age and continue progressively ... Purposeful swims can be carried out alone, with

[53] R. Winterton and C. Parker, '"A Utilitarian Pursuit": Swimming Education in Nineteenth-Century Australia and England', *International Journal of the History of Sport* 26 (2009), p. 2110.

[54] C. Love, *A Social History of Swimming in England: Splashing in the Serpentine* (London, 2007), pp. 12–13, 88–92; D. Day, 'London Swimming Professors: Victorian Craftsmen and Aquatic Entrepreneurs', *Sport in History* 30 (2010), pp. 39–45.

[55] Royal Life Saving Society, *The Life Saving Society Handbook*, 2nd edn (London, 1893), p. 6.

[56] Annison, *Swimming*, pp. 127, 158.

a friend, or in a group or school class'.[57] The assumption was that young people and adults trained in this way would be self-possessed and confident in situations of danger. In the words of a handbook published by the Royal Life Saving Society in the 1970s, 'the lifesaver must take charge of the situation from the outset. He must keep calm and comfort the casualty to minimize shock. He must control bystanders, and make use of any who are able to assist'.[58]

It was partly, then, a question of fostering a certain capacity for self-governance, one which, when and if required, could be pressed into action to govern endangered others. Yet this was impossible to dissociate from other concerns, not least those of health and a more robust population. 'Purposeful' pro-swimming initiatives were often advertised as boosting national efficiency, just as they had been in the pre-war era: the swimming champion William Francis wrote as early as 1937 that 'the sport of swimming does play an important part in the growth and development of the nation. It is what one might call a "stretchy exercise" … One has only to watch a breast stroke swimmer in action to realize the value of the exercise for a growing youth'.[59] The means by which national competitiveness continued to be emphasized in this arena was elite sport: the first months of the Sports Council and the initial work of a Minister for Sport, both announced by Labour in 1964, were dominated by publicity about the Tokyo Olympics and the subsequent World Cup.[60]

Equally, participating in more sport was supposed to dissuade juvenile delinquency at sport's 'grass roots'. This was very much Labour's approach in policy statements such as *Leisure for Living*, approved by the party's conference in the autumn of 1959.[61] Physical recreation was still perceived as a way of enjoying novel leisure time 'enjoyably, beneficially and healthily—for our own sakes [and] for the sake of our children', as a Labour flyer entitled 'A Sporting Chance' put it during the 1970 election. Denis Howell, the Sports Minister, featured on the cover, sitting proudly by a swimming pool and surrounded by children.[62] Official and

[57] Jarvis, *Lifesaving*, p. 14.

[58] Royal Life Saving Society, *Life Saving and Water Safety Handbook, Vol. 5: Resuscitation and First Aid* (London, 1978), p. 7.

[59] W. Francis, *Swimming* (London, 1937), pp. 1–2.

[60] K. Jefferys, *Sport and Politics in Modern Britain: The Road to 2012* (Basingstoke, 2012), pp. 78–86.

[61] Labour Party, *Leisure for Living* (London, 1959), pp. 39–40.

[62] Labour Party, *A Sporting Chance* (London, 1970), p. 1.

semi-official campaigns to secure child safety via the teaching of swimming therefore proliferated in these years: the Royal College of Surgeons Convention of 1963 had looked to Australia as the home of a happy, confident and vigorous youth, 'where learning to swim and the provision of trained rescue personnel and equipment are matters of national pride and urgency'. The Australian example, the College argued, showed exactly why 'in this country more baths, more instructors and a considerable amount of propaganda are needed'. More first-aid training in schools and more life-savers were also required.[63]

Such concepts did feed through into practice. Between 1960 and 1970, 197 new public indoor pools were built; a further 450 opened between 1970 and 1977.[64] Relatively generous spending on public pools undoubtedly raised the number of people subject to swimming instruction and exposed to the eyes of lifeguards when swimming. At the end of the 1960s, the Government Social Survey found that 44 % of teenage men and boys, and 31 % of girls and women, claimed to have been swimming in a pool at an average of once a month.[65] A total of 7.5 % of the population had been swimming indoors in just the 4 weeks before one 1977 Birmingham University study, a figure that was higher (at 10.2 %) among 16–19-year-olds. The annual average had risen by 67 % since similar figures were gathered in 1973. Nonetheless, important limitations remained, for the numbers swimming *outdoors*, in lakes and the sea, were 7.3 % among the populace as a whole and 14.7 % for older teenagers. Clearly more young people (though figures for younger children were not given) were still swimming in potentially dangerous waters than in supervised municipal and private pools, especially during the hotter months between July and September.[66] By contrast, in the still more safety-conscious twenty-first century, not only do young people seem to swim rather less than in the 1970s (17 % had been swimming anywhere in the lead-up to the 2002 General Household Survey), but the order of outdoor and indoor water's popularity had been reversed. More respondents now swam in pools than outdoors.[67]

[63] Royal College of Surgeons, *Accident Prevention*, pp. 52, 56–8.

[64] Gordon and Inglis, *Great Lengths*, pp. 229, 257.

[65] K.K. Sillitoe, *Planning for Leisure: An Enquiry into the Present Pattern of Participation in Outdoor and Physical Recreation* (London, 1969), Tables 63–4, pp. 122–3.

[66] A.J. Veal, *Sport and Recreation in England and Wales: An Analysis of Adult Participation Patterns in 1977* (Birmingham, 1979), Table 3, p. 9, Table 7, p. 35 and Table 18, p. 81.

[67] K. Fox, *Sport and Leisure: Results from the Sport and Leisure Module of the 2002 General Household Survey* (London, 2004), Table 1, p. 21, Table 3, p. 23 and Table 5, p. 25.

Public Information Campaigns

Public information was the second—and more novel—element of attempts to govern the dangers of accessing water, especially drowning. This served as a way of compromising between a highly interventionist role for the state and inculcating self-reliance in the individual, for such campaigns would theoretically allow a role for both approaches. Water safety conferences, 'codes of conduct', publications and propaganda, as well as resources for parents, flourished in the post-war public sphere. It was a process guided, though by no means always initiated, by a public sector that seems to have been more reactive than proactive in this area. Especially notable were the actions of charities. Established in 1957, the British Safety Council (BSC) issued a series of safety surveys that attracted a great deal of attention. The BSC was a controversial competitor to RoSPA, earlier established in 1916, which rather resented its much smaller and less well-equipped rival: in 1961, RoSPA officials wrote to the BSC when the latter body issued a Highway Code for small boats, reminding it that they had already issued a Water Safety Code.[68] Still, the BSC's publicity was very strident about the risks of seaside holidays: 'hazard signs warning of dangerous currents and rocks are frequently not being replaced … Lifeguards are still something of a rarity … speedboats operating from the shore are a real danger [and], finally, many local authorities leave broken glass and sharp tins on the beach'.[69]

Government propaganda films could be, if anything, more impressionistic and shocking than private efforts. Here at least, government departments did take the lead. Given that many more children were pursuing leisure activities both within their families and beyond, one of the key tactics was to encourage more responsible parenting and attentive parental supervision. In the Central Office of Information (COI)'s 1967 series of animated films, *All at Sea*, the two children of the Robinson family hold a net and a fishing line while they await an ill-fated trip in a dinghy with their parents.[70] One frightening film, deliberately designed to make an emotional impact, was the COI's *Reach, Throw, Wade, Row*, which

[68] U. Fox, *Nautical Code (International)* (London, 1961); Royal Society for the Prevention of Accidents Archives, Birmingham (hereinafter RoSPA Archives), D266 4/1/24, Stoney to Fox, 2 January 1961, Tye to RoSPA Executive Committee members, 25 January 1961.

[69] RoSPA Archives D266/4/1/10, BSC Press Release, 'Britain's Stinking Beaches', December 1966.

[70] British Film Institute (BFI), COI, *All at Sea: Overboard* (1967).

opened with a terrifying point-of-view series of screams from a lake. When the camera pans back to reveal who is screaming, a young girl is thrashing about in the water. A man dives in to save her, gets in trouble himself and goes under. The voiceover is stark: 'she survived. But you drowned'. A series of vignettes then lays out the film's advice: reaching out from a tree, throwing out an inflatable, testing the depth with a branch before wading out, or finding a boat, are all outlined as alternatives to losing one's life in a futile attempt to play the hero. Throughout, it is the frank, stark naturalism that is the most arresting element of the piece.[71]

RoSPA itself began a Water Safety Campaign in 1960, proceeding to issue a series of pamphlets on the subject. Interviews were given on the BBC; a Water Safety Code was released for sale at resorts, which proceeded to sell 106,000 copies within a year; a 'Learn to Swim' campaign was kick-started by the Central Council of Physical Recreation.[72] Details were provided, for instance, on what to do if one fell from a pleasure boat, discovered a cold and shivering victim, or found oneself in trouble in the water.[73] Once the campaign was formalized via a Water Safety Committee in 1962, a great deal of RoSPA activity was dedicated to its water-based campaigns over the next few years. It organized conferences of local government representatives, meeting for instance in the Lake District during the autumn of the campaign's first year; worked with the English Schools Swimming Association to encourage the adoption of pre-fabricated swimming pools in schools; and mounted joint stalls with the Ministry of Transport at industry events such as the National Boat Show.[74]

These campaigns did attract some public funding, though many in government were reluctant to circumvent or dissuade the efforts of civil society, fearing that this would undermine their role, and consequently the idea that individuals and families should be to the fore in these campaigns. RoSPA separated its Water Safety Section from the general Home Safety Division during 1966–7, assisted by a £3500 grant from the Home Office.[75] Such activities continued throughout the 1960s and into the

[71] BFI, COI, *Reach, Throw, Wade, Row* (n.d., late 1960s).

[72] 'Home Safety Activities on Many Fronts', *Safety News* 286 (May 1960); 'Water Safety Campaign Spreads its Message', *Safety News* 290 (September 1960); 'Progress on the Water Safety Front', *Safety News* 302 (September 1961).

[73] See e.g. RoSPA, *Cold Water Can Kill* (London, 1975), pp. 1–4.

[74] RoSPA Archives D 266/2/14/3, RoSPA National Safety Education Committee, minutes, 20 July 1962.

[75] *Ibid.*, RoSPA National Safety Education Committee, minutes, 30 June 1967.

1970s, providing 'filler' films for cinemas and television that were also part-sponsored by the Home Office, and bringing bodies such as the Royal Life Saving Society, the Surf Life Saving Association and tourist groups together to look at improving beach safety and other water-related public education activities. Their campaigns were also funded by subscribing local authorities, who paid to participate in RoSPA's water safety activities in return for posters, pamphlets and advice. This raised a great deal of money, with the 1967–8 financial year seeing the Water Safety Committee able to raise £3200 from publicity material and spend up to £12,000.[76]

One notable element of this campaign was the insistence that children should be both highly educated as to water's dangers and watched when they were near it, work that was overwhelmingly pictured as conducted by parents (see Fig. 10.1). This was about fostering the same kinds of subjectivity noted in the previous section: more informed and responsible children, that is, as well as more involved and watchful parents. In 1965, the Ministry of Housing and Local Government agreed to issue a circular drawing councils' attention to a RoSPA press campaign entitled 'Where There's Water, There's Danger—Watch Your Child'.[77] As 1968's *On the Water, In the Water* insisted:

> Children must be taught the dangers of water and to understand warning signs … yes, tell your child about the fun of a pond that is made for paddling (though even shallow ponds can be dangerous without supervision), but the dangers of: playing near canals, flooded excavations and gravel pits, mill dams and open drains.[78]

The year 1967 was RoSPA's 'Stop Accidents Year' and it produced a plan entitled 'Get Wise to Water', which listed a number of 'lucky escapes' when adults had saved children who had got into trouble in the water from drowning. It pointed out that two out of three young people who left school at this point could not swim. It called for much more swimming and water training throughout young people's lives, for, as it noted, 'people panic in the face of real or fancied danger, and by thrashing around quickly become exhausted and reduce their chances of survival; whereas

[76] *Ibid.*, D 266/2/26, RoSPA Sub-Committee on Publicity Material of the National Water Safety Committee, minutes, 21 July 1969; National Water Safety Committee, minutes, 19 September 1967, 20 February 1968, 19 November 1968.

[77] *Ibid.*, National Water Safety Committee, minutes, 21 April 1965.

[78] RoSPA, *On the Water, in the Water* (London, 1968), pp. 3–4.

Fig. 10.1 RoSPA, *The Water Safety Book* (London, 1976), p. 4. Published with the kind permission of the Royal Society for the Prevention of Accidents

if they remembered to turn on their backs and put their heads back they would float'.[79]

During the late 1960s and early 1970s, RoSPA launched a campaign on 'The Prevention of Drowning Accidents', producing a series of glossy brochures that offered charts and posters for schools and parents. Most of the available images contained graphic or forbidding scenes of danger familiar from the genre, though there was an increasing tendency to contain images that might mean just as much to children as to the relevant responsible adults. Campaigns featuring Theodore the Water Wise Cat

[79] RoSPA, *Get Wise to Water* (London, 1967), p. 3.

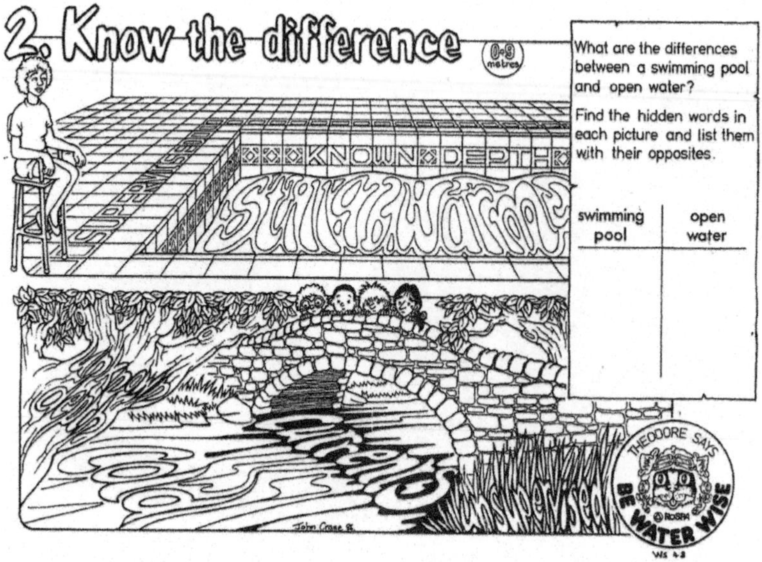

Fig. 10.2 RoSPA, *Be Water Wise* (n.d., 1980s), p. 2. Published with the kind permission of the Royal Society for the Prevention of Accidents

were prominent in this respect during the 1980s (see Fig. 10.2).[80] Many RoSPA pamphlets did, however, focus on the role of parents in ensuring child safety near and on water. Women were more likely to be pictured teaching children to swim or instructing them about safety; fathers' roles as managers of recreation—fishing, or on the beach with their children—were also to the fore.[81] RoSPA, indeed, held publicity conferences for its 'Watch Your Child' campaign explicitly for 'women journalists' during February 1965.[82] The growth of paid leisure allowed fathers to spend just such time in supervisory roles: it was they who gained more advantage from the expansion of paid holidays, for they were both more likely than their wives or partners to be in full-time work and less likely to be busy

[80] D. Parker and J. Raven, *Theodore the Water Wise Cat* (London, 1985).

[81] Glamorganshire, BB/C/8/351, 'National Water Safety Campaign 1970': leaflet, charts and posters.

[82] RoSPA Archives, D 266/2/26, National Water Safety Committee, minutes, 21 April 1965.

with the housework that many girls had absorbed as duty or regimen while they were still living with their mothers.[83]

Other organizations responded to similar challenges by issuing their own guidelines. The Central Council of Physical Recreation published a Water Sports Code in 1970 to provide advice on how to deal with 'the very great increase of interest in water sports in recent years'.[84] The Royal Life Saving Society picked up on the increased interest in water sports when it first published a practical guide to *Life Saving and Water Safety* in 1963. A second edition followed in 1969, which added a guide to help teachers instruct pupils in life-saving and safety. Given the spread of deep water across urban and suburban environments, it was natural for this guide to single out the dangers of 'streams, canals, rivers [and] gravel pits near home'. But under the chapter heading 'Teach Them Young', the Society warned parents and children even more strongly than other organizations about the dangers of open water. One did not even need to swim to get into trouble, it advised: 'water is a great attraction but slippery and crumbling banks, weeds, loose or slippery stones can cause loss of balance'. 'Required', it concluded: 'MAXIMUM SUPERVISION'.[85]

Many of the accompaniments of popular seaside holidays became objects of some public concern during the 1960s. One example of this was an oft-expressed worry about inflatables. In 1965, RoSPA issued a public warning about the Stingray, available on the presentation of empty Golden Wonder crisp packets and a small cash payment. 'DO NOT use as a life saver', ran a series of RoSPA flyers, issued in an alarming red colour.[86] The Society issued a public information film towards the end of the decade, providing the advice that airbeds should not be used on the sea at all. It did so despite private Home Office concerns that this might throttle a legitimate business and the advice that 'there are places around our coast where airbeds and inflatable toys can be used in calm, shallow water without much risk'.[87] Airbeds were also the subject of an animated

[83] Hill, *Sport, Leisure and Culture*, p. 9; S. Todd, *Young Women, Work, and Family in England, 1918–1950* (Oxford, 2005), pp. 205–8.

[84] Central Council of Physical Recreation, *The Water Sports Code: Some Recommendations for Recreational Users of Inland Waters* (London, 1970), p. 4.

[85] Royal Life Saving Society, *Life Saving and Water Safety*, 2nd edn (London, 1969), p. 14, emphasis in original.

[86] 'Dangerous Toy, Says Society', *Evening News and Star* (Essex), 20 August 1965.

[87] RoSPA Archives D 266/2/26, RoSPA National Water Safety Committee, minutes, 12 November 1969.

COI film entitled 'Keep Airbeds off the Sea'. A howling wind overwhelms a terrified sea swimmer; an official narration intones 'don't at any time take them on to the sea ... Wind can make airbeds uncontrollable and dangerous'.[88] Commander Charles Thompson, Director of the National Coastal Rescue Centre, made a similar point when he appeared on BBC Radio 4's *Woman's Hour* in 1971, again emphasizing the importance of parental watchfulness: 'one of the ... problems which parents should look out for is the number of air beds ... that children are using on the edge of the water. Now these things are enormous fun ... [but] the snag is that if the wind changes from off shore to on shore or vice versa, then the craft are simply carried out to sea, and the children have got no method ... to bring them back'.[89]

The Working Party on Water Safety

The third and final element of the public policy response was the search for a national co-ordinating council on water safety. Such a representative body might draw all of these varied efforts together and again—as with their propaganda efforts—allow successive governments to encourage the self-reliant efforts of charities and families without imposing solutions from Whitehall and Westminster. It was RoSPA that first urged the creation of an interdisciplinary working party on the matter, which would combine governmental and charities' expertise to look at making Britain's waterways and beaches safer. Though the Conservative government of Edward Heath rejected the Society's idea of a central body responsible for water safety, judging the concept too clumsy and likely to be slow to produce recommendations, it did agree to a much narrower inquiry. Roy Jenkins inherited and accepted the proposal when he returned to the Home Office after Labour won the 1974 General Election. This committee contained representatives from central government and local authorities from all over the UK, but also drew on the expertise of members from the Sports Council, the Royal Life Saving Society, the Royal National Lifeboat Institution, RoSPA itself, the Royal Yachting Association, local water authorities and the Surf Life Saving Association.[90]

[88] BFI, COI, *Don't Take Airbeds on the Sea* (1965).
[89] BBC Written Archives, Caversham, BBC *Woman's Hour* transcript, 7 July 1971.
[90] Home Office, *Water Safety*, pp. 1–2 and Appendix A, pp. 129–30.

The Working Party recommended a raft of measures: the creation of a central Water Safety Council to guide local authorities' efforts; better liaison between councils, police and coastguard authorities; Sports Council funding for safety activities (which had not been permitted previously); and water safety committees within local government bureaucracies. Finally, the Working Party urged that the new Water Safety Council, in concert with central government and the charitable sector, should redouble the efforts being made to educate the public about the dangers of even shallow water.[91] Increased publicity did ensue, as well as enhanced links with RoSPA, while official statistics were further bolstered by a Home Office Scientific Advisory Branch pilot study set up in 1974, covering the period 1975–7. The Home Office's new breakdown of drowning by age, sex, time, region and activity eventually became available in 1980.[92]

The idea of a Water Safety Council, however, fell foul of the public spending austerity of the mid- to late 1970s. Both the Treasury and the Civil Service Department (CSD) warned the Home Office that, as the Working Party was a 'mixed' commission of outside members and civil servants, there could be no commitment to carrying through its recommendations. The CSD referred to 'recommendations which do not appear to have taken much account of current constraints on public expenditure' and, had it been possible politically, would have published only a list of recommendations rather than the full report. The reaction of Joel Barnett, Chief Secretary to the Treasury, is worth quoting in full:

> Apart from the suggestion of nation-wide publicity, which is potentially very costly, there are several recommendations for measures to be taken by local authorities, and I need hardly remind you how sensitive those authorities are—and rightly—about additional burdens being imposed on them. Even the proposed Water Safety Council, while it might not cost a great deal in itself, would allow the voluntary bodies to focus their pressure for more and earlier action.[93]

Even the Home Office itself only agreed to full publication because any partial effort might do 'more harm than good' in terms of bad publicity.[94] Though ministers welcomed the report when it was eventually published

[91] *Ibid.*, pp. 4–9.
[92] Home Office, *Drowning Statistics, England and Wales, 1975–77* (London, 1980), p. 6.
[93] TNA HO 381/43, Russell to Owen, 4 August 1977, Barnett to Rees, 21 July 1977.
[94] *Ibid.*, Home Office memorandum for Secretary of State, 8 August 1977.

in October 1977, they admitted only to be 'consulting' on the idea throughout 1978 and early 1979. The public sector cuts that had begun with the sterling crisis and the International Monetary Fund mission of 1976 meant that there was simply no money for any such new initiative, desirable as it might have seemed.[95]

The accession to power of the new Conservative government under Margaret Thatcher, dedicated to further and deeper public spending cuts, saw the Home Office offer up the idea as one of its first savings. The concept of a central co-ordinating body on water safety was dead: further initiatives would have to emerge from local or charitable efforts.[96] A London Home Safety Council did expand its remit to become the London Home and Water Safety Council in 1981, but this drew public bodies and councils together from across the capital alone, and in a grass-roots fashion, rather than taking its inspiration from Westminster and Whitehall or reaching out into the whole of the UK. The idea of a government committee that would oversee the whole question had to wait until the creation of a new Water Safety Forum encouraged by the Department of Transport, but drawing its secretariat from RoSPA, under a resumed period of Labour government in 2005.[97]

Conclusion: Affluence and Anxiety

Swimming and water sports were an integral part of British society in the post-Second World War era. The nature writer Robert Macfarlane remembers his father's joy at such events: 'during my childhood, whenever we drove from our home in the Midlands up to the Highlands ... he would stop the car at the same bay on Loch Lomond's western shore, and plunge into the water for a few minutes, regardless of the weather. Then—smiling, damp, restored—he would get back in and drive on north'.[98] The late environmentalist Roger Deakin, a friend of Macfarlane's for many years, began his account of his 1990s swim across Britain with the stirring words 'you see and experience different things when you're swimming in

[95] M. Rees, 'Water Safety', Written Answers, *H. of C. Debs.*, vol. 936, cols 786–7; 'Action Urged on Deaths by Drowning', *The Times*, 27 October 1977.

[96] W. Whitelaw, 'Water Safety', Written Answers, *H. of C. Debs.*, vol. 971, cols 539–40, 27 July 1979; 'Rolling Back the Frontiers of Government', *The Guardian*, 3 September 1979.

[97] RoSPA, 'Saving Lives and Reducing Injuries ... at Leisure'. Available at: www.rospa.com/about/annualreview/leisure-safety.aspx (date accessed 20 November 2015).

[98] R. Macfarlane, *The Wild Places* (London, 2007), p. 59.

a way that is completely different from any other. You are *in* nature, part and parcel of it, in a far more complete and intense way than on dry land, and your sense of the present is overwhelming ... There is a feeling of absolute freedom and wildness that comes with the sheer liberation of ... weightlessness in natural water'.[99]

Joy and abandon there certainly was, but this was not without the shadows cast by a profound consciousness of what might—and occasionally did—go catastrophically wrong. Theorists of the post-war 'risk society' have tended to focus on the malign consequences of the development of large-scale scientific-industrial complexes and energy-hungry megacities: the fear—and fact—of nuclear accidents, chemical pollution and, more recently, global warming. The work of Ulrich Beck and others on such threats, and the insecurity that attends them, is undoubtedly seminal. But as this chapter suggests—and as Otter and Cooper have also argued in this volume—the risk society is also a matter of the personal and the familial. Certainly the new histories of the everyday pioneered by Joe Moran and Daniel Miller might be brought to bear in examining how intimate and personal fears, not least for one's offspring, were also critical to the experience of risks and dangers in the so-called nuclear age.[100]

This was not without intense ironies. Physical exercise and outdoor leisure were seen as an antidote to the stresses and strains of modern life, and yet release from these strains came with its own dangers. Beach swimming, for instance, might now be enjoyed in out-of-the-way locations, given the post-war expansion of car ownership, and yet in remote locations, surveillance of one's children was all the more important, making for enjoyment and anxiety in equal measure.[101] It is telling that this did not escape notice at the time as an issue not just for individuals and families, but for society as a whole. In 1963, Norman Carpener, chairman of the Royal College of Surgeons' Working Party on Accident Prevention, suggested that the accidents that often resulted when heedlessly trying to give vent to the frustrations of modern life constituted a 'social disease' which merited 'epidemiological study'. In an era when the church, the press and politicians were becoming less respected, doctors, he thought, 'could play an important role ... because the prevention of accidents is a social issue

[99] R. Deakin, *Waterlog* (London, 1999), pp. 3–4.

[100] J. Moran, *Reading the Everyday* (London, 2005); D. Miller, *The Comfort of Things* (Cambridge, 2008).

[101] J. Walvin, *Leisure and Society, 1830–1950* (London, 1978), p. 155.

affecting individual action and national policy, depending ultimately on education and good citizenship'.[102]

As we have seen, charities, schools, local authorities, professionals and central officials hastened to respond, in what was more a matter of governance than state intervention more narrowly cast. Between them, these multiple agents emphasized the importance of learning to swim and the responsibilities of parents and children, doing so in all sorts of ways, from the tried-and-tested provision of swimming lessons to the more novel use of taxpayer-funded and semi-official literature and films. They even aspired to co-ordinate these efforts centrally. Ultimately, perhaps, what united these efforts was an attempt to answer the human fears and worries that came with a dynamic society that was stretching established norms of consumption and self-control.[103] The official and charitable responses involved rather mechanical meetings, agendas and training initiatives that, even where they succeeded on their own terms, sometimes did little to still the deep-seated worries about safety that sat in the background of everyday existence throughout this apparent age of leisure. This approximates to what the social commentator Jeremy Seabrook meant when he wrote in the 1980s that 'the leisure society … belongs securely to the growth-and-expansion dynamic of capitalist society … it is yet another mechanism whereby economic processes that are increasingly disarticulated from human need may survive'.[104] Perhaps this chapter has revealed another dynamic: the enjoyment of increasing amounts of free time, ever more haunted by its risks, and never entirely stilled by the varied 'answers' proposed—a dynamic, as it might be put, of affluence and anxiety.

[102] N. Carpener, 'Final Note', in Hunt (ed.), *Accident Prevention and Life Saving*, pp. 304–5.

[103] See A. Offer, *The Challenge of Affluence: Self-Control and Well-Being in the United States and Britain since 1950* (Oxford, 2006).

[104] J. Seabrook, *The Leisure Society* (Oxford, 1988), p. 182.

PART IV

Occupational Risks

CHAPTER 11

Risk, Responsibility and Robens: The Transformation of the British System of Occupational Health and Safety Regulation, 1961–74

Christopher Sirrs

Over the last 20 years, three short words have come to dominate many discussions about the control of risks: 'health and safety'. In colloquial use, the term embodies a multitude of concerns about the impact of everyday actions on the bodies and minds of individuals; it also commonly conflates what are often separate areas of statutory regulation, particularly road safety, food safety and environmental regulations. Together with two other words often uttered in the same sentence, 'gone mad', 'health and safety' is often used as a kind of shorthand for bureaucracy, and the whole gamut of rules and regulations that have evolved in response to the risks of everyday life.[1]

[1] *Oxford Dictionaries* defines 'health and safety' as 'Regulations and procedures intended to prevent accident or injury in workplaces or public environments'. See www.oxforddictionaries.com/definition/english/health-and-safety (date accessed 21 November 2015).

C. Sirrs
Centre for History in Public Health, London School of Hygiene and Tropical Medicine, 15–17 Tavistock Place, London WC1H 9SH, UK

T. Crook, M. Esbester (eds), *Governing Risks in Modern Britain*,
DOI 10.1057/978-1-137-46745-4_11

The equation of 'health and safety' with protective rules and regulations in general may not be (for want of a better word) accidental, since over the last 50 years in Britain and other industrialized countries, regulatory systems addressing the 'health and safety' of workers and other key groups, such as the public, have undergone a period of unprecedented expansion. Universal legislative protection has been extended to employees against the risks of work, whilst occupational safety legislation has become decentred from its historical focus, the workplace, to address the impact of work on the wider public and environment. New regulatory agencies, such as Britain's Health and Safety Executive, have been established with the dedicated aim of protecting people from risk, while the health and safety of workers has been given explicit recognition in the legislation underpinning the European Union. As the legal and administrative arrangements surrounding 'health and safety' have become more sophisticated, a health and safety 'industry' has also emerged, providing advice and services to companies attempting to fulfil their legal obligations. New chartered bodies representing health and safety professionals, such as the Institution of Occupational Safety and Health (IOSH), have formed alongside voluntary organizations that have long campaigned for improvements in safety, such as the Royal Society for the Prevention of Accidents (RoSPA). This expansion in scope of 'occupational' legislation has blurred the boundaries between what were, historically, separate areas of labour, industrial and environmental legislation. The scale and speed of these changes not only give the impression that 'health and safety' is a monolithic entity, but also that it is a comparatively recent phenomenon, when in fact its roots stretch back over two centuries.

What allowed 'health and safety' to be spoken about in such an all-encompassing manner? Focusing on the period 1961–74, this chapter analyses a pivotal transformation in the law, which established the basis for the modern, integrated system of 'health and safety' regulation in Britain. Enshrined in the landmark Health and Safety at Work etc. Act 1974 (HSWA), this transformation marked a movement from a reactive, fragmented and piecemeal system, one which left some 5–8 million workers outside its remit, to a system thought to be more comprehensive, flexible and proactive, premised on the notion of 'self-regulation' by employers and employees. Analysing existing arrangements for worker protection, this chapter highlights how the establishment of the modern regulatory system was intimately bound up with the changing political discourse on risk in the 1960s and wider concerns about the economy and industrial relations. Over the course of the decade, several circumstances converged, calling into question long-established ways of thinking about and regulating workplace hazards. These circumstances transformed what was, by the mid-1960s, an administrative desire to revise and consolidate the law into a far more fundamental re-examination of the role of the state.[2]

Much of this chapter is devoted to the role of the Committee on Safety and Health at Work (henceforth the CSHW or the Robens Committee), an independent inquiry set up under the chairmanship of Lord Robens in the early 1970s that recommended many of the significant changes underpinning the modern system noted above.[3] While the work of the Robens Committee is widely recognized among academics and health and safety professionals (and also widely criticized), this chapter offers a new perspective on its work by examining its conclusions in light of debates surrounding health and safety in the 1960s.[4] Such an analysis reveals the important historical contingencies and continuities of the Committee's key ideas as they informed the modern system. It demonstrates that although the Committee's logic continues to shape the way we think about health and safety in Britain to this day, its 'philosophy' was very much a construct of its time.

A Fragmented and Piecemeal System

In Britain, occupational health and safety has been an important area of statutory regulation for over 200 years, although the shape, scope and objectives of this regulation have evolved only gradually. It initially emerged in the early nineteenth century out of attempts to control the working hours and conditions of children. 'Safety' was an early concern of British labour legislation, with the 1844 Factory Act including provisions for the fencing of dangerous machinery. However, it was not until later in the nineteenth century that legislation addressed the health of workers in the so-called dangerous trades, and the bias of British legislation towards safety over health continued into the twentieth century, with

[2] The National Archives, London (hereinafter TNA), LAB 96/465, RCP18, 'Background Paper by DEP on Preparation of Comprehensive Safety, Health and Welfare Legislation'.

[3] Lord Robens, *Safety and Health at Work: Report of the Committee 1970–72* (Parl. Papers 1972 [Cmnd. 5034]).

[4] A notable exception is M. Beck and C. Woolfson, 'The Regulation of Health and Safety in Britain: From Old Labour to New Labour', *Industrial Relations Journal* 31 (2000), pp. 35–49.

a senior official in the Ministry of Labour (MoL) commenting as late as 1960 that: 'In practice we classify the work as "safety, health and welfare", which is a more realistic appraisal of its balance, both from the official and industrial point of view.'[5]

Protective legislation gradually expanded across British industry, developing reactively in response to social and political concerns and sudden events, such as disasters.[6] In the process, the law became more complex and detailed, focusing on the problems of particular industries, such as manufacturing, agriculture and mining. Although the British government made several attempts to consolidate the law and make it more flexible, most notably in the Factory and Workshop Act 1901, there was no attempt at a broad solution that encompassed these various industries. Effectively, there was not one 'system' of health and safety regulation, but several. According to one early twentieth-century commentator, the economist Sidney Webb: 'We seem always to have been incapable even of taking a general view of the subject we were legislating upon. Each successive statute aimed at remedying a single ascertained evil.'[7]

It was not until 1963 that this legislation expanded to encompass workers in certain non-industrial settings, such as offices. However, by this point, British health and safety legislation had developed into a labyrinthine and fragmented mass of law, much of which was obsolete. Five separate acts governed the health and safety of workers in particular industries, while other acts extended control over specific hazards, such as radiation. These acts were accompanied by almost 500 detailed regulations, covering everything from lead to lighting.[8] Despite the quantity of law as of 1974, eight million workers, one-third of Britain's working population, received no statutory protection from occupational hazards (see Fig. 11.1).[9] These included

[5] P. Bartrip and S. Burman, *The Wounded Soldiers of Industry: Industrial Compensation Policy, 1833–1897* (Oxford, 1983), p. 15; P. Bartrip, *The Home Office and the Dangerous Trades: Regulating Occupational Disease in Victorian and Edwardian Britain* (Amsterdam, 2002), p. 9; TNA LAB 14/934, K. Kenney, memo, 15 September 1960.

[6] In the twentieth century, for example, fire precautions were tightened up in the 1959 Factory Act following a devastating mill fire in Keighley, West Yorkshire, which killed eight people, and new regulations on tips were introduced following the catastrophe at Aberfan in 1966. See Robens, *Safety and Health at Work*, p. 4.

[7] B.L. Hutchins and A. Harrison, *A History of Factory Legislation*, 2nd edn (London, 1911), p. ix; *Annual Report of H.M. Chief Inspector of Factories, 1968* (Parl. Papers 1969 [Cmnd. 4146]), p. 2; Robens, *Safety and Health at Work*, pp. 4–5.

[8] Robens, *Safety and Health at Work*, pp. 6–7.

[9] *Ibid.*, p. 10; HSC, *Report 1974–76* (London, 1977), pp. 2–3.

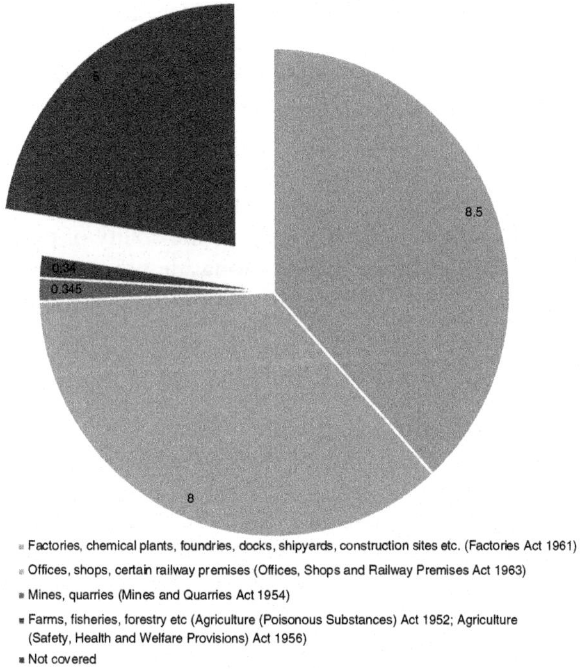

Fig. 11.1 The proportion of workers covered by principal health and safety laws in 1972 (millions of workers). Lord Robens, *Safety and Health at Work: Report of the Committee. 1970–2* (2 vols, London, 1972), I, p. 5

workers in premises such as schools and hospitals, which were deemed to fall outside the ambit of existing laws. In addition, members of the public received only incidental protection from industrial harms, a distinction that became fraught with difficulty over the 1960s, as risks increasingly intruded into the public space and consciousness, with dramatic and deadly effect.

Before the HSWA in July 1974, British health and safety legislation tended to be prescriptive, laying down detailed minimum standards for physical conditions in the workplace, such as temperature, ventilation and the design of dangerous machinery. Far less of a priority were social and organizational arrangements, such as safety committees, which could raise awareness of hazards and promote safety in general.[10] By the early 1960s,

[10] Robens, *Safety and Health at Work*, p. 8.

however, inspectors and officials in the British government, and many trade unions and safety charities, were increasingly vocal about the need for such arrangements. Factory inspectors highlighted the lack of safety arrangements in many firms and the need for employers to accept their legal responsibilities.[11] Between 1958 and 1961, the reported number of accidents under the Factories Acts increased by almost 15 %.[12] The rising tide of industrial accidents and the perceived reluctance of many employers to adopt safety measures cast doubt on the ability of prescriptive legislation to promote health and safety. Alongside other developments, the effectiveness of the existing prescriptive approach came into question.

Inculcating Safety Consciousness in Industry

By the early 1960s, therefore, British regulatory attention increasingly focused on the social conditions of work, which were seen to underpin general safety performance in firms.[13] While legislation remained fixated on physical conditions, industry was urged to bear greater responsibility for its own actions, as opposed to relying on statutory intervention in the form of legislation, inspection or prosecution. This development was not new; it formed part of a much longer trend over the twentieth century in which voluntary organizations, in conjunction with government, attempted to educate workers about safety and foster a more positive attitude. Since 1917, safety posters produced by institutions such as RoSPA were one of the principal ways in which this was achieved.[14] Films, exhibitions and promotional campaigns were also used to publicize safety efforts and raise awareness of protective controls, such as eye protection. The need to educate workers about safety was supported by prevailing 'human factor' models of accident causation, which emphasized the individual and psychological dimensions of accidents. Developed in the early twentieth

[11] *Annual Report of H.M. Chief Inspector of Factories, 1961* (Parl. Papers 1962 [Cmnd. 1816]), p. 8.

[12] *Ibid.*, p. 7.

[13] This concern also manifested itself in increased scientific attention on the underlying causes of accidents, as evidenced by a 4-year comparative study undertaken by the National Institute of Industrial Psychology, *2000 Accidents: A Shop-Floor Study of their Causes Based on 42 Months' Continuous Observation* (London, 1971).

[14] M. Esbester, 'The Discipline of Safety: Preventing Accidents in Britain after 1913'. Presented at the 'Accidents and Emergencies' conference, Oxford Brookes University, September 2013.

century by psychologists and safety engineers such as H.W. Heinrich, these models entrenched the assumption that the worker was principally to blame for industrial accidents, as opposed to negligent managements or deficient regulation.[15] By the 1960s, however, these models widened beyond a concern with the individual to address managerial or organisational factors behind accidents. Not only did statistics reveal stark discrepancies between the accident records of firms in the same industry, but insurers and politicians increasingly used accidents as a gateway into wider industrial problems. Frank E. Bird's 'total loss control' model, for example, drew attention to the financial costs of workplace accidents in terms of damage to plant, property and equipment as well as injury.[16]

Connected to wider perceived problems in British industry (see below), in the 1960s, this movement in regulatory attention gained further momentum. In the 'industrial self-help campaign', the British government, alongside trade unions, employers and safety charities, embarked on a broad educative mission of promoting health and safety as part of efficient management. Drawing upon a range of methods including conferences, speeches, posters and exhibitions, the government attempted to foster the active participation of employers and workers in health and safety, including the uptake of joint safety committees (bringing representatives of management and employees together to discuss safety matters), training schemes, industrial health services and professional safety officers.[17] Importantly, this drive did not stem from any fundamental desire to legislate. Instead, it was motivated by a paternalistic concern with helping industry help itself, and avoiding legislation—a process described as inculcating 'safety consciousness'. This was summed up by one former Chief Inspector, T.W. McCullough, in 1963 when he wrote: 'Safety consciousness ... is a form of foresight or alertness, a quality of mind which has to be developed and nurtured.'[18] The industrial self-help campaign was primarily an exercise in governance: finding means to establish within industry a

[15] See in particular J. Burnham, *Accident Prone: A History of Technology, Psychology and Misfits of the Machine Age* (Chicago, 2009).

[16] See S. Mannan (ed.), *Lees' Loss Prevention in the Process Industries: Hazard Assessment, Identification and Control* (Oxford, 2005), section 1.

[17] An example of a conference on the theme of 'industrial self-help' was the British Employers'' Confederation Conference on 'Safety and Health in Industry' held in Brighton in February 1962. See TNA LAB 14/1197.

[18] *Annual Report of H.M. Chief Inspector of Factories, 1962* (Parl. Papers 1963 [Cmnd. 2128]), p. 56.

positive disposition towards safety, which enabled the state to moderate its own role regulating the work environment.

This exercise was founded on a deep-seated belief: inspectors believed that the law was a blunt instrument to secure improvements. First, inspectors thought—despite the proliferation of legal requirements—that the law could be counter-productive if over-rigorously applied or enforced. For instance, Bryan Harvey, the Chief Inspector of Factories, remarked in 1970 that:

> It is no more thinkable that there should be so many Inspectors that one could be permanently stationed in every works than that, say, every fifth motor car should be a police car to enforce the Road Traffic Acts ... If a situation ever arose in which the Inspectorate were to attempt rigid enforcement of everything that could be driven through the Courts, so that industry ceased to turn to it for advice and guidance, the standards of safety, health and welfare set over the years in the great majority of workplaces would indeed suffer.[19]

Thus, inspectors considered that persuasion, advice and education were the most important 'weapons' in their arsenal, and they prized themselves on developing an amicable, 'conciliatory' relationship with industry, an idea that, as Peter Bartrip and Kit Carson have shown, extends back to the early nineteenth century.[20]

Second, drawing on dominant ideas about accident causation, inspectors believed that the most common accidents included an intrinsically 'human' element that defied legislative control. Referred to as the 'Big Five', these included accidents resulting from manual handling, falls, the use of hand tools, strikes against objects and strikes from falling objects. In 1962, they accounted for almost two-thirds of all reported accidents under the Factories Act. As the Chief Inspector R.K. Christy remarked: 'Passing a law does not prevent a man from dropping something on another man's head.'[21]

[19] *Annual Report of H.M. Chief Inspector of Factories, 1969* (Parl. Papers 1970 [Cmnd. 4461]), p. xii.

[20] Bartrip, *The Home Office and the Dangerous Trades*, p. 38; W. Carson, 'The Conventionalization of Early Factory Crime', *International Journal of the Sociology of Law* 7 (1979), pp. 41–60.

[21] *Annual Report of H.M. Chief Inspector of Factories, 1966* (Parl. Papers 1967 [Cmnd. 3358]), p. 8.

While these beliefs were therefore part of inspectors' historical 'DNA', they were reinforced over the 1960s. Statistical trends, for example, revealed that despite the growing mass of law, safety continued to be neglected in many workplaces. From 1959, the number of reported accidents under the Factories Acts increased, with a further, more worrying spike recorded in 1964. The total of 268,648 accidents that year represented the highest reported figure since the Second World War.[22] While the causes of this increase were unknown, inspectors thought that improved reporting, increased industrial production and the harsh winter of 1962–3 were important factors.[23] Despite a fall in fatal workplace accidents, however, the scale of the increase generated significant political attention. At a parliamentary debate on accident causation in 1965, the Parliamentary Secretary to the MoL, Ernest Thornton, argued that 'a new spirit of determination' and more 'active safety consciousness' was required to combat the problem.[24]

The rising number of accidents compounded concerns among officials that certain parts of industry were flouting their responsibilities. A 1962 survey by the MoL highlighted that less than 60 % of all notifiable accidents were being correctly reported by industry.[25] A follow-up survey in 1964 revealed the damning verdict that industry was incorrectly reporting two out of every five notifiable accidents, including 70 % of all accidents to young persons in construction.[26] Other studies also painted a grim picture of industry's willingness to engage with safety. Since 1956, the National Joint Advisory Council, a tripartite body advising the MoL on industrial relations, had called for joint safety committees to prevent accidents.[27]

[22] *Annual Report of H.M. Chief Inspector of Factories, 1964* (Parl. Papers 1965 [Cmnd. 2724]), pp. 7, 44.

[23] *Ibid.*, p. 13; TUC archive, Modern Records Centre, University of Warwick (hereinafter TUC). MSS.292B/146.17/1, report of ISSC meeting 2 June 1964.

[24] *Hansard*, HC Deb 25 February 1965, vol. 707, col. 781.

[25] *Annual Report of H.M. Chief Inspector of Factories, 1963* (Parl. Papers 1964 [Cmnd. 2450]), p. 20. TUC MSS.292B/146.17/1, 'Failure to Report Accidents', memo prepared for ISSC.

[26] TUC MSS.292B/146.17/1, Note for ISSC meeting 17 November 1964 prepared by National Union of Dyers, Bleachers and Textile Workers. Comments on 'Non-reporting of accidents' (paper 58) prepared by Safety, Health and Welfare Department of MoL; *Annual Report of H.M. Chief Inspector of Factories, 1964*, p. 24.

[27] Ministry of Labour and National Service, *Industrial Accident Prevention: A Report of the Industrial Safety Sub-Committee of the National Joint Advisory Council* (London, 1956); *Annual Report of H.M. Chief Inspector of Factories, 1965* (Parl. Papers 1967 [Cmnd. 3080]),

A 1964 paper prepared by its Industrial Safety Sub-Committee showed that, despite efforts by the Ministry, the Trades Union Congress (TUC) and some progressive employers, the number of safety committees in the largest and supposedly better-equipped workplaces had actually decreased since 1956 rather than increased.[28] Consequently, the TUC, which had previously adopted a voluntarist position to industrial relations, threatened legislation as a means to compel the appointment of safety committees, and the 1964–70 Labour government followed suit.[29]

By the end of the 1960s, therefore, factory inspectors and other officials were increasingly sceptical about the power of prescriptive legislation to prevent accidents. In addition, inspectors increasingly believed that most accidents preventable by longstanding engineering means, such as machinery guards, had already been prevented: they were suffering from diminishing returns.[30] As John Plumbe, the Chief Inspector of Factories, explained in 1969:

> [I]n a large proportion—perhaps 50 percent—of accidents no reasonably practicable precautions, at least of a physical kind, could have been taken to prevent them ... a very considerable number of the remainder result from poor industrial housekeeping of a kind which is susceptible to improvement by efficient management, so that well-run firms are very much tidier and safer in every way than far too many others.[31]

This implied that progress in accident prevention lay less in prosecution, enforcement or new regulations, than in the promotion of 'better attitudes' in industry. Harvey was unequivocal: 'Some of the traditional hazards of the physical environment have been brought under control over the past years. What we must now increasingly tackle is the social or management environment which may underlie poor safety performance.'[32]

p. 19; V. Long, *The Rise and Fall of the Healthy Factory: The Politics of Industrial Health in Britain, 1914–60* (Basingstoke, 2011), p. 169.

[28] TUC MSS.292B/146.17/1, comments on paper 59 by National Union of Dyers, Bleachers and Textile Workers.

[29] TUC MSS.292B/146.17/1, comments on paper 60; *Hansard*, HC Deb 11 July 1966 vol. 731 cols 954–5.

[30] *Annual Report of H.M. Chief Inspector of Factories, 1968*, p. xiv; *Annual Report of H.M. Chief Inspector of Factories, 1969*, p. xiv.

[31] *Annual Report of H.M. Chief Inspector of Factories, 1968*, p. xiv.

[32] *Annual Report of H.M. Chief Inspector of Factories, 1970* (Parl. Papers 1971 [Cmnd. 4758]), p. xiv.

The Productive Workplace

Historians have revealed how concerns about productivity fuelled government interest in health and safety during the First World War and interwar period, when the needs of the worker and the militaristic demands of the British state came into alignment.[33] A similar phenomenon occurred in the 1960s, although the background this time was the perceived inefficiency of British industry against its major international rivals. In the late 1950s and early 1960s, Britain's share of world trade declined, from approximately 20 % in 1955 to just 13 % in 1970.[34] By 1965, comparative levels of real output per worker were 32 % higher in West Germany and a remarkable 84 % higher in the USA.[35] Britain's diminishing productivity resulted in a growing trade deficit, culminating in Prime Minister Harold Wilson's decision in November 1967 to devalue sterling.[36] Within this context, the economic cost of absenteeism, sickness and injury resulting from occupational accidents and disease was an increasingly contentious issue. In the 1965 parliamentary debate, Thornton highlighted 'the human suffering and waste of our scarce manpower resources' which the deteriorating accident figures represented.[37] By 1967, these costs were quantified at 23 million lost working days, ten times greater than the comparable figure lost to industrial disputes.[38]

The British government increasingly thought that poorly organized and inefficient management lay at the root of these problems. In an era of full employment, amid rising concern about inflation and the need for unions to exercise wage restraint, the key to improved productivity was increasingly seen to be improving the everyday efficiency of the firm, of which health and safety was a core component. The drive to promote 'safety consciousness' was thus deeply enmeshed within these concerns. The government identified industrial training as one particular area where economic and safety needs converged, and it expended significant effort in

[33] See in particular Long, *The Rise and Fall of the Healthy Factory*; H. Jones, *Health and Society in Twentieth-Century Britain* (London, 1994).

[34] Alfred Robens, *Human Engineering* (London, 1970), p. 8.

[35] Lord Donovan, *Royal Commission on Trade Unions and Employers' Associations; 1965–1968* (Parl. Papers 1968 [Cmnd. 3623]), p. 74.

[36] Robens, *Human Engineering*, p. 8.

[37] *Hansard*, HC Deb 25 February 1965, vol. 707, col. 781.

[38] This figure was later used by the Robens Committee, *Annual Report of H.M. Chief Inspector of Factories, 1967* (Parl. Papers 1968 [Cmnd. 3745]), p. xi; Donovan, *Royal Commission*, p. 97; Office for National Statistics, *Social Trends 30* (London, 2000), p. 78.

the 1960s trying to improve the quantity and calibre of industrial training schemes.[39]

The relationship between health and safety and efficiency was also evident in industrial relations. Between 1956 and 1966, the annual number of strikes in industries other than mining increased by 142 %.[40] The growing problem of strikes motivated the 1964–70 Labour government to appoint the Royal Commission on Trade Unions and Employers' Associations (Donovan Commission) in 1965. Its 1968 report recommended statutory intervention in British industrial relations, including an Industrial Relations Act, to shore up and formalize workplace-level industrial relations, which it thought undermined collective bargaining at a wider industry and national level. The report included workplace safety as a central objective, ensuring 'regular joint discussion of measures to promote safety at work'.[41] The British government's movement to legislate for joint safety committees after 1966 was thus intimately bound up with its changing industrial relations policy. Barbara Castle's infamous 1969 White Paper, *In Place of Strife*, proposed giving union members the right to take part in management decisions, for instance, by sitting on company boards.[42] Her subsequent Employed Persons (Health and Safety) Bill advanced on this policy by proposing that recognized trade unions have the exclusive right to appoint workplace safety representatives, a proposal enshrined in the HSWA and Safety Representatives and Safety Committees Regulations 1977.[43]

The Changing Dimensions of Occupational Risk

While these developments highlighted the need for industry to take greater responsibility for safety, they left intact the underlying structure of the existing system, namely the vast and fragmented corpus of law that left up to one in three British workers without statutory protection. A convergence

[39] See *Industrial Training: Government Proposals* (Parl. Papers 1963 [Cmnd. 1892]), p. 3; *Annual Report of H.M. Chief Inspector of Factories, 1965*, p. 16.

[40] Donovan, *Royal Commission*, pp. 19, 98–9.

[41] *Ibid*., p. 45.

[42] *In Place of Strife. A Policy for Industrial Relations* (Parl. Papers 1969 [Cmnd. 3888]), pp. 16–17.

[43] The incoming Labour government in 1974 legislated for safety committees as a 'quid pro quo' for union support of the 'Social Contract'. See Arthur McIvor, *Working Lives: Work in Britain since 1945* (Basingstoke, 2013), p. 182.

of pressures in the latter half of the 1960s, however, demanded a fundamental rethink of the way in which the system worked, including the contribution of the British state. The changing nature of British industry and technology, and associated changes in occupational risk, in particular, conferred a new sense of urgency and immediacy upon reform.

While the focus of trade unions during the 1960s was not merely the extension of worker protection, but their desire to extend political control over the workplace (for example, via safety committees), factory inspectors were keenly aware of changes in the industrial environment that were transforming the risks confronted by workers.[44] As early as 1967, the Chief Inspector of Factories expressed concern about the growing scale of industrial processes. Chemical plants, for instance, were storing dangerous substances (such as liquid oxygen) in ever-growing quantities, which increasingly jeopardized the safety of surrounding communities.[45] As the Chief Inspector wrote in 1970:

> We now face a new technology. The Inspectorate is now concerned with an industrial system where virtually anything is possible. Not only can natural materials be handled and worked in totally new ways, but we can manipulate molecular structures to make new materials with virtually any property or characteristic which we desire. Above all, we can now do this on a scale which only a few years ago would have been regarded as wholly unbelievable.[46]

He expanded in 1972: 'It is clear that we can no longer afford to take a chance in many plants. In these circumstances a very detailed calculation of the sorts of problems which are likely to arise will be necessary.'[47]

Such anxieties were dramatically vindicated in June 1974, just as the HSWA was being finalized: the Nypro chemical plant in Flixborough, Humberside exploded, killing 28 workers and injuring 36 others. The explosion, equivalent to 15–45 tons of TNT, was described by the official inquiry set up afterwards as one of 'warlike dimensions', and until recently it was one of the largest Britain has ever seen. The explosion

[44] See, for instance, TNA LAB 96/483, RCP 70, 'Oral Evidence—Trades Union Congress' (August 1971); Robens, *Safety and Health at Work. Report of the Committee*, vol. 2, 'Selected Written Evidence', p. 670.

[45] *Annual Report of H.M. Chief Inspector of Factories, 1967*, pp. xii–xiii.

[46] *Annual Report of H.M. Chief Inspector of Factories, 1970*, p. xii.

[47] *Annual Report of H.M. Chief Inspector of Factories, 1971* (Parl. Papers 1972 [Cmnd. 5098]), p. xvi.

caused significant damage to properties in the local area, including homes and factories.[48]

Health risks were also rapidly changing. While the British government had for some time been concerned with acute occupational diseases, such as asbestosis, pneumoconiosis and lead poisoning, by the late 1960s, chronic occupational diseases were increasingly intruding into the regulatory consciousness. Industry was producing toxic chemicals at an accelerating speed, and the risks associated with these substances, such as cancer, were being identified which eluded the direct perception of workers and employers. These risks were the object of increasing political and public concern in the 1960s, and garnered considerable media exposure: in 1968 alone, the press reported adeno-carcinoma of the nose among furniture workers, scrotal cancer among workers handling mineral oil, and mesothelioma among asbestos workers.[49] The controversies surrounding these risks revealed how, unlike 'traditional' physical hazards such as dangerous machinery, these substances often asserted their effects invisibly, with a long delay between exposure and the onset of symptoms. This complicated risk perception, reinforcing the focus on industrial self-help. For example, in the absence of immediately visible dangers that could be corrected ad hoc, it became necessary for many employers to proactively measure, evaluate and control risks through routine environmental monitoring.[50]

The increasing profile of risks such as cancer was intimately linked to their growing detectability. Technical improvements in toxicology and industrial hygiene rendered risks visible by providing tools to identify, measure and control them. While industrial hygiene has a long history—Sellers points to its origins in the early twentieth-century USA—it was only in the late 1960s that the science began to play a prominent role in setting the policy agenda in Britain, for example, in setting quantitative 'threshold limit values' for exposure to workplace chemicals.[51] The 1969 Asbestos Regulations explicitly recognized this new quantitative approach, although at the time, the British government continued to rely on values prepared by the American Conference of Governmental Industrial

[48] *The Flixborough Disaster: Report of the Court of Inquiry* (London, 1975), pp. 1–14.

[49] *Annual Report of H.M. Chief Inspector of Factories, 1968*, pp. xvi–xvii.

[50] *Annual Report of H.M. Chief Inspector of Factories, 1967*, p. xiii.

[51] C. Sellers, *Hazards of the Job: From Industrial Disease to Environmental Health Science* (Chapel Hill, 1997). See also T. Carter, 'British Occupational Hygiene Practice, 1720–1920', *Annals of Occupational Hygiene* 48 (2004), pp. 299–307.

Hygienists, as opposed to its own scientists.[52] The rising prominence of industrial hygiene in British health and safety regulation was reflected in the decision to establish a dedicated Industrial Hygiene Unit in 1966. From 1967, field inspectors were equipped with portable instruments, enabling them to measure contamination more precisely without relying on laboratories in central London.[53] Between 1966 and 1973, tests of toxic substances in the new unit increased by 836 %.[54]

These changes in the risk environment added impetus to warnings by officials such as Harvey that existing arrangements could not keep up with technological change. However, the period was marked by a more dramatic development that implied urgent change was needed: the industrial disaster. Alongside Flixborough, one disaster above all indicated the urgent need to rethink British health and safety regulation.

On 21 October 1966, 144 people, including 116 schoolchildren, died when a spoil heap from a mine collapsed over the Welsh mining village of Aberfan, burying a school and 18 houses (see Fig. 11.2).[55] At the tribunal appointed to examine the causes of the disaster, evidence pointed to a basic failure in regulation and deficiencies in regulatory risk perception. Giving evidence, a representative of HM Mines and Quarries Inspectorate suggested that spoil heaps had never been considered dangerous before. While recorded inspections were a legal requirement underground, no such requirement extended to the surface. Nor was there a legal requirement for colliery owners to report accidents and dangerous occurrences affecting the public, only mine employees. Hence, since no miner was injured or killed that day, Aberfan's colliery manager was not obliged to report a single casualty.[56]

Alongside an earlier incident in 1964, when a construction crane in North London collapsed on a passing coach, Aberfan and Flixborough highlighted the 'delocalized' effects of many modern risks and how regulation could no longer end at the factory gates. Industrial accidents

[52] *Annual Report of H.M. Chief Inspector of Factories, 1970*, p. xvi; *Annual Report of H.M. Chief Inspector of Factories, 1969*, pp. 14–15; *Annual Report of H.M. Chief Inspector of Factories, 1973* (Parl. Papers 1974 [Cmnd. 5708]), p. 62.

[53] TUC MSS.292B/145.85/2, Copy of letter from Secretary of State for Employment and Productivity to TUC, 26 Mar. 1969, p. 2.

[54] *Annual Report of H.M. Chief Inspector of Factories, 1973*, pp. viii, 62. The number of tests made of toxic substances increased from 1373 in 1966 to 12,850 in 1973.

[55] *Report of the Tribunal Appointed to Inquire into the Disaster at Aberfan on October 21st, 1966* (Parl. Papers 1967 (HC 553)), p. 26.

[56] *Ibid.*, pp. 35–6.

Photograph showing general view of flowslide and mud run. 21st October 1966, approx. 1 p.m

Fig. 11.2 The 1966 Aberfan disaster. *Welsh Office: A Selection of Technical Reports Submitted to the Aberfan Tribunal* (2 vols, London, 1969), I, p. 33. Published with the kind permission of the Bodleian Library, Oxford

could kill members of the public and devastate entire communities.[57] With the enactment of remedial legislation in 1969, the reactivity of the existing regulatory system was once again demonstrated.[58]

The Failure of Reform, 1967–70

Although disasters such as Aberfan lent new urgency to reform, by the late 1960s purely administrative concerns had raised the issue. By 1967, the Minister of Labour, Ray Gunter, and his colleagues believed that the Factories Act was overly long and confusing, both for those who administered the law and for those it protected. Much of its wording was inconsistent or vague, and many of its provisions were antiquated, with some dating back to the nineteenth century. Further, with two acts administered by the Ministry in force side by side—the Factories Act 1961 and the Offices, Shops and Railway Premises Act 1963—demarcation problems arose where it was difficult to tell which act applied. If one act and its subordinate regulations had to be revised, so did the other.[59]

By December 1967, therefore, plans were afoot to revise and consolidate these acts into a single statute. Proposals were circulated, seeking to 'meet the needs of a rapidly developing industrial society' by advancing a new comprehensive statute of a more widely applicable character.[60] While the proposals envisaged covering all work premises, however, and certain defined 'work operations' wherever they were performed (such as window cleaning), the 1967 proposals contained significant exceptions: premises subject to statutes administered by other government departments, such as mines, were excluded, as were provisions concerning the self-employed, homeworkers and, critically, the public.[61] Effectively, the 1967 proposals left intact the existing fragmented arrangements.

[57] *Report of the Investigation of the Crane Accident at Brent Cross, Hendon, on 20th June 1964* (Parl. Papers 1965 [Cmnd. 2768]). The idea of risk delocalization, of course, underpins Ulrich Beck's notion of the 'risk society'—that in recent decades, the risks of industrial society have become delocalized and global in their effects. See Ulrich Beck, *Risk Society: Towards a New Modernity* (London, 1992).

[58] The Mines and Quarries (Tips) Act 1969. See Robens, *Safety and Health at Work*, pp. 4, 90.

[59] TNA LAB 96/332, CSHW: DEP Background Paper, p. 1.

[60] TUC MSS.292B/145.85/1, First Consultative Document, covering letter, 1 December 1967, par. 3.

[61] TUC MSS.292B/145.85/1, First Consultative Document, December 1967.

Although consultations with trade unions, employers' associations and other interested parties continued throughout 1968, they were not fruitful. By 1969, Barbara Castle and her colleagues at the Department of Employment and Productivity (DEP), which inherited the proposals, were dissatisfied at the lack of progress. The wider government shared this view: in January 1969, the Home Affairs Committee ruled out comprehensive health and safety legislation in the 1969–70 parliamentary session.[62] Castle's interim Employed Persons (Health and Safety) Bill, which was lost upon the dissolution of Parliament in 1970, consequently focused on just two policy issues requiring immediate attention: joint consultation and proposals for a new Employment Medical Advisory Service.

By 1969, therefore, the DEP accepted that a more radical solution was necessary if contemporary needs were to be met. That year, it mooted the prospect of a National Authority for Safety and Health at Work, as well a wide-ranging inquiry into health and safety regulation, among other government departments. Although some departments raised concerns about the scope of this inquiry and the potential costs associated with the expansion of legislation, Castle was convinced of its necessity. In a revealing memo to her Cabinet colleagues, she argued that an 'independent' committee would give the government significant leverage if it recommended a significant break with the old system. The 1967 proposals had in any case 'virtually committed' the government to reform and alternative approaches, such as commissioning research, would suggest that the government was kicking the issue into the long grass. What was necessary, she argued, was a fresh start and a small committee, composed of just a few members, would be more likely to get results.[63] In a letter to Victor Feather, the General Secretary of the TUC, she explained:

> The conclusion I have come to is that the matter can be satisfactorily dealt with only by having a high-level outside enquiry. I have in mind a small body—perhaps a chairman and 3 or 4 members—who could, without going into the detail of the existing legislation, take a general look at the way the present system works right across the field.[64]

[62] TNA LAB 96/447, Memorandum by the First Secretary of State and Secretary of State for Employment and Productivity; TNA CAB 134/2862, H(69), 2nd Meeting (24 January 1969), p. 7.

[63] TNA LAB 96/447, Memorandum by the First Secretary of State; Doc 1, summary of replies to Sir Derek Barnes' letter of 5 September 1969.

[64] TUC MSS.292B/145.85/2, Castle to Feather, 24 February 1970.

At Feather's suggestion, on 29 May 1970, Castle appointed Lord Alfred Robens to head this inquiry.

The Industrial Philosophy of Lord Alfred Robens

Alfred Robens was an interesting choice of Chair for the Committee on Safety and Health at Work. As a former trade union official, Labour MP for the northern England constituency of Blyth, and briefly Minister of Labour, Robens was a close associate of the trade unions and a passionate advocate of industrial safety. In the mid-1950s, he had lobbied the then Conservative government to expand industrial health and safety legislation to non-industrial premises.[65] Later in the decade, the Prime Minister, Harold Macmillan, invited Robens to chair the organization running the nationalized coal industry in Britain, the National Coal Board (NCB). There, he became closely acquainted with health and safety in a major and still very hazardous industry, albeit one in serious decline.[66]

Following Aberfan, however, the media lambasted Robens as NCB Chair for his mishandling of the relief effort. Notoriously, rather than attend the scene of the disaster immediately, he preferred to honour his instalment as Chancellor of the University of Surrey.[67] At the Aberfan tribunal, he was criticized for his inconsistent evidence. It was demonstrated that while he had suggested to a TV reporter that 'it was impossible to know that there was a spring in the heart of this tip which was turning the centre of the mountain into sludge', the NCB actually had technology at its disposal that could have detected its presence.[68]

Despite the reputational damage that Robens incurred, the fact that it was Victor Feather who proposed his name to Castle suggests Robens retained credibility among the trade union movement.[69] Indeed, having been appointed to the NCB by a Conservative Prime Minister, Robens had a degree of political acceptability across 'both sides of industry' and was

[65] *Hansard*, HC Deb 1 April 1955, vol. 539, col. 757.

[66] Output contracted from 194 million tons per year in 1960 to 142 million by the 1970s. Geoffrey Tweedale, 'Robens, Alfred, Baron Robens of Woldingham (1910–1999)', *Oxford Dictionary of National Biography* (Oxford, 2010); Alfred Robens, *Ten Year Stint* (London, 1972).

[67] *Report of the Tribunal*, pp. 92–3; Tweedale, 'Robens, Alfred, Baron Robens of Woldingham (1910–1999)'.

[68] *Report of the Tribunal*, pp. 89–92.

[69] TNA LAB 96/447, Safety and health inquiry: membership. Brief for the First Secretary's meeting with Mr Feather on 20 April, p. 1.

well versed in arbitrating between employers and trade unions, which was seen by the DEP as key to reducing accidents. In the 1960s, Robens was a member of the Donovan Commission and became familiar with the link between safety and productivity. Then, in 1970, before he was appointed chair of the CSHW, Robens published an insightful book called *Human Engineering* that demonstrates the influence of these considerations on his thinking.[70] In this book, he cited inefficient management as the overriding explanation for Britain's economic and industrial decline. The primary reason Britain was uncompetitive, he argued, was because it could not properly utilize labour, unlike the USA, which set the example to follow.[71] Industrial accidents were symptomatic of a poorly managed workplace, where workers had little stake in the management decisions affecting their work. Arrangements that encouraged worker participation, and health and safety as a matter of good practice, should thus be promoted and used in preference to prescriptive legislation, which in his view encouraged the notion it was government, not employers and employees, who had primary responsibility for health and safety. 'Not until wise managements recognise the importance of safety at the place of employment as an integral part of efficiency will the requirement for inspectors and enforcement virtually disappear.'[72] In *Human Engineering*, Robens devised a redistribution of responsibility that he later elaborated on as chairman the CSHW.

The Committee on Safety and Health at Work

The members of the CSHW were assembled from across the political spectrum. Besides Robens, the seven members of the Committee included a legal professor (John Wood), a Conservative MP (Mervyn Pike), a radiologist (Sir Brian Windeyer), a trade unionist (Sydney Robinson), a chairman of a major standard-making body (George Beeby) and a management consultant (Anne Shaw). Shaw's place on the Committee is particularly insightful, highlighting the importance of 'management' to the Committee's thinking when industrial efficiency was a top political priority.[73]

[70] Robens, *Human Engineering*.

[71] *Ibid*., p. 10.

[72] *Ibid*., pp. 123–4.

[73] H. Williams, 'Roots: The Pioneers—Anne Shaw, CBE, 1904–1982', *Management Services* 35 (1991), pp. 26–8.

The CSHW was the first ever 'across the board' inquiry into British health and safety legislation, and its terms of reference were correspondingly vast: to examine both the statutory and voluntary arrangements for occupational health and safety in Britain, and (following the Brent Cross crane collapse and Aberfan) to consider whether any further action was necessary to protect the public from hazards arising from work activity.[74] These terms were diligently drafted to avoid contention with issues considered to be outside the domain of 'health and safety' at this time, such as environmental pollution. However, the fact that hazards were increasingly delocalized and had effects beyond the workplace meant that the Committee found it difficult to confine itself. 'Safety and health at work', Robens conceded, 'is not a subject that is easily delimited.'[75]

The CSHW's first meeting was held on 23 June 1970.[76] In addition to its main members, the Committee was assisted by a Secretariat composed of seconded civil servants, led by Matthew Wake of the Department of Employment (DE). The Secretariat and the DE played an essential role administering the Committee's work, scheduling meetings and visits, processing evidence, and preparing background documents that helped the Committee get underway. These documents, as well as notes of informal meetings, provide a unique insight into the Committee's developing ideas. What becomes apparent is how closely exposed the Committee was to the agenda of its sponsoring department, the DE, and thus how its recommendations closely followed the template of existing priorities. For example, an early background paper painted a picture of the regulatory landscape that was unquestioningly adopted by the Committee, highlighting 'the multiplicity of enforcing agencies, the multiplicity and overlap of statutes, the distinction between safety and health of employed persons and safety and health of members of the public, [and] gaps in the coverage of the legislation'.[77] Further, an early review of evidence just 6 months into the inquiry emphasized the Factory Inspectorate's belief that 'the existence of a mass of detailed restrictive legislation may inhibit the natural development of self-help and continuous self-regulation by industry itself'.[78] This was uncannily

[74] Robens, *Safety and Health at Work*, p. 5.

[75] *Ibid.*, p. xv.

[76] TNA LAB 96/481, minutes, RCM1, 23 June 1970.

[77] TNA LAB 96/465, Document 4.

[78] TNA LAB 96/465, RCP37, November 1970.

similar to the Committee's eventual conclusion that 'the existence of such a mass of law has an unfortunate and all-pervading psychological effect. People are heavily conditioned to think of safety and health at work as in the first and most important instance a matter of detailed rules imposed by external agencies'.[79]

The similarity of these arguments suggests that the CSHW was cognitively 'captured' by the prevailing ideas of the DE and the Factory Inspectorate. Such an interpretation is further supported by examining the Committee's evidence gathering. Over the course of its inquiry, the CSHW collected evidence from over 200 individuals and organizations with an interest in health and safety, including government departments and inspectorates, local authorities, trade unions, employers' associations, insurers, medical and voluntary organizations. It also embarked on a series of overseas visits to West Germany, Sweden and the US. Before the CSHW invited formal written evidence, informal talks were held with senior figures of some of these organizations, helping the Committee to form a preliminary impression of the state of the system. Many of these officials' comments, particularly 'expert' members of the Factory Inspectorate, found their way directly into the Committee's Report—for example, Plumbe's assertion that the Factory Inspectorate's enforcement work suffered from diminishing returns.[80] These beliefs were accepted by the Committee without question, and indeed were closely in line with Robens' own ethos (as articulated in *Human Engineering*). In contrast, the strongly held beliefs of other parties were largely dismissed out of hand and relatively early in the CSHW's life. The Committee did not share the trade unions' view, for instance, that the answer to accidents was more detailed regulation or more inspectors. It also discounted the views of other government departments and inspectorates, who emphasized the benefits of independence, such as specialism. By January 1971, the CSHW had already largely determined that there should be a new single act applying to all employees and that there should be greater emphasis on better attitudes, organization and responsibility in the workplace; there was a limit to what legislation alone could achieve.[81]

[79] Robens, *Safety and Health Work*, p. 7.

[80] TNA LAB 96/481, 'Note of Committee's informal discussion with W.J.C. Plumbe, 21 July 1970'.

[81] TNA LAB 96/481, Minutes of 18th meeting, 19 January 1971.

The Robens Report

Accompanied by a widespread publicity campaign, the Robens Report was published on 19 July 1972. Its primary conclusion was that the existing regulatory system no longer served the needs of people in the 1970s. Fragmented, overly complex and confusing, while failing to protect millions of workers, the system suffered from diminishing returns and discouraged voluntary effort. The continuing humanitarian and economic costs of accidents and ill health revealed the failure of existing approaches, estimated at 1000 fatalities per year, half a million injuries and 23 million lost working days.[82] Statutory effort, the Committee argued, should be refocused on encouraging voluntary compliance with the law: '*There are severe practical limits on the extent to which progressively better standards of safety and health at work can be brought about through negative regulation by external agencies. We need a more effectively self-regulating system.*'[83]

This conclusion followed logically from the Report's central premise, which was that 'apathy' rather than weak regulation or enforcement was primarily to blame for workplace accidents.[84] While controversial to this day, this belief made sense in terms of Robens' industrial philosophy and the experiences of inspectors and administrators in the British government, to whose expertise the Committee deferred. These actors genuinely believed that the law was deleterious if over-applied or enforced, even if other actors (namely trade unions) passionately disagreed. In Robens' view, the maze of rules on the statute book was counter-productive, since it obscured the actual responsibilities of employers and employees. The primary responsibility for securing safe and hygienic working conditions lay not with the state, but with those who generated risk, and the role of the state was to support industry in fulfilling its obligations.[85] Moreover, rapid changes in industry and technology rendered the existing system obsolete. As disasters such as Flixborough demonstrated, prescriptive legislation could not keep pace with changes in the risk environment. A more flexible and forward-looking system was needed.

Robens' approach to workplace safety drew on his industrial philosophy and experience in the NCB, and was closely inspired by the Factory Inspectorate's paternalism. Just as he advocated in *Human Engineering*,

[82] Robens, *Safety and Health at Work*, p. 1.
[83] *Ibid.*, p. 12, emphasis in original.
[84] *Ibid.*, p. 1.
[85] *Ibid.*, p. 2.

Robens emphasized that health and safety was an essential feature of good management and needed to be treated in the same way as other business activities, such as industrial relations and personnel management.[86] Safety performance could only be improved, he asserted, if everyone pulled their weight; from the chairman to shop floor, accidents could only be reduced if everyone was clear about their responsibilities. Integral to this shared effort was his recommendation that companies produce written safety policies, detailing safety arrangements in the workplace.[87] He was also acutely aware of the power of joint consultation in stimulating this effort. On the question of safety committees, he stopped short of calling for their statutory compulsion, as demanded by the TUC, believing that industrial conditions varied so widely that it was unwise to impose particular arrangements. Nevertheless, he advised that employers should consult their employees about health and safety issues.[88]

Robens' most far-reaching recommendations focused on the British state's contribution. He recommended that the various acts and regulations littering the statute book should be scaled back, simplified and reorganized under the umbrella of a single 'enabling' act, administered by a new quasi-independent National Authority for Safety and Health at Work.[89] By 'enabling', Robens envisaged a central act detailing the general principles of health and safety, applying to all workers and workplaces. Specific matters, such as precautions applying to particular industries, would be detailed in an organized framework of subordinate regulations, codes of practice and standards. Concordant with his ideas about 'self-regulation', he argued that codes of practice and voluntary standards should be used in preference to detailed statutory regulation, unless the scale of risk rendered this necessary. In general, the quantity of regulations should be reduced.[90]

[86] *Ibid.*, pp. 15–16; Robens, *Human Engineering*, p. 10.

[87] Robens, *Safety and Health at Work*, pp. 23–4.

[88] *Ibid.*, pp. 21–2.

[89] A critical feature of this new body was that it would be managed by a board composed of representatives of trade unions and employers' associations, thus institutionalizing the philosophy of self-regulation. By 'quasi-independent', it was meant that the Authority would ultimately be responsible to Parliament, although it would have autonomy in its day-to-day operations. The Health and Safety Commission, founded in October 1974, would ultimately realize this goal, also extending representation to local authorities as representatives of the public. See Robens, *Safety and Health at Work*, pp. 31–9.

[90] *Ibid.*, p. 45.

The Committee thought that this new approach had multiple benefits: it was more flexible and amendable with technical progress, allowing the system to keep pace with change; it was comprehensive, bringing under protection all workers, regardless of workplace or industry; it was also more comprehensible, outlining the fundamental responsibilities of employers, employees and other groups, such as manufacturers. The use of subordinate regulations and codes would permit the gradual replacement of existing rules, while by emphasizing the primacy of voluntary standards and (quasi-legal) codes, this approach supported a wholesale redistribution of effort on to industry.

Robens' use of the term 'self-regulation' to express this idea, however, was problematic, since he did not envisage the complete abandonment of regulations to control hazards, merely their rebalancing. He asserted that his proposals did not weaken workers' legal protection, but rather permitted the more 'discriminating' use of legislation.[91] Indeed, for some areas of potentially catastrophic risk, such as major hazards, he advocated even stronger legal requirements. The idea of a single 'enabling' act was strongly influenced by the DE's previous proposals, and in this way Robens' proposals can be seen as a logical extension of Ray Gunther's reform programme, which began in 1967. Seen against this background, the originality of the Robens Committee has been much exaggerated.

Conclusion

It is beyond the scope of this chapter to describe the events that resulted in the HSWA. Briefly, while 'both sides of industry' and the main political parties broadly supported the Robens Report, they disagreed on matters of detail, which still needed to be worked out on an administrative level. Some government departments with existing responsibilities, such as the Department of the Environment, were resistant to Robens' recommendation that their functions should be hived off to a new national authority—what ultimately became two new institutions, the Health and Safety Commission (HSC) and the Health and Safety Executive (HSE). Ministers feared that the loss of their inspectorates to a new authority would undermine the links with industry and technical expertise they relied upon for policy-making. Consequently, the Robens Report generated what was euphemistically termed by the Labour Employment

[91] *Ibid.*, p. 46.

Secretary, Michael Foot, as 'a prolonged and intensive period of interdepartmental consultation'.[92]

Despite the significant administrative problems that resulted from the Report, the cross-party political support that greeted its publication became central to the ongoing development of the regulatory system. The political consensus around occupational health and safety, seen in other areas of British public policy in the 1960s and 1970s, became embodied in the constitution of the HSC, which became the primary vehicle for making new standards, codes and regulations after 1974. Following the lead of other quasi-independent authorities at this time, such as the Manpower Services Commission, the HSC adopted a tripartite structure, bringing together representatives of employers and trade unions and the state to secure agreement on health and safety matters. The consensual nature of their decision-making, according to the socio-legal scholar Graham K. Wilson, has contributed to the widespread political acceptance of British health and safety policy, in contrast to occupational health and safety in the USA, by ensuring that a wide range of interests are taken into account when making regulatory decisions.[93] It has certainly contributed to the longevity of the HSE as a regulator in Britain, although the HSC was merged into the HSE's management structure in 2008.

In this and other respects, the regulatory approach laid down by the Robens Committee continues to shape the way in which health and safety risks are confronted in Britain to this day, over 40 years after the HSWA was passed. One of the most important outcomes of the reform process was a system that put voluntary effort, or 'self-regulation', at the heart of the control of risk. Events that took place over the course of the 1960s exposed the need for employers to evaluate work that could potentially endanger workers and others affected by their activity, and implement controls accordingly. While the events described here pre-date the use of the phrase 'risk assessment' in health and safety policy, it is pertinent to note that later moves in the 1980s and 1990s to formalize 'risk assessment' as part of the everyday control of risk were conditional on these earlier moves to prioritize self-regulation. The qualification 'so far as is reasonably practicable', spread throughout the HSWA, implied a form of risk assessment in the control of risk: the idea that controls should be

[92] *Hansard*, HC Deb 3 April 1974, vol. 871, col. 1287.

[93] G. Wilson, *The Politics of Safety and Health: Occupational Safety and Health in the United States and Britain* (Oxford, 1985), pp. 151–2.

proportionate to risk, taking into account time, trouble and expense.[94] By emphasizing how excessive legal requirements could damage safety by standing in the way of employers understanding their legal responsibilities, these developments paved the way for extensive deregulation of health and safety law in the 1980s, although it is important to note that Robens did not entirely condone this.[95]

Significantly, efforts to inculcate safety as part of efficient management in the 1960s and early 1970s demonstrate that risk regulation 'may proceed by means other than by the application or promulgation of rules'.[96] Formal regulations have been just one instrument at the disposal of regulators to promote safety and have generally been discouraged in favour of softer approaches such as codes of practice, education and consultation. While this chapter has focused on statutory efforts, it is important to recognize that regulation can encompass a diverse field of actors: not just trade unions and employer's associations, but also charities, insurers, professional and trade bodies and other organizations.

Perhaps the most significant outcome of Robens' vision, however, was a wider and more all-embracing conceptualization of 'health and safety' itself, one that continues to frame how we think about and regulate occupational risks—and, indeed, contest and critique this regulation, as the next chapter suggests. As a consequence of his recommendations, 'occupational' health and safety legislation expanded to encompass virtually all workers, as well as 'third persons' such as members of the public who could be injured or made ill by work activity. Only domestic servants in private households, covered under civil law, were ultimately excluded. Robens realized that since risks crossed the factory or work gates and did not merely affect employees, it was inefficient to deal with them under separate laws, administered by separate government departments and inspectorates. The implication of this idea, as enacted in the HSWA, was staggering: prisons had responsibility for the health and safety of prisoners, schools their pupils, and factory owners the people who lived in the communities around their factories.[97] The Robens Report established the

[94] 'So far as is reasonably practicable' was given legal definition in the case *Edwards v. National Coal Board* [1949] 1 All ER 743.

[95] See S. Tombs and D. Whyte, 'A Deadly Consensus: Worker Safety and Regulatory Degradation under New Labour', *British Journal of Criminology* 50 (2009), pp. 46–65.

[96] R. Baldwin, *Rules and Government* (Oxford, 1995), p. 3.

[97] J. Locke, 'The Politics of Health and Safety: Text of the Alexander Redgrave Memorial Lecture', 1981, p. 10.

conditions for a truly universal system of health and safety, reflected in the fact that much of the work of the twenty-first-century HSE is devoted to issues of 'public', as opposed to worker, health and safety. Paradoxically therefore, while the Robens Report streamlined health and safety law, it greatly increased the scope, power and reach of health and safety over our work and everyday lives. Ironically, current ideas in Britain about the over-zealous application and extent of health and safety law were made possible, implicitly, by these historic changes. While Robens and inspectors in the early 1970s saw the public as an enthusiastic recipient of reform, the modern-day belligerence and even 'apathy' of the British public towards health and safety is surely not something they anticipated.

CHAPTER 12

Il/Legitimate Risks? Occupational Health and Safety and the Public in Britain, c. 1960–2015

Paul Almond and Mike Esbester

The last 20 years have seen the emergence of a popular climate of antipathy towards occupational health and safety regulation in the UK, particularly within the mainstream British media.[1] The emergence of a narrative of 'health and safety gone mad' has been mirrored by a hardening of government policy around risk regulation, including a reduction of resources, a rolling back of the legislative framework, and the adoption of

[1] P. Almond, 'The Dangers of Hanging Baskets: "Regulatory Myths" and Media Representations of Health and Safety Regulation', *Journal of Law and Society* 36 (2009), pp. 352–75; D. Ball and L. Ball-King, 'Safety Management and Public Spaces: Restoring Balance', *Risk Analysis* 33 (2013), pp. 763–71; S. Lloyd-Bostock, 'Public Perceptions of Risk and "Compensation Culture" in the UK', in B. Hutter (ed.), *Anticipating Risks and Organising Risk Regulation* (Cambridge, 2013), pp. 90–113.

P. Almond (✉)
School of Law, University of Reading, Foxhill House,
Whiteknights Road, Reading RG6 7BA, UK

M. Esbester
School of Social, Historical and Literary Studies, University of Portsmouth,
Milldam, Burnaby Road, Portsmouth PO1 3AS, UK

T. Crook, M. Esbester (eds), *Governing Risks in Modern Britain*,
DOI 10.1057/978-1-137-46745-4_12

a policy-making rhetoric of 'red tape' and 'sensible regulation'.[2] The governance of health and safety has thus become an increasingly visible and contested public and political issue.

The extent of this contestation and its impact on health and safety in the workplace and beyond requires explanation and historicization. Why, in recent years, has public rhetoric about health and safety become so important in framing the ways in which the state might legitimately act? Where does public opinion fit into the longer history of preventing deaths and injuries in post-war Britain? In a volume interested in pluralizing notions of how risk has been governed and by whom, it may seem counter-intuitive to focus on the state, an institution thoroughly explored by an earlier generation of historians, as Chapter 1 in this volume has noted. Yet, we can affirm the agency of the state whilst also attending, as this chapter does, to the shifting place and input of the public, and more especially to how public opinion came to exercise a key role in the formation and legitimacy of health and safety regulation, which is largely a product of recent decades.

This development forms part of a broader history of governance in which the state has taken account of constituencies far beyond the realms of formal regulatory processes. Indeed, the state was never a monolithic or domineering agent, even during the heyday of the so-called classic post-war welfare state. Actions were always negotiated with multiple interested parties, collectively forming what Christopher Sellers and Joseph Melling have recently called the 'industrial hazard regime'.[3] As we shall see, there were peaks and troughs in the extent to which the many actors involved were able to influence the state's approaches to health and safety. Trade unionism was particularly significant up to the 1970s, whereas employers became increasingly influential in the 1980s. Meanwhile, safety organizations (such as the Royal Society for the Prevention of Accidents) and

[2] S. Tombs and D. Whyte, 'A Deadly Consensus: Worker Safety and Regulatory Degradation under New Labour', *British Journal of Criminology* 50 (2010), pp. 46–65; P. Hampton, *Reducing Administrative Burdens: Effective Inspection and Enforcement* (London, 2005) (hereinafter the Hampton Review); R. Löfstedt, *Reclaiming Health and Safety for All: An Independent Review of Health and Safety Legislation* (London, 2011) (hereinafter the Löfstedt Review); R. Macrory, *Regulatory Justice: Sanctioning in a Post-Hampton World* (London, 2006) (hereinafter the Macrory Review); Lord Young, *Common Sense, Common Safety* (London, 2010) (hereinafter the Young Review).

[3] C. Sellers and J. Melling (eds), *Dangerous Trade: Histories of Industrial Hazard across a Globalizing World* (Philadelphia, PA, 2011).

pressure groups (such as the Society for the Prevention of Abestosis and Industrial Diseases) struggled to gain long-lasting purchase throughout, commanding attention only at particular moments. But what is most striking is that from the 1980s, one set of actors assumed an increasingly important and influential role, both as an actor and as a point of reference: 'the public'.

To be sure, the public was never a uniform entity, something that was recognized at the time. As Bill Simpson, Chair of the Health and Safety Commission (HSC)—the management board overseeing the post-1974 regulatory system—observed in 1982: 'I even find it difficult to grasp sometimes what "public concern" actually means, or what "the wider public" means.'[4] Temporary coalitions of opinions emerged at particular points and the public always expressed a multiplicity of views. Nonetheless, the public gradually assumed a central place in debates about the legitimacy of health and safety. This was not, however, simply a product of growing governmental accountability per se; rather, it reflected a new *kind* of accountability that emerged in the wake of a gradual dissolution of more tripartite forms of governance. It also reflected the advent of a new political and administrative culture that was pro-business, sceptical of 'red tape' and keen to embrace more efficient styles of public management. As we shall see, the key change was from a relatively longstanding and limited conception of governance focused around industrial stakeholders—employers, workers and regulators especially—to one rooted in a much more diffuse coalition of interested parties, including the public. This began, we suggest, in the mid-1980s, followed by a period of consolidation in the years after 2000.

A Culture of Tripartism: 1960–85

The modern regulatory system governing occupational health and safety (OHS) reaches back into the early nineteenth century. It began with the creation of an official Factory Inspectorate in 1833, which remained the lynchpin of the system beyond the Second World War. The creation and longevity of this body might be seen in terms of a sustained climate of progressive opinion, a view famously put forward by the jurist A.V. Dicey

[4] *The Working of the HSC and E: Achievements since the Robens Report* (Parl. Papers 1981–2 [HC 400–ii]), minutes of evidence, 23 June 1982, p. 15.

in the early twentieth century.[5] It is certainly true that factory inspection was gradually better resourced and that inspectors were slowly equipped with greater powers of enforcement. Regulations became more exacting, especially in relation to working conditions: the Factories Act of 1937, for instance, was a mammoth piece of legislation, specifying sanitary conditions, the safeguarding of machinery, the provision of fire exits and procedures for notifying accidents, among many other things.

In fact, as historians have shown, these achievements were only secured through intensely complex processes of negotiation and compromise, and there was little, if any, direct engagement with public opinion more broadly.[6] Instead, the public dimension, such as it was, was restricted to employers, employees and trade unions. As early as the mid-Victorian period, inspectors were urged to practise diplomacy when advising or admonishing employers. It was axiomatic that persuasion was more reliable—and cheaper—than legal action: a sentiment that was just as pronounced in the interwar period. Similarly, tactics of education and consultation were judged critical throughout, and by the 1930s, as Helen Jones has described, a loosely tripartite culture of governance had arisen in which inspectors regularly liaised with manufacturers' associations and trades unions.[7] Firms, for instance, voluntarily introduced safety committees that featured representatives of labour and management. Although none of this necessarily made for consensus, direct dialogue and tripartite consultation between the state, employers and employees was a part of both the formulation and implementation of health and safety measures.

This culture of broadly consensual, tripartite governance persisted into the post-war period, when further legislation was passed, such as the Factories Act of 1961. Inspectors, for instance, continued to insist on the limits of legislation and the need to educate (rather than coerce) workers and employers. As the Chief Inspector of Factories noted in his 1963 report, 'both employers and workers are morally bound to accept responsibilities that are wider than those imposed by law … Legislation

[5] A.V. Dicey, *Lectures on the Relation Between Law and Public Opinion in England During the Nineteenth Century* (London, 1905).

[6] On diplomacy and negotiation, see D. Roberts, *Victorian Origins of the British Welfare State* (New Haven, CT, 1960), pp. 287–93; and P.W.J. Bartrip, 'State Intervention in Mid-Nineteenth Century Britain: Fact or Fiction?', *Journal of British Studies* 23 (1983), pp. 63–83.

[7] H. Jones, 'An Inspector Calls: Health and Safety at Work in Inter-War Britain', in P. Weindling (ed.), *The Social History of Occupational Health* (London, 1985), pp. 223–39.

cannot be a complete guide to what should be done'.[8] Likewise, if moving in the other direction, trade unions and local authorities continued to lobby for greater state involvement. To give but one example, in the early 1970s, the Dock and Harbour Authorities' Association requested better and more extensive inspection, complaining of 'a considerable shortage of trained personnel in the Factory Inspectorate, particularly those familiar with dock operations and ports generally'.[9]

At the same time, debate remained largely confined to those groups with a direct and vested interest in OHS. Matters of workplace safety and health were not afforded great public importance.[10] In 1972, the TUC General Secretary could note that: 'More people are interested in the antics of a certain lady and her butler or the Provost of Portsmouth Cathedral than in safety in industry.'[11] Officials within the Factory Inspectorate seem to have held only a limited conception of public opinion, which was constructed largely in terms of knowledge about the workplace. In 1972, the Chief Inspector of Factories recorded that 'it is part of the job of the Inspectorate to develop an informed public and to harness the force of its informed opinion to the improvement of industrial conditions'.[12] Although the same report noted that 'we are considering a much more active approach to the development of public opinion', this was conceived in terms of informing the public about the work of the Inspectorate.[13] On rare occasions, perhaps, significant disasters sparked considerable public interest and intense debate in the press regarding questions of industrial safety. This was true of the disaster at Aberfan, South Wales, in October 1966, when a primary school and adjacent houses were engulfed by a collapsed colliery spoil heap, resulting in the death of 144 people, the majority of whom were children. Yet media coverage was invariably short-lived and it was not necessarily related to the precise question of OHS.[14] As Rex

[8] *Annual Report of H.M. Chief Inspector of Factories, 1963* (Parl. Papers 1964 [Cmnd. 2450]), p. 47.

[9] Written evidence of Dock and Harbour Authorities' Association to the Robens Committee (c. 1972), p. 3. The National Archives, London, LAB 96/57.

[10] J.L. Williams, *Accidents and Ill-Health at Work* (London, 1961).

[11] *Daily Telegraph*, 9 August 1972.

[12] *Annual Report of H.M. Chief Inspector of Factories, 1972* (Parl. Papers 1972 [Cmnd. 5398]), p. vi.

[13] *Ibid.*, p. xv.

[14] I. McLean and M. Johnes, *Aberfan: Government and Disasters* (Cardiff, 2000); M.K. Pantti and K. Wahl-Jorgensen, '"Not an Act of God": Anger and Citizenship in Press Coverage of British Man-Made Disasters', *Media, Culture & Society* 33 (2011), pp. 105–22.

Symons, a former member of the HSC, has recently observed: 'Aberfan didn't strike one as being a health and safety issue, it struck you as being a public safety issue.'[15]

The approach taken by the Robens Committee and the subsequent Health and Safety at Work etc. Act 1974 (HSWA) at once built on and formalized the existing culture of corporatist, tripartite governance. As Christopher Sirrs' chapter in this volume shows, the approach taken by Robens was driven by an ethos of 'industrial self-regulation' and a perceived 'identity of interests' between workers and employers. Underlying the Robens philosophy was a particular vision of risk governance that sought to co-opt the self-regulating capacities of workers and employers alike, whilst limiting the role of the state and the use of formal methods, such as legally enforcing the precise specifications of factories acts. The result was the creation of the Health and Safety Executive (HSE), which was charged with implementing the HSWA and developing more formal and permanent consultative mechanisms.[16] Crucial here was the HSE's management board, the HSC, which was essentially tripartite, comprising representatives from industry, trade unions and local government, as well as safety experts and policy-makers—all those actors that were understood as having a direct interest in OHS. In this way, by incorporating the input of a range of stakeholders, Robens sought to ensure that the new system of risk management was viewed as publicly acceptable, even if public opinions were not formally solicited within the tripartite structure.

Until the end of the 1970s, the governance of OHS was thus characterized by a general lack of direct engagement with public opinion. It was not necessarily that members of the general public had no opinions on the issue of workplace safety and the risks that they faced—it was more that there was no means of expressing these opinions formally. As the Chair of the HSC observed in 1982 before a parliamentary select committee inquiring into the work of the HSE: 'We are structured the way we are because of the Act of Parliament [the HSWA] which laid down in broad terms the sort of representative groups that would be appointed there.' The public was not one of them, although he went on: 'I am not saying

[15] R. Symons interview, 18 November 2014, para. 10.

[16] Lord Robens, *Safety and Health at Work: Report of the Committee 1970–72* (Parl. Papers 1972 [Cmnd. 5034]), p. 21.

there that we do not take a note of public concern, of course we do.'[17] It seems the general understanding was that the public would be represented via the existing groups sitting on the HSC. As the General Secretary of the Associated Society of Locomotive Enginemen and Firemen informed the same committee: 'The public interest is still well safeguarded by the local authority representatives on the Commission, especially the general public interest.'[18]

There are two key reasons for the lack of attention paid to general public opinion at this time. One is that health and safety was seen as a matter that only really concerned the workplace. As an article in *The Times* summed up in 1971: 'Industrial safety is a dry subject which arouses the passions of a limited number of people directly concerned with preventing accidents at work.'[19] Although section 3 of the HSWA extended the responsibilities of employers to 'persons not in employment who may be affected' by business activities, the full implications of this had not yet been developed: at this point, the attention of employers, unions and regulators remained very much focused on workers. For the most part, regulators and policy-makers remained wedded to viewing the relevant constituencies in narrow, tripartite terms, as was indeed reflected in the very structure of the HSC.[20] The assumption was that 'the public' was not really separable from 'the working population' and that the interests of this group were represented by trade unions. As the Chair of the HSC noted in 1982: 'I often quarrel with the idea that, because a person contributes to a trade union, he automatically disqualifies himself from being a member of the public.'[21]

The second reason is that the policy-making process was principally concerned with a small and immediate range of issues relating to the day-to-day operation of OHS rather than bigger issues which might make health and safety more politically contentious.[22] In part, this reflected

[17] *The Working of the Health and Safety Commission and Executive* (Parl. Papers 1981–2 [HC 400-iii]), minutes of evidence, 23 June 1982, pp. 15–16.

[18] *The Working of the Health and Safety Commission and Executive* (Parl. Papers 1981–2 [HC 400-ii]), minutes of evidence, 16 June 1982, p. 25.

[19] *The Times*, 5 May 1971, p. 23.

[20] S. Dawson, P. Willman, A. Clinton and M. Bamford, *Safety at Work: The Limits of Self-Regulation* (Cambridge, 1988); B. Hutter, *Compliance: Regulation and Environment* (Oxford, 1997).

[21] *The Working of the Health and Safety Commission and Executive* (Parl. Papers 1981–2 [HC 400-iii]), minutes of evidence, 23 June 1982, p. 25.

[22] M. Moran, *The British Regulatory State: High Modernism and Hyper Innovation* (Oxford, 2003), p. 138.

longstanding aspirations to impartiality and attempts to depoliticize health and safety by removing it, as far as possible, from the wider (and often fraught) industrial relations context of the time. In 1972, the Chief Inspector of Factories stated that 'impartial we must be, for no side—employer or workforce—has a monopoly of rectitude in safety and health at work. We must also exercise a strict impartiality if we are to hold—and deserve to hold—the trust of managers and workers'.[23] In the absence of any institutional reason to look at public opinions, health and safety therefore retained a relatively narrow focus on issues which could be addressed via the existing approaches of the regulator. This even reflected what might be called the technocratic nature of the regulator at this time and its status as a body that was constituted to deal with a particular range of considerations in an avowedly scientific, apolitical way. It is telling that the prevailing culture of regulation was sometimes criticized on these grounds: in the early 1980s, the Labour MP John Golding questioned whether the HSC was not in fact a 'conspiracy of science between workers and employers'.[24]

A Change of Focus: 1985–2000

During the 1980s, fractures began to appear in the relative consensus surrounding health and safety that had emerged in the preceding decades. The underlying principles of tripartite management and mediated public consultation were compromised as 'health and safety' became a more contested and politicized arena of state regulation. It became more and more difficult to conceive of health and safety as a narrow area of concern, fit only for the attention of employers, employees and unions. Accordingly, state agencies such as the HSC had to pay attention to a much wider cross-section of opinion, including that of the public. In short, the governance of health and safety broadened and this impacted on the ways in which the state governed risks.

How might this be explained? Underlying the shift were significant social and economic changes. Most notably, traditional heavy industries such as mining and shipbuilding declined, whilst service and office-based

[23] *Annual Report of H.M. Chief Inspector of Factories, 1972*, p. xiii.

[24] A.R. Hale and J. Hovden, 'Management and Culture: The Third Age of Safety—A Review of Approaches to Organizational Aspects of Safety, Health and Environment', in A. Feyer and A. Williamson (eds), *Occupational Injury: Risk, Prevention and Intervention* (London, 1998), pp. 129–65; *The Working of the Health and Safety Commission and Executive* (Parl. Papers 1981–2 [HC 400-ii]), minutes of evidence, 16 June 1982, p. 26.

work increased in scale. Employment in mining and quarrying, for example, fell from over 527,000 in 1961 to around 164,000 in 1981, whereas jobs in administration and management rose from 643,000 in 1961 to over 1,342,000 in 1981.[25] These trends continued in the 1980s, dramatically reshaping the economic landscape in which risks were produced and governed. At the same time, the obligations and powers set out in section 3 of the HSWA, which imposed a duty on employers and the HSE to consider the impact of occupational activities on people beyond the workplace, were increasingly developed and realized. One instance is gas safety in the home. In January 1985, an explosion at the Newnham House flats in Putney, London killed eight people, which was thought to have been caused by the faulty installation of gas appliances by engineers. The HSE was called in to investigate, marking the first time the body had dealt with the problem of domestic gas safety.[26] As David Eves, then Chief Inspector of Factories, later recalled:

> That accident was significant because it really elevated gas safety as an issue ... then everybody became aware that about 30 people a year were being gassed in their homes ... so we became involved with domestic gas issues. Now I think I'm right in saying this was the first time ... that we had powers, or even the willingness to enter domestic premises.[27]

In short, health and safety reached broader and more varied constituencies than it had previously: it was no longer synonymous with 'industrial safety'.

Yet changes in the social and economic context and the nature of health and safety regulation do not by themselves explain the increased prominence of the public. In fact, we should acknowledge at least three other factors in what was also a contested and contingent period of transition in the culture of regulation: a politicization of regulation under the Conservative governments of Margaret Thatcher and John Major; a run of large-scale disasters that prompted concerns about public safety; and the development of new ideas about assessing risks and measuring levels of public tolerability. In terms of the first factor, the neoliberalism espoused by the Conservative governments of the 1980s and 1990s made

[25] B.R. Mitchell, *British Historical Statistics* (Cambridge, 1988), p. 107.
[26] *The Guardian*, 11 January 1985, p. 1; *The Times*, 11 January 1985, p. 2.
[27] D. Eves interview, 22 September 2014, para. 57.

for a hostile ministerial and administrative environment. Many accounts of HSE policy and practice during this period have highlighted the impact of a more avowedly anti-regulatory political climate on the way in which health and safety was directed. This included, among other elements: the imposition of cost-benefit-oriented decision-making processes around regulations; scepticism about the value of personnel invested in inspection and enforcement; and greater pressure for political and legal accountability around decision-making.[28]

The presumption, certainly, was that regulation constituted a negative, burdensome intervention, but this was also—and increasingly—subject to explicit articulation. According to a 1986 government White Paper *Building Businesses … Not Barriers*, health and safety regulations amounted to a form of 'red tape' that 'forces people running businesses to follow a particular pattern or administrative process which is not related to that business'.[29] Together with other White Papers such as *Lifting the Burden* (1985), *Building Businesses* recommended that 'along with a concerted effort to reduce the volume and burden of existing regulations, new arrangements should be established to ensure that the business dimension is properly taken into account in the framing of new regulations *where these remain necessary*'.[30] Such sentiments were widespread: in 1988, *The Guardian* quoted a 'senior government official' who asserted that a 'culture which is about enterprise, competition and profitability doesn't want to concern itself too closely with issues of health and safety'.[31] Health and safety was thus targeted for substantive reductions in the number of regulations, and there was a shift towards increased self-regulation and freedom from inspection.

The elevation of health and safety into an object of party-political antipathy also broke with the more consensual and consultative culture of the 1960s and 1970s. Business interests were seen as both dominant and more

[28] Health and Safety Executive (HSE), *The Scrutiny Programme: Problems of Assessing the Costs and Benefits of Health and Safety Requirements and the Techniques Available* (London, 1985), pp. 1, 16–17; R. Baldwin, 'Health and Safety at Work: Consensus and Self-Regulation', in R. Baldwin and C. McCrudden (eds), *Regulation and Public Law* (London, 1987), pp. 132–58; Dawson et al., *Safety at Work*, pp. 251–65; K. Hawkins, *Law as Last Resort: Prosecution Decision-Making in a Regulatory Agency* (Oxford, 2002); B. Hutter and P. Manning, 'The Contexts of Regulation: The Impacts upon Health and Safety Inspectorates in Britain', *Law and Policy* 12 (1990), pp. 103–36.

[29] *Building Businesses … Not Barriers* (Parl. Papers 1986 [Cmnd. 9794]), p. 2.

[30] *Ibid.*, p. 10, emphasis added.

[31] *The Guardian*, 9 March 1988, p. 23.

legitimate compared to the interests of organized labour.[32] The crude equation was of health and safety with trade union influence, declining traditional industries, unaccountable bureaucracy and 'outdated' welfare politics.[33] Yet, besides pronounced Tory antipathy towards the labour movement, the movement itself was suffering from falling membership, declining from a peak in union membership of 13,212,000 workers in 1979 to 7,898,000 in 2000.[34] As a result, it became increasingly difficult for state agencies to overlook public opinion or, just as crucially, to assume that it was captured via the existing tripartite structure. In this context, reference to a wider public became unavoidable, whether one was for or against regulation.

The second development was the sudden and dramatic visibility of health and safety issues in the mid- to late 1980s. Over 4 years, a spate of high-profile industrial, organizational and public disasters occurred, involving significant loss of life. The King's Cross London Underground fire in 1987 (31 fatalities), the *Herald of Free Enterprise* sinking in 1987 (189), the Piper Alpha oil rig fire in 1988 (167), the Clapham Junction rail crash in 1988 (35) and the Hillsborough football stadium disaster in 1989 (96), among others, created a particular moment of public safety crisis. This was exacerbated by a backdrop of terrorism (IRA, ongoing during the 1980s; Lockerbie, 1988) and nuclear meltdown (Chernobyl, 1986), and had a significant effect on both the public and government. As *The Guardian* noted in 1988, additional responsibilities demanded by the government and EEC regulations, 'combined with a series of disasters ... has put worker and public safety high on the agenda and the role of the HSE is being closely examined'.[35]

This increased scrutiny led to major changes in the systems of regulation in particular industries and in the approaches and methods that were used.[36] The offshore and rail industries, for instance, were now brought within the HSE directly (previously these pockets of safety work had been retained by the government departments responsible for running the industries), and the 'safety case' regime was more widely applied, whereby operators were granted licences to practise on the basis of documentation submitted in

[32] A. Gamble, *The Free Economy and the Strong State: The Politics of Thatcherism*, 2nd edn (London, 1994); D. Harvey, *A Brief History of Neoliberalism* (Oxford, 2005).

[33] Hutter and Manning, 'Contexts of Regulation', pp. 107–10.

[34] 'Trade Union Membership 2013: Statistical Bulletin', Department for Business, Innovation and Skills (2014), p. 21.

[35] *The Guardian*, 16 November 1988, p. 1.

[36] C. Wells, *Corporations and Criminal Responsibility*, 2nd edn (Oxford, 2001).

advance to show that effective risk management procedures were in place. This was a much more anticipatory regime, with organizations taking responsibility for governing potential risks rather than reacting to specific incidents and interventions as and when they occurred.

Crucially, public scrutiny also served as a bulwark against the deregulatory instincts of the governments of the day, providing a protective shield to regulators. As one Labour MP later recalled, 'for virtually all of Margaret Thatcher's governments, I think that they probably would have liked to have done things with the Health and Safety at Work Act but there were so many disasters, it was very difficult'.[37] Following some of the large-scale disasters, a number of actors—including the public, the Trades Union Congress (TUC) and the Labour Party—put pressure on the government about the reduced resources for the HSE. In response, the Director-General of the HSE was reported in the press as 'smiling discretely and welcom[ing] the political weight they are able to put behind his requests for more money and resources'.[38]

It thus became very difficult for even a deregulatory government to take action that might be construed as exposing the general populace to risk, and post-disaster reforms tended to strengthen the hand of the regulators rather than weaken them. For example, at select committee hearings in 1988, the HSE was able to make a play for greater responsibility in the areas of offshore (following Piper Alpha), underground (following King's Cross) and ferry (following the *Herald of Free Enterprise*) safety.[39] By 1992, the same committee welcomed the HSE's management 'back here with responsibilities which we thought you should have back under your belt'.[40] Starting in this period, government and regulators took a much greater interest in public attitudes to health and safety risks. Roger Bibbings, at that point Health and Safety Advisor at the TUC, recalled a meeting in the late 1980s:

> He [the Director-General of the HSE] invited me to come and present from a TUC perspective to get the discussion going amongst his senior colleagues. So I said, 'oh you need to look again at worker safety, and need

[37] F. Doran interview, 22 October 2014, para. 46.

[38] *The Guardian*, 16 November 1988, p. 1.

[39] *Health and Safety Matters* (Parl. Papers 1987–8 [HC 704-i]), minutes of evidence, 8 November 1988, pp. 6–7; Moran, *British Regulatory State*, p. 136.

[40] *The Work of the Health and Safety Commission and Executive* (Parl. Papers 1991–2 [HC 263]), minutes of evidence, 12 February 1992, p. 2.

> to have a bigger view of worker safety' ... not very long into this, he put his hand up and said, 'no, no, no, stop my boy, stop ... that's worker safety. That's a dead volcano', he said. 'The live volcano is public safety. That is what's going to energise everyone.'[41]

Not only, then, was the public becoming more prominent in directing political attention, it was becoming increasingly noted by the regulators.

The third development was more technical: the idea of the 'tolerability of risk'. This continued a long-established trend for new technologies to become sites around which debates about safety and risk crystallized—for instance, factories in the early Victorian period, the railways and the mines in the late nineteenth and early twentieth centuries, and, by the 1980s, the nuclear industry. The Sizewell B nuclear power station planning inquiry of 1982–7 in particular raised questions about how the safety calculations around nuclear sites should be made. It was proposed during the inquiry that the HSE should explicitly assess 'tolerable levels of individual and societal risk to workers and the public' in relation to nuclear power.[42]

This led to the publication in 1988 of a new framework for calculating the 'tolerability of risk' in which health and safety regulators would seek to weigh probabilistic assessments of risk and the costs of prevention alongside a more informed sense of what was deemed appropriate by the public.[43] This model embodied a new approach to governing risk. In particular, it allowed regulators like the HSE to frame calculations of what level of risk exists (how serious, how likely) and what is possible in terms of risk control (feasibility, costs and benefits) against the backdrop of judgements about the social acceptability of those risks (from 'broadly acceptable', through 'tolerable' to 'unacceptable').[44] This then allowed for a more principled assessment of risk control to take place in high-hazard areas like nuclear power, where the potential risks (and public attitudes towards them, especially after Chernobyl) might be extreme. As the then

[41] R. Bibbings interview, 8 September 2014, para. 19.

[42] F. Layfield, *Sizewell B Public Inquiry: Report by Sir Frank Layfield* (London, 1987), 'Summary of Conclusions and Recommendations'.

[43] HSE, *The Tolerability of Risks from Nuclear Power Stations* (London, 1988); J. McQuaid, 'A Historical Perspective on Tolerability of Risk', in F. Bouder, D. Slavin and R. Löfstedt (eds), *The Tolerability of Risk: A New Framework for Risk Management* (London, 2007), pp. 87–92.

[44] T. Bandle, 'Tolerability of Risk: The Regulator's Story', in Bouder, Slavin and Löfstedt (eds), *The Tolerability of Risk*, pp. 93–103.

Chair of the HSC observed during select committee hearings in 1988: 'technological change is now probably swifter ... the public has become increasingly conscious of and knowledgeable about its implications. The reassurance provided by a fully effective and respected state regulatory body is more and more important'.[45]

The tolerability of risk framework became a highly influential document, and was revised in 1992 and 2001 to make it applicable to a broader range of industries and sectors.[46] It became widely admired for its efforts to put the balancing of public concerns and expert-led risk assessment on a systematic footing. At the same time, the HSE began to commission research into public opinion by organizations such as MORI. Many of these studies took the form of investigations into public attitudes towards and tolerance of high-risk industries, particularly among the specific populations who co-existed and interacted with them. All of these studies identified a public desire for regulation in these areas of technological change and risk.[47] Indeed, risk-generating industries were not necessarily trusted and this created an opportunity for an agency like the HSE to stake a claim as a trusted agency that acted to advance the 'public interest', as opposed to the interests of profit-hungry businesses.[48] The claim that regulation could and did counter incipient risk insecurity was thus reinforced by evidence that positioned health and safety as a matter of 'externalities', or costs accruing to parties not directly involved in the employment exchange.[49] This served to rebut the characterization of regulation as a burden imposed illegitimately from outside upon autonomous organizations. If risk was not internal to businesses in the complex, interconnected modern world, then risk regulation from outside was implicitly legitimated.

[45] *The Work of the Health and Safety Commission and Executive* (Parl. Papers 1987–8 [HC 267]), minutes of evidence, 20 January 1988, p. 2; Hawkins, *Law as Last Resort*, Appendix 1.

[46] Bandle, 'Tolerability of Risk'.

[47] G. Walker, P. Simmons, A. Irwin and B. Wynne, *Public Perception of Risks Associated with Major Accident Hazards* (London, 1998); J. Elgood, N. Gilby and H. Pearson, *Attitudes Towards Health and Safety: A Quantitative Survey of Stakeholder Opinion [MORI Social Research Institute Report for the HSE]* (London, 2004); S. King, M. Dyball and L. Waller, *Public Protection Consultation Study [Research Report RR541]* (Sudbury, 2005).

[48] N. Pidgeon, J. Walls, A. Weyman and T. Horlick-Jones, *Perceptions of and Trust in the Health and Safety Executive as a Risk Regulator [Research Report 100]* (Sudbury, 2003), pp. 15–16.

[49] R. Baldwin and M. Cave, *Understanding Regulation: Theory, Strategy, and Practice* (Oxford, 1999), p. 11.

Regulating in Public: 2000 Onwards

The period after approximately 2000 witnessed a consolidation and intensification of the trends that emerged from the mid-1980s. Two aspects might be highlighted: first, the systematic targeting of regulation, itself a product of increasing political sensitivity to perceptions of public opinion; and, second, an increase in public scrutiny and demands for accountability. In terms of the former, the 'better regulation' agenda pursued by the New Labour governments of the late 1990s and early 2000s was significant. Established in 1997, the Better Regulation Task Force reflected values that were articulated during the previous Conservative governments. These were seen in the Force's five guiding principles, which included a commitment to cost-benefit analyses, an ability to justify decisions publicly and ideas about assessing the impact of regulations on business efficiency. The intention was to ensure that policy and practice meshed with wider ideological and economic goals. Likewise, risk management continued to be devolved to a range of partner institutions, which in the case of health and safety included businesses. As regulations were increasingly questioned from within government and as further actors were brought into play, the governance of OHS broadened still further.[50]

One important step was the Revitalizing Health and Safety strategy of 1999, which was designed to reposition health and safety 25 years after the HSWA. It re-stated a need to focus on high-frequency risks and for the first time set targets for improvements in safety performance, reflecting pressures for increased public accountability. At the same time, central government's capacity to exert direct control over regulatory outcomes was weakened. This was a result of both the continuation of the self-regulatory agenda, which moved responsibility for risk management outside the state, and the associated government desire to step away from direct control of day-to-day delivery.[51] According to Bill Callaghan, formerly of the TUC and Chair of the HSC during the years 1999–2007:

> I do recall a conference ... Brown and Blair were there ... the finger was being pointed at a number of regulators. Not HSE, I think, directly ... [but] there was a very strong view in New Labour that there was too much regulation ...

[50] R. Baldwin, 'Is Better Regulation Smarter Regulation?', *Public Law* 49 (2005), pp. 485–511; A. Dodds, 'The Core Executive's Approach to Regulation: From "Better Regulation" to "Risk-Tolerant Deregulation"', *Social Policy & Administration* 40 (2006), pp. 526–42.

[51] J. Black, 'Tensions in the Regulatory State', *Public Law* 51(2007), p. 64.

> in the City and in the retailing sector there were a lot of complaints to the political powers that be about what they saw as excessive regulation … It then led to [the] Hampton and Macrory [reviews] and so on.[52]

The 2005 Hampton Review, entitled *Reducing Administrative Burdens*, recommended an easing of some regulations and the creation of a business-led body at the heart of government.[53] The Macrory Review of Regulatory Penalties, which reported in 2006, also embraced notions of proportionality and accountability.[54]

New Labour thus continued in the direction of travel started under previous administrations. Indeed, the climate of anti-regulatory sentiment that developed from the mid-1980s only hardened, making for an ongoing cycle of public review and reflection about the purpose and legitimacy of health and safety regulation. This was partly fuelled by a highly politicized media narrative of 'health and safety gone mad' and the now regular provision of stories of regulatory excess, which was especially pronounced in the tabloid press.[55] Equally, attacks on the idea of regulation emerged with increasing ferocity from the business lobby and the Conservative Party, which sought to create a public perception that it was a matter of 'petty or restrictive' rules.[56] In 2008, the then leader of the Conservative opposition, David Cameron, argued that 'this whole health and safety, human rights act culture, has infected every part of our life … it's not a bigger state we need: it's better, more efficient government'. In 2012 and now in office, he stated that his government's 'New Year's resolution' was 'to kill off the health and safety culture for good. I want 2012 to [be] the year we get a lot of this pointless time wasting out of the British economy and British life once and for all'.[57]

[52] B. Callaghan interview, 9 September 2014, para. 31–3.

[53] Hampton Review.

[54] Macrory Review.

[55] Almond, 'The Dangers of Hanging Baskets'.

[56] Pidgeon et al., *Perceptions of and Trust in the Health and Safety Executive as a Risk Regulator*, pp. 28–30.

[57] Speech to Conservative Party Conference, reported in *The Guardian*, 1 October 2008. Available at: www.guardian.co.uk/politics/2008/oct/01/davidcameron.toryconference1 (date accessed 21 November 2015); 'Coalition Plans to Kill off "Health and Safety Monster" with Limits on Lawyers' Fees', *Daily Telegraph*, 5 January 2012. Available at: www.telegraph.co.uk/news/politics/8995276/Coalition-plans-to-kill-off-health-and-safety-monster-with-limits-on-lawyers-fees.html (date accessed 21 November 2015).

The desire to reshape the regulatory system in order to respond to 'public opinion' led to the Young (2010) and Löfstedt (2011) reviews, which both paid attention to the problem of public standing, recognizing its potential to impact adversely upon the ability of regulators to fulfil their mandates. The report of the Löfstedt review was, significantly, entitled *Reclaiming Health and Safety for All*, explicitly putting the public at the heart of debate.[58] Although Löfstedt determined that the existing regulatory system was broadly fit for purpose, Conservative Minister for Employment Chris Grayling claimed that '[b]y accepting the recommendations of Professor Löfstedt we are putting common sense back at the heart of health and safety', suggesting that regulation had run out of control and away from public opinion.[59] The promise of these reviews tended to reflect the deregulatory desires of the incumbent government, something noted in *The Guardian* following the announcement of the Young Review into the operation of health and safety law: 'The review will delight the Tory leader's spurned right wing, with the issue of over-restrictive rules filling many MPs' postbags.'[60] The tendency for reforms to go beyond the conclusions of the reviews, however, suggests that those conclusions were not always to the liking of the commissioning politicians. Although Löfstedt recommended that 35 % of health and safety regulations might be cut, the government announced that over 3 years it expected to cut up to 50 % of regulations.[61]

The second theme evident in relation to regulation in general, and health and safety regulation in particular, was the persistence of public scrutiny and a desire for public accountability. This found expression in attempts to use corporate manslaughter rules to find senior management figures criminally culpable for deaths. Attempts to reform corporate manslaughter laws had been tied to public opinion since the mid-1980s, following the failures of prosecutions arising out of the *Herald of Free Enterprise* disaster of 1987 and the Southall rail crash of 1997, both of

[58] Löfstedt Review.

[59] Department for Work and Pensions press release, 'Report Calls for One Million Self-Employed to Be Exempt from Health and Safety Law', 28 November 2011. Available at: https://www.gov.uk/government/news/report-calls-for-one-million-self-employed-to-be-exempt-from-health-and-safety-law (date accessed 21 November 2015).

[60] *The Observer*, 13 June 2010. Available at: www.theguardian.com/politics/2010/jun/13/tories-start-health-safety-rules-cuts (date accessed 21 November 2015).

[61] 'Report Calls for One Million Self-Employed to Be Exempt from Health and Safety Law'.

which were linked to a lack of high-level managerial accountability. This particular facet was thus not entirely new, but it gathered momentum after 2000. Commentators and government continued to cite public concern as a central reason for introducing revisions of corporate homicide liability law, and significant reform was eventually secured in 2006.[62]

Equally, public attitudes remained hugely complex, characterized either by ambivalence about or lack of concern with health and safety issues. Research published by Gary Slapper in 1999 argued that there was a broader public view that health and safety was, in Kit Carson's term, 'conventionalized'. Offences, for instance, were not viewed as 'proper' crimes.[63] Although people might be aware of health and safety as an issue, it was perceived as a minor irritant rather than something more serious. This was certainly the view of Lawrence Waterman, a leading corporate health and safety consultant and formerly Head of Health and Safety at the Olympic Delivery Authority, who identified a 'public perception of health and safety being a bit trivial, a bit interfering, getting in the way of the lives that we want to lead ... Although there's a degree of political maliciousness about it ... it does definitely weaken the opportunity we have for achieving what we want'.[64]

Nonetheless, it is clear that in 2015, health and safety and risk governance remain contested issues, and most of all in the media and for politicians.[65] The focus groups conducted as part of the wider research project which underpins this chapter found evidence of an interplay between, on the one hand, an instinctive cynicism and rejection of 'health and safety' as boring and restrictive, and, on the other, more considered and positive evaluations.[66] It was thus perfectly possible for participants to regard the diffuse mechanisms currently in place to manage health and safety as interfering, overly risk-averse and contrary to 'common sense', *and*

[62] Wells, *Corporations and Criminal Responsibility*, p. 122; Home Office, *Reforming the Law of Involuntary Manslaughter: The Government's Proposals* (London, 2000); Home Office, *Corporate Manslaughter: The Government's Draft Bill for Reform* (London, 2005).

[63] G. Slapper, *Blood in the Bank: Legal and Societal Aspects of Workplace Deaths* (London, 1999), p. 155.

[64] L. Waterman interview, 24 September 2014, para. 66.

[65] Slapper, *Blood in the Bank*, p. 157; see also Wells, *Corporations and Criminal Responsibility*, p. 12.

[66] P. Almond and M. Esbester, 'The Changing Legitimacy of Health and Safety, 1960–2015', Institution of Occupational Safety and Health (IOSH) Research Report (unpublished, 2015). Eight semi-structured focus groups were conducted, each containing between seven and ten participants (total number 67).

as something that empowered workers and had brought about major improvements in working conditions. And while negative media perceptions and public opinions were shared, they were also understood as representing a particular political agenda. Perhaps surprisingly, despite holding these negative opinions on some level, the idea of health and safety as a morally 'correct' thing was still almost universally endorsed as a vital part of modern society:

> As a citizen you feel, when people have got their act together as far as health and safety's concerned, confident, that you're being looked after, and that's what you want ... over the years we've got more confident about asking for these things, so there's a sense of safety, people have got their act together.[67]
>
> [Interviewer] Do you think it's important to have health and safety laws in place? ... [Participants all together] YES![68]

Conclusion

In 2015, the health and safety system might be characterized as being subject to 'critical trust' by the public at large.[69] It is accepted at the level of general principle, but is subject to heavy criticism at the level of implementation and experience. While the abstract principle of state intervention to ensure health and safety has remained robust, the pursuit of this has become increasingly politicized and fragmented in recent years. The regulatory system has increasingly bifurcated so as to split efforts by central government to change the political character of health and safety away from the implementation and delivery of day-to-day outcomes by non-state actors such as safety professionals.[70] On both fronts, there is evidence of a disjunction between the ways in which health and safety is talked about and what it means in practice.

As we have argued, the present situation is a product of a complex set of developments which relate to changes both in the nature of regulation and in the broader social and political context. Since the 1960s, the place

[67] References are structured by focus group identifier ('A' to 'H'), the participant identifier within that group ('1' to '10') and the point in time during the recording/transcript where the comment was made. C4: 1.00.22–1.00.52.

[68] G1–7: 43.03.

[69] Pidgeon et al., *Perceptions of and Trust in the HSE.*

[70] Black, 'Tensions in the Regulatory State'.

of the public in the governance of health and safety has been of increasing importance. Conceptions of key stakeholders in health and safety altered slowly, if radically, moving from the longstanding 'industrial' interests of capital and labour to a more nuanced and diffuse group, including the public as a key player. Perhaps more significantly, since the mid-1980s, the place of public *opinion* in the state's governance of health and safety risks has assumed a greater prominence. This grew out of the changing political and economic structure of the UK at this time, not least the gradual decline of trade unions and tripartite models of governing, coupled with the rise of a neoliberal agenda: all developments that made health and safety and state intervention matters of significant political dispute. These developments also meant that the state—which had long paid heed to public opinion, if in relatively informal or intangible ways—took increasing steps to respond to public attitudes about health and safety at work and beyond. Crucially, this recognition of the role of the public further complicated the diffuse nature of risk governance. State action had always been but one mode of governing risks in modern Britain, and towards the end of the twentieth century, public opinion added a further and significant layer of complexity.

From a wider historical perspective, it might be pointed out that there have long been points of conflict about what health and safety means and how far the state ought to intervene in the activities of businesses and the lives of individuals. What is noticeable, however, is the degree to which efforts to systematize public attitudes as a factor within bureaucratic decision-making have co-existed with a recasting of these attitudes within broader political and social debates. On the one hand, these trends are connected, in that formal regulatory accountability to public scrutiny is a major element of the neoliberal, managerial state.[71] On the other hand, however, it seems that the emergence of a public anti-health and safety narrative has relatively little to do with formal issues of accountability, and more to do with the re-emergence of longstanding tensions around the role that state regulation should play in the settlement of competing interests around the everyday realities of work and public lives. If anything, these tensions are now less deep-seated than in the past, but their expression is more prominent than it has been for some time.

[71] C. Hood, 'A Public Management for All Seasons?', *Public Administration* 69 (1991), pp. 3–19; Moran, *The British Regulatory State.*

CHAPTER 13

Conclusion: Governing Risks in Britain and Beyond

Arwen P. Mohun, Thomas Le Roux, Tom Crook, and Mike Esbester

Collectively, the chapters contained in this volume have sought to argue that risk and risk-related problems constitute a useful means for rethinking how Britons have been governed over the past 200 years and more. This field of questioning and enquiry is still in its infancy, as discussed in Chapter 1. The preceding studies suggest at least four significant themes that might lend this field a better sense of some of its guiding threads and

A.P. Mohun (✉)
Department of History, University of Delaware,
46 W. Delaware Avenue, Newark, DE, 19716, USA

T. Le Roux
Centre de Recherches Historiques (CNRS/EHESS), 190 avenue de France,
75013, Paris, France

T. Crook
Department of History, Philosophy and Religion, Oxford Brookes University,
Tonge Building, Headington Campus, Gipsy Lane, Oxford OX3 0BP, UK

M. Esbester
School of Social, Historical and Literary Studies, University of Portsmouth,
Milldam, Burnaby Road, Portsmouth PO1 3AS, UK

T. Crook, M. Esbester (eds), *Governing Risks in Modern Britain*,
DOI 10.1057/978-1-137-46745-4_13

critical co-ordinates. The first is perhaps the most important: namely, the composite nature of risks and dangers, in the sense that they are at once physical and environmental, technological and economic, and social and cultural. Evidently, as Otter's chapter argued, it is impossible to ignore the profound changes that have occurred in the material and technological composition of British society as a result of the first and second Industrial Revolutions. New technologies meant that bodies were mangled and mutilated in new ways; novel synthetic substances meant that human cells underwent novel kinds of cancerous mutation. To return to Chapter 1, we should certainly affirm that governing risk relates not just to the administration of persons, but also to the administration of things, and these things in the form of infrastructures, machines and natural and artificial substances have a material agency of their own.

Yet things of this sort exercise agency only once they have been invented, networked and objectified by humans, who themselves are enmeshed in equally complex webs of shifting social, economic and cultural relations. Luckin's chapter, for instance, showed how, for all the human damage inflicted by drunk driving in Victorian Britain, both popular and legal attitudes in the motor age largely came to side with drivers, reflecting the development of a broader socio-cultural commitment to pro-motorism. Similarly, as Crook's chapter argued, the danger of sewer gas emanating from novel large-scale sewerage systems cannot be understood without reference to middle-class idealizations of the home as a place of privacy and moral and physical safety. Other examples might be given, but the importance of a social and cultural dimension was especially evident in Vieira's chapter, which demonstrated that the emergence of single accident articles in the press during the 1820s cannot be explained by a sudden increase in accidents or the advent of new and dangerous technologies. The railway industry, which did so much to provoke popular interest in accidents, was still to come. Rather, it was the emergence of a new middle class and the simultaneous erosion of the aristocracy's social authority that was the principal factor behind this transformation. To put it another way, the chapters in this volume suggest that the history of risk demands a non-reductive approach that views the production and governance of dangers and accidents as complex phenomena, partaking of and combining various forces and relations in any given moment or place.

Our second theme builds on the first: the situated and mutable nature of the expert and official knowledge that informs how dangers and accidents are governed. Certainly the history of governing risk is related to the growth of professional and official authority and multiple forms of specialist knowledge. Statistics, bacteriology, chemistry, medicine, engineering and the law: the work and prestige of all of these forms of knowledge is evident in the preceding pages. Health and safety itself emerged as a discrete and specialist field of administration over the two centuries or so covered in this book, culminating in the formation of Britain's Health and Safety Executive (HSE) in 1974, the birth of which was examined in Sirrs' chapter. Yet we should also recognize the contingent and partial nature of expert and official authority. Williams' contribution, for instance, recovered how the police at once fashioned their authority in relation to governing motor traffic risks and used this authority to privilege long-term engineering solutions over those that entailed greater manpower resources. In short, professional interests were in play. Equally, as Cooper's chapter argued, we also need to develop a fuller, more political sense of the limitations of expert knowledge—of what it includes *and* excludes. This is so not just in relation to the interests it serves, which for Cooper are ultimately those of a capitalist society dedicated to the maximization of economic value; it also concerns the limited temporal horizons of this knowledge—that is, the way it authorizes practices and interventions with only a limited sense of the enduring impact they might have on those who have to live with them daily.

This is not to deny the agency of the public or its political representatives. Indeed, all of the chapters in the book make reference to acts of Parliament, which of course relied on the support of MPs and the sponsorship of ministers. Likewise, the chapters detail multiple instances in which members of the public, knowingly or otherwise, variously complied with and resisted practices designed to secure their safety. This is partly what makes governing risks so fraught and difficult: the need—in a broadly liberal society such as modern Britain at least—to work with agents whose support may or may not be forthcoming. But this is clearly not the only factor at work. It is also a product of the sheer scale, ambition and dynamism of modern society. This is our third theme: namely, complexity, even irony, and the way in which governing risks was defined by a wide-ranging struggle to deal with the unfortunate and unintended consequences of practices and technologies otherwise deemed to be useful and essential, and even the very embodiment of 'progress'. There are, perhaps, some obvious and dramatic technological instances of this. As the cultural theorist Paul Virilio has put it, in typically provocative fashion: 'To invent the train is to invent the rail accident of derailment. To invent the family automobile is to produce the pile-up on the highway. To get what is heavier than air to take off in the form of an aeroplane or dirigible is to invent the crash, the air disaster.'[1]

However, as this volume suggests, this is much too restrictive, obscuring the way in which this dynamic played out across *all* areas of life, making risk a kind of obsessive, sprawling preoccupation. The case of carbolic disinfectant preparations explored in Whyte's chapter was among the more striking instances. Designed to save lives and to prevent the risk of infection, carbolic disinfectants also doubled as a means of suicide in the hands of some. In the bigger scheme of national mortality, carbolic suicides were altogether rare, but clearly the need to balance safety with germicidal efficiency was a matter of much debate and, eventually, regulatory action. Another striking instance was provided by O'Hara's chapter, which examined the anxieties that attended the recreational use of open waters. This was supposed to be relaxing, entertaining and edifying; yet, as the likes of the Royal Society for the Prevention of Accidents so keenly publicized, open swimming was also fraught with danger and in particular the risk of drowning. To put it another way, governing risks concerns the mundane and the everyday as much as the disastrous and catastrophic (or what one scholar has called the 'accidental sublime'), and it inhabits both leisure and workplace practices.[2] It is vigilant, persistent and unceasingly adaptive and inventive.

This feeds into our fourth and final theme: the multiple agents and the diffuse practices that have been mobilized in order to govern risks. As we suggested in Chapter 1, governing risk involves agents and practices that extend far beyond the state. Judges, police officers, ministers and inspectors have certainly featured in the preceding pages, all of which, quite rightly, might be characterized as agents of the state. Yet we have also seen the crucial role played by voluntary and commercial actors, which themselves sought to shape and mould the daily habits of members of the public. To adopt the idiom now used in relation to the history of welfare, this was very much a 'mixed economy' of governing. Indeed, risk-based forms of governing have no necessary connection with a state. As Dodsworth's chapter argued, the genesis of risk-based policing in the mid- to late eighteenth century should be sought in a medley of informational and (commercial) actuarial practices that were variously adopted and reworked by local authorities, magistrates and members of the public; at this point, the state was still a distant presence. Conversely, even where the state does

[1] P. Virilio, *The Original Accident*, trans. J. Rose (Cambridge, 2011), p. 10.

[2] R. Hamilton, *Accident: A Philosophical and Literary History* (Chicago, 2007), Chapter 7.

play a significant role in governing risk, this need not preclude the involvement of other actors. This is true of the HSE, an institution examined by two chapters in this volume. As Sirrs argued, the very birth of the HSE was informed by ideals of 'self-regulation' and devolved responsibility for workplace risk management, and as Almond and Esbester then showed, during the 1980s, as a tripartite culture of governance went into decline, the public became a crucial actor in terms of defining the legitimacy and function of health and safety.

Connecting and Comparing Britain

These themes, we suggest, might help to guide further research which builds on—much as the present volume does—the emergent work on the history of risk and accidents outlined in Chapter 1. They arise, however, from a set of studies that concern modern Britain and we are conscious, not least because of the global and transnational historiographical turns, that this offers only a limited geographical perspective. Although international actors and movements have made occasional appearances, they have not assumed the importance they might, and perhaps should, have. We end, then, with some brief remarks regarding how the British experience of governing risk might be opened up and situated within a more expansive comparative and connected framework.

In terms of the bigger, more structural considerations that have shaped the governance of risk in particular national contexts, surely among Western nations the rise of the modern liberal state is significant. In particular, if we work on the basis that the most important function of the modern liberal state is to secure both liberty and safety, and therefore to manage risk on behalf of its citizens—and whether indeed that risk is invasion from a foreign power, economic instability or the possibility of being killed in a road accident by a drunk driver—then we have a very broad framework with which to examine different national experiences. Crucially, it opens an important window on to the vexed relationship of liberty and security and how to balance the two, not least with respect to changing and nationally specific ideas about the rights and responsibilities of citizenship. Put simply, what does the state owe the individual? Conversely, what does the individual owe the state? What is the relationship between individual liberty and the collective good? How can conflicting interests be reconciled in a peaceful, productive and indeed safe way?

In his *Leviathan*, Thomas Hobbes put forward the idea of the social contract underlying the liberal state, in which people should willingly surrender some of their freedom to govern themselves to the state, which in turn should leave citizens free to do whatever was not explicitly forbidden by law. He famously said that without such a social contract, life would be 'solitary, poor, nasty, brutish and short'. As he suggested, the security that a state offered was both social and embodied, but it also concerned risk, in the sense that protection was offered not just in the present moment but also in the future. It is here perhaps that we might locate the birth of a recurrent and variously expressed political problem that goes to the heart of governing risk and danger. Indeed, the social contract first introduced by Hobbes was never settled or fixed; rather, it was continually renegotiated, tested and critiqued, and part of the fractious and indeterminate working-out of this problem was different visions of risk management, varying across time and national space. Should the pursuit of industrial profit be at the expense of the safety of workers? Should citizens be allowed to drive as they please, even if their actions might endanger fellow citizens? These might be styled as political dilemmas but they are also social, of course, reflecting the fact that different groups of people—capitalists and workers, for instance—have fundamentally different interests.

Industrial capitalism, new technologies and urbanization all shaped new understandings of risk that tested liberal ideologies in the years after 1800. The scale and scope of dangers and risks increased, and there were new imperatives to act, expanding the scope and reach of the state and stirring the regulatory energies of voluntary actors. Equally, however, interests and liberties were thereby threatened, generating opposition and hostility, especially on the part of employers and industrialists. This was evident in Britain, but it extended to all those places where liberal conceptions of governing and the social contract took root. Although liberalism and its descendants trace their origins to English political thought, a variety of other liberalisms emerged across the world, first in France, Germany and the British colonies in North America, and eventually further afield.[3] In each of these contexts, the balancing of personal freedom with the management of risk in the name of safety and security was interpreted in different ways.

The tension between liberty and security thus offers one dynamic in which we might situate the generation of national peculiarities. Another,

[3] I. Wallerstein, *The Modern World-System IV: Centrist Liberalism Triumphant* (Berkeley, CA, 2011).

however, is the interplay of the production of national peculiarities on the one hand, and the emergence of transnational dialogues and the diffusion of legislative templates, administrative structures and forms of expertise on the other. The USA, for instance, was—and remains—a liberal state that both borrowed from the British example and diverged from it. The Industrial Revolution was written into the US Constitution in the form of the patent clause, along with one of the guiding threads of liberalism, namely, the protection of 'life, liberty, and property'. Over subsequent decades, the material conditions of economic development—mills, steamboats, railways and cities—and the logic of industrial capitalism gradually challenged and eventually transformed the variant of liberal ideology, republicanism, embraced by the Founding Fathers.[4] Yet private groups and private interests assumed and retained some of the functions of governing risk that were the responsibility of the state in Europe, most notably perhaps health insurance. Then, as now, the USA embraced a peculiar model of managing industrial and urban risks compared to Western Europe, even if it routinely borrowed both expertise and techniques of risk management from Britain and Germany.[5]

Looking within Western Europe, we find a similar story of the joint production of national peculiarities and international connections amid the pressures generated by industrialization and urbanization. Legal frameworks, for instance, were transformed by the proliferation of industrial risks.[6] But whereas in France, laws on pollution and hazardous industries were passed in 1810, 1823 and 1824, in Britain there was no such active regulation until the middle of the century. Until this point, employers were trusted to judge the safety of their equipment, and the extent of tolerable risk was negotiated directly with employees. Conversely, though France was judged to be a leader in public health innovations during the early nineteenth century, prompting interest from British sanitary reformers such as Edwin Chadwick, by the mid-nineteenth century, Britain was judged to have taken the lead, and most of all in the field of sanitary

[4] J.F. Kasson, *Civilizing the Machine: Technology and Republican Values in America, 1776–1900* (New York, 1976).

[5] A.P. Mohun, *Risk: Negotiating Safety in American Society* (Baltimore, MD, 2013).

[6] R. Harris, *Industrializing English Law: Entrepreneurship and Business Organization, 1720–1844* (Cambridge, 2000); J. Bell and D. Ibbetson, *Comparative Studies in the Development of the Law of Torts in Europe, Volume 4: The Development of Liability in Relation to Technological Change* (Cambridge, 2010).

engineering.[7] Hereafter France looked to Britain for inspiration in the design of water and sewerage systems. This complex dynamic of national innovation and transnational borrowing and international comparison would persist into the twentieth century. Ongoing work by Claas Kirchhelle, for instance, on the use of antibiotics in agriculture and livestock production in post-war Germany, Britain and the USA shows three distinct responses, all rooted in peculiar national cultures regarding the organization of expertise and the art and possibilities of governing. And yet these national differences have co-existed—and continue to co-exist—in a thoroughly internationalized culture of governance.[8]

Other examples might be given. Chief among these is the development of actuarial technologies, which as Robin Pearson has argued were essential to the development of industrial capitalism from a very early stage.[9] In Britain, sharing financial risk among artisanal, industrial and domestic subscribers underpinned the entire insurance system until the 1850s, whereby the revenue generated by insuring residential buildings compensated the overall losses from industrial sectors. These approaches to distributing risk crossed the Channel and started to develop in Germany, for example, during the first decades of the nineteenth century, marginalizing established systems of municipal insurance.[10] Another instance is the use of cartography to rationalize the management of fire risks in the late nineteenth century, as pioneered by the engineering firm Goad.[11] Developed in London, this technique of mapping risk eventually spread throughout the British Empire and from there into mainland Europe—though only slowly in France in the face of resistance dating back to the period before 1818, when fire insurance was not permitted. Novel practices not only flowed from Britain outwards, however: as is well known, Britain's

[7] A.F. La Berge, *Mission and Method: The Early Nineteenth-Century French Public Health Movement* (Cambridge, 1992), Chapters 8–9.

[8] C. Kirchhelle, 'Pyrrhic Progress: Consumer Attitudes towards Agricultural Antibiotics (1951–2012)' (PhD thesis, University of Oxford, ongoing).

[9] R. Pearson, *Insuring the Industrial Revolution: Fire Insurance in Great Britain, 1700–1850* (Aldershot, 2004).

[10] C. Zwierlein, *Der gezähmte Prometheus. Feuer und Sicherheit zwischen Früher Neuzeit und Moderne* (Göttingen, 2011).

[11] N. Van Manen, 'Les plans d'assurance incendie de Goad: cartographie des risques d'incendie et normalisation des risques industriels (1885–1903)', *Le Mouvement Social* 249 (2014), pp. 163–85.

landmark 1911 National Insurance Act was directly modelled on schemes pioneered in Germany in the 1880s.[12]

The legal regulation of occupational risks and workplace accidents also developed out of transnational exchanges and international comparisons.[13] Between 1880 and 1900, most industrial European countries promulgated laws redefining workplace accidents and schemes of compensation, notably in 1897 in Britain and in 1898 in France, in both cases drawing on innovations in Germany.[14] These laws made employers liable for workers' safety, whilst protecting workers through the generalization of compulsory compensation systems. Yet, if reformers were keenly aware of developments abroad, the pressures of international economic competition introduced political complications and meant, among other things, that industrialists frustrated the adoption of common standards. Instead, as Julia Moses has argued, a degree of transnational harmonization only developed through international conferences on industrial hygiene and workplace accidents in the years after 1890 and through the lobbying of bodies such as the International Labour Organization, which dates from 1919.[15]

In the process, of course, the very meaning of the state was transformed, forming another renegotiation of the social contract and the relationship between security and liberty. Indeed, it is here that scholars commonly locate the birth of the welfare state and the advent of nascent social democratic forms of governance, at least in Western Europe.[16] Freedom itself was redefined in terms of a commitment to common standards of safety and 'social security', and the assumption of collective responsibility for risks that were now judged to lie beyond the control of individuals and families. Beyond the state, however, the importance of national innovations and transnational connections is also evident in the emergence of

[12] E.P. Hennock, *British Social Reform and German Precedents: The Case of Social Insurance, 1880–1914* (Oxford, 1987).

[13] P.-A. Rosental, 'Health and Safety at Work: An Issue in Transnational History – Introduction', *Journal of Modern European History* 7 (2009), pp. 169–73.

[14] C. Gersuny, *Work Hazards and Industrial Conflict* (Hanover, NH, 1981); J.F. Witt, *The Accidental Republic: Crippled Workingmen, Destitute Widows and the Remaking of American Law* (Cambridge, MA, 2004).

[15] J. Moses, *The First Modern Risk: Workplace Accidents and the Origins of European Welfare States* (forthcoming, 2016).

[16] P. Baldwin, *The Politics of Social Solidarity: Class Bases of the European Welfare State, 1875–1975* (Cambridge, 1990).

safety as a specialized arena of technical expertise and regulatory initiative, something that was also pioneered by an eclectic array of agents. In 1855, for instance, steam boiler owners in Britain seeking to adopt common standards of safe and efficient construction established the Association for the Prevention of Steam Boiler Explosions. France followed suit by creating the *Association pour prévenir les accidents de machines* (Association for the Prevention of Accidents Caused by Machinery) in 1867, which carried out a substantial amount of work collecting data and compiling proposals for reform.[17] Likewise, if the USA looked to Europe for direction on risk and accident prevention during the nineteenth century, then the tide began to turn during the twentieth century, when American techniques became paradigmatic for the rest of the world. There is no better example of this than the term 'Safety First', which was first coined in the US steel industry at the turn of the century, before enjoying an international career as the archetypal expression of risk-aversion in all of its multiple manifestations and applications.[18]

In sketching the above two lines of enquiry—the political problem of reconciling liberty and security, and the production of both national peculiarities and transnational connections—we join other historians who have recently urged the importance of perspectives that move beyond the nation-state whilst emphasizing the importance of the particular and the local. Geographers and environmental historians, for instance, have begun to reframe histories of the regulation of industrial pollution and responses to natural catastrophes in terms of the interaction of multiple levels of governance, from the local and the national to the international and the global.[19] Most notably, Christopher Sellers and Joseph Melling have offered the framework of 'industrial hazard regimes' as a means of grasping the ways in which knowledge of risks, dangers and accidents

[17] For further comparative discussion on this front, see T. Le Roux, 'Editorial. L'émergence du risque industriel. France, Grande-Bretagne, XVIIIe–XIXe siècles', *Le Mouvement Social* 249 (2014), pp. 3–20.

[18] M. Aldrich, *Safety First: Technology, Labor, and Business in the Building of American Work Safety, 1870–1939* (Baltimore, MD, 1997).

[19] Special issue of *Environment and History* 17 (2011), 'Uncertain Environments'; G. Quenet, *Les Tremblements de terre aux XVIIe et XVIIIe siècles. La naissance du risque* (Seyssel, 2005); C. Mauch and C. Pfister (eds), *Natural Disasters, Cultural Responses: A World History* (Lanham, MD, 2009); F. Walter, *Catastrophes. Une histoire culturelle, XVIe–XXIe siècle* (Paris, 2008); M. Elie and K. Gestwa, 'Zwischen Risikogesellschaft und Katastrophenkulturen. Zur Einführung in die Katastrophengeschichte des östlichen Europas', *Jahrbücher für Geschichte Osteuropas* 62 (2014), pp. 161–79.

is created, translated and contested both within and between countries. Crucially, it is a framework that also seeks to embrace developed and developing, Western and non-Western, nations.[20]

In short, the work of situating Britain within a broader, more expansive comparative and connected framework is already under way and seems set to intensify. Nonetheless, if we need more comparative and connected histories of governing risks, we also need histories that rethink and question this very activity and probe how, why and when risk became central to practices of governing, and indeed such a rich and abundant field of initiatives and anxieties. The two should no doubt inform one another, and although Britain is not the only place where such questions might be explored and posed anew, we offer the above conclusions in the hope that they will invite critique and stimulate further research—in Britain and beyond—in what remains an emerging area of historiography.

[20] C. Sellers and J. Melling, 'Towards a Transnational Industrial-Hazard History: Charting the Circulation of Workplace Dangers, Debates and Expertise', *British Journal for the History of Science* 45 (2012), pp. 401–24; C. Sellers and J. Melling (eds), *Dangerous Trade: Histories of Industrial Hazard across a Globalizing World* (Philadelphia, PN, 2012).

Index

A

Aberdeen, 156
accidents. *See also* Royal Society for the Prevention of Accidents (RoSPA); safety
  human factors model, 254–5, 256
  meanings and definitions of, 15–22, 61–4, 73–5, 89, 172, 207–9, 301
  prevention of, 62, 175–6, 182–4, 192, 198, 223, 231, 238–42, 245–6, 258, 306
  reporting, 19, 55–76, 180, 208–9, 254, 256–7, 263
affluence, 222, 224, 229, 244–6
Amateur Swimming Association, 232
anxiety, 14, 15, 35, 82, 102, 118, 146, 162, 224, 229, 232, 244–6
Arsenic Act 1851, 134
Asbestos Regulations 1969, 262
automobile. *See* car
Automobile Association (AA), 173, 174

B

bacteriology, 107, 113–15, 126, 129, 136–7, 299
Bassom, Arthur, 196, 205–8, 210
Bazalgette, Joseph, 109, 125
Beck, Ulrich, 2, 9, 12–14, 17, 23, 24, 33, 37, 52, 55–8, 74, 80–2, 100, 103, 106, 150, 245
'better regulation' agenda, 291
Beveridge, William, 5
bicycles, 190
Birkenhead, 177
Birmingham, 43, 63, 109, 110, 123, 134, 225
boating, 225, 229
Boston, 172
Bow Street Runners, 43, 48
British Broadcasting Corporation (BBC), 199, 212, 226, 237, 242
British Medical Association (BMA), 141, 199
British Medical Journal, The, 94, 138

T. Crook, M. Esbester (eds.), *Governing Risks in Modern Britain*,
DOI 10.1057/978-1-137-46745-4

British Safety Council (BSC), 236
British Waterways Board, 226
Bromley (Kent), 185
Buchanan, Colin, 216
Buchanan, George, 112, 113

C

canals, 225–6, 229, 232
cancer, 82, 92, 94, 95, 160, 262
car, 173–6, 185–8, 191, 196, 202, 217, 218, 221, 231, 244, 245, 256
carbolic acid (phenol), 24, 95, 132, 137–47
Castel, Robert, 12, 34, 35, 38, 53
Castle, Barbara, 174, 260, 266, 267
Central Council of Physical Recreation, 237, 241
Central Office of Information (COI), 236, 242
Chadwick, Edwin, 5, 108, 110, 303
Charity Organization Society, 41
children, 69, 178, 182–3, 196, 208, 210–12, 224, 225, 227–31, 232–3, 235, 236, 238–42, 245–6, 251, 263, 281
Civil Service Department (CSD), 243
class, 13, 29–30, 35, 55–9, 65–72, 75, 100, 116–17, 119–21, 123, 132–3, 150, 156, 178–9, 182, 193, 298
Committee on Safety and Health at Work (CSHW; Robens Committee), 251, 267–73, 282
Contagious Diseases Acts, 52
crime prevention, 29–54, 204, 214

D

Department of Employment (DE), 269
Department of Employment and Productivity (DEP), 266, 268
Department of Transport, 244
Derby, 187
Devonport, 158, 159
disasters
  Aberfan, 263, 264, 267, 281–82
  Chernobyl, 287, 289
  Flixborough, 100, 261, 263, 271
  Herald of Free Enterprise, 287, 288, 293
  Newnham House explosion, 285
disinfection, 24, 128–37, 146. *See also* carbolic acid (phenol)
Dock and Harbour Authorities' Association, 231, 281
domestic safety. *See* home safety
Donovan Commission. *See* Royal Commission on Trade Unions and Employers' Associations
Dostoevsky, Fyodor, 180
Douglas, Mary, 9
drink-driving, 171–94
Dundee, 114, 187

E

electrical safety, 85, 87
Employers' Liability Act 1880, 89
enforcement, 94, 122, 141, 195–6, 199, 217, 218, 256, 270–1, 286
engineering, 20, 40, 70, 90, 96, 109, 110, 116–19, 122–3, 181, 196–218, 255, 258, 299, 303
environmentalism, 149–54, 166–7
environmental risks, 79–103, 106–7, 118, 126, 149–68, 221–46, 306–7
Ewald, François, 11, 12, 18, 38
expertise, 5, 11, 14, 15, 93, 107, 126, 149–53, 155–7, 159, 161, 163–5, 166, 197–8, 205–6, 207, 242, 270, 271, 273, 282, 298, 303–5. *See also* professionalization

F
Factory Act
  1844, 251
  1937, 280
  1961, 265, 280
Factory and Workshop Act 1901, 252
Factory Inspectorate, 269–71, 279–81
fear, 74, 107, 118, 119, 123, 126, 143, 155, 156, 160, 164, 166, 224–31, 245. *See also* anxiety
Fielding, Henry, 37, 47–9
Fielding, John, 43, 47–9
fire
  insurance, 18, 44, 45, 86, 304
  prevention, 8, 39–40, 90, 121
Foucault, Michel, 33, 52, 121
France, 34, 111, 162, 303–6

G
gas, 85–7, 105–26, 285
gender, 63–6, 72, 132–4, 150, 165, 227, 235, 240–1
General Board of Health (GBH), 108, 110–12, 127
General Register Office, 19, 204, 229
Germany, 259, 270, 303–5
germ theories. *See* bacteriology
Giddens, Anthony, 1, 37
globalisation, 10, 13, 33, 56, 81, 100–1, 154, 161, 166–7, 301, 306
Gordon Riots, 48
Guardian, The, 158, 286, 287, 293

H
Habitual Criminals Act 1869, 51
Habitual Drunkards Act 1879, 52
Hampton Review (2005), 292
health and safety, 26, 249–76, 277–96, 299. *See also* safety
  opposition to, 26, 248, 286, 294, 299
Health and Safety at Work etc. Act 1974 (HSWA), 250, 253, 260, 261, 273–5, 282, 283, 285
Health and Safety Commission (HSC), 273–4, 279, 282–4, 290
Health and Safety Executive (HSE), 16, 20, 26, 250, 274, 276, 282, 285–9, 290, 299, 301
Health Protection Agency, 159
Heinrich, H.W., 255
Highway Code, 199, 236
Hobbes, Thomas, 302
Home Office, 51, 96, 138, 200–3, 207, 209, 216, 218, 231, 237–8, 241–4
home safety, 85, 105–26, 128, 130–1, 134, 237, 244, 285
horses, 83, 175, 185, 186, 190, 194
Huxley, Thomas, 79, 103

I
industrial hygiene, 262–3, 305
Industrial Hygiene Unit, 263
industrialization, 14, 16–17, 38, 53, 55–8, 65, 76, 82, 172, 193, 302, 303
industrial relations. *See also* tripartism
Industrial Revolution
  first, 83, 92, 303
  second, 84, 92
Infectious Disease (Prevention) Act 1890, 130
infectious diseases, 17, 80, 113, 115. *See also* bacteriology; disinfection
  notification and prevention of, 19, 128, 130
  outbreaks of, 110–11, 113, 130, 146

information. *See* systems, information
Inland Waterways Association (IWA), 226, 229
inspection, 20–1, 89, 90, 94, 263, 286. *See also* surveillance
  factory inspection, 19, 90, 254, 258, 269, 279–81
  sanitary inspection, 123–4
  vehicle inspection, 199, 210
Institute of Transport, 198, 207, 214
Institution of Occupational Safety and Health (IOSH), 20, 250
insurance, 2, 11–12, 18–19, 30, 32, 38–9, 43–5, 49, 50, 53, 62, 90, 304
  state-sponsored (*see* National Insurance Act 1911)
International Labour Organization, 305

L

Lancet, The, 138, 143
Leicester, 112, 191–2
leisure safety, 221–46
liability, 22, 294. *See also* Employers' Liability Act; Workmen's Compensation Act
liberalism, 3, 6, 121, 299, 301–3
liberty, 301–3, 305
Liverpool, 123, 203, 225
local authorities, 32, 108–9, 122, 125, 128, 130, 146, 162, 198, 207, 211–12, 227, 229, 231, 238, 242–3, 270, 281, 283, 300
Local Government Board (LGB), 112–13, 115, 121–2, 125, 142, 145, 188
Löfstedt Review of Health and Safety (2011), 293
London, 20, 30, 42, 43, 47–51, 55–76, 86, 109–11, 123, 157–8, 172, 175, 176, 179–81, 183, 190, 191, 198, 200, 202, 205–12, 225, 227, 244, 263, 285, 287, 304
London Building Act 1774, 121
London County Council, 114, 211
Luhmann, Niklas, 9–11, 17

M

Manchester, 20, 85, 109, 119, 123, 131, 180, 183, 185, 189
Medical Officer of Health (MOH), 111, 113, 115, 130, 131, 134, 136, 139, 145, 156
Metropolitan Board of Works, 109
Metropolitan Buildings Act 1844, 121
Metropolitan Police (Met), 29, 51, 181, 191, 196, 198, 200, 202, 205, 206, 208–11, 213–14
Ministry of Labour (MoL), 252, 257
Ministry of Transport (MoT), 21, 192, 198, 199, 202, 203, 208, 237
mobility, 17, 171–94, 195–219
Morning Chronicle, The, 58–9, 60, 63, 64, 67, 68
Morning Post, The, 58–61, 63–5, 66–70, 72, 73
Morrison, Herbert, 199
Motor Car Act 1903, 175, 188, 199
Motor Union, 189
motor vehicles, 83, 173–5, 185–94, 195–219, 228–9, 231

N

National Coal Board (NCB), 267, 271
National Health Service, 4
National Insurance Act 1911, 4, 19, 305

National 'Safety First' Association (NSFA), 20, 198, 199, 205. *See also* Royal Society for the Prevention of Accidents (RoSPA)
National Water Safety Conference, 231
neo-liberalism, 6, 285–6, 296
New Labour, 291–2
New Scotland Yard. *See* Scotland Yard
New York, 172, 173
Nottingham, 109, 113, 212
nuclear safety, 245, 287, 289
nuisances, 107, 116, 125, 156

O
Offices, Shops and Railway Premises Act 1963, 265
Orpington, 213
outward Bound, 223

P
Paris, 172, 173
pedestrians, 173, 175, 182–4, 189–90, 193–4, 197, 217
Peel, Robert, 29
Pharmaceutical Society, 141–2
Pharmacy and Poisons Act 1868, 138, 140–2, 146
phenol. *See* carbolic acid
poisons, 86, 93–6, 98, 101, 134–45, 230, 262
policing, 29–53, 195–219
  'risk-based policing,' 31–41, 47
  of traffic, 173, 176, 190, 197–204
pollution, 10, 107, 269, 303–4. *See also* refuse disposal; waste disposal
  air, 81, 87, 100, 101, 156
  water, 93, 109, 113, 228
Privy Council, 112, 142–3, 145, 146
professionalization, 19–20, 42–3, 53, 110, 112, 114–15, 119, 124, 129, 133–7, 141, 144, 176, 196, 198–9, 215, 250, 299
pro-motorism, 173–4, 193, 198, 203
public health, 24, 105–26, 127–48, 159, 192, 232, 303
Public Health Act 1875, 130
public opinion, 137, 278–9, 281–6, 291–5
public safety, 137–47, 209, 250, 264–5, 275–6, 282, 283, 285, 289

R
railways, 7, 8, 16, 19–21, 61, 73, 110, 121, 126, 190, 230, 289, 298
'red tape,' 278, 279, 286
Reducing Administrative Burdens (2005). *See* Hampton Review
refuse disposal, 153–60, 165. *See also* waste disposal
responsibility, 4, 11, 18–19, 22, 42, 56, 89, 121, 146, 174, 182, 193, 210, 211, 218, 233, 254–8, 260, 268, 272, 288, 289, 291, 301–2
Revitalising Health and Safety (1999), 291
risk. *See also* Beck, Ulrich; Douglas, Mary; Ewald, François; Giddens, Anthony; Luhmann, Niklas
  assessment of, 20–1, 32, 34, 53, 274–5, 289–90
  meanings and definitions of, 9–22, 32–41, 55–8, 74–6, 80–3, 100–3, 150–2, 166–8, 249–53, 277–9, 300
  perception, 9, 80, 125–6, 151–2, 231–4, 262, 263, 289–90
  tolerability, 289–90
Road Research Laboratory, 198, 200

roads, 25, 87, 97, 171–94, 195–219
Road Safety Act 1967, 174, 218
Road Traffic Act 1930, 199
Road Union, 189
Robens, Alfred (Baron Robens of Woldingham), 267–8, 270–3
Robens' Committee, the. *See* Committee on Safety and Health at Work
Royal Automobile Club (RAC), 173, 174, 198, 202
Royal College of Surgeons, 223, 228, 230, 235, 245
Royal Commission on Motor Cars 1906, 188, 201
Royal Commission on Trade Unions and Employers' Associations, 260, 268
Royal Humane Society, 62, 231
Royal Life Saving Society, 228–31, 233, 234, 238, 241, 242
Royal National Lifeboat Institution, 242
Royal Society for the Prevention of Accidents (RoSPA), 20, 198, 230, 236–41, 242, 243, 245, 250, 254, 278, 300. *See also* National 'Safety First' Association (NSFA)
Royal Yachting Association, 225, 242

S

safety, 6, 19–20, 22, 26, 49, 62, 134–8, 143, 147, 157, 183–4, 301, 305, 306. *See also* health and safety
safety education, 20, 196, 212, 216–17, 223, 237–41, 256, 280
Safety First movement, 20, 198, 306
Salford, 156–7, 186
Sanitary Act 1866, 130
Scarborough, 117, 187
Scotland Yard, 51, 205, 207, 210
security, 7, 32, 301–3, 305
Select Committee on Motor Traffic
  1913, 190, 191, 206
  1919, 208
self-regulation, 26, 198, 250, 269, 272–301. *See also* voluntarism
sewerage systems, 105–26
Sheffield, 87, 181–2
Society for the Prevention of Accidents and Industrial Disease, 279
Society for the Prevention of Street Accidents and Dangerous Driving, 182, 183
standards, 107, 121–3, 137, 201, 253, 268, 272–3, 305, 306
statistics, 17–19, 22, 32, 33, 38–9, 53, 138, 197, 204–9, 229–31, 257, 304–5
streets. *See* roads
suicide, 137–43
Surf Life Saving Association, 238, 242
surveillance, 32, 34, 38, 49, 52, 217, 245. *See also* inspection
swimming, 164, 225–9, 232–5, 237–8, 244–6
synthetic materials, 79–104
systems. *See also* sewerage systems; water supply systems
  information systems, 47–52, 204–5
  technological systems, 10, 20, 34, 83–7, 110

T

temporality. *See* time
Thames Tunnel accidents, 70–1
Thatcher, Margaret, 244, 285–7, 288
time, 101, 149–67, 213
Times, The, 58–60, 67–73, 117, 118, 138, 190, 191, 283

Torrey Canyon oil tanker spill, 161–5
Towcester, 184
Trades Union Congress (TUC), 258, 266, 272, 281, 288, 291
trade unions, 254, 255, 260, 261, 266, 267, 270, 274, 283, 287. *See also* tripartism
  decline of, 296-7
traffic. *See also* motor vehicles; pedestrians
  regulation of, 171–94, 195–219
Transport Act 1968, 226
tripartism, 257, 274, 279–84, 287, 296. *See also* trade unions
Tripp, Herbert Alker, 196, 214–17

U
United States of America, 8, 172, 173, 259, 262, 268, 274, 303, 304, 306
urbanization, 38, 53

V
Vernon, H.M., 192
Virilio, Paul, 299–300
Voluntarism, 5, 20, 22, 43–4, 123, 132–3, 232, 244, 250, 254, 258, 269–74, 280, 300, 302. *See also* National 'Safety First' Association (NSFA); Royal Society for the Prevention of Accidents (RoSPA); self-regulation

W
waste disposal, 111, 154–62. *See also* refuse disposal; sewerage systems
water supply systems, 85, 87, 94, 108–9
Woolf, Virginia, 185
Workmen's Compensation Act 1897, 4, 22, 305
workplace accidents, 60, 75, 87–8, 103, 249–75, 277–96, 305

Y
Yiewsley, 157–8
York, 113, 180
young people, 183, 222–3, 228–9, 233, 235, 241, 257
Young Review of Health and Safety (2010), 293